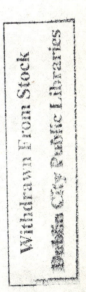
Mr Parnell's Rottweiler

To the Williams women, Nerys and Gwyneth Owen

Diolch yn fawr iawn cariad.

Mr Parnell's Rottweiler

Censorship and the United Ireland
Newspaper, 1881–1891

MYLES DUNGAN

IRISH ACADEMIC PRESS

First published in 2014 by
Irish Academic Press
8 Chapel Lane
Sallins
Co. Kildare, Ireland

© 2014 Myles Dungan

British Library Cataloguing in Publication Data
An entry can be found on request

ISBN: 978 0 7165 32330 (cloth)
ISBN: 978 0 7165 32347 (paper)
ISBN: 978 0 7165 32354 (ebook)

Library of Congress Cataloging-in-Publication Data
An entry can be found on request

Printed in Ireland by SPRINT-print Ltd

Contents

Acknowledgements

I would first like to thank Professor David Dickson, Trinity College, Dublin, for his for all his help, patient advice and guidance and Professor Jane Ohlmeyer, also of Trinity College, Dublin, for her initial encouragement.

I must also record my thanks to Conor Graham of Irish Academic Press, for his interest in this and other projects and for his championing of much of the best Irish historical writing of recent years. Professor Donal McCartney, Professor Emeritus, University College, Dublin, made a number of invaluable suggestions after his highly informed reading of the text. This was followed up by the appraisal and approval of Professor Pauric Travers, St Patrick's College, Drumcondra, and Professor Patrick Geoghegan, Trinity College, Dublin.

The staff of the National Library (main reading room and manuscript room) offered their friendship, good humour and created a warm and comforting home from home. Likewise the staff of the National Archives of Ireland in Bishop Street and, in particular, Caitriona Crowe. She, amongst other valuable services, reminded me how to navigate the Chief Secretary's Office registered papers after a gap of a few decades.

To Ciaran Wallace, Léan ni Cléirigh, Eamon Darcy, Maeve Ryan and Donnacha Sean Lucey of Trinity College, Dublin, thanks for the coffee and nuggets. To the History department of the University of California, Berkeley, my eternal thanks for the use of office and library facilities during a period of heavy writing in late 2011 and in particular Professors Thomas Brady, Mark Brilliant and James Vernon. 'Cal' also offered me the first and, so far, the only office I have ever had at my disposal.

My gratitude and love go out to my children Amber, Rory, Lara, Ross and Gwyneth Owen – especially Lara, whose own PhD work and a large competitive streak spurred me on. Well done Dr Dungan.

And finally my undying love and thanks to my patient wife Dr Nerys Williams for her indulgence, previous experience, advice, encouragement and affection. This book and the work of the last four years are dedicated to her and to our lovely daughter Gwyneth Owen.

List of Abbreviations

Titles

AG	Attorney General
DMP	Dublin Metropolitan Police
IRB	Irish Republican Brotherhood
MP	Member of Parliament
RIC	Royal Irish Constabulary
RM	Resident Magistrate

Sources

BL	British Library
CSORP	Chief Secretary's Office, Registered Papers
NAI	National Archives of Ireland
NLI	National Library of Ireland
TNA, PRO	The National Archive / Public Record Office, Kew
TCD	Trinity College, Dublin

Introduction

The liberty of the press has its inconveniences, but the evil which may result from it is not to be compared to the evil of censorship.[1]

(Jeremy Bentham, *Principles of Penal Law*)

The worst means of governing the Irish is to give them their own way. In concession they see only fear, and those that fear them they hate and despise.Coercion succeeds better, they respect a master hand, though it be a hard and cruel one.[2]

(J.A.Froude, *The English in Ireland*)

Anthony Trollope's final, and incomplete, 1882 novel, *The Land Leaguers*, written by an indignant opponent of the Irish agrarian movement, introduces the reader to a gallery of Irish stereotypes. This includes Carroll, the embittered ribbon-man, Gerard O'Mahony, the dilletantish Irish-American nationalist, and Florian Jones, the impressionable and vulnerable young aristocrat. It also encompasses radical priests, boycotting, the despatch of threatening letters, the intimidation of juries, stopping the hunt, and agrarian murder. Assertive Irish agrarianism was, *d'apres* Trollope, the new aristocracy of violence. His embittered valedictory does not, however, include a figure familiar from many of his more celebrated works, a newspaper editor. Undoubtedly, had the great Victorian novelist seen fit to include one, assuming of course that he was of a nationalist persuasion, he would have been as devious and loathsome as the detestable Quintus Slide of the *People's Banner*, a character who recurs throughout Trollope's fiction.

Trollope died just a few weeks before the first attempt by the Gladstone administration to convince a jury to jail a national newspaper editor, William O'Brien of *United Ireland*, for seditious libel. The prosecution of O'Brien was an atavistic, almost seigneurial, reaction, albeit a response to egregious provocation. It was something of a reversion to type, of a polity that appeared to have divested itself of a variety of convenient but oppressive penal methodologies in a genuinely progressive attempt to govern Ireland by means other than the exercise of arbitrary power.

Back in the halcyon days of Union, the early 1800s, the Irish executive had little difficulty in consigning bothersome newspaper editors to jail. Hostile journalists were, in any case, few and far between, as most newspapers were, of necessity, favourably disposed towards the policies of the Castle. Subsidies, pensions, bribes and intimidation ensured that this was the case.[3] The trial of John Magee, independent editor of the *Dublin Evening Post* in 1813, before a 'packed' jury, had little to do with natural justice or the 'rule of law'. Magee, volubly, though not necessarily ably, defended by Daniel O'Connell, had given offence to the new chief secretary, Robert Peel, in an editorial critical of the administrative capacities of the recently departed viceroy, the Duke of Richmond. Peel used the libel legislation of the time – 'a mere mechanism of political censorship, with cruel penalties being imposed retrospectively for breaches of an unspecified and unpromulgated code'[4] – to jail and fine Magee. The *Post* editor later chose discretion rather than sustained valour, and became a subsidized advocate of Castle policy.

Two years before the trial of Magee the mercurial Walter 'Watty' Cox, editor of the pugnaciously independent *Irish Magazine*, had been arrested and tried for publishing an article advocating Irish separatism. He was fined £300 and sent to jail for a year.[5] Cox emigrated to the US in 1816 after agreeing to close down his journal in return for a government pension.

In his survey of press censorship in pre-Famine Ireland, *The Freedom of the press in Ireland, 1784–1841*, Brian Inglis remarks:

Various expedients were used to deprive the press of the protection which the jury system theoretically gave them. Juries were packed, or intimidated, or circumvented by legal tricks. The executive and legislature joined with the judiciary in employing devices to harass newspaper owners, or silencing them by force or with favours.[6]

Even after the concession of Catholic emancipation there was little relaxation of censorship. In 1831 Thomas Edgerton Browne, known as 'the Irish Cobbett' and motive force behind the literary and political magazine *The Comet*, published a pamphlet entitled *The Parson's Horn Book*, an attack on the tithe system. Browne was prosecuted for criminal libel, fined £100 and sentenced to a year in jail. He secured his early release when he agreed, like Cox, to migrate with his family to the US.[7] Not that Browne, himself a member of the Church of Ireland, would have necessarily found much succour for his independent views under the wing of the Liberator. Inglis writes of Daniel O'Connell, that he considered the non-unionist press should be instruments of the national cause, 'that independent newspapers should set aside their various opinions, and range themselves under his leadership'.[8] Such sentiments were rather in keeping with the philosophy of that other great charismatic nationalist leader, Charles Stewart Parnell.

In mid-century the administration had no legal difficulty in suppressing, however briefly, the *Nation* and also John Mitchel's *United Irishman*, the latter after only sixteen editions. In 1844 John Gray of the *Freeman's Journal*, Charles Gavan Duffy of the *Nation*, and Richard Barrett of the *Pilot* had accompanied Daniel O'Connell to jail for conspiracy in the state trials of that year. The Fenian journal, the *Irish People*, was closed down in 1865 after its offices were raided. As the functioning adjunct and archive of a revolutionary organization the *People* had, of course, left itself open to suppression on grounds other than that it was merely a treasonable and seditious publication.

'Fenian fever' coercion legislation in the 1860s and 1870s provided for penal consequences should a newspaper be adjudged by the lord lieutenant (as opposed to being found by a jury) to have published 'matter, or expressions encouraging or propagating treason or sedition'. Penalties included seizure of the offending edition of the paper and confiscation of 'all printing presses, engines, machinery, types'.[9] Even the more enlightened administrations of the mid-Victorian period ensured they had sufficient weapons in their legislative arsenals to deal with a seditious Irish press. There was, however, as the century wore on, an increasing reluctance to deploy those weapons as the notion of 'freedom of the press' moved from elusive ideal to functioning principle.

Between the emergence of Davis, Blake Dillon and Gavan Duffy's *Nation* in the 1840s, and the appearance of William O'Brien's *United Ireland* in 1881 there had been a revolution in the publication, distribution and supervision of newspapers. Between 1851 and 1881 the number of newspapers in Ireland virtually doubled. Literacy rates went from 47 per cent of the population to 75 per cent. In the 1850s stamp duty and other 'taxes on knowledge' had been removed, making the mass-circulation one-penny paper a reality. An expanded railway network made rapid nationwide access to metropolitan newspapers readily available. The use of the telegraph revolutionized news-gathering. In the period 1880–92 thirty-one new provincial newspapers began publication.[10] Two thirds were overtly nationalist in their politics. Reading rooms sponsored by the Land League/Irish National League and the likes of the Catholic Young Men's Association ensured that nationalist papers were widely circulated and read. On more than one occasion Lord Spencer, Liberal lord lieutenant from 1882 to 1885, bemoaned the absence of a viable ministerialist alternative to oppose vociferous nationalist commentary. During the heyday of Parnellite politics in the 1880s a highly partisan, politically motivated nationalist press establishment placed its powers of persuasion and propaganda at the disposal of the forces of agrarian reform and separatism. The Irish executive and British governments, initially thrown out of kilter by what was described, in hyperbole worthy of their opponents, as the 'journalism of murder',[11] responded to the threat with determination and, occasionally, a measure of ruthlessness.

Surprisingly little historiographical attention has been devoted to studies of the Irish press in the late Victorian period. Indeed the study of Irish journalistic history in general has, up to now, been somewhat neglected. While newspapers are ubiquitous as a crucial research resource, little scholarly attention has been paid to their impact, their political value and the exertions of various administrations to restrain their influence. The valuable work of Brian Inglis in *The freedom of the press in Ireland, 1784–1841* has yet to be expanded beyond the pre-Famine period.[12]

This work will seek to underscore the significant role played in the 1880s – both in a proactive and reactive sense – by the Parnellite weekly newspaper *United Ireland*, edited from July 1881 to December 1890 by William O'Brien. The treatment to which *United Ireland* was subjected reflected its importance at a time of fluctuating levels of nationalist opposition to the political and agrarian status quo. Inspirational or infuriating, depending on one's political perspective, *United Ireland* gave militancy coherence. Its adhesion to an internalized, self-defined logic, and the apparent absence of any subscription to doubt, made it a highly effective standard-bearer for an easily demoralized movement. On a weekly basis it created a narrative – often fictional – that suggested, and consequently encouraged, a high level of organizational co-ordination and cohesion in Irish nationalism and agrarianism. This sometimes reflected, but often belied, reality. Just as the Land League and the Irish National League brought form and structure to dissent, so *United Ireland* fashioned the narrative. The plot, however, was not always as carefully contrived as the presentation sought to suggest.

Often seen, in a sort of Irish *Bildungsroman*, as an extension of the personality of its editor, William O'Brien, *United Ireland* was more than an expression of the beliefs, principles and personality of one man. It functioned without O'Brien for lengthy periods, though his absence was never absolute. Even while incarcerated he managed to exercise a surprising level of editorial control. But the fact that, for example, during the 'Kilmainham' period (October 1881 to May 1882) when he and the other nationalist leaders were incarcerated, O'Brien still had a paper to edit, was a function of its importance to the Land League and to Irish agrarianism at that time.

Irish nationalist journalism during the Parnellite period was bifurcated in nature. Newspapers like the *Nation* and the *Freeman's Journal*, with legacies derived from the relatively moderate 'repeal' nationalism of Charles Gavan Duffy and Sir John Gray, represented a slightly perturbed conformism. There was an air of irritated and bourgeois conventionality, albeit one laced with an appealing urbanity, about their nationalist rhetoric.

There was, on the other hand, precious little that was urbane about the 'new' nationalist journalism of the period. This was vocal, angry, and the 'textual reproduction of a communal voice'.[13] Without being as socially radical, it adapted many of the campaigning elements of the leftist press of William Cobbett and Feargus O'Connor in mid-century Britain. Newspapers like *United Ireland* (and the *Kerry Sentinel*) functioned superbly as noticeboard, sandwich-board and sounding board. But they also operated in a vigilantist milieu. The 'new' nationalist rhetoric regularly strayed well beyond mere cajolery into a manifest coercion of its own. *United Ireland's* policing, propagandistic and repressive functions meant that it was often akin to a Parnellite *Dublin Gazette*. An aggressively supportive press was of paramount importance to the Land League and the Home Rule movement. A free press was at the heart of late-nineteenth-century democracy. However, in an Irish context the two were often mutually exclusive.

In addition the 'communal voice' was ultimately subverted. *United Ireland*, while never entirely abandoning its iconoclastic remit, was also pressed into service as icon-maker and its editorial rhetoric was placed at the disposal of an insider elite. Ironically, Parnell, while happy to exploit the paper's hagiographic tendencies where his own reputation was concerned, was, as will be clear, more *ad idem* with the conservatism of the *Freeman's Journal*.

This book seeks to explore one of the significant imperatives of the two governments of the period 1881–91: to restrict the transmission of certain kinds of information from an aggressively partisan nationalist press to its highly politicized readership. In the words of newspaper historian Marie Louise Legg, 'between 1880 and 1887 various legislative possibilities were canvassed, tried and discarded by both political parties'.[14] In the process the Gladstone administration exceeded its powers and dented its principles, while that of Salisbury exercised its brief over-zealously. In the process, while neither was oppressively heavy-handed, both seriously damaged their claims to legitimacy as administrative partners in a functioning union. Their tactical approaches may have been marginally different, but the governing strategy of the Gladstone and Salisbury governments towards an irksome nationalist press was neatly defined, in a moment of illiberality on the part of the Liberal Prime Minister, in a letter to his chief secretary, William E. Forster, when he wrote, 'what we want is to enforce silence'.[15]

If the challenge was to achieve this end without the use of arbitrary power, the abuse of freedom of expression, or overt manifestations of repression, then both governments signally failed in that enterprise. Of course this presupposes a relatively benign intent on the part of those administrations. In fact their philosophies were more informed by Machiavellian principles in which the end was of greater relevance than the means. This was especially true in the case of the Conservatives.

The British response to the increased efficacy of nationalist press propaganda and advocacy can be divided into three distinct phases. From 1881 to 1882 chief secretary W.E.Forster employed the Protection of Person and Property (Ireland) Act of 1881, a piece of legislation devoid of any dedicated press clauses, to pursue an aggressive policy of internment without trial of significant journalistic figures. However, Forster's approach, though excessive and counter-productive, was not exclusively confined to recalcitrant newspaper editors. It was of a piece with a much wider regime of repression, one that, in the words of one of Gladstone's leading chroniclers, J.L.Hammond, 'enabled the viceroy to lock up anybody he pleased and to detain him as long as he pleased'.[16]

From 1882 to 1886, during a period of wary *rapprochement* between the Irish party and the Liberal administration, characterized by F.S.L.Lyons as an inexorable movement 'towards the fulcrum',[17] the lord lieutenant, Earl Spencer, adopted a more nuanced but equally resolute approach. A press clause inserted into the 1882 Crimes Act proved supernumerary, but a variety of legislative alternatives were used to stifle *United Ireland* in particular. Before leaving office, and before any intimation of the future legislative consummation of the Irish/Liberal courtship, Spencer had concluded that much more stringent measures were required to make anti-press legislation fit for purpose.

From 1886 to the death of Parnell in 1891 the Tory administration in Ireland, largely under the aegis of Arthur Balfour, while cannily avoiding overt press clauses in its own 1887 Crimes act, adopted an approach that was as aggressive as Forster's but, arguably, less severe than that advocated by Spencer.

Despite the critical necessity to restrain the nationalist press it will be seen that the Liberal and Tory governments of the 1880s found it almost impossible to use the common law, statute law, special legislation or quasi-legal improvization to stifle the often seditious narrative that dominated nationalist newspaper discourse. This predicament was a function of popular British attachment to the principle of freedom of the press, the recalcitrance and tenacity of nationalist editors and proprietors, and the reluctance of Irish juries to convict in cases brought under common or statute law. Almost intractable difficulties arose despite special legislation designed for the purpose, the relative acquiescence of the judiciary and magistracy and, especially in the case of the Tories, the enthusiastic co-operation of the unionist press in Ireland and England. Ultimately it was only the resolute application of controversial policies by the redoubtable Arthur Balfour and, more particularly, the mutually destructive infighting of the Parnellite split, that eroded the capacity and the will of nationalist editors to overstep the subliminal boundary that – in the view of the government at least – separated acerbic criticism and hostile commentary from outright incitement and sedition.

Failures of policy and resolve often emboldened nationalist newspapers like *United Ireland*. This led to sustained editorial attacks on government policies and procedures as well as illegal defiance of special legislative provisions against the promotion of the activities of the Land League and the Irish National League in proscribed areas. The former was difficult but not impossible for the administration to neutralize. The latter was vital for Dublin Castle to frustrate and counteract. But where action *was* taken against individual editors, proprietors, journalists, printing staff or news vendors, it was often inconsistent, ill-advised, inept, badly timed or simply counter-productive. Government jousts with William O'Brien and other nationalist editors served to enhance their credibility, popularity and the circulations of their journals to the point where the weekly purchase by supportive nationalist subscribers of papers like *United Ireland* amounted to a virtual Parnellite 'Catholic rent'.

What does the punitive British response to this unbridled animus – communicated through the nationalist press in general and *United Ireland* in particular – tell us about British policy in Ireland? Was it a blatant and logical extension of Liberal home secretary William Harcourt's belief – as expressed to Spencer – that, 'we do and can only hold the country by force'.[18] Was it, in other words, the mere use of *force majeure* by the guardians of a 'grand colony'[19] bereft of legitimacy? Was it the strict, neutral and impersonal implementation of fundamental notions of the sanctity of law and order? Was it premised on the reality that Irish freedom of speech was not as sacrosanct or inviolable as that of Britain? Was it a proportionate response to egregious abuses of the freedom of expression by Irish nationalist journals?

It certainly did not involve the equal application of British law to Ireland in keeping with the logic of a politically and legally integrated union. The word 'special' became the euphemism that often distinguished the statute law applied to Ireland as opposed to that governing the rest of the United Kingdom. Ireland was a 'special' case requiring copious applications of 'special' legislation. However, in general, although often inconsistently applied and occasionally of dubious legality and questionable legitimacy, official sanctions against the nationalist press were a largely proportionate, if generally ineffective, response to an orchestrated chorus of contumely that constituted a weekly 'insurrection in print'.

While the Parnellite split brought an end to the stand-off between newspapers and government, the nationalist press was highly successful in purveying a narrative of victimhood before the intra-party bloodletting began. The almost universal, and only partly justified, perception that *United Ireland* and other elements of the nationalist press had been subjected to unwarranted penal repression helped to undercut the authority and legitimacy of the British administration in Ireland.

Although, in purely arithmetical terms, the press regime in operation under the Salisbury administration outscored its Liberal predecessors in the incarceration and harassment of journalists, this was not true in the case of *United Ireland*. Bar a single prosecution under the new chief secretary Arthur Balfour's 1887 Crimes Act, the main Parnellite newspaper appeared oddly untouchable from 1887 to 1891. The sources, however, suggest that appearances were deceptive. Were it not for the fact that O'Brien, arising out of Plan of Campaign offences, spent much of the late 1880s in jail, *United Ireland* would have been as frequent a target of legal action as were certain local newspapers during that period. Punitive action against *United Ireland* was often contemplated by the Tories but, informed by the travails of the Gladstone administration against the newspaper, and conscious that they generally had its principal motive force under lock and key anyway, discretion prevailed.

Notwithstanding the arithmetic of incarceration there was no fundamental difference between the approach of the Liberals from 1881 to 1886 and the Tories thereafter. The two administrations were distinguished less by any essential contrast in philosophy than an inclination towards appeasement on the part of certain senior Liberal politicians (Chamberlain, Dilke) in the years before the Irish party/Liberal alliance rendered unthinkable the threatened Liberal administration policies which were ultimately introduced by the Tories under Balfour. If there was a minor distinction between their policies it related to the issue of how best, rather than whether, to punish the railing scribes of the Irish national press. As policy developed towards the middle of the decade during the internal Liberal debate on the extension of the 1882 Crimes Act, the preferred method of retribution was to be property-related – involving seizure and confiscation. The Tories, ever the steadfast defenders of property rights, chose direct action against the person. Both governments wanted to revert to coercion regimes of old. The Liberals favoured a return to a variation of their own anti-Fenian and anti-Ribbon Peace Preservation Acts of the 1860s and 1870s. The Conservatives introduced a regime more reminiscent of the post-Union anti-press repression of the early 1800s, minus the acquiescent juries of that era.

The two governments therefore cast about for an appropriate and effective legal mechanism to deal with the nationalist press while advancing warily into the minefield planted by British champions of freedom of expression. They tried – in chronological order – internment without trial, outright seizure, indictment for sedition, prosecution for incitement and intimidation, and the encouragement of civil suits for defamation. Finally the Conservatives sought to wave a magic wand and make the issue disappear by denying that the use of summary jurisdiction posed any threat to conscientiously exercised press freedom. They, of course, got to define the meaning of the word 'conscientious'.

One distinction between the strategy of the two governments was in overall approach. This revolves around issues of centrality and peripherality in dealing with the nationalist press. Essentially, in the intense struggle of the Gladstone administration with Irish nationalism and agrarianism, the conflict with the press was peripheral. However, in the course of that clash the Liberals engaged with the centre and largely ignored the periphery. Thus, their most crucial battle was with *United Ireland*. Only a small number of local newspaper editors were jailed by Forster or Spencer.[20] The opposite was the case with the Salisbury government. After the installation of Balfour as chief secretary the struggle with the nationalist press was of central importance to the Tory strategy of 'coercion and conciliation'.[21] Unlike the Liberals, however, Balfour chose, in the main, to engage with the periphery in taking on the provincial rather than the national press. *United Ireland* was largely, though not entirely, out of the frame.

During the land war (1879–82) the battle with the press was a very small part of a much larger conflict. It was only one of many serious challenges facing William E. Forster. The suspension of *habeas corpus* and the convenient participation of a number of local newspaper editors in Land League activities allowed the Castle to remove many of them, as it were, from circulation. The exception was *United Ireland*. Like the legendary hydra, as each head – in the shape of editors, managers, reporters, clerks, compositors and printers – was cleaved from the body it was immediately replaced. The Protection of Person and Property (Ireland) Act, 1881 was ineffective against the Parnellite weekly. Having established *United Ireland* as its journalistic vehicle a recently proscribed Land League could not allow it to close.[22] Having banned the League, Forster could not permit its chief propaganda outlet to continue to function. Accordingly,*United Ireland* became as much a surrogate for the League as the autonomous Ribbon activity of the post-October 1881 period. Much official ingenuity was exercised and a number of different legal routes were travelled in a dogged, and unsuccessful, attempt to close *United Ireland* down.

The peripherality of the press struggle in the early part of the decade was actually an important element of Liberal policy. This was because of the reluctance of sections of the party to countenance anything too closely resembling outright suppression of press freedom. The seizure of thousands of copies of *United Ireland* and the arrest of more than a dozen members of its staff between October 1881 and May 1882 could be represented as a logical extension of the proscription of the Land League. The newspaper was, after all, in the vanguard of the futile struggle that followed from the introduction of the 'no rent manifesto'. The implication, for British consumption, was that *United Ireland*, as proxy for the lawless League, by dint of its perceived encouragement of violence and outrage, had sacrificed any legitimate entitlement to absolute freedom of expression.

The Conservative administration of Lord Salisbury, though required to respect the democratic norms of late Victorian Britain, had fewer concerns about upsetting influential factions of 'free speech' advocates within its ranks. Vocal radicals like Charles Conybeare[23] and Joseph Cowen[24] were in short supply on the Conservative back benches. Indeed, some of its own influential philosophers, like the distinguished jurist A.V.Dicey, argued that no clearly defined right of freedom of expression even existed in English law.[25] Notwithstanding, the formidable Arthur J.Balfour was wary of appearing to circumscribe such a commonly accepted principle.[26]

Faced with a plethora of intimidatory and seditious commentary promoting the aims of the Plan of Campaign, Balfour had no option but to make the battle with the nationalist press central to his policy of containment. However, outside of initial forays against the editors of the *Nation* (successful) and *United Ireland* (unsuccessful), Balfour concentrated exclusively on the periphery. This reflected the nature of the opposition. Forster had faced an agrarian campaign that, while not conducted on a nationwide basis, was organized across much of the country. The Plan of Campaign was essentially a series of conflagrations that broke out in a more localized fashion. While the involvement of William O'Brien, in particular, in a leadership role, meant that the Plan received the full support of *United Ireland*,[27] the more detailed attention of editors in affected areas was of just as much consequence to the Tory administration. The upshot of this focus on the periphery was the incarceration by the Conservative government, via summary jurisdiction enforced by two magistrates, of more than a dozen local newspaper editors and half a dozen newsagents.

Untrammelled by any hand-wringing philosophical ambivalence, Balfour's press policies were proving to be more of a deterrent than those of his predecessors when they became largely redundant owing to the cannibalism of the Parnellite split. Internecine journalistic warfare turned nationalist invective inwards. The policies of the once-reviled Castle administration became almost incidental as denunciation and polemic was reserved for erstwhile allies.[28] *United Ireland* was at the heart of this communal journalistic *felo de se*.

But this mutual self-destruction was merely an exacerbated instance of a familiar strain that characterized the nationalist press of the 1880s. Nationalist newspapers, *United Ireland* being one of the main offenders, became adept at 'enforcing silence' themselves. Mirroring the concentration and centralization of nationalist power in the Irish National League and the Irish Parliamentary Party, the Parnellite 'apologist-in-chief' policed diversity and promoted uniformity. *United Ireland* became a disseminator of Parnellite orthodoxy. It had to be capable of excoriating and then lionizing Earl Spencer. It was required to castigate William O'Shea as a Whig and a 'nominal' nationalist politician and then justify his selection as an unpledged Irish party candidate for Galway in 1886. Prevailing Parnellite convention always won out over consistency.

In 1881 Parnell found it convenient to silence the quasi-Fenian newspapers of Richard Pigott by purchase. The *Irishman*, the *Shamrock* and the *Flag of Ireland* were bought out and the latter was replaced by his own apologist *United Ireland*. While he could not hope to conscript the entire nationalist press, any more than could Daniel O'Connell, Parnell made use of *United Ireland* to ensure that an influential newspaper like the *Freeman's Journal* became more malleable and Parnellite in its editorial line.

While resistant to any effort at infringement of their own liberties, journals like *United Ireland* practised an often-strident form of censorship of nationalist dissent. This perennial struggle against nuance had its ugly apotheosis during the rupture brought on by the O'Shea divorce. Elements of a nationalist press, most of which had dutifully canonized Parnell, now unpicked their handiwork in the struggle for the means of propaganda production. A government which had expended much energy and some ingenuity devising a formula to achieve a measure of press silence, and which had borne with much frustration in the process, simply had to move aside as the force they had been battling set about creating a new clamour that posed no threat to establishment interests.

After a decade of dextrous and tenacious deflection of the best efforts of two governments to neutralize nationalist press antagonism, after the largely ineffectual incarceration of more than twenty editors and journalists, an increasingly defiant and resourceful cadre, led by a resolutely Parnellite *United Ireland*, succumbed to a self-inflicted wound.

Notes

1   Cited in Alan J.Lee, *The origins of the popular press, 1855–1914* (London, 1976), 23.

2   J.A.Froude, *The English in Ireland in the eighteenth century* (2 vols, London, 1874), vol.1, 22.

3   See Brian Inglis, *The Freedom of the Press in Ireland, 1784–1841* (London, 1954), 113–34.

Stephen J.Brown, *The Press in Ireland* (New York, 1971), 21–3.

4 Oliver MacDonagh, *The Hereditary Bondsman: Daniel O'Connell 1775–1829* (London, 1988), 120.

5 He was also pilloried but rather enjoyed what was supposed to be an indignity as a large crowd of supporters came to see him in the stocks. (Myles Dungan, *Conspiracy: Irish Political Trials* (Dublin, 2010), 56.

6 Inglis, *The Freedom of the Press in Ireland*, 16.

7 James D. Birchfield, 'Banned in Dublin: The Parson's Horn-Book',*The Journal of Library History*, vol.10, no. 3 (July, 1975), 231–40.

8 Inglis, *The Freedom of the Press in Ireland*, 16.

9 *Public General Statutes Passed in the Thirty-third and Thirty-fourth Years of the Reign of Queen Victoria* (London, 1870), 141.

10 For a discussion of the expansion of the newspaper business see Marie-Louise Legg, *Newspapers and Nationalism: the Irish Provincial Press, 1850–1892* (Dublin, 1999) and Brian Farrell, (ed.), *Communications and Community in Ireland* (Cork, 1984).

11 *Daily News*, 13 April 1882.

12 In addition to the important work of Legg mentioned above a useful contribution on nineteenth-century print culture has been made by Christopher Morash in his wide-ranging *A History of the Media in Ireland* (Cambridge, 2009) and the subject is given a more detailed airing in the recent Kevin Rafter (ed.), *Irish Journalism before Independence* (Manchester, 2011).

13 Martin Conboy, *The Press and Popular Culture* (London, 2002), 68.

14 Marie-Louise Legg, *Newspapers and Nationalism* (Dublin, 1999), 161.

15 Gladstone to Forster, 25 October 1880, Gladstone papers, British Library (BL), Add. Mss 44157, ff.184–5. Cooke and Vincent contend that, 'in 1881–2, the cabinet contained no stronger supporter of coercion than Gladstone'. A.B. Cooke, and John Vincent, *The Governing Passion: Cabinet Government and Party Politics in Britain 1885–86* (Brighton, 1974), 50.

16 J.L.Hammond, *Gladstone and the Irish nation* (London, 1938), 211.

17 F.S.L.Lyons, *Charles Stewart Parnell* (London, 1977), 275.

18 Harcourt to Spencer, 21 September 1884, BL, Althorp papers, Add. Mss. 76933.

19 Charles Townshend, *Making the Peace: Public Order and Public Security in Modern Britain* (Oxford, 1983), 23.

20 They were Edward Walsh of the *Wexford People*, John MacPhilpin of the *Tuam News*, Edward Harrington of the *Kerry Sentinel* and John Callanan of the *Western News*.

21 The general consensus is that *Coercion and Conciliation in Ireland, 1880–92* (Princeton, 1963) by L.P.Curtis has yet to be surpassed as a survey of the Irish policies of the Salisbury administration.

22 Even the radical Liberal MP Joseph Cowen came to Dublin to assist with the preparation of the paper after the arrest of O'Brien in October1881.

23 Liberal MP for Camborne, 1885–95.

24 Liberal MP for Newcastle upon Tyne, 1874–86. Proprietor of the Newcastle *Daily Chronicle.*

25 'At no time has there in England been any proclamation of the right to liberty of thought or to freedom of speech.' A.V. Dicey, *Introduction to the Study of the Law of the Constitution* (London, 1902), 242.

26 'I am afraid of the freedom of the press.' Balfour to Buller, 13 March 1887, Balfour Papers, BL, Add.Mss. 49826, f.29.

27 On whose front page it was launched. *United Ireland*, 23 October 1886.

28 Appendix, 96–9.

CHAPTER ONE

'A Weekly Insurrection in Print': *United Ireland*, 1881

'Mr. T.P. O'Connor once described the struggle which began with the utter prostration of the National movement and ended with the overthrow of Earl Spencer, as "a long and lonely duel" between that intrepid Viceroy and myself. Substituting *United Ireland* for my own then unfamiliar personality, the description is not an untrue one. The paper was literally a weekly insurrection in print. To its columns behind the barricades gathered all the stormy passion, all the insuppressible resolve of a country panting to escape from its galling chains.'[1]

(William O'Brien, *Evening Memories*)

'The history of *United Ireland* is an epic in itself. Since the *Nation* of Thomas Davis there had been no paper like it in Ireland, and there has been none since. It instantly became a power.'[2]

(T.P. Gill, *Studies*, December 1928)

United Ireland meets the Liberal government – August 1881

When William E. Forster, the beleaguered chief secretary for Ireland, cast his eye over the first issue of the new nationalist journal *United Ireland,* on or about 13 August 1881, he is rumoured to have demanded of his associates

'Who on earth is this new madman?'[3] The querulous comment was a reference to the editor of the weekly newspaper. The offender was William O'Brien, late of the *Freeman's Journal* and a man with whom Forster would have ample time to become familiar before his departure from office in May 1882.

The chief secretary's chagrin was hardly surprising given the opening lines of the first column on page one of the first issue. This should have been a routine call for Land League notices to reach the editorial section of the paper by Tuesday of each week. Instead the notice concluded with the aspiration 'that the columns of *United Ireland* may form a Weekly National Monster Meeting which cannot be dispersed with buckshot'.[4] Even in the formulation of a banal housekeeping item O'Brien was unable to stifle either his grandiloquence or his innate polemical tendencies.

During what remained of Forster's controversial tenure, the chief secretary and his associates would find themselves in the front line of a struggle to neutralize O'Brien's dissident journal. This would incorporate the seizure of individual copies, the attempted interdiction of entire print runs, the confiscation of stereotypes, and arbitrary arrest. Despite the attentions of the executive, the law officers, the Dublin Metropolitan Police (DMP) and the Royal Irish Constabulary (RIC), the sustained campaign to stifle *United Ireland* waged by the Liberal administration from October 1881 to May 1882 was largely futile.

The political landscape in which the Land League founded its own newspaper is well-known and has been thoroughly documented.[5] The League's direct collective confrontation with the entire basis of land tenure in Ireland and the implied challenge to the underlying legitimacy of British rule was already firmly established by the time *United Ireland* began to add a significant measure of journalistic cohesion to the often disparate 'supra-local' struggles that marked the land war of 1879–82. Throughout the decade of the 1880s *United Ireland*, and a small number of regional weeklies, would severely test the commitment of government to the rule of law. They acted as *provocateurs* and goaded successive administrations into tacit contravention of a burgeoning attachment to the notion of freedom of expression in print. This willful and highly effective flow of incitement and sedition emanating from elements of the nationalist press openly invited exclusion from the protective convention of press freedom. The repressive consequences that flowed from such manifest provocation served merely to reinforce the exceptionalist narrative of Irish nationalism and invite repudiation of the legitimacy of a rule of law supplemented by decree and coercion.

From a legal perspective, the landscape into which *United Ireland* was launched was dominated by the Protection of Person and Property (Ireland) Act (PPP Act).[6] This piece of coercion legislation had become law on 2 March 1881. It was one of two pillars – the other being the 1881 Land Act – underpinning the efforts of the Liberal government of William Gladstone to return to the *status quo ante bellum* and restore the authority – through a combination of resolve and concession – of the country's political and social elite. The PPP Act provided for the suspension of *habeas corpus* in 'proclaimed' districts and the detention, without trial, of persons suspected of agrarian or treasonable offences.[7] There was no dedicated press clause included in the legislation but it was still considered adequate to deal with recalcitrant newspapers which might give too much aid and succour to Land League activities in parts of the country plagued by unrest. Should, for some reason, the provisions of the coercion act prove unequal to the task, the extant laws of seditious libel could, theoretically at least, be invoked.

Cherished ideals of press freedom made at least one alternative option undesirable or impracticable. The continental concept of 'caution money', in effect a recognizance entered into by a newspaper proprietor not to publish treasonable or seditious material,[8] was alien to British law, which was based on an *ex post facto* rather than a preventive model. Essentially, under British law, a newspaper only faced penalties after it had published actionable material. Penalties were based on court judgments rather than on a prior assessment by government officials of the amount of 'caution money' to be retained in anticipation of an infraction.

The journalistic backdrop of the time was not overly conducive to the inculcation of either Parnellite or Land League principles. The nationalist press was dominated by the Whiggish daily, the *Freeman's Journal*, owned by the moderate Home Rule MP Edmund Dwyer Gray. He had voted against Parnell in the 1880 contest for party Chair.[9] To the 'left' of the *Journal* was the long-established weekly, the *Nation,* the former Young Ireland newspaper, owned by Alexander Martin Sullivan from 1858 and edited by his brother Timothy Daniel Sullivan from 1876.[10] It was closer in sympathy to Parnell than to the moderate 'nominal'[11] nationalist faction of the party led by William Shaw. Both papers, while broadly supportive of Parnell's policies and tactics, once he assumed the party leadership, were capable of displays of independence, especially in the case of the *Journal*. Neither, for example, supported parliamentary opposition to the Land Bill of 1881, a cause of considerable irritation to Parnell. In addition neither paper devoted much space to coverage of anything other than the most significant of Land League meetings and activities. Both were also too metropolitan in their outlook for the leadership of an organization whose overwhelming support came from rural Ireland. For these, and other, reasons Parnell felt the need to establish a newspaper that would be more directly subject to his political control.

Unionist newspapers still circulated widely and extensively in the 1880s. The national dailies, the ultra–conservative *Dublin Evening Mail*,[12] the *Daily Express,* and the rather more Liberal–Unionist *Irish Times*, had stable readerships while in the provinces newspapers describing themselves as Conservative or Liberal–Conservative, like the *Clare Journal* or the *Cavan Weekly News*, also had healthy circulations. The 1880s, however, saw a growth in the number of new nationalist weeklies. Twenty of the thirty-one provincial newspapers established between 1880 and 1892 claimed to be nationalist, while twenty-four others switched their allegiance to nationalism during a similar period.[13]

At the other political extreme, militant Fenianism was also, on the face of it at least, well provided for. Circulating fitfully through the country was Jeremiah O'Donovan Rossa's militant and eccentric Irish-American journal *United Irishman*, founded in 1876. The newspaper was described by John Devoy as 'the queerest Irish paper ever published. It was a purely personal organ, giving his own views on everything.'[14] It was supported by subscription – described by Rossa as 'rent' – and supplied on a weekly basis to his 'tenants'. Essentially a platform for the old Fenian's extremist views, which included the use of dynamite as a political tool, its interdiction was a weekly ritual for the RIC and the DMP.[15] Catering for a similar readership were two of the three newspapers under the proprietorship of Richard Pigott, the *Irishman* and the *Flag of Ireland*. Pigott, avowedly at least, a staunch champion of O'Donovan Rossa, had enhanced his reputation as a journalist with Fenian sympathies when he was jailed for six months for the publication of an article on the executions of Allen, Larkin and O'Brien in Manchester in 1867.[16] The line taken by Pigott's papers was often doctrinaire and anti-Land League. Pigott purported to oppose political activity that might subvert single-minded devotion to the revolutionary cause.[17]

Hovering somewhere between the idiosyncratic militancy of the *United Irishman* and the relative moderation of the *Nation* was Patrick Ford's New York weekly the *Irish World*. The newspaper had a circulation in excess of 60,000 readers in the USA and shipped up to 20,000 copies to Ireland on a weekly basis. Ford had allowed Rossa to use the pages of the *World* in 1876 to launch his infamous Skirmishing Fund, dedicated to raising subscriptions to support militant action, including the use of dynamite, against Britain. Although Ford's own politics were more nuanced and moderate than those of Rossa in 1881 (he drifted towards greater militancy after the Kilmainham Treaty before reverting to moderation in the 1890s), the Irish Executive was as keen to prevent the circulation of copies of the influential *World* as they were of the more abrasive *United Irishman*. Issues of the *Irish World* were distributed free of charge throughout the country, with the co-operation of the Land League.[18] This was despite the fact that the newspaper was actually out of kilter with the dominant conservative ethos of Irish nationalism in that its editorial line was socialistic, and Ford, an advocate of land nationalisation in 1881, was an admirer of the radical American social reformer Henry George.

In the summer of 1881 Parnell and the Land League treasurer, Patrick Egan, moved to, simultaneously, silence the carping criticism of Pigott's publications, which reflected both Fenian orthodoxy and the proprietor's own bile, and to launch a newspaper supportive of the policies of the League. In doing so they may have anticipated a similar move by the Fenians themselves.[19] The perennially impecunious Pigott was persuaded to part with the *Irishman*, the *Flag of Ireland* and his literary newspaper the *Shamrock* for £3,000. James O'Connor, prominent Fenian and sub-editor of the *Irishman* wrote that they were 'not worth a fourth of the money'.[20] However, the acquisition of the presses and offices at 33 Lower Abbey St and a guarantee of the permanent departure of the irksome and amoral Pigott from the publishing business, a condition of the sale, made it a worthwhile expenditure for the Land League. In 1889 Parnell told the *Times* commission unambiguously that 'we purchased it in order to terminate Mr. Richard Pigott's journalistic existence in Ireland'.[21]

Under the proprietorship of journalist Denis Holland, the *Irishman*, originally established in Belfast in 1858 before moving to Dublin the following year, had been an overtly 'advanced' nationalist newspaper. It was acquired in 1862 by the former Young Irelander, the irascible P.J. Smyth MP. He proceeded to deviate from Fenian orthodoxy and was duly punished with the establishment by the IRB of the rival *Irish People* the same year. Smyth began to neglect his new enterprise before handing it over to Richard Pigott in 1865. Pigott's acquisition of the title proved fortuitous, for him at least, when the *Irish People* was suppressed shortly after Smyth had handed over the reins. The Fenian perturbation in the mid 1860s meant sales of the *Irishman* rocketed from a few thousand copies a week to an estimated 50,000.[22] The imprisonment of Pigott in 1868 for sedition, arising out of the editorial disparaging of the 'Manchester martyr' executions, had added to his extremist lustre.

But by the time of the purchase of his three titles in 1881 Pigott was a thoroughly discredited figure who had, on more than one occasion, offered his services to the Castle as a paid informant and who was known to have appropriated IRB funds from the organization's treasurer and his chief sub-editor, James O'Connor. His editorial attacks on the Land League, written from a faux-doctrinaire Fenian perspective, were suspected by nationalists of being inspired by inducements from the 'Secret Service Fund'.[23] Michael Davitt described him as an 'unconscionable rogue' who was 'impartial in his scheming propensities'.[24] At his most successful Pigott may have earned up to £2,000 a year from his various enterprises but, as O'Connor wrote, 'between the theatres and the Model Yacht Club he spent his leisure hours, and freely spent his money'.[25] Hence the urgent need to sell his titles, the most prominent of which, *The Irishman*, had reverted by the early 1880s to a sales record equivalent to that which obtained when Pigott had acquired it in 1865.[26]

The vehicle used for the purchase of the Pigott titles was the newly created Irish National Newspaper and Publishing Company. In his opening address to the *Times* commission the British attorney general, Sir Richard Webster, alleged that the money used to purchase Pigott's newspapers had come from O'Donovan Rossa's Skirmishing Fund.[27] Shares were issued at £10 each. Parnell and Egan were the principal shareholders with 237 shares apiece.[28] Senior nationalist MPs Justin McCarthy and Joseph Biggar were given a small stake, as was the editor William O'Brien. The 'shareholders' were also the directors of the Irish National Newspaper and Publishing Company. According to O'Brien this arrangement changed when the paper became embroiled in a series of potentially crippling lawsuits. The directors quietly melted away and O'Brien was left, or so he claimed, in sole possession of the field.[29]

The original plan was to replace the *Irishman* with the new Parnellite title, *United Ireland*,[30] and kill off the loss-making *Flag of Ireland* and *Shamrock*. In the end only the publication of the *Flag of Ireland* was terminated. It was replaced by *United Ireland* and the other two titles were retained, largely at the behest of O'Brien.[31] A somewhat less overtly extreme *Irishman*, under the stewardship of Dr George Sigerson and James O'Connor, remained as an 'advanced', i.e. quasi-Fenian, publication, while the *Shamrock* continued as a literary magazine.

A waspish Pigott, endeavouring to ingratiate himself with the chief secretary, wrote of his two former employees in October, 1881, 'When I had the place he [O'Connor] used to pretend to be a ferocious Fenian. Since I left he has turned an equally ferocious Land Leaguer – for more pay. Sigerson too is as culpable as any of them for he was trusted to revise and tone down anything dangerous in what the others wrote.'[32]

The Fenian response to the disappearance of the *Flag of Ireland* (and the modification of the political line of the *Irishman*) was to establish the *Irish Nation* on 13 November 1881. This was a New York newspaper edited by John Devoy – the establishment of an alternative journal in Dublin in the context of the suppression of *United Ireland* at that time would have been foolish and a waste of resources.[33] Attempts by the DMP and the RIC to interdict the distribution of copies of the *Irish Nation* and Patrick Ford's *Irish World* were vigorous, all the more so as the fact that they were published outside the state meant that, unlike Irish publications, their authors were not amenable to the laws of libel and sedition in Ireland

'A weekly Monster meeting'

When William O'Brien was offered the editorship of *United Ireland* he was only twenty-nine years old. As a reporter with the *Freeman's Journal* O'Brien had become something of a protégé of the proprietor Edmund Dwyer Gray. In 1877, as a young reporter, he had managed to secure an interview on Kingstown pier with Gladstone on his only visit to Ireland.[34] His series of articles the same year, 'Christmas on the Galtees', brought him to the attention of a wide readership. He had been dispatched by Gray to Tipperary to write about unrest on an estate owned by the wealthy English manufacturer Nathaniel Buckley. His vivid, personal and highly partial account of oppressive landlordism on the meagre pastures of Skeheenarinka on the Cork/Tipperary border, marked him out as a thorough and politically engaged journalist.

His first encounter with the rising Irish nationalist politician, Charles Stewart Parnell, came when he reported on a meeting addressed by the MP for Meath in Tralee, Co. Kerry on 16 November 1878. 'He spoke under cruel difficulties,' he wrote of Parnell, 'but fired them all before he sat down. The country is with him in a half-hearted way, so far as it has any heart in anything.'[35] O'Brien became quickly enchanted with Parnell on a personal level. They travelled back to Dublin together. O'Brien's assessment of Parnell was of a man who was, 'as romantic as Lord Edward Fitzgerald, but not to be shaken from prosier methods. In any case a man one could suffer with proudly. He has captured me, heart and soul, and is bound to go on capturing.'[36] F.S.L. Lyons has described O'Brien's relationship with his chief as 'little less than hero-worship'.[37] He retained his personal affection for Parnell up to the party leader's death in 1891, and beyond. Despite his political opposition to Parnell in the aftermath of the great rift of 1890 O'Brien wrote a sympathetic biography of his chief, *The Parnell of Real Life*, in 1926.

The abiding relationship between the two men was, on the face of it, an unlikely one. As indeed were many of the personal political alliances forged by the aristocratic, landholding, Irish leader. O'Brien came from Fenian stock (his brother was a member of the organization) though he told the Special Commission on Parnellism and Crime that he had never taken the oath himself.[38] O'Brien's philosophy is perhaps best summed up in a line from a speech he made in Phoenix Park on 1 March 1885, in which he described Ireland's association with England as 'simply the relations of civil war, tempered by the scarcity of arms'.[39] It was the personal chemistry between Parnell and O'Brien that helped their relationship survive some quite fundamental political differences, especially surrounding the Plan of Campaign, in the years ahead. In addition to Parnell's affection for O'Brien their friendship was informed by the leader's knowledge that O'Brien, despite his prominent position within nationalist polity, posed no real threat to his leadership. O'Brien 'lacked judgment and was too volatile to inspire awe or obedience'.[40]

O'Brien was reluctant to leave the *Freeman's Journal*. Despite its relative political moderation (he had resisted becoming a leader writer for the paper because of his own more 'advanced' political convictions), O'Brien had great respect and personal affection for the proprietor, Edmund Dwyer Gray MP. The original approach from Parnell was couched in highly flattering terms. He wrote that he was 'very anxious that you should undertake the editing and general management as I feel sure from your well known ability and great experience, you would conduct the undertaking to success'.[41] This was followed by further communications from Land League treasurer Patrick Egan,[42] neo-Fenian MP James O'Kelly[43] and T.P. O'Connor MP, the latter themselves distinguished journalists, urging O'Brien to accept the offer. He overcame his reluctance to offend Gray, a personal disinclination towards the establishment of a rival to the *Nation*,[44] his aversion to be seen to step into the shoes of Richard Pigott[45] and the prospect of a reduction in salary to £400 per annum,[46] and agreed to take the editorship. It was only when he did so he discovered that John Dillon and other members of the so-called 'Kilmainham party' – jailed Land Leaguers of considerable influence, like Dillon, Andrew Kettle and Thomas Brennan – were opposed to the expenditure of League money on a newspaper. Their fear was that the 'parliamentary' approach of Parnell would dominate coverage in the paper at the expense of agrarian activism. Dillon apologetically but firmly informed O'Brien that he was opposed 'to the course adopted by the Parliamentary Party towards the Land Bill' adding that 'it is quite impossible for me – just now – to allow my name to be identified with a newspaper which must of necessity put the best face on Parnell's action'.[47]

O'Brien's response was to seek assurances from Parnell, who responded by effectively granting O'Brien licence to develop the newspaper along radical lines. Parnell wrote to his wavering editor on 15 July 1881, 'I think the feeling you allude to would not be a persistent one, if the newspaper were managed on straightforward and advanced lines'.[48] The 'Kilmainham party' was sufficiently mollified to agree to a benevolent neutrality. In a letter to Dillon the new *United Ireland* editor set out his mission statement.

> So long as I may have any voice in the management of the new
> paper it will never be an instrument of faction, but will devote
> itself to the development of a fearless and manly spirit among
> the people.[49]

While there can be no doubt that O'Brien came up to the mark in the latter respect he fell well short of his stated ambition to eschew factionalism.

Edmund Dwyer Gray, while he had been personally magnanimous at the loss of his most tenacious and talented reporter, and while he had begun to reconsider his earlier opposition to Parnell by 1881, was always concerned lest the upstart journal should move towards publication on a daily basis. There is little doubt that this was under consideration, but plans appear to have been abandoned in the wake of the almost crippling harassment of the newspaper in late 1881 after the banning of the Land League.[50] Nonetheless, the threat of a competitive eclipse, as well as Gray's own personal Damascene conversion, prompted a reappraisal of the temperate political line of the *Journal*. Coincidental or otherwise, the appearance of *United Ireland* on newsagent's counters seemed to stimulate the *Journal's* search for its radical soul. The unionist journalist, Michael J.F. McCarthy, an inveterate polemicist who wrote for the *Freeman,* claimed that 'the starting of *United Ireland* brought Edmund Dwyer Gray to his knees, making the *Freeman* the subservient mouthpiece of Parnell and the Land League.'[51] The maverick nationalist, Frank Hugh O'Donnell, recorded how Dwyer Gray had once told him of a warning he had received from Davitt 'that if the *Freeman's Journal* did not come into line with the organs of the League, "he would have the *Freeman* burned on the same Sunday afternoon on a hundred platforms throughout Ireland, and start on the Monday a new daily paper with the American money."'[52] *United Ireland* was Davitt's nightmare scenario come true as far as the proprietor of the *Journal* was concerned.

The pique of the *Nation* at the appearance of *United Ireland* was unconcealed and unambiguous. The venerable weekly was more directly in the commercial firing line of the Parnellite newspaper than the *Freeman's Journal*. Its editor, T.D. Sullivan, still harboured resentment at the launch of *United Ireland* many years after the demise of both publications, as is apparent from his 1905 memoir, *Recollection of Troubled Times in Ireland*:

> This transaction was secretly planned and silently effected. I was a member of the Executive of the Land League at the time, but I got no hint of the project until the arrangements had been completed, and the new journal was about to be launched. The proceeding was unfair to the *Nation* and to me; I made some protests against it privately, but in the interests of the party and the movement I refrained from referring to the subject in print.[53]

Sullivan's chagrin may have been exacerbated by comparisons made between *United Ireland* and the 1840s *Nation* of Davis, Blake Dillon and Gavan Duffy.[54] Such was Sullivan's ire that Tim Healy, his nephew, wrote to his own brother Maurice that Sullivan might abandon the Parnellites. Healy claimed the *Nation* editor had 'half-hinted at the formation of a *Nation* party'.[55] Adding insult to injury Healy, who had been writing a parliamentary diary for the *Nation*, subsequently defected to *United Ireland*.

In his dealings with Parnell, O'Brien expressed confidence that a total capital of £10,000 would be sufficient to launch and sustain the newspaper.[56] Before finally accepting the job he reminded Parnell that he would be guided by his own quasi-fundamentalist philosophy. He advised his proprietor that 'if the object is to preach moderation, or to save the paper from the Castle, I am the last man to be placed at the helm'. Parnell's instructions were 'you are to go as far as you please. Short of getting yourself hanged – or us, you know'.[57] O'Brien was convinced after his conversation with Parnell 'that I should have a free hand as to the name, conduct, and policy of the new paper – a freedom which he never once attempted in the slightest degree to interfere with until the tragedy of the split in 1890'.[58] So 'free' was his hand that he appears, in the initial weeks at least, to have written virtually the entire paper. In 1889 he told the *Times* commission that, 'I had the whole burden of starting this new paper *United Ireland* on my shoulders. It occupied me night and day. I had to write the whole of the leading pages of it for every number up to my imprisonment.'[59] In addition to his journalistic duties he filled most of the management roles as well, supervising the commercial operation of the newspaper.

During the Land War, and in the years after, Parnell constructed a vital bridge between agrarian activism and parliamentarianism. *United Ireland* was to be an important prop in that edifice, often by dint of misdirection and obfuscation. By October 1881, when he was jailed under the Protection of Person and Property Act, and certainly by May 1882 when he was released from Kilmainham, Parnell was moving inexorably away from even the appearance of irredentism towards a policy of moderation and accommodation. He had, therefore, good reason to indulge his zealous young editor. His move to appoint O'Brien to the stewardship of *United Ireland* had not simply been based on the latter's fine journalistic credentials but on the Irish party leader's identification of the constituency to which O'Brien's writing principally appealed. As F.S.L. Lyons has noted, 'Parnell needed an organ which would be so much his mouthpiece that he could use it to inflate or deflate the agitation as he chose, without having to explain himself to third parties.'[60]

But *United Ireland* under O'Brien offered much more than a convenient mouthpiece. It afforded Parnell vital protection on his left flank as he maneuvered his party back towards the acceptable (to reformist British opinion) centre of nationalist politics. O'Brien managed to cover this strategic retreat without obviously vitiating his own activist narrative. With the assistance of *United Ireland*, according to Frank Callanan, 'Parnell could institutionalise a "soft left" within the movement he led. He could rely on O'Brien to articulate an agrarian nationalism which deferred to his leadership, upheld parliamentary methods, and accepted the primacy of home rule over land reform.'[61]

The Irish leader did not intend to re-traverse all of the ground already abandoned in the struggle against the discredited political legacy of Isaac Butt. But he was aware that any move back to the centre would be resisted and must be finessed with the collaboration of a skilled communicator. It was just such an eventuality that Dillon had feared when he expressed his opposition to the newspaper project. The choice of O'Brien as editor had already played a significant role in pacifying the radical faction within the broad church of Irish nationalism. The irony was that O'Brien was himself a committed member of that faction and was a forceful apologist for its principles. In his masterly assessment of Parnellism, *Parnell and His Party*, Conor Cruise O'Brien points out that *United Ireland*, with 'its stirring language and boundless enthusiasm served without doubt to combat the general tendency towards apathy in the ranks of the Land League, and especially the declining popularity of Parnell on the left'. 'Violence', O'Brien once said, 'is the only way of securing a hearing for moderation.' Those words might well have been inscribed on the masthead of *United Ireland*.[62]

In the course of the 1880s O'Brien was prosecuted nine times and spent a total of two years in jail.[63] Only the period from October 1881 to April 1882, when he was detained without trial under the Protection of Person and Property (Ireland) Act was directly related to his editorship of *United Ireland*. He was, according to Lyons 'a young man of real, if erratic genius'.[64] T.P. O'Connor often feared for O'Brien on account of his delicate health. He describes a driven man whose physical appearance reflected his personality. 'A long thin face, deep set and piercing eyes, flashing out from behind spectacles, sharp features, and quick, feverish walk – the whole appearance of the man speaks of a restless, fierce, and enthusiastic character.'[65] O'Connor was aware of O'Brien's journalistic background and experience but may have underestimated his true capability. 'Great as was his reputation as a writer of nervous and picturesque English, he had hitherto been unknown as the author of editorial and purely political articles, and few were prepared for the political grasp and feverish and bewildering force of the editorials he contributed to the new journal.'[66]

Michael MacDonagh, biographer of O'Brien, described his subject as 'a journalist of the highest rank, both as a descriptive writer and as a commentator on public affairs. In attack his pen was often unsparing, and wrote phrases that were bitter as gall to his opponents'.[67] It was this quality that made O'Brien many enemies. He could be unstinting in his vitriol and rarely contented himself with restrained or calibrated coverage of individuals he perceived as acting in a manner inimical to Irish agrarian or nationalist interests. This tendency to behave like a latter-day Savonarola and give vent to a form of nationalistic neo-Calvinism, as well as drawing retaliatory salvoes from Dublin Castle, failed to endear him even to some of his own political allies. Andrew Kettle writing of their mutual incarceration in Kilmainham (October 1881–April 1882) described O'Brien as 'impossible' and while acknowledging that he did 'great work' in the pages of *United Ireland* added that 'as a leader of men in the actual affairs of ordinary business, he is a rather dangerous personality'.[68]

The insurrection begins

O'Brien told the *Times* commission in 1889 of his almost physical aversion to the offices of his new enterprise, given the dubious legacy of Richard Pigott. 'The first time I ever entered the place, from the traditions of the place, and the hopeless air of bankruptcy about the place I had the feeling of entering a sepulchre.'[69] Despite this antipathy to 33 Lower Abbey St O'Brien got down to work and produced the first edition of *United Ireland* at 1d a copy[70] for Saturday, 13 August.

The front page, unlike the normal practice of the times, was not devoted to advertisements. It originally included a political cartoon drawn by J.D. Reigh that would become a regular feature, but whose humour, while always apposite, rarely rose above the ponderous. There were letters of congratulation from Parnell, Archbishop Croke and the lord mayor of Dublin, Charles Dawson.[71] In keeping with the nationalist meta-narrative of confiscation and dispossession there was a front-page article entitled 'Who Are the Landlords?' tracing the origins of the landholding elite back to feudalism and the invasion of Henry II. Page four saw the debut of the weekly column 'The World's Week's Work', later abbreviated to 'The Week's Work'. Part commentary, part political gossip, it was regularly used by O'Brien as a forum for personalized abuse of political opponents of Parnell, the Land League or the Irish Parliamentary party. Designed to keep enemies at bay and wavering allies in line it regularly featured scathing and convenient attacks from which Parnell could distance himself but of which he tacitly approved.[72]

The introductory editorial, on page five of the newspaper, promised a regime of fearless commentary:

> To some cautious persons it may seem that these are perilous times for an enterprise like ours [but] it is not an altogether discouraging state of things in which it takes forty thousand fixed bayonets, and a corresponding army of spies and jailers, to keep Irish landlordism, and with it English misgovernment, from crumbling to pieces like the walls of Jericho at the shout of a nation.[73]

It was a clarion call to the constituency, many of whose members Parnell, notwithstanding his tactical opposition to the Land Bill, would be in danger of alienating when the logic of his desire for a political realignment became apparent.

In his evidence to the *Times* commission eight years later, O'Brien displayed an oddly insouciant attitude towards some of the more immoderate material included in his newspaper. This was copy for which he took, as he acknowledged, full responsibility. Nonetheless he insisted that he did not even read news items or pieces cut and pasted from other newspapers. Most of this work he left to James O'Connor, who continued to work on the *Irishman* while sub-editing *United Ireland*. O'Connor's position, and even his desire to remain on the staff, had been in some doubt. But despite his Fenian background,[74] he proved to be a loyal and enterprising employee. However, O'Connor's judgement of the line between fair comment and incitement was occasionally skewed and caused his editor some embarrassing moments under cross-examination in 1889 by the attorney general, Sir Richard Webster.[75]

One example of a potentially seditious and certainly problematic extract, not cited by Webster in his interrogation, appeared on page seven of the debut issue of 13 August. This was a bloodcurdling warning from O'Donovan Rossa to Irish landlords:

> Henceforward a record will be kept of every landlord who exercises the power of eviction in Ireland, and for every such death sentence executed on a tenant a death sentence will be recorded by the Irish race against the murderer's house and the Irish race all the world over will give encouragement to the avenging angel.[76]

In the debate on the Queen's speech in February 1882 the Irish attorney general, William M. Johnson, singled out the piece and suggested that *United Ireland*, in reproducing the item, was advancing seditious propaganda as 'news'. 'The promoters of that journal had an ingenious way,' he told the House of Commons, 'of conveying information, under cover of collecting news of public interest, which was of the most odious and atrocious character, and which struck at the root of all morals and of all law … Was there ever a more direct incitement to murder?'[77]

On the back page of the newspaper, in the absence of any substantial amount of advertising copy, *United Ireland* carried a People's Trade Directory. This was a list of traders across different parts of the country with whom readers were recommended to do business. It was not extensive and the basis for the selection of certain businesses above others was not explained. The directory tallied with a line from Parnell's letter on page one which congratulated the newspaper on its intent 'to make the development of the industrial resources of the country and the encouragement of native manufactures a leading feature of your paper'.[78]

There was an odd paradox in two of the advertisements carried by the paper in its first edition. One was for 'Cheap emigration to Canada' via the Beaver line which offered farm labourers passage in steerage, on government-assisted crossings, for £4 15s. The advertisements, and others like them, remained a feature of *United Ireland's* back page despite O'Brien's regular fulminations in the editorial pages against assisted emigration. The second was an advertisement for 'Hair Destroyer – Alex Ross Depilatory – removes hair from the face, neck and arms, 3s 6d a bottle'. To avoid embarrassing the customer this product was available to be 'sent by post, secretly packed'. Within four months this would become the only means of distributing the newspaper itself throughout the country.

The bottom of the right-hand column on page eight bore the legend 'Printed and Published at the offices 33 Lr Abbey St, Dublin, by William O'Brien, to whom all communications should be addressed.' That was how it remained until, and indeed well after, the Parnellite split. Notwithstanding O'Brien's lengthy periods of incarceration, his Parliamentary committments after his election to the Mallow constituency in 1883, and his involvement with the Plan of Campaign from 1886, he retained editorial control. While he would prove loath to admit authorship of some of the contents of the newspaper before the *Times* commission in 1889, he never shirked his legal responsibility for anything that was published.[79]

O'Brien's biographer, Joseph O'Brien, has described the first edition of the newspaper – and the description is valid for most of the subesquent issues – as 'eight pages of unrelieved news and comment on the land problem and the activities of the branches of the Land League. It was a stark contrast to the cosmopolitan and inoffensive *Freeman's Journal*. Nothing quite like it had ever before been offered for the delectation of the village sages.'[80]

The first edition of the newspaper also carried a snippet relating to what would become a recurring phenomenon. An over-enthusiastic Royal Irish Constabulary sub-Inspector in Midleton, Co. Cork, had espied 'a placard announcing the appearance of this journal. He, in the most dashing manner, invaded the shop and, at the point of a bayonet, hauled down the placard, and retreated in good order upon Dublin Castle. It is, we suppose, a service both of profit and glory under the present *regime* in Ireland; but it is possible that a jury in a court of law may not take precisely the same view of the freedom of the Press as a "village tyrant" with a braided jacket on.'[81] The eager Midleton policeman may have been a 'single spy' on that occasion but the 'battalions' would soon follow.

The Land League and Irish Parliamentary party leadership professed itself well pleased with O'Brien's maiden effort. 'Wonderful, sparkling all over'[82] was Parnell's verdict. The paper quickly came to the attention of the inveterate and well-informed diarist, Florence Arnold-Forster (adopted daughter of the chief secretary). She wrote that 'I read the rebel papers.[83] The new one *United Ireland* is the cleverest of all of them. Very violent about the Ch.Sec [*sic*] … calling him every kind of opprobrious name, and indulging generally in language worthy of Billingsgate whenever having occasion to allude to him.'[84] The following day one of Forster's dinner guests, Irish solicitor general John Naish, described O'Brien to her as 'a very clever fellow, but a born rebel, and always will be'.[85]

As F.S.L. Lyons has written, the first issue of the newspaper struck 'the intransigent note that was to be the hall-mark of O'Brien's editorship for the rest of the decade'.[86] The tone was pugnacious and carping, the writing style robust and aggressive. The *Irish Times* was moved to reflect on how 'unpoetic' Irish patriotism had become. The *United Ireland* response was utilitarian. 'If the *Irish Times* means that our paper is not so beautiful reading as the old *Nation* in the days of Davis, it is quite right. The time was, and will be, for cultivating literary graces; but that time is not now.'[87] Apparently the new *Nation* was unimpressed with its competitor. In the issue of the *Nation* of 20 August T.D. Sullivan didn't deign to refer to the arrival on the newspaper scene of *United Ireland*. Neither did the *Freeman's Journal* of Monday, 15 August deem the launch of a new nationalist weekly, under the aegis of the Land League, to be a newsworthy event. *United Ireland* itself drew the attention of its readers to the stand-offish attitude of the *Freeman* in a sarcastic *World's Week's Work* vignette on 17 September 1881 after the *Journal* had sought to place an ad. 'We see by an advertisement in another column that the *Freeman's Journal* has at last discovered, not only our existence, but our address. We feel quite six columns bigger for its gracious notice. It was violent exercise ignoring us so vigorously and long. And it was surely the strangest thing in the world that without its notice we should have attained a circulation which – well makes it desirable for the *Freeman* to advertise with us largely.'[88]

United Ireland would eventually attain a circulation that would have made daily publication feasible. However, in its first months of existence it was not as financially successful as suggested by Joseph O'Brien, who asserts that the newspaper 'within weeks achieved a steady circulation of between 70,000 to 100,000'.[89] The first year of its existence saw a steady rise in circulation to 30,000. The paper did not reach sales of 100,000 until the heady period of the General Election and Home Rule fever in 1885/6.[90] Its reach, however, went far beyond the raw statistics of its sales figures. Even on the basis of the accepted industry norm – five readers per paper in circulation – the readership at its height would have been at least half a million. However, the operation of Land League reading rooms throughout the country may have ensured an even wider readership.

The *Freeman's Journal* may have chosen to ignore the debut of *United Ireland* but there was a perceptible change in its politics from late 1881. This could be attributed to a number of causes. These include the arbitrary arrests of the nationalist political leadership under the PPP Act, the oppressive Crimes Act regime of 1882 and the influence of a radicalized proprietor.[91] But Florence Arnold-Forster, for one, was in no doubt that the threat of competition from *United Ireland* was the decisive factor. She wrote in her diary on 28 September 1881, 'Apropos of the *Freeman* and its apparently lurking desire to see a fair trial given to the [Land] Act, notwithstanding Mr. Parnell, I was told that its spasmodic but violent Parnellism is caused to a great extent by dread of successful competition on the part of their paper *United Ireland*.'[92] By the time of the Land League Convention in September 1881 the Parnellite policy of 'testing the Act', had already become, according to the *Journal*, one of 'moderate counsel and caution'.[93] This contrasted sharply with its position only weeks before when the *Journal* had acted as advocate for the legislation.

However, though the *Freeman* may have shifted its political direction, it always strove to differentiate and distance itself from the vituperative tone of its rival. In January 1882, at a time when the Land League leadership was incarcerated and *United Ireland* was struggling to maintain its existence, the *Freeman* set out an alternative political philosophy. 'We are no advocate of extreme or visionary doctrines in connection with the distribution of land … We are opposed to all violence and all illegality. We have never encouraged those who dream of a separation of Ireland from England.'[94]

O'Brien's first major task was that of opposition to the 1881 Land Bill, described in the first issue as 'an arrant fraud from beginning to end'[95] and, subsequently, denigration of the land courts which were created, via a Land Commission, to arbitrate between landlord and tenant when the bill was enacted. This piece of legislation was a complex and flawed vehicle, both in its original analysis of the problems faced by Irish tenant farmers and its template for resolution.[96] It was designed to address issues of fair rent, free sale and fixity of tenure (the elusive '3Fs') but ignored and excluded from its provisions the thousands of tenant farmers in arrears of rent. Partly for fear of contamination of the contractual basis of the relationship between British tenant farmers and their landlords, it also deliberately avoided the inclusion of Irish leaseholders in its terms of reference. Though not necessarily the direct responsibility of the framers of the legislation itself the crucial issue of the modernization of Irish agriculture was not addressed either.[97]

Displays of enthusiasm for the Bill risked incurring the wrath of significant American supporters and commentators like Patrick Ford, proprietor of the New York *Irish World*, who characterized the legislation as 'Gladstone's sham Land Bill'.[98] Ford's support was more than moral in nature. By the first quarter of 1882 his readers had contributed more than $300,000 to the Land League.[99]

The Land League, prompted by Parnell, had advised its members to boycott the land courts and await the arbitration of a number of 'test' cases advanced by the League itself. One of O'Brien's initial tasks was to hold the line against mass defections of tenant farmers eager to 'test' their own particular case. According to Frank Hugh O'Donnell, *United Ireland* 'made the intimidation of the Land Courts a fundamental tenet of its policy from the very outset'.[100] To this end, for example, one of the iconic founders of the *Nation* newspaper, the former Young Irelander Charles Gavan Duffy, was censured for his support of the legislation.[101] In pursuit of this agenda, as thousands of tenant farmers put their faith in the Land Act, *United Ireland* focused on the downside of the process. Headlines like 'In the Land Court – Throwing off the Disguise – The farmers beginning to discover the delusion'[102] proclaimed, in defiance of reality, the foundering of the courts. There was no coverage of the ever-increasing number of cases where substantial reductions, of the order of 20 to 30 per cent, were being granted. Stories of instances where no reduction was forthcoming, with tenants bearing the costs of the proceedings, were favoured.

Oddly O'Brien later represented this policy as allowing the Land Act to 'have a fair trial', though in his own opinion the legislation 'would turn out to be a fraud'. In the wake of the Land League Convention of September 1881, convened to adopt a uniform approach to the Act, O'Brien had editorialized in *United Ireland* that the policy of testing the Act was designed 'to see whether that Act can be used as an instrument to destroy landlordism and English rule, and, if it cannot, to put the Act contemptuously aside, and destroy landlordism and English rule without it'.[103] He later acknowledged to the *Times* commission, 'I am perfectly sure that it is a statement that Mr. Parnell would not have approved at the time, and that it went a great deal further than Mr. Parnell's attitude towards the Land Bill; but it is perfectly and absolutely consistent with a fair trial of the Land Act'.[104] These views, expressed to the Special Commission at a time when he might have been anxious to downplay his past opposition to the palliative measures of a Liberal government, would appear to contradict Sally Warwick-Haller's suggestion, in her biography of O'Brien, that his opposition to the Act was almost as circumscribed as that of his leader and that 'what O'Brien was saying was really fairly mild, but his colourful and inflammatory language was, as Parnell had hoped, of the kind that would appeal to extremists'.[105] She does, however, also refer to his letter to Archbishop Croke, a personal friend of O'Brien's and a keen supporter of the Land Act, in which he observed that, 'anything like general acceptance of the bill would be a calamity and plunge the country in all sorts of dissension'.[106]

By the end of the year the campaign against the land courts had, more or less, petered out. The efforts of the Land League, via *United Ireland* and more direct forms of moral suasion, had failed to bear fruit. The incarceration of the 'suspects' under the terms of the PPP Act (see chapter two) had radically changed the nationalist agenda. 'No rent' rather than 'fair rent' was the main criterion, as a campaign of civil and contractual disobedience, not to mention an upsurge in 'outrages' and violence, had taken hold. In its issue of the 17 December 1881 (produced in fraught circumstances) the newspaper, not for the last time, changed direction. Almost haughtily, it brought down the curtain on the struggle against the land courts. The principle of the judicial rent was by then well-established in all parts of the country. 'We don't care to waste our space today with much about the rambles of the sub-commissioners,' *United Ireland* sniffed. 'Their decisions are doing some small service, though not quite in the direction that Mr. Gladstone anticipated. They are showing that the rents of all sorts of tenants, on all sorts of estates, were mere robbery, and that the tenants were slaves and fools to have paid them so long.'[107]

But the paper made clear that it was not waving a white flag, and even in the death-throes of the campaign re-iterated its scorn for the land courts, insisting that 'their work is like that of ants removing a mountain. The tenants of the Duke of Leinster the other day demanded a reduction of 20 per cent, and the Duke promptly surrendered. This one reduction upon a single estate, leaves more money in the pockets of the farmers than all the Land Commissions put together have deprived the landlords of since their first sitting.'[108] Not unexpectedly the journal was being disingenuous. It failed to point out that many landords, like the Duke of Leinster, caved in because they were accepting of the inevitable: an inevitability largely brought about by the land courts. Conscious of the new arbitration regime the landlords were aware that if they didn't concede substantial rebates the tenants would simply secure the reduction from the land courts anyway. For many of the landowners who resolutely declined to offer rebates it would prove to be merely a delaying tactic.

O'Brien had ten issues of *United Ireland* (before his arrest in October along with Parnell and the other Land League leaders) to make his mark on Irish nationalist opinion, arouse the antagonism of Irish unionists and landlords, and bring himself and his journal to the attention of Dublin Castle. He used his time well in the conduct of what was described in the paper as 'a Holy War against Saxon rule'.[109] O'Brien quickly established a template to which he remained faithful for the duration of his association with *United Ireland*.

Editorial policy comprised an entirely uncritical attitude towards Parnell and, to a lesser extent, his supporting cast of lieutenants. This went hand-in-glove with the execration of landlords, 'land-grabbers', the Irish Executive, British officialdom in Ireland, the Orange Order,[110] recalcitrant nationalists, socialists and land nationalisers. Readers were encouraged to withhold rent, boycott their neighbours and refrain from co-operation with the police. In this context it is difficult to accept the contention of Sally Warwick-Haller in her biography of O'Brien that *United Ireland* was less than fulsome in its opposition to the coercion regime instituted under the Protection of Person and Property (Ireland) Act of 1881. She maintains that O'Brien's real invective was reserved for the Crimes Act of 1882. While O'Brien was acerbic in his frequent tirades against the latter piece of legislation, it is hardly the case that 'by comparison O'Brien's utterances in 1881 were mild'.[111] His rhetoric was anything but restrained and even though Dublin Castle chose to take no direct legal action against *United Ireland* the content of the newspaper was often privately described by the authorities as seditious.[112]

Joseph V. O'Brien in his 1976 biography of the *United Ireland* editor characterizes it thus.

> The tone of the paper was vituperative and not a little tiresome, neglecting all news values not directly connected with the Nationalist movement. Its more extreme exhortations were no doubt not meant to be taken seriously, but its pages were both an arsenal against the Dublin Castle regime as well as the exemplar of a revived Nationalist spirit of defiance.[113]

While it might be unsafe to assume that the somewhat self-important O'Brien did not intend his every word to be taken at face value, it is certainly fair to say that almost all copy was spurned unless it was of some relevance to the cause. *United Ireland*'s news columns were based on the publication of 'news' that was of a certain propagandistic value. Almost the only item in the first edition of the paper that was unrelated to the Land War was a report on the back page of a man's arm being eaten by a cob-horse in Maynooth, Co. Kildare.[114]

O'Brien made it clear within a fortnight of his initiation that even his indulgence towards nationalist inadequacies had its limits. In the issue of 27

August 1881 he railed against the forty-four 'supposed Home Rulers' who had failed to go through the lobbies in support of a motion relating to the incarceration of Michael Davitt. The rhetoric he deployed on that occasion would become familiar, over time, to his growing readership. 'Whoever was absent from that list without satisfactory cause committed a high treason against the Irish cause. "Remember Davitt" will be their death knell in Irish politics.'[115] O'Brien's use of emotive and hyperbolic terms like 'high treason' were typical of his style. In this instance, given that only nineteen Irish MPs had voted on the motion, a number of members of the tight, pre-1885, circle around Parnell would have been counted amongst the abstentionist 'traitors'. O'Brien, who was utterly unsentimental when it came to the business and the ruthless logic of propaganda, prompted T.P. O'Connor, by and large an admirer, to observe that he separated the world into two unequal parts, 'his slaves and his enemies'.[116]

But O'Brien's contumely was largely reserved for two strands of nationalist 'opposition'. The first was the group of so-called 'nominal Home Rulers'. These MPs, men like William Shaw, George Errington, Richard O'Shaughnessy, The O'Donoghue and Captain William O'Shea,[117] largely took up positions on the Liberal benches and were derided even in their own constituencies as 'Whigs'. They were swept away by the Parnellites in the election of 1885. The second group, seen as renegades, were more militant nationalists who had strayed from the fold. These included two of Parnell's allies during the 'obstructionist' period of the mid to late 1870s, John O'Connor Power and Frank Hugh O'Donnell, who took what O'Brien described as 'The Banshee's Kiss'.[118] The most common explanation for the antagonistic stands taken by O'Connor Power and O'Donnell (mercilessly lampooned in *United Ireland* as 'Crank Hugh O'Donnell') was that they were driven by their jealousy at being usurped by Parnell, who had occupied a subaltern role in the 1874–80 parliament. In his highly subjective, idiosyncratic, entertaining and generally unreliable *A History of the Irish Parliamentary Party*, written in 1910, O'Donnell describes *United Ireland* as 'the new organ of misrepresentation and menace' and a 'cheap and incendiary sheet'.[119]

Those elements of *United Ireland's raison d'etre* related to O'Brien's diatribes against Irish Tory papers and journalists will be dealt with elsewhere.

Likewise the iconographic part played by *United Ireland* in the creation of Parnell's 'cult of personality'. In the latter case *United Ireland*'s coverage of the activities of the Irish party leader tended towards the hagiographical. It was 'totally uncritical of Parnell'.[120] Not that O'Brien was guilty of mindless sycophancy. As a talented propagandist he was simply conscious of the need to create a mythic, imposing, efficacious and unifying figure directing Irish nationalism. Parnell was 'our chief, our guide'.[121] In his assessment of the constitutional nationalist movement of the 1880s in *Parnell and his Party*, Conor Cruise O'Brien reflected on the role and importance of the newspaper in creating an iconic Parnell. '*United Ireland*, unlike the moderate *Nation*, was totally uncritical of Parnell, and the ingenious irrelevancies of its vocabulary undoubtedly did much to keep national opinion in Ireland solid behind him, and much also to prevent mass defections among Irish American nationalists.'[122]

In the formative period of *United Ireland*'s existence Parnell's principal antagonist was the chief secretary, William E. Forster. He was victim of an unfortunate syndrome identified by Virginia Crossman in *Politics, law and order in nineteenth-century Ireland*, where she points out that 'ministers made the mistake of thinking that good intentions and a principled dislike of repressive measures would soften the impact of coercion and reconcile the Irish people to its imposition'.[123] He was to discover that the Irish people were more conscious of harsh practice than notional principle in their interaction with his regime. Although he never quite understood his casting, Forster became the villain of the *United Ireland* narrative. His espousal of stringent coercion policies earned him the nickname 'Buckshot', an appellation rigorously and regularly applied by *United Ireland*. Forster was anathemized and lampooned as the epitome of English misrule. He was 'Her Majesty's Chief Turnkey in Ireland – The Right Honourable Gentleman whose name is associated in Ireland with ammunition'.[124] In May 1882 Forster's function as *bête noire* would pass to Earl Spencer, the new lord lieutenant, with the replacement chief secretary, George Otto Trevelyan, occupying a prominent supporting role.

Florence Arnold-Forster, as already noted, made it her 'unpleasant duty' to read 'rebel papers'. She, rather generously, given its treatment of her father, compared *United Ireland* to the *Nation* of the days of Davis and Gavan Duffy. She described it, dispassionately, as a journal that 'evidently wishes to appeal to the more educated class of Irishmen for their respect'. However, she also exemplified how the paper was uniquely capable of antagonizing its primary targets by describing her reaction to its frequent anti-Forster phillipics:

> The amount of lying, the misrepresentation, the gratuitous insolence they contrive to compress into a small compass is sickening, and yet at the same time there is a fervour of nationalism, an enthusiasm of hatred, a spirit of genial camaraderie of Irishmen of which I can quite understand the attraction. If ever there is a civil war between England and Ireland, the *United Ireland* may fairly claim credit for a large share of the responsibility.[125]

However, she also testified to an urbane indifference on the part of her father in relation to the attacks upon him in the newspaper. In her diary entry for 28 January 1882 she writes, 'Father in cheerful spirits – read aloud to us the latest abuse of himself in *United Ireland*, and a poem in the same paper. Which he thought very spirited.'[126] One of the paper's favourite targets, the activist Special Resident Magistrate, Clifford Lloyd, also ignored in his own memoir the lightning bolts aimed at him by O'Brien. In *Ireland Under the Land League* he expressed annoyance at the time required to answer the myriad questions posed about his activities by Irish MPs in the House of Commons – 'The answers mattered little so long as the charges were made' – [127] but makes no reference to the (often scurrilous) commentary aimed at him in *United Ireland*.

While maligned officials could afford to adopt an attitude of haughty *sang-froid* towards the upstart journal, its obvious popularity and its almost immediate impact meant that it was soon a force to be reckoned with. And that is precisely what Dublin Castle did. The reckoning took the form of confiscation, suppression, imprisonment without trial, indictment for seditious libel and probable covert support for a proxy campaign of civil suits. *United Ireland* would emerge, relatively unscathed, from this litigious onslaught but in the course of a concerted drive against the newspaper, the Liberal government would stretch beyond breaking point vaunted notions of freedom of the press.

'A Holy War against Saxon rule' – October–December 1881

The first civil right to disappear was freedom from arbitrary imprisonment. The escalating rural violence of 1880 and 1881, which had seen instances of agrarian murder rise from an average of five a year in 1878 to seventeen during the period of the land war, and that of lesser crimes increasing by a multiple of twenty-five, persuaded the British government of the wisdom of the aggressive counsel of Forster. The Protection of Person and Property (Ireland) Act allowed the government to suspend ordinary law in proclaimed districts and arrest 'any person who is declared by warrant of the Lord Lieutenant to be reasonably suspected of having at any time since the thirtieth day of September one thousand eight hundred and eighty been guilty as principal or accessory of high treason, treason-felony, or treasonable practices'.[128]

The legislation had become inevitable after the failure of the administration to secure convictions against Parnell and the Land League leadership in a landmark 'state' trial in January 1881. The arrest of 'suspects', based on information received from the RIC on the activities of known political activists, began almost immediately after the passage of the coercion act. The effective suspension of *habeas corpus*, opposed by Gladstone six months before,[129] allowed the government to dispense with legal niceties and bypass a jury system signally failing to secure convictions in cases of serious crime against local Land League militants. In a direct attack on the Land League leadership, the 'ticket of leave' secured by Davitt in 1876 was revoked and he was re-arrested.

An assertive response to this *demarche* was required of Parnell. This took the form of renewed parliamentary disruption on a scale not seen since the obstruction campaign of the late 1870s. Gladstone might have anticipated just such a response from a man who was, after all, still seen as a belligerent radical by a Liberal leadership personally unacquainted with his pragmatism and growing moderation. But the Prime Minister might, legitimately, have expected a more supportive attitude from the Irish leader on the Land Bill. When this was not forthcoming, and with agrarian violence mounting despite Parnell's stated opposition, the logic of the January trial was now pursued within the context of Forster's new coercion powers. With some prompting from the chief secretary, Gladstone, in a speech in his son Herbert's Leeds constituency on 7 October 1881, pointedly reminded

Parnell that, where his liberty and independence of action was concerned, 'the resources of civilisation were not exhausted'. Thenceforward the phrase would be referenced, repeated and satirized incessantly in *United Ireland*.

Another, equally assertive, response was forthcoming from the Irish leader. In a speech of his own in Wexford two days later Parnell referred to Gladstone as a 'masquerading knight-errant' and a 'pretending champion of the rights of every nation except those of the Irish nation' who was supporting the landowning class by 'bayonets and buckshot'.[130] On 13 October 1881 Parnell was arrested by Superintendent John Mallon, head of 'G' Division of the DMP in his room in Morrison's Hotel and taken to Kilmainham Jail where he would reside for the next six months.

The reaction of *United Ireland* to the arrest was, unsurprisingly, apoplectic. In an extravagantly aggrieved front-page 'Stop Press' – which opened with the phrase 'Saxon cowardice has done its worst' – O'Brien accused Gladstone of political hypocrisy. 'Gladstone's argument at Leeds was shattered to bits by Parnell's argument at Wexford. The old hypocrite has mended his argument by the help of his police, and has answered his opponent by garotting him.' The conclusion was vintage O'Brien. 'Let the cowards yell with joy as they may, this last outrage upon Irish liberty has changed nothing, and least of all, either the resolve or the power of our race to wage more relentless war than ever against landlordism and against the miscreant government that backs it with the gag of a garotter.'[131]

O'Brien's record as Parnellite propagandist-in-chief had already made his own arrest inevitable when the government deemed it necessary to lodge Parnell's lieutenants in Kilmainham along with their leader. But had sanctions against him not already been pre-ordained his call for 'relentless war' against landlordism and the government would probably have guaranteed his incarceration. O'Brien's 'Recommendation for Arrest' form, under the Protection of Person and Property (Ireland) Act was actually prepared on 9 October 1881[132] by John Mallon. The 'G' Division Superintendent fully accepted that, 'His character apart from politics is good.' But Mallon was seriously misinformed as to O'Brien's age. His delicate health (he came from a consumptive family) may have aged the *United Ireland* editor, because Mallon gives this as 'about 42 years old'. O'Brien posed a threat because of his 'treasonable and seditious writing in the *United Ireland* newspaper ... the character of the matter published in his newspaper and his own declarations from time to time'. Mallon added, somewhat incongruously, 'It is a matter of notoriety that when the members of the Dublin Press contemplated dining together for the purpose of celebrating a reunion of some kind William O'Brien would not permit the health of Her Majesty to be on the list of toasts, and the dinner had to be abandoned.'[133] The head of detectives may have felt it necessary to gild the lily by reference to O'Brien's egregious offence against royalty but it is unlikely, in the event of its omission, that the lord lieutenant would have denied the application to arrest O'Brien.

O'Brien was arrested in Sackville Street a few hours after Parnell had been safely committed to Kilmainham. He was on his way to the offices of the *Freeman's Journal* and asked to be allowed to conclude his business there first. Because of the presence of large and threatening crowds in the vicinity this request was refused by the arresting officer, Inspector Thomas Kavanagh. O'Brien was taken to the Detective Office in Dublin Castle where he was met by Mallon, who had just lodged James O'Kelly in Kilmainham. O'Brien appealed to Mallon to be allowed to communicate with *United Ireland* deputy editor James O'Connor and to be permitted to write a cheque to meet staff wages. Mallon, hinting at the rather benign nature of the incarceration that awaited the obstreperous editor, reported to the Police Commissioner that 'I told him that the anxiety of Government was that no one should suffer unnecessary inconvenience and that I was quite prepared to give him every facility to communicate with James O'Connor at the office of the newspaper.'[134]

The *United Ireland* issue of 22 October carried the news of its editor's fate. In a column headed 'The Arrests – Garrotting continued – The Press struck down – Our Editor dragged to the dungeon', the newspaper observed that 'The Editor of *United Ireland* is now reaping the hereditary penalty of those who, among his countrymen in the past, have most distinguished themselves in the cause of humanity and reform.'[135] The newspaper also apologized, 'for the many shortcomings of the present issue of *United Ireland*. The arrest of its able and energetic editor was a loss which at any time would be deeply felt, but occurring as it did, with such sudden unexpectedness and at such a crisis, it was absolutely irreparable.' The ill-effects, it has to be said, are not immediately obvious. O'Brien was arrested in spite of a fear on the part of the administration that they were, in so doing, adding a name to the roll of virtuous martyrs. *United Ireland* had already made significant inroads on the psyche of the nationalist population; the arrest of its editor added immeasurably to its cachet.

O'Brien's first task upon his committal was to articulate the Land League response to the jailing of its leaders, the 'No Rent Manifesto'. This appeared on the front page of the 22 October edition of *United Ireland* as 'A Proclamation from the Irish Executive' and sought to lower the boom on the administration and its propertied allies.

For most of the next six months *United Ireland* doggedly espoused the cause of the 'No Rent Manifesto' and testified to its efficacy. Such 'testimony', however, was tantamount to perjury. The campaign against the payment of rent – disapproved of even by radicals like Dillon and Davitt – was doomed from the outset. The 'Manifesto', issued on 18 October, offered Forster whatever cover he required for the proclamation of the Land League. Deprived of its organizational infrastructure – though not its covert muscularity – any League campaign based on the moral suasion of tenant farmers was operating at a distinct disadvantage from the start. They had already espied Eden in the form of the land courts. In the face of the apathy of a majority of tenant farmers and the antipathy of their clerical mentors, *United Ireland* (and the *Irish World*) relentlessly promoted the wisdom of the non-payment of rent and predicted the triumph of a programme that was, in effect, an active encouragement of a form of civil strife – Parnell's 'Captain Moonlight'. While a protracted campaign of agrarian 'outrage' ultimately brought the Liberal government to the negotiating table, the failure of the 'No Rent Manifesto' meant this achievement was a Pyrrhic victory for the Land League.

As will be discussed elsewhere, *United Ireland* readers were kept well-informed of the 'successes' of the 'no rent' policy. Anything up to an entire page of tightly condensed print was normally devoted to the campaign in each issue of the newspaper from October 1881 to May 1882. Concerted and communal refusals to pay rent were lauded. Rebates extracted from landlords made amenable by the Land League programme were highlighted. More menacingly, fatal or injurious outcomes sustained by those who failed to support the campaign were diligently reported, either without adverse comment or with the use of provocative terminology. For example, in the same edition in which the death of one of the Manifesto's clerical antagonists, the celebrated 'Lion of the West', Archbishop John MacHale of Tuam, was reported, the paper carried a news item on the murder of Peter Doherty of Craughwell, Co. Galway. He 'took a farm surrendered by another tenant … [and] was shot dead at his own door on Wednesday night. Shots were fired the same night into the home of a cousin of his, who joined in taking the surrendered farm.'[136] There was no condemnation of the killing by the newspaper. In the case of the murder of a 'respectable farmer' in Co. Limerick the victim was described as having been '*formally executed* [my italics] a few nights ago by neighbouring tenants, whom he had displeased by paying his rent without consultation with them'.[137]

In contrast the *Freeman's Journal* expressed its own lack of enthusiasm for the 'No Rent Manifesto' the day after it was first promulgated. 'We regret it deeply and sincerely. We deplore it from our hearts. We cannot anticipate the end of such a contest. Who can? We can foresee dire confusion, ruin to individuals, possible strife and bloodshed.'[138] The *Nation* was non-commital. For two weeks it studiously avoided editorializing on the manifesto before acknowledging in its issue of 5 November that 'we shall not discuss the merit of the No Rent Manifesto in these columns'. It wondered aloud if the document was 'wise or unwise, moral or immoral'[139] without, ultimately, coming down on either side of the argument.

In a gesture of frustration with a nationalist press that was less than supportive of the 'no rent' campaign, *United Ireland* complained, on 19 November, of self-censorship on the part of the *Nation* and the *Freeman's Journal*. 'We are perfectly certain that not more than a tenth of the refusals to pay rent have obtained publicity in the Irish Press. If only one week's list were prepared from private as well as from public sources we are convinced that it would fill every inch of our 48 columns.'[140] In its Christmas Eve, 1881 edition, in an attempt to provide a statistical underpinning for its philosophical certainty that the 'no rent' campaign had indeed taken hold, the paper published a comprehensive list of estates around the country upon which it claimed rents were not being paid. These included the substantial holdings of Lord Dillon (89,000 acres – probable annual rental £40,000), the Earl of Kenmare (91,080 – £49,400), the Earl of Bessborough (43,545 – £40,000), the Duke of Devonshire (27,483 – £29,000) and Lord Castletown (22,241 – £25,000).[141]

Long after the 'no rent' movement itself had effectively ended *United Ireland*, when it was formally possible to do so in the wake of the 'Kilmainham

Treaty', abandoned its crusade and replaced it with a much less ambitious but more productive campaign for the democratization of the often aristocratic and elitist Poor Law Boards of Guardians.[142]

A campaign against the payment of rent, tantamount to unarmed insurrection, 'was seen by some as a prelude to that total conflict with British power in Ireland that the new departure had been intended to initiate', wrote R.V. Comerford. 'But,' he added, 'if the farmers ever possessed the stomach for that they no longer did in October 1881.'[143] The proclamation of the Land League as an illegal organization, the incarceration of its political leadership, the relative success of the land courts (which implied a perception that Irish tenant farmers had been misled by their leaders) and the promise of legislation designed to deal with tenants in arrears who did not benefit from the 1881 Act, ensured that the seeds of civil disobedience fell on largely barren soil. The opposition of leading nationalist clerics, such as Archbishop Croke, emboldened tenant farmers who might otherwise have been inclined to succumb to the intimidation of more bellicose elements within the Land League.

The newspaper's fulsome support of the 'No Rent Manifesto' – which copper-fastened the reputation of *United Ireland* as being on the outer extremities of constitutional nationalism – was the principal, though by no means the sole, reason for the government's campaign of interdiction waged against the newspaper under the aegis of the PPP Act during the period of its editor's detention. *United Ireland*'s loyal, and ultimately futile, adherence to the prosecution of the campaign against rent left it open to forms of punitive action at which the government might otherwise have baulked. The coercion act, as already discussed, was a blunt instrument. It contained no specific provision for measures to be taken against newspapers. However, in order to transgress against the act, all that was required was that a person or persons be declared by warrant to be 'reasonably suspected' of 'inciting to an act of violence or intimidation, and tending to interfere with or disturb the maintenance of law and order'.[144] It was on this basis that O'Brien was only the first of a number of *United Ireland* employees to be incarcerated.

The most common offence cited in the arrest of various *United Ireland* employees was for 'instruction against payment of rent'.[145] The all-embracing nature of the coercion legislation allowed the government to be indiscriminate in its arrest of editorial, administrative and printing staff. While only the former might reasonably have been sanctioned for such 'incitement' in a courtroom under common or statute law, Forster's sweeping legislation made it possible to arrest and detain employees in the latter two categories as well. It was assumed that their detention would make it impossible for production of the newspaper to continue. The attorney general, W.M. Johnson, in a note appended to a DMP memo on 23 November 1881, suggested that 'The only practical way of dealing with this mischievous paper is to arrest under the PPP Act [*sic*] each successive person who undertakes the management of the paper.'[146]

Of course there already existed a corpus of legislation and precedent in relation to the utilization of the laws of seditious libel under which the journalistic staff of the paper might have been prosecuted. But the government chose not to, nor was it really required to, adopt that course of action. A comment of the solicitor general, A.M. Porter, on perusal of the 27 December 1881 edition of the paper is revealing. In reference to a report in *United Ireland* on the Irish Convention in Chicago that month, at which a number of provocative speeches were made – Porter highlighted that of the activist priest Fr Eugene Sheehy– he made the point that:

> There would, however, be considerable difficulty in selecting particular passages from the paper to support an indictment for seditious libel. But there is no doubt that the greater part of the paper is intended and calculated to encourage combinations against payment of rent, and to further the aim of the No Rent Manifesto [and] of the Land League.[147]

In the months ahead, in its determined efforts to still the rhetoric of *United Ireland* the government would, by default, have recourse to the rapier of seditious libel. But in its first concerted foray against the newspaper it contented itself with the broadsword of Forster's coercion provisions.

Notes

1   William O'Brien, *Evening Memories* (Dublin and London, 1920), 14–15.

2   T.P. Gill, 'William O'Brien: Some aspects', *Studies: an Irish Quarterly Review*, vol.17, no.68, December 1928, 614.

3 Joseph V. O'Brien, *William O'Brien and the Course of Irish Politics 1881–1918* (Berkeley, Los Angeles, London, 1976), 14.

4 *United Ireland*, 13 August 1881.

5 In, for example, Paul Bew's – *Land and the National Question in Ireland, 1858–82* (Dublin, 1978) and Samuel Clark, *Social Origins of the Irish Land War* (Princeton, 1979).

6 The Newspaper Libel and Registration Act, 1881, which was also a salient piece of legislation, will be discussed elsewhere.

7 R.V. Comerford, 'The Politics of Distress, 1877–82' in Vaughan, W.E. (ed.) *A New History of Ireland* (Oxford, 1996) 6 volumes, vol. vi., 46.

8 Irene Collins, *The Government and the Newspaper Press in France 1814–1881* (Oxford, 1959), 182.

9 http://dib.cambridge.org/viewReadPage.do?articleId=a5043 and, Felix Larkin, 'Parnell, politics and the press in Ireland', *The Parnell Lecture*, Parnell Summer School, Avondale, 11 August, 2010, 1. [My thanks to the author for a copy of his paper.]

10 http://dib.cambridge.org/viewReadPage.do?articleId=a8386 (17 September 2013)

11 The phrase was first used by Gladstone to describe nationalists elected in 1880 who opposed the leadership of Parnell and sat with the Liberals in the House of Commons.

12 'Writing for a select upper class readership' according to Patrick Maume. (Patrick Maume, 'This Proteus of politics': the *Dublin Evening Mail* on 'Gladstone', 1868–1898' in Daly and Hoppen, *Gladstone: Ireland and Beyond* (Dublin, 2011), 106.)

13 Marie-Louise Legg, *Newspapers and Nationalism*, 125–8.

14 John Devoy, *Recollections of an Irish Rebel* (New York, 1929), 329.

15 6 January 1882, Order of lord lieutenant for the seizure of *United Ireland*, the *United Irishman* and the *Irish World*. NAI, CSORP 1882/45842.

16 James O'Connor, *Recollections of Richard Pigott* (Dublin, 1889), 10.

17 Epitomized by Charles Kickham in a letter to Land League secretary P.J. Quinn, in which he wrote, 'I would not like to seem to throw cold water on anything that might serve the tenant farmer but the land agitators seem to keep doing their best to demoralise the people. I am told the West is in a bad way, but the intelligent Nationalists have seen the danger and I hope will keep clear of it.' (Kickham to Quinn, 27 May 1880, P.J. Quinn papers, NLI, MS 5930.)

18 Remarks of the attorney general, *Special Commission* (London, 1890), 11 volumes, vol. 6, 89.

19 Owen McGee, *The I.R.B: The Irish Republican Brotherhood from the Land League to Sinn Fein* (Dublin, 2005), 90. However, a memo from Superintendent John Mallon written in November 1880, suggests that while the Supreme Council wanted to establish a newspaper 'they think that unless the *Nation* or *Irishman* was discontinued, it would

not pay'. Mallon to Talbot, 20 November 1880, TNA, PRO, CAB 37/24, 1889, no. 21, 10. *Copies of Secret Official Reports made by the Officers of the Dublin Metropolitan Police between December, 1880 and March, 1883 on the Subject of Secret Societies and the Nationalist Movement in Ireland.*

20 James O'Connor, *Recollections of Richard Pigott* (Dublin, 1889), 14.

21 2 May 1889, *Special Commission*, (London, 1890) 11 volumes, vol. 7, 165, 60318.

22 O'Connor, *Recollections of Richard Pigott*, 6–10.

23 William O'Brien, *Recollections* (London, 1905), 300.

24 Michael Davitt, *The Fall of Feudalism in Ireland* (London, 1904), 565.

25 O'Connor, *Recollections of Richard Pigott*, 11.

26 James O'Connor alleges that Pigott had received a large sum of money from Isaac Butt and Patrick Egan in 1873 to sell his newspapers to the Home Rule movement. Money had changed hands but 'the sale was never completed, nor, of course, was the money returned'. (O'Connor, *Recollections of Pigott*, 13.)

27 Monday, 22 October 1888, *Special Commission*, vol. 1, 52.

28 HC Deb. 16 February 1882, vol. 266, c802.

29 O'Brien, *Recollections*, 308fn. O'Brien wrote 'As prosecutions and actions for libel thickened, Parnell and the others wisely withdrew from their nominal Directorship. The entire responsibility was thenceforward my own.'

30 Parnell to O'Brien, 1 July 1881, *Cork Free Press*, 27 September 1913.

31 21 May, 1889 *Special Commission*, vol.8, 89. O'Brien told the commission 'I would not be a party to depriving the extreme nationalists of what they might regard as their organ.' He claimed that his hope was to see the *Irishman* die a natural death as its dwindling circulation continued to fall. However it was only finally discontinued in 1885 at the insistence of Parnell. O'Brien admitted to paying scant attention to its content though he had editorial responsibility for its output.

32 Pigott to Forster, 15 October 1881, *Special Commission*, vol. 5, 580.

33 According to Owen McGee in *The IRB* the paper was imported, by a newsagent, Mrs Catherine Keogh, of 141 Dorset St (Owen McGee, *The IRB:The Irish Republican Brotherhood from the Land League to Sinn Fein* (Dublin, 2005), 91fn). She also imported the *Irish World* (NAI, CSORP, 1882/3283).

34 Kevin McKenna, 'From private visit to public opportunity: Gladstone's 1877 trip to Ireland' in Daly and Hoppen, (eds.) *Gladstone: Ireland and beyond*, 80.

35 Michael MacDonagh, *The Life of William O'Brien, the Irish Nationalist: a Biographical Study of Irish Nationalism, Constitutional and Revolutionary* (London, 1928), 50.

36 MacDonagh, *The Life of William O'Brien*, 50–1.

37 F.S.L. Lyons, *The Fall of Parnell, 1890–91* (Toronto, 1960), 24.

38   21 May, 1889 *Special Commission*, vol. 8, 72.

39   *United Ireland*, 7 March, 1885. 23 May, 1889 *Special Commission*, vol. 8, 182.

40   Lyons, *The Fall of Parnell*, 25.

41   Parnell to O'Brien, 1 July, 1881, from *Cork Free Press*, 27 September 1913.

42   'Your answer to our proposal must be yes nothing else will do.' Egan to O'Brien, 3 July 1881, O'Brien papers, UCC, WOB-PP-AA, f.12.

43   'In your newspaper you will be advancing directly and to the fullest of your ability the course and interest of your people and country.' O'Kelly to O'Brien, 2 July 1881, O'Brien papers, UCC, WOB-PP-AA, f.11. O'Kelly had been a distinguished foreign correspondent with the *New York Herald*.

44   21 May 1889 *Special Commission*, vol. 8, 88.

45   He wrote in his diary of 'a physical repulsion for the Pigott concern as for an ugly disease'. (O'Brien, *Recollections*, 299)

46   He rarely ever paid himself his full salary, normally subsisting on half that amount and residing in a room in the Imperial hotel living out of the contents of two trunks, the contents of which he put at the disposal of all potential libel litigants as his only tangible assets (Michael J.F.McCarthy, *The Irish Revolution* (Edinburgh, 1912), 281).

47   Dillon to O'Brien, 12 July 1881, O'Brien papers, UCC, WOB-PP-AA, f.14.

48   Parnell to O'Brien, 15 July 1881, from *Cork Free Press*, 27 September 1913.

49   O'Brien to Dillon, 18 July 1881, from *Cork Free Press*, 27 September, 1913

50   'The project of starting it as a daily paper on the 1st January has been almost abandoned.' Confidential report of Superintendent John Mallon to the Commissioner of the Dublin Metropolitan Police, 8 November, 1881, NAI, Police and Crime Division Reports, Compensation Cases, Crimes Act, 1882, Carton 6, 1881/38894.

51   Michael J.F. McCarthy, *The Irish Revolution* (Edinburgh, 1912), 187.

52   Frank Hugh O'Donnell, *A History of the Irish Parliamentary Party* (London, 1910), 2 vols, vol. 2, 150.

53   T.D. Sullivan, *Recollection of Troubled Times in Ireland* (Dublin, 1905), 73.

54   By, for example T.P. Gill MP – 'Since the *Nation* of Thomas Davis there had been no paper like it in Ireland, and there has been none since.' T.P. Gill, 'William O'Brien: Some Aspects', *Studies*, vol. 17, no. 68 (Dec. 1928), 614.

55   Frank Callanan, *T.M. Healy* (Cork, 1996), 62.

56   Parnell to Dr Kenny, 9 July, 1881, R. Barry O'Brien, *The Life of Charles Stewart Parnell* (London, 1910), 232.

57   MacDonagh, *The Life of William O'Brien*, 53.

58   *Cork Free Press*, 27 September 1913. In addition to his journalistic duties O'Brien filled most of the management roles as well, supervising the commercial operation of the newspaper. He was also responsible, in the early weeks of publication, for writing most of the editorial and news 'copy'.

59   21 May 1889, *Special Commission*, vol. 8, 90.

60   F.S.L. Lyons, *Charles Stewart Parnell* (London, 1977), 162. Frank Hugh O'Donnell described the newspaper as Parnell's 'personal instrument'. (Frank Hugh O'Donnell, *A History of the Irish Parliamentary Party* (London, 1910), 2 vols, vol. 2, 31.

61   Callanan, *T.M. Healy*, 60.

62   Conor Cruise O'Brien, *Parnell and His Party* (Oxford, 1957), 69.

63   MacDonagh, *The Life of William O'Brien*, 19.

64   F.S.L. Lyons, *Charles Stewart Parnell*, 162.

65   T.P. O'Connor, *The Parnell Movement* (London, 1886), 508.

66   O'Connor, *The Parnell Movement*, 507–8.

67   MacDonagh, *The Life of William O'Brien,* 14.

68   Andrew Kettle, *Material For Victory*, ed. Laurence Kettle (Dublin, 1958), 75.

69   21 May 1889, *Special Commission*, vol. 8, 88.

70   The *Nation* sold for 2d but was sixteen pages long, twice the length of *United Ireland*.

71   In subsequent issues most letters to the editor were unsigned, prompting the suspicion that some, at least, were the work of O'Brien or other members of the editorial staff.

72   A case in point was the shrill criticism of a proposed tour of Ireland in 1885 by Joseph Chamberlain and Sir Charles Dilke (*UI*, 27 June 1885). Parnell, for whom the radicals had outlived their usefulness, was asked by Chamberlain to instruct O'Brien to desist. Parnell, while publicly deprecating the tone of the article, placed responsibility for the invective squarely on the shoulders of O'Brien. The campaign continued for some time (Myles Dungan, *The Captain and the King: William O'Shea, Parnell and late Victorian Ireland* (Dublin, 2010), 199).

73   *United Ireland*, 13 August 1881.

74   He had been treasurer of the IRB (Owen McGee, *The IRB* (Dublin, 2005), 44).

75   21 May 1889, *Special Commission*, vol. 8,121. 22 May, vol. 8, 151.

76   *United Ireland*, 13 August, 1881. There is no indication of the source but it was probably extracted from the *United Irishman*.

77   HC Deb. 16 February 1882, vol. 266, c801.

78   *United Ireland*, 13 August 1881.

79   22 May 1889- Special Commission, vol.8, 120–214 [cross examination of O'Brien by

the attorney general].

80 Joseph V. O'Brien, *William O'Brien and the Course of Irish Politics 1881–1918*, 17.

81 *United Ireland*, 13 August 1881.

82 MacDonagh, *The Life of William O'Brien*, 53.

83 By 25 November 1881 she was styling them 'the Sedition papers'. T.W. Moody and R.A.J. Hawkins, *Florence Arnold-Forster's Irish Journal* (Oxford, 1988), 322.

84 Diary entry, 22 September 1881, Moody and Hawkins, *Florence Arnold-Forster*, 248.

85 Diary entry, 23 September 1881, Moody and Hawkins, *Florence Arnold-Forster*, 249. Naish would find out just how clever when O'Brien defeated him in the Mallow by-election two years later.

86 F.S.L. Lyons, *Charles Stewart Parnell*, 162–3.

87 *United Ireland*, 18 February 1882.

88 *United Ireland*, 17 September 1881.

89 O'Brien, *William O'Brien*, 15.

90 23 May 1889, *Special Commission*, vol. 8, 199.

91 Gray's move towards 'Parnellism', already begun by 1882, was hastened in August of that year when he was jailed for contempt of court as a result of the fallout from the Hynes case, the first prosecution for murder taken under the 1882 Crimes Act.

92 Diary entry, 28 September 1881, Moody and Hawkins, *Florence Arnold-Forster*, 251.

93 *Freeman's Journal*, 17 September 1881.

94 *Freeman's Journal*, 14 January 1882.

95 *United Ireland*, 13 August 1881.

96 Its entire basis has been questioned by much modern scholarship, beginning with Barbara Lewis Solow, *The Land Question and the Irish Economy, 1870–1903* (Cambridge, Mass. 1971) and including William E. Vaughan, *Landlords and Tenants in Ireland, 1848–1904* (Dublin, 1984).

97 Solow, for example, suggests that the 1870 Land Act 'signaled [*sic*] the end of landlord investment' (198) and contends that 'the Irish sacrificed economic progress on the altar of Irish nationalism' (204). Vaughan concurs. 'Irish landlords did not invest in their estates as lavishly as was common in Britain' though he goes on to argue that 'the social significance of this was probably more important than its economic effects' (25).

98 *Irish World*, 7 January 1882.

99 *Irish World*, 15 April 1882.

100 O'Donnell, *A History of the Irish Parliamentary Party*, vol. 2, 74.

101 *United Ireland*, 27 August 1881.

102 *United Ireland*, 24 November 1881.

103 *United Ireland*, 24 September 1881.

104 22 May, 1889 Special Commission, vol. 8, 163, 71546, 71553a, 71554.

105 Sally Warwick-Haller, *William O'Brien and the Irish Land War* (Dublin, 1990), 52.

106 Sally Warwick-Haller, *William O'Brien and the Irish Land War* (Dublin, 1990), 53.

107 *United Ireland*, 17 December 1881.

108 *United Ireland*, 17 December 1881.

109 *United Ireland*, 8 October, 1881, from a congratulatory telegram sent by Patrick Egan to Fr Eugene Sheehy on the occasion of his release from prison. Endorsed by O'Brien with the headline 'A Holy War'.

110 This included the simianization of working-class members of the Order in a number of *United Ireland* cartoons, much along the lines for which English magazines like *Punch* and the likes of Thomas Nast in the USA, have been criticized (*United Ireland*, 14 June 1884).

111 Sally Warwick-Haller, *William O'Brien and the Irish Land War* (Dublin, 1990), 54.

112 For example, a memo of attorney general A.M. Porter having viewed the 24 December 1881 issue of *United Ireland*. 'The particular number in question is I think seditious in its tone.' 27 December 1881, NAI, CSORP, Police and Crime Division Reports, III, Carton Six, 1881/46048.

113 Joseph V. O'Brien, *William O'Brien and the Course of Irish Politics*, 17.

114 *United Ireland*, 13 August 1881.

115 *United Ireland*, 27 August 1881.

116 T.P. O'Connor, *Memoirs of an Old Parliamentarian* (London, 1928) 2 vols, vol. 1, 143.

117 O'Shea, husband of Parnell's mistress, came in for rather less abuse than the other Irish Shaw-ite MPs. This may have been connected to his surprising vote, cast for Parnell for party chair in 1880. It may have also been related to O'Brien's knowledge of Parnell's affair and a desire to leave well enough alone. Alternatively, although this is highly unlikely, it may merely have been an oversight on the part of the editor.

118 Michael MacDonagh, *The Home Rule Movement* (Dublin & London, 1910), 169.

119 O'Donnell, *A History of the Irish Parliamentary Party*, 31–2.

120 O'Brien, *Parnell and His Party*, 81.

121 *United Ireland*, 15 October 1881.

122 Conor Cruise O'Brien, *Parnell and His Party* (Oxford, 1957), 81.

123 Virginia Crossman, *Politics, Law and Order in Nineteenth-century Ireland* (Dublin, 1996), 151.

124 *United Ireland*, 10 September 1881.

125 Diary entry, 8 October 1881, Moody and Hawkins, *Florence Arnold-Forster*, 262.

126 Diary entry, 28 January 1882, Moody and Hawkins, *Florence Arnold-Forster*, 364.

127 Clifford Lloyd, *Ireland Under the Land League* (Edinburgh and London, 1892), 146.

128 *Public General Statutes Passed in the Forty-fourth and Forty-fifth Years of the Reign of Her Majesty, Queen Victoria, 1881* (London, 1881), 3.

129 'I look on it with feelings not only of aversion on general grounds but of doubt and much misgiving as to the likelihood of its proving efficacious in the particular case.' Gladstone to Forster, 25 October 1880, British Library, Gladstone papers, Add.Mss 44157, ff.184–5.

130 O'Brien, *The Life of Charles Stewart Parnell*, 238–40.

131 *United Ireland*, 15 October 1881.

132 9 October 1881, NAI, CSORP, 1882/19234. The actual document itself, NAI, CSORP, 1881/39049, is erroneously dated 9 November 1881.

133 9 October / 9 November 1881, NAI CSORP 1882-19234.

134 Mallon to Police Commissioner, 21 October 1881, NAI, CSORP, 1882/19234.

135 *United Ireland*, 22 October 1881.

136 *United Ireland*, 12 November 1881.

137 *United Ireland*, 12 November 1881.

138 *Freeman's Journal*, 19 October 1881.

139 *Nation*, 5 November 1881.

140 *United Ireland*, 19 November 1881.

141 *United Ireland*, 24 December 1881.

142 *United Ireland*, 8 April 1882. 'Ejecting the Lords – Purging the Poor Law Boards – some Poor Law Union results'.

143 R.V. Comerford, 'The Politics of Distress, 1877–82' in Vaughan, W.E. (ed.) *A New History of Ireland* (Oxford, 1996), 9 vols, vol. VI, 48.

144 *Public General Statutes Passed in the Forty-fourth and Forty-fifth Years of the Reign of Her Majesty, Queen Victoria, 1881* (London, 1881), 3.

145 Note of J.M. Naish, 25 November 1881, NAI, CSORP, Police and Crime Division Reports, III, Compensation Cases, Crimes Act 1882–83, Carton Six, 1881/42170.

146 Note of W.H. Johnson, 23 November 1881, original memo of Insp. James Smyth to Captain Talbot, 19 November, 1881, NAI, CSORP, Police and Crime Division Reports, III, Compensation Cases, Crimes Act 1882–83 Carton Six, 1881/40550.

147 Memo of A.M. Porter to T.H. Burke, 27 December, 1881, NAI, CSORP, Police and Crime Division Reports, III, Compensation Cases, Crimes Act 1882–83, Carton Six, 1881/46048.

CHAPTER TWO

Enforcing Silence: The Liberal Government and the Attempted Suppression of United Ireland, October– December 1881

'Its entire tone is suggestive of outrage; and, in many instances, its disgraceful attacks upon particular members of the Government could hardly fail to be understood by some of its readers as incitements to murder. In some instances … its teaching is distinctly and undisguidedly *treasonable,* and its language is nearly always seditious.'[1]

(Memo to Cabinet on *United Ireland,* Andrew Marshall Porter, solicitor general for Ireland, 23 January 1882)

'If anybody or anything showed signs of comparative sanity, *United Ireland*, under the spirited editorship of Mr. William O'Brien, was ready to apply the requisite ginger in the largest available doses.'[2]

(Frank Hugh O'Donnell, *A History of the Irish Parliamentary Party*)

The *United Ireland* bulletin board

Dublin Castle had a long history of dealing with unsympathetic newspaper commentary. But in an era where bribery and arbitrary suppression were more problematic than they had been at the turn of the nineteenth century, *United Ireland* offered the administration a unique challenge. Unlike intractable local newspapers like Timothy Harrington's *Kerry Sentinel* or Jasper Tully's *Roscommon Herald*, it had a national reach. The *Irish World,* while a serious irritant, was erratically distributed and had an underlying socialistic ethos seriously out of kilter with the philosophy of most Irish tenant farmers. Furthermore any imperative on the part of the Land League to continue its widespread distribution disappeared after the establishment of *United Ireland*. The *Freeman's Journal* and the *Nation*, other national newspapers, were relatively moderate in tone and rarely required punitive action on the part of the Castle. Gladstone felt in a position to write of the *Freeman's* proprietor in October 1881, 'With Gray we have a real power on our side.'[3]

The potentially more contentious, and avowedly Fenian, the *Irishman* had a rapidly dwindling circulation and, probably as a consequence of its irrelevance, the authorities never found it necessary to take repressive steps against it.[4] Furthermore the information that might be gleaned from its columns made its continued publication more useful to G Division than its curtailment or repression. However, some of its more extreme editorial copy was used in an attempt to discredit O'Brien and Parnell in cross-examination before the *Times* commission in 1889. O'Brien had made the decision, against the better judgment of Parnell, to keep the *Irishman* going. He later told the commission that 'we paid no attention to the *Irishman*. It was a mere thing that was kept going for no particular purpose or object' and that when it was finally closed in 1885 the weekly sales amounted to 1,204.

But *United Ireland* abjured, even abhorred, moderation and the politics of deference. Its zealotry resonated with Irish tenant farmers. Its news columns, however factional, offered some evidence to rural Land League branches that they were not campaigning in isolation. Its simultaneous fulfilment of both a narrative and facilitative function created a declamatory bulletin board. As governmental assumptions that the arrest of its editor would inhibit its effectiveness proved overly optimistic, the journal became the primary target for a series of *ad hoc* measures designed to silence it.

It should not have been necessary for the government to improvise its strategy for the curbing or outright suppression of the newspaper. Outside of the gamut of the recently introduced coercion legislation the government had powers to deal with what were viewed as seditious or treasonable publications through the ordinary libel laws. While correspondence between the law officers and the Executive testifies to the prevailing view that much of the content of *United Ireland* was seditious,[5] no action was taken against the newspaper for seditious libel during this period. This reluctance was based on the assumption that it would be difficult to secure a conviction from an impartially constituted jury. In his *Introduction to the Study of the Law of the Constitution,* first published in 1885, A.V. Dicey wrote that 'a man may publish anything which twelve of his countrymen think is not blamable'.[6] But the reality in Ireland was that a man facing trial by jury, might well expect to be able to publish anything which even two jurors of like mind thought was 'not blamable'. The result would be a hung jury and a probable *nolle prosequi* thereafter.

The decisions made by the Castle also suggested a debilitating apprehension. This was based on uncertainty surrounding the legality of many of the actions taken against the paper. Documentary evidence confirms that there were protracted and anxious internal legal debates and the approach adopted was often improvised in nature. Ironically an earlier Liberal administration led by Gladstone (1868–74) had introduced coercion legislation in the shape of the 1870 Peace Preservation Act whose press provisions might well have dealt the fatal blow to *United Ireland's* vitriolic rhetoric that Forster's Irish legal regime was eager to inflict but unable to administer.

Of course the philosophical context of the entire campaign of suppression waged against *United Ireland* was a notional Liberal party attachment to the concept of freedom of the press, and a reluctance to be seen to transgress in a blatantly oppressive fashion against what was regarded as one of the fundamental rights of a democratic society. In her work on the Irish provincial press during this period Marie-Louise Legg has written of the Liberal leadership that 'their willingness to prosecute newspapers was still hampered by their concern about the freedom of the press'.[7] This is reflected in the relative infrequency of such prosecutions between 1880 and 1885. Tampering with the right of an Irish journal to publish material that was objectionable, merely because it was inimical to the policy of an incumbent government, also had potential consequences for the English press, the implications of which the Liberals did not wish to have to confront. Even newspapers, otherwise supportive of government coercive policies in Ireland, like the *Times*, were wary of attempts to smother the Irish radical nationalist press. In the wake of the Fenian unrest of the late 1860s the *Times* had expressed regret at a draconian press clause in the 1870 Peace Preservation Act but deemed the action of the authorities to be 'indispensable'.[8] It took a similarly nuanced line a decade later with the attempted suppression of *United Ireland*.

The justification offered for the restraint of freedom of expression in the 1880s was that such freedom was being abused by the polemicists of the Irish nationalist press. As a result, so the argument went, the rights of such journals were forfeit because of their own transgressions. In addition adherence to the concept of press freedom was far from absolute anyway. It was, for instance, circumscribed by a patently undemocratic sentiment that such liberty was only genuinely valid in the upper reaches of an hierarchical society. Writing in the 1870s Gladstone described press freedom as 'a safety valve of passions'.[9] But he also distrusted what the political elite saw as the undifferentiated and unsophisticated approach of the masses to politics. Freedom of expression was potentially subject to proletarian abuse. That mind-set was, almost axiomatically, extended to the ungovernable Irish. This was especially true in the 1880s, when public order was deemed to have been jeopardized by the subversive rhetoric of certain Irish nationalist newspapers. William O'Brien, *primus inter pares* in that regard, scoffed at Liberal pretensions with editorial reminders in *United Ireland* that the government was behaving in a fashion reminiscent of, 'the Sultan of Turkey, or the military Governor of St. Petersburg'.[10] On 11 February 1882

United Ireland proclaimed that 'John Bull has become the grinning satyr of Europe. A *soi-disant* apostle of liberty, he has been forced to swallow his own professions of faith, and to trample on the prerogative of his rather too-much-vaunted Constitution.'[11]

Not that Britain had ever adopted a US-style 'First Amendment' approach to the notion of press freedom in any case. Dicey has pointed out that there was actually no specific recognition of the concept in British legislation. In his *Introduction to the Study of the Law of the Constitution* he wrote that,

> the phrases 'freedom of discussion' or 'liberty of the press' are rarely found in any part of the statute-book nor among the maxims of the common law. As terms of art they are indeed quite unknown to our Courts. At no time has there in England been any proclamation of the right to liberty of thought or to freedom of speech ... Above all, [the law] recognises in general no special privilege on behalf of the press. [12]

This was in contrast to other European countries, like Belgium, where it was enshrined in constitutional law. Dicey went on to observe that the latitude afforded newspapers varied and could range from, 'unrestricted license to very severe restraint, and the experience of English history during the last two centuries shows that under the law of libel the amount of latitude conceded to the expression of opinion has, in fact, differed greatly according to the condition of popular sentiment'.[13]

United Ireland: the succession – October/November 1881

The most frenzied period of government suppression of *United Ireland* stretched from the arrest of O'Brien in October 1881 to that briefest of respites in the sustained combat between Irish nationalism and the Liberal government, in April/May 1882. During that time the newspaper, by its very survival, provided activists with a reflection of their own tenacity. It offered itself as a weekly instruction manual in civil disobedience, and implicit incitement or, at the very least, encouragement to trespass into areas of activity outside of the law. The latter encroachment alone offered comfort to the government in its policy of suppression. The unrestrained nature of *United Ireland*'s commentary during the early days of the 'Kilmainham' interlude calls into question the view of Lyons that the accompanying upsurge in agrarian crime was inchoate in nature, 'the anarchy of lost leadership, not of imposed tyranny'.[14] The Land League's newspaper, while not exactly imposing tyranny, was certainly offering leadership. Neither was it seen to condemn the more extreme actions of the 'village tyrants' of the Liberal narrative. On the contrary, it assiduously reported on their activities. In so doing it made a significant contribution to the success of 'Captain Moonlight' in extracting concessions from the Gladstone government.

Both *United Ireland's* strident advocacy of the 'No Rent Manifesto' and the manner in which it reported both egregious and petty episodes of agrarian crime in a weekly column with the unambiguously bellicose title 'Incidents of the Campaign', clearly left the paper vulnerable to legal sanctions. Over the period in question the Irish Executive, in consultation with the Dublin Castle law officers, adopted a number of different approaches designed to hamper the activities of the newspaper. All ended in failure. The first phase involved the arrest of 'essential' employees. When this was counteracted by an influx of volunteers – at least one of whom was a DMP informant – the policy adopted was the more questionable one of seizing copies of the paper from newsagent's shops. This presented the government with a potential influx of claims for compensation from vendors. Latterly the authorities resorted to a policy of wholesale interdiction of the newspaper before it even reached any retail outlets. This left it vulnerable to legal action from *United Ireland*. Though each individual element of a largely piecemeal strategy presented the newspaper with a series of difficult challenges, none proved insurmountable.

After the arrest of O'Brien, a highly motivated group that included the journalist Edward O'Donovan, barrister James Bryce Killen and sub-editor James O'Connor,[15] managed to maintain *United Ireland's* presence in the shops of willing newsagents, in the hands of street vendors, and even circulating via the Irish postal service. At the apex of an adminstrative, technical and editorial triangle was Patrick Egan, resident in Paris with the Land League funds at his disposal, who 'acted as the nominal proprietor'.[16] While the newspaper continued to be printed in Dublin, O'Connor and Killen played a significant role in its assembly. The first replacement editor, Edward O'Donovan, 'barely had time to escape to France'[17] after a warrant was issued for his arrest shortly after he took over the reins.

Presumably because of his own journalistic connections Thomas Sexton MP was 'credited' by the *Times* in early November 1881 with the editorship of the newspaper. With, no doubt, some element of pique and bruised vanity, *United Ireland* informed its readers on 12 November, that 'we desire it to be made known that a malicious statement in the Irish correspondence of the London *Times,* that Mr Sexton "has assumed the chief direction of *United Ireland*," is totally without foundation. Mr. Sexton is not now, and has not been at any time, connected with this journal.'[18]

Among the other journalists actually associated with the enterprise were Eugene Davis, who 'edited' the paper for six weeks in Paris, T.P. Gill, later MP for Louth[19], John Augustus O'Shea, who had reported on the Franco-Prussian war for the London *Standard* and William O'Donovan, brother of Edward O'Donovan and former Paris Correspondent of the *Irish Times*.[20] Davis, a Fenian – Parnell described him to the *Times* Commission as 'a man of physical force opinions'[21] – was a regular contributor to the *Irishman*. He would later become notorious as the alleged (and fictional) source of the Pigott/*Times* letters in 1886.

William O'Donovan was the epitome of the professional journalist. Despite his covert existence as a senior member of the IRB he was, unlike the more squeamish O'Brien during his time with the *Freeman*, capable of writing editorial copy for the Unionist *Irish Times*. John Devoy, himself a New York journalist, pointed out that while O'Donovan, a Fenian, was doing editorials for the *Irish Times*, Jack Adams, an atheist, was 'doing Catholic articles' for the *Freeman*. They used to meet in the Ship Tavern in Abbey St 'and have a good laugh over their articles, of which they didn't believe a word'.[22] Reporting to the Police Commissioner on 21 October 1881 Chief Superintendent Mallon, at this point getting most of his information from constables posted outside the offices at 33 Lower Abbey St, and from his own journalistic sources,[23] reported that 'William O'Donovan, who was up to a recent date on the literary staff of the *Irish Times*, has gone to the *Irishman* office, supposed to take charge of it.'[24]

A lesser light, in a journalistic sense, was sub-editor Arthur O'Keeffe, whose brother Francis worked for the paper as business manager. O'Keeffe, arrested on the premises on 15 December 1881, was described by the redoubtable secret policeman Sir Robert Anderson as 'one of Parnell's fellow prisoners in 1882, and who was sometimes employed by him as an amanuensis'.[25]

One of the more unexpected volunteer journalists who attempted to facilitate the survival of *United Ireland* was the English Radical MP and newspaperman Joseph Cowen, Liberal MP for Newcastle and proprietor and editor of the *Newcastle Chronicle*. In February 1882 *United Ireland* would declare that only he and Henry Labouchere 'keep the name of Parliamentary Radical from stinking'.[26] According to a report sent by Superintendent Mallon to the DMP commissioner, Cowen arrived in Dublin to offer his services shortly after the arrest of O'Brien. The intervention appears to have been facilitated by the prominent Land Leaguer and future MP, Dr Joseph Kenny. Mallon arrested Kenny on 24 October and observed to Talbot, the DMP Commissioner, that 'it is singular that Mr Cowan's [sic] name was written on the slate in Dr Kenny's hall on this morning when he was taken into custody'.[27] Nothing came of the visit or the offer of assistance.[28]

An element of uncertainty surrounds the extent to which O'Brien himself continued editing and/or contributing to the newspaper during his incarceration in Kilmainham. Certainly the prisoners appeared to have no difficulty in smuggling out anything from the 'No Rent Manifesto' to Parnell's passionate and troubled correspondence with Katharine O'Shea. O'Brien had the leisure and the facilities in Kilmainham to write at will.[29] He himself offered two different versions of the truth of his continuing involvement with his paper.

When questioned on the issue at the special commission in May 1889 O'Brien admitted to 'irregular' contributions to the newspaper while he was in jail. But he downplayed the extent or significance of those contributions. 'Owing to the constant arrests and to the constant shifting of the place of publication it was utterly impossible to keep an effective control of the paper'.[30] However, fifteen years later, in the first volume of his memoirs, *Recollections*, O'Brien was less inclined to relinquish credit for the output of the paper, writing that 'it was another of the singularities of the Forsterian tragi-comedy, that I was able throughout the No-Rent movement to supply the journalistic stimulus and direction of the movement weekly from within the walls of Kilmainham Jail'.[31]

O'Brien's *Times* commission evidence, suggesting minimal involvement, came at a time when it was incumbent upon him to distance himself from some of the material and commentary that had brought about the strenuous government efforts to close down the paper in 1881/2. He spent much of his cross-examination on the back foot, disowning the authorship and decrying the tone of many articles that appeared in *United Ireland* during his incarceration. While he accepted full responsibility for everything that was printed, he appeared somewhat chastened on many occasions by the character of some of the more extreme 'copy' carried in the newspaper. However, his later version of events is supported by others associated with *United Ireland* from October 1881 to May 1882.

John Denvir, a journalist and former Fenian, had an established printing business in Liverpool and was responsible for the publication of a number of Irish political newspapers in the UK.[32] He played a major role in the survival of *United Ireland* and frequently printed the newspaper in his Liverpool works. In his memoir, *Life Story of an Old Rebel*, Denvir reproduced a letter from Patrick Egan in which the former Land League Treasurer recalled the process by which the newspaper was published in Paris. According to Egan, 'all the leading articles that appeared in "U.I" [*sic*] during those fateful months (or almost all of them) were written by William O'Brien in Kilmainham prison, smuggled out by the underground railroad, which ran upon regular scheduled time, and were despatched by trusty messengers to me in Paris'.[33]

A fortnight after the arrest of O'Brien *United Ireland* carried a leading article announcing a severe curtailment of editorial comment. Claiming that 'freedom of opinion is for the moment at an end in Ireland' the editorial continued, 'under these circumstances a journal which has no aptitude for apostacy [*sic*] can continue to exist only by ceasing to express any opinion at all, and confining itself to collecting the bare facts concerning the great struggle which is only now commencing'. It advised its readers to draw their own conclusions in the future about the stance of the newspaper on political developments and to 'interrogate their own hearts for our opinions'. Running alongside the editorial was something that would become familiar to readers in the weeks that followed, a blank, black-bordered column stretching to the bottom of the page bearing the heading 'Freedom of the Press in Ireland in 1881'.[34]

However, despite deliberately denying itself the traditional use of the editorial page, a multiplicity of stratagems was devised to ensure that the readership was never reduced to the interrogation of its own 'hearts and opinions' in order to divine the position of *United Ireland* on any given topic. The front-page cartoon (restored on 12 November for the first time since the arrest of Parnell and O'Brien) afforded the opportunity of a satirical swipe at Castle policies and functionaries. Also on the front page the letters column allowed the newspaper to vent, while claiming some distance from any inflammatory opinions expressed. This was, of course, of absolutely no value when it came to potential retaliatory legal action on the part of the authorities. The newspaper was responsible for every word printed, whatever the source.

How 'remote' the correspondence columns were is, at any rate, a moot point. O'Brien, before his arrest, had tried to impress on correspondents the necessity to sign all letters to the editor. However, increasingly, the newspaper carried unsigned and pseudonymous letters on its front page. On a typical week (5 November 1881) during this period there were letters from, 'Harvey Duff', 'Erin Oge', 'A Munster Boy', 'An Irish Papist', '*Nil Desperandum*', 'One of the Civilised', 'Pro Bono Publico', and 'A True Leaguer'. Of eighteen letters only three are in any way traceable and only one of those, from a J. Smallhorne, 43 Lower Gardiner Street, gives a full address.[35] There are three possible explanations. The letters were received unsigned and published anyway. They were signed but the editorial staff exercised discretion on behalf of correspondents by deleting their names. Or they were actually written by *United Ireland* staff as a useful adjunct to the propaganda being purveyed elsewhere in the newspaper.

'Incidents of the Campaign'

But it was not the front-page cartoon or indeed the 'letters to the editor' that set the newspaper on a collision course with Dublin Castle. Since its inception *United Ireland,* in common with the *Freeman's Journal* and the *Nation*, had reported on criminality associated with the Land War. After the arrest of Parnell and the other leaders the incidence of agrarian crime increased rapidly. *United Ireland*, rather than simply reporting on the most newsworthy 'outrages' in standard fashion, that of the *Freeman* for example, adopted a more provocative approach. On 5 November much space was devoted to a column entitled 'The Spirit of the Country'. This was an exhortatory collation of the details of dozens of assaults, attacks, threatening notices and boycotting incidents which had taken place over the preceding week. Arranged around the paper in haphazard fashion each incident, in isolation, might have attracted little enough attention. But when assembled in combination, often accompanied by inflammatory headings, the effect was intimidatory. This juxtaposition of a series of examples of petty and serious violence also contributed to a sense of pervasive anarchy, and even *anomie*, any notions of which Dublin Castle was eager to dispel.

While some of the forty snippets first collated under the heading 'The Spirit of the Country' were intended to be heartening and morale-boosting in nature, a total of fourteen items related to incidents of violence, intimidation and boycotting associated with the land agitation. One paragraph, headed 'Captain Moonlight in Kildare', for example, read,

> The following threatening notice was found posted on the Athy Catholic Church gate on Sunday morning: – 'Notice to the Kavanaghs of Chapel Lane, Athy. Drive no more Preseners [*sic*] or Police. As I am Captain Moonlight I will visit you by a nearly date and leave youse [*sic*] an example to all mankind. – Captain Moonlight.' At the bottom were two coffins carefully and tastefully drawn. The notice was written in a female hand.

Other stories referred to the burning of crops on a farm where the tenants 'were suspected of paying their rent', the refusal of farmers to cut a boycotted neighbour's hay and the, apparently, more innocuous 'A Midnight Warning', in which the object of the warning had actually been murdered.[36]

The militancy of its coverage of the land agitation was reinforced when 'Spirit of the Country' gave way to a new column later in November entitled 'Incidents of the Campaign'. Its arrival was heralded by an open letter to officers of suppressed branches of the now-proscribed Land League. This read: 'As people are now deprived of the ordinary means of exchanging ideas between one part of the country and another, it becomes more necessary than ever to obtain full and reliable information of what is passing upon every estate in the country at this all-important time.' Accordingly past secretaries of League branches were asked 'to forward weekly, or as often as may be necessary, to this office short accounts of what is happening in their several districts.'[37]

In taking on what was, in essence, a quasi-organizational function by exchanging details of the levels of agrarian activity between different regions of the country, *United Ireland* stepped outside its propaganda remit and invited an even greater quantum of repression from Dublin Castle. It left itself open to the accusation that, if not actually guilty of incitement, it was certainly giving form and structure to anarchic resistance. H.O. Arnold Forster, the chief secretary's adopted son suggested, in correspondence with the *Pall Mall Gazette*, that *United Ireland* was also abetting the quasi-judicial functions taken upon itself by the Land League through the *ad hoc* tribunals (often called 'Land League courts') established by local branches. He maintained 'that the Land League decrees have constantly been enforced by outrage ... and in confirmation of my statement I refer your readers to the columns of *United Ireland*, where they will find the whole proceeding – the crime, the tribunal and the punishment – over and over again described'.[38]

Most of the items carried were cautionary tales of one kind or another. A typical example was the following:

> 'A Bitter Punishment' – John R. Heffernan, of Blarney, now in Kilmainham, who procured his release lately by a contrite petition to Mr. Forster for his honour's clemency, is not spoken to by the Kilmainham suspects, his crops are lying derelict, as nobody can be got to save them, and the testimonial which was being organised in his interest in Cork before the disclosure of his letter to Mr. Forster has been abandoned in disgust.

> 'A Farmer Shot Dead' – Peter Doherty, a young farmer living at Carrigan, near Craughwell, county Galway, who took a farm surrendered by another tenant, who was refused a reduction, was shot dead at his own door on Wednesday night. Shots were fired the same night into the home of a cousin of his, who joined in taking the surrendered farm.[39]

In some instances the levels of information on the travails of the boycotted 'land-grabber' or payer of rent were even more detailed.[40] The headlines were often morbid and sinister, and there was a singular lack of even implied disapproval of the violence in the accompanying reportage. It was an undisguised warning to potential renegades. The column practically introduced an element of 'No Rent' competition between League branches in different parts of the country and left *United Ireland* open to the accusation that it was deliberately ratcheting up tension, dissent and violence by publishing such reports in such a fashion. Later the column was cited specifically by the attorney general as an egregious example of incitement in his opening statement to the *Times* commission in 1888.[41]

In his own evidence before the *Times* commission in 1889 O'Brien was, essentially, forced to disown the column. By way of self-exculpation he pointed out that it had appeared while he was incarcerated in Kilmainham and was then discontinued by him after his release 'owing to the hateful insinuations that were made in reference to this heading.'[42] Among the 'hateful insinuations' was a charge by Arnold-Forster that *United Ireland* was an 'accessory to crime'.[43]

While accepting full responsibility for the content of *United Ireland* O'Brien refused to accept any personal blame for the material contained in 'Incidents of the Campaign'. Instead he placed that squarely on the shoulders of James O'Connor and insisted that it was O'Connor's job to clip news reports from daily papers and reproduce them in *United Ireland*. O'Brien acknowledged that O'Connor had often exceeded his brief in the choice of headline. He was referred, for example, to a story entitled 'Bathing a Bailiff'. The language of the actual report was factual and neutral, but it dealt with the 'tarring' of a bailiff who was then thrown in a canal. O'Brien was forced to accept that 'that is an exceedingly objectionable thing to publish under that particular heading but it is a paragraph cut out of some daily newspaper as an ordinary item of news. It was probably in precisely the same words in the London *Times*.'[44] O'Brien, however, was unable to divorce himself entirely from the column. He was forced to admit that before he was imprisoned, 'the heading, "The Campaign" appeared, for which I am undoubtedly responsible'. But this was, 'started for the purpose of including such incidents as sheriff's sales, arrests of suspects, and matters of that sort'.[45]

In February 1883, as an embittered backbench MP, W.E.Forster singled out the 'Incidents of the Campaign' column as evidence of what he alleged to be Parnell's tacit approval of 'outrage'.[46] This was a logic pursued by the *Times* and the Tories later in the decade. Forster pointed out that Parnell was a major shareholder in a newspaper where 'murder, arson, robbery, insults to the dead, attacks upon women were habitually described ... as "Incidents in the Campaign?"'[47] However, in a conversation during the most intense period of 'no rent' activity in November 1881, he seemed reluctant to act against the journal for fear of increasing its popularity. Florence Arnold Forster recorded in her diary, 'I spoke to him about *United Ireland* and its "No Rent" propaganda: he does not think so much of this – the circulation of the paper, Mr. Johnson[48] tells him, has fallen off by one half,[49] and a prohibition or prosecution would only give it a new lease of life.'[50] In a game of risk and reward the creation of martyr-journalists was a disadvantageous consequence that had to be considered by every serving chief secretary of the 1880s.

In February 1882, *United Ireland* claimed that its own apotheosis had, indeed, taken place, abetted by Forster's policies. O'Brien wrote that 'on the whole we are pleased with the measures Mr. Forster is taking to suppress *United Ireland*. If he consulted our own feelings we would scarcely dare to request him to advertise us so well and hurt us so little. It was he who first opened the eyes of the public, or indeed our own, to the full merits of our paper.'[51]

Eight years later, in his own evidence to the *Times* Commission Parnell, like O'Brien, separated himself from the *United Ireland* of the Kilmainham incarceration period. He disingenuously told the Attorney General in his cross-examination that, 'There was an attempt made to carry on "United Ireland" at that time, but it was carried on in a variety of ways by shifts under no settled management, *and it could not be described as the Land League organ* [my emphasis].'[52] It was a classic example of Parnell's occasional economy with the truth. While its leadership was incarcerated in jails around the country *United Ireland* was one of the few functioning organs of a rapidly disintegrating association.

Legislating for silence: arrest and seizure – November/December 1881

In its edition of 12 November 1881 *United Ireland* announced that it intended to take legal action of its own against RIC constables who, up to that point, had been instructed merely to remove sheets advertising the contents of the newspaper on the shop fronts of newsagents.

We simply want to give notice to all whom it may concern that we mean to have the question tried out with the least possible delay, whether newspaper property is as hopelessly as newspaper liberties at the mercy of Sub Constable Snooks and his masters.[53]

As to the legality of the actions contemplated and taken against *United Ireland* over the winter of 1881/2, the subject was debated and discussed at the highest levels of the Irish government. There were numerous options, but equally there were snares and pitfalls into which an unwary administration could stray. The Protection of Person and Property act gave the state virtually unlimited powers when it came to the arrest and detention of individuals 'guilty as principal or accessory … [of] an act of violence or intimidation, or inciting to an act of violence or intimidation, and tending to interfere with or disturb the maintenance of law and order'.[54] But it did not, for example, specifically bestow upon the administration the capacity to remove placards advertising the availability of a newspaper in retail outlets. When *United Ireland* 'launched writs against every policeman so offending, and prepared to take the verdict of Irish juries as to our treatment … that little plan was frustrated'.[55] This particular form of punitive action ceased as it had been carried out on no discernible legal basis.

The subsequent approach of the authorities to the newspaper was dictated by the attorney general, William Moore Johnson, in a November 1881 memo. He advised that 'the only practical way of dealing with this mischievous paper is to arrest under the PPP [*sic*] Act each successive person who undertakes the management of the paper'.[56] When it came to *United Ireland* the powers vested in the Castle by the coercion act were liberally availed of. O'Brien's was merely the first of fourteen arrests or attempted arrests between October 1881 and January 1882.[57]

William O'Donovan escaped to America after a warrant was filed for his arrest on 15 November.[58] James Bryce Killen was jailed two weeks later on the recommendation of Johnson.[59] James O'Connor followed on 8 December. In order to damage the newspaper logistically, as well as journalistically, punitive action was also taken against clerks, printers and the business manager. The ground for most of the arrests under the PPP act was 'for instruction against payment of rent'.[60] Measures against the office staff were taken on the advice of Mallon who reported to commissioner Talbot on 1 December, in relation to Edward Donnelly (printer), Francis O'Keeffe (business manager), Arthur O'Keeffe (clerk and occasional contributor) and Thomas Noonan (printer) that 'should the government deem it advisable to arrest these persons it would, I think, cripple the publication'.[61]

It signally failed to do so. Francis O'Keeffe and Edward Donnelly escaped arrest by travelling to London. *United Ireland* continued in production. A defiant 10 December editorial goaded Forster:

> We have committed no offence against the law, and he knows that. Else why not try the question out before his tribunals? He cannot lay a finger on our property without breaking the law himself, and (what is of more importance) suffering for it at the hands of an Irish jury. We are aggravatingly within our legal right in printing and selling our paper.[62]

The editorial continued by condemning the policy of arbitrary arrests. However, by invoking the PPP act against named individuals the government was clearly operating within the remit of its own emergency legislation. Outside of those arrests, in dealing with *United Ireland*, the Castle otherwise tended to wander into questionable legal territory. On 9 December 1882, attorney general Johnson announced a change of approach. He recommended that the DMP raid the premises of *United Ireland* and seize the entire issue as it left the presses while the RIC seized individual copies that might have reached rural newsagents. He accepted that,

> This is a very serious step and therefore we would have to be prepared to defend claims for damages. Therefore it would be very necessary to be quite clear that the particular issue justified the proceeding by its illegality and violence.[63]

There were, as Johnson suggested, a number of inherent risks associated with this change of policy. As *United Ireland* itself would point out, the authorities had no legal right to seize any newspaper in advance of publication on the basis that it *might* prove to be seditious or treasonable. It was only after ascertaining that the newspaper contained seditious matter that the law could take its course. However, establishing that any individual issue contained such material was problematic. A copy of the 'suspected' edition of the newspaper had to be obtained, read and ruled upon. As Mallon pointed out, by the time one of his officers was able to purchase a copy in the *United Ireland* offices at 10.00am on any given Thursday morning 'the edition will have been sent to the country and Dublin agents'.[64] The authorities could seize whatever was left, or they could 'test' the law and confiscate an entire edition in advance without first ascertaining that the paper contained actionable material. They could, in theory at least, base such a proceeding on prior information obtained on the contents of the paper. In either event they left themselves open to compensation claims from O'Brien. Were they to extend this policy to the seizure of copies of the paper directly from the shops of newsagents or the supplies of street news-vendors, they left themselves vulnerable to claims from those sources as well. As it transpired this is precisely what occurred.

On 15 December, John M. Naish, the Castle's law officer, ordered the DMP to seize the *United Ireland* print run for that week. The only *caveat* was that the police were instructed 'not to go breaking doors for it'.[65] The edition of 17 December would have appeared that morning but there is no indication in the chief secretary's office registered papers as to whether or not it was examined before the order was made. The previous day Mallon had reported to Talbot that an informant within the newspaper was inclined to think the tone of the issue would actually be quite moderate.[66] This suggests that the administration had pre-determined to take the action advised by attorney general Johnson irrespective of the content of the newspaper.

The DMP raid on 33 Lower Abbey Street took place at 5.20 on the evening of Thursday, 15 December. Three detectives and four constables entered the premises with warrants for the arrest of five employees (the O'Keeffes, Donnelly, William McDonnell – a printer and Henry Burton – a clerk) and with orders to seize copies of the issue of 17 December. 4,200 copies of *United Ireland* were confiscated but printing of the 'Fenian' newspaper, *The Irishman,* was allowed to proceed unhindered. Arthur O'Keeffe and Henry Burton were found on the premises and arrested.

Quickly on the scene was Parnellite MP Edmund Leamy and a number of members of the Ladies Land League who were centrally involved at the time in keeping the newspaper in operation. Mallon was asked for his warrant for the seizure. He responded that he was acting on orders but was unable to produce these when requested to do so. The Superintendent was told that 'the whole thing was robbery and that I was a robber' and was asked 'who will indemnify us?' Mallon later visited fourteen newsagents and seized a further 81 copies of the newspaper. He reported to Talbot that 'the demand for this paper in Dublin was not considerable at any time, and the 2nd and 3rd editions were usually supplied to Dublin vendors and sold over the counter in the office. The first edition was invariably sent to the country and to England ... today copies of it are being sold at 1/- each.'[67]

The reaction of *United Ireland* in its next issue was entirely predictable:

> Mr. Forster thinks ... he can stifle our voice and ruin our property without incurring the consequences of illegally and violently suppressing a newspaper. We intend to ask an Irish jury whether Mr. Forster's cheap and cowardly thievery is to their liking.[68]

On 17 December the *Freeman's Journal* reported that *United Ireland* was 'to forthwith take the necessary steps for the purpose of testing the legality of the action of the authorities in seizing the newspaper, and that, acting under the advice of eminent counsel, writs against the responsible officials of the Government will be served within the next few days.'[69] *United Ireland* would, shortly thereafter, begin a suit against the government for £20,000. The damages sought included the value of the confiscated newspapers and the cost of lost production.

United Ireland itself claimed that, as Mallon forewarned, 37,000 copies had already been dispatched to rural destinations before the arrival of the DMP. The newspaper begged the indulgence of its readers in the event that 'within the next few weeks they cannot get our paper in time, or quite to their taste.'[70] In order to circumvent further attempts at seizure readers were asked to form clubs. 'Arrangements should be made locally by which each copy shall pass from hand to hand, until the paper shall reach every corner of the island.'[71] The paper also reiterated its call for local information to be forwarded to the *United Ireland* offices, 'so that the men of every district shall know what their neighbours are doing.'[72]

The *Times* referred to the 15 December raid as a 'vigorous blow' not just to the newspaper but to the recently proscribed Land League. Recognizing the systemic importance of *United Ireland* to the 'no rent' agitation it commented that 'the journal has been a means of keeping up excitement in the country'.[73] Just over a week later the *Times*, however, was forced to acknowledge that 'the seizure of *United Ireland* last week and the warning given to persons in the office against assisting in its publication have had no effect in preventing the continued issue of the paper'.[74] It railed against 'the futility of half measures' and observed that 'if the government meant to give it the *coup de grâce*, the blow which they struck was feeble, and was interpreted as an indication that they were not sure of their legal powers'. The 'Thunderer' recalled, with obvious regret, a time when newspaper seizures were newspaper seizures, 'the whole plant was taken, and the means of publication shut off'.[75] The *Times* also commented on the fact that, in some instances, receipts had been given to newsagents for confiscated copies and commented, prophetically as it happened, that 'the seeds of a prolific crop of litigation are being sown'.[76]

The era to which the *Times* was harking back had been instituted in 1870 by the Peace Preservation (Ireland) Act.[77] Sections 30–4 of that particular piece of coercion legislation, introduced by Gladstone's first administration, dealt directly with the press in a way that the 1881 Protection of Person and Property Act failed to do. Under the terms of the Peace Preservation Act, after a preliminary warning, any newspaper adjudged to contain 'any treasonable, seditious engraving, matter, or expressions, or any incitements to the commission of any felony … was liable to forfeit, all printing presses, engines, machinery, types, implements, utensils, paper, and other plant and materials used or employed, or intended to be used or employed, in or for the purpose of printing or publishing such newspaper'.[78] The seizure of copies of newspapers was also sanctioned, and, crucially, the legislation ensured that 'no action … shall be brought or maintained against any person for the issuing of such warrant, or for any entry, search, or seizure, or other act, matter, or thing done in pursuance or under the authority of any such warrant'.

The latter provision meant, in effect, that the authorities were indemnified against actions for compensation in the event of any confiscation of property, provided the search and seizure operation was legally sanctioned. Having given itself such extensive powers the government then, by and large, failed to use them. The press provisions of the Act were repealed in 1875 by the Disraeli administration.[79] That the second Gladstone government might have done well to cut and paste the 1870 press provisions into the Protection of Person and Property (Ireland) Act, 1881 was essentially the argument of the *Times*.

In its analysis of the 'half measures' being taken by the Castle, based on the available legislation, the *Times* tentatively drew attention, *inter alia*, to the availability of the laws of seditious libel. This was not, however, in order to berate the government's failure to make use of the libel laws against *United Ireland*. The *Times* was under no illusions as to the potential worth of such a course of action. *United Ireland* had regularly challenged the government to pursue it through the courts. The *Times* countered that O'Brien knew he was on safe ground 'as a single "boot-eater" in the jury-box would make the trial abortive. There have been successful prosecutions of papers for sedition, as the *Nation* and *Irishman* can testify; but they were ... before the organisation of the Land League, with its mysterious terrorism, had a footing in the country.'[80] Given the record of nationalist acquittals – most notably that of Parnell and his lieutenants in the state trial of December 1880–January 1881 – in agrarian or 'political' trials, the government could hardly be sanguine about securing a guilty verdict.

Solicitor general Andrew Marshal Porter tacitly accepted as much in a memo to Cabinet written in January 1882. In relation to the tactics used against *United Ireland* he noted of the alternatives that 'it would have been quite idle to institute prosecutions. Acquittals or disagreements of the juries would have been their certain result.'[81] In a country no longer governed by consent, which required the suspension of *habeas corpus* for the law to function, the very term 'seditious' was contested. The Castle's sedition was the Land League's advocacy and the bulk of the population sided with the League. It was preferable to invoke the blunt instrument that was the 1881 coercion act, albeit *sans* press clause.

Essentially the government was in a quandry once it moved outside of the aegis of the impolitic and somewhat disagreeable sanctuary of the PPP Act. While the administration, under the powers it had voted itself, could sanction however many 'persons' who undertook to keep *United Ireland* in print, actions against the 'property' of the newspaper were more problematic. This dilemma was highlighted by *United Ireland* itself and exploited by the Tory opposition. In the debate on the Queen's speech in the House of Commons in February 1882 Lord Randolph Churchill disparaged the government's procedures. He 'wished to know whether Government considered that they had acted legally in suppressing *United Ireland*?' Churchill claimed that theirs was an 'action without precedent'. Regarding the seizure of copies of the paper 'he wanted to know under what Act it had been done?'[82] The Tory gadfly then came to the nub of the difficulty as far as the administration was concerned. He contended that they should have asked for specific powers against the nationalist press in 1881:

> Which always, from an English point of view, had a tendency
> towards sedition; and they ought not to have hesitated to ask
> Parliament to give them the necessary powers to deal with it,
> so that they might have kept themselves within the law.[83]

Churchill suggested that, were there any doubt as to the legality of the moves against *United Ireland*, it behoved the government to introduce an Act of Indemnity. This would have protected the administration from the consequences of any action taken by its agents in excess of jurisdiction. Such a measure had been built into the 1870 legislation. The response of the solicitor general for Ireland, Andrew M. Porter, was that the issue was 'the subject of legal proceedings', before venturing the simultaneously anodyne and sweeping proposition that he, 'hope[d] to defend the action of the Government upon legal and Constitutional grounds'.[84]

The previous month Porter had written an *ex post facto* opinion on the legality of the 15 December 1881 *United Ireland* raid. While acknowledging the unprecedented nature of the procedure he pointed out that the course pursued had the sanction of the lord chancellor, the master of the rolls, and the law officers. The defence against the anticipated legal action by *United Ireland* would be 'that the paper was of a seditious character; that its dissemination, besides being a crime, was attended with great danger to the public peace'. Porter accepted that while there was, 'no precedent for such a defence … in my opinion, the suppression of this most dangerous publication was an absolute necessity'.[85]

However, law officials were not especially confident that such an argument would prevail in court. In fact, despite his instructions to Cabinet, even Porter was not entirely convinced by his own case. On 16 April 1882, law adviser John Naish dined with Forster. In her diary Florence Arnold Forster recorded that Naish was 'very anxious that the Chief Sec. [*sic*] should put a stop to the *United Ireland* action by getting a Bill of Indemnity[86] passed, which would cover any technical illegalities that may possibly prove to have been committed in the struggle to maintain or assert the law … some of the lawyers (notably the solicitor general) are of opinion that, by strict law, the seizure of the papers cannot be justified'.[87]

The chief secretary was adamantly opposed to any form of indemnification. He told Naish (according to Florence Arnold Forster) that 'he would rather pay £200 (the claim for £20,000 is, as Mr Naish says, "poetry") out of his own pocket than have to carry a Bill of Indemnity for himself through the House'.[88]

Indemnification was quite common where the suspension of *habeas corpus* was concerned. Dicey referred to Indemnity Acts as 'the supreme instance of Parliamentary sovereignty'[89] and demonstrated that such legislation was codified and ratified on, virtually, an annual basis the century before the accession of Queen Victoria. Indemnification might, for example, have overcome any ambiguity about the interception of copies of *United Ireland* in the mails. While the government was legally entitled to prevent the distribution of seditious material by post it was caught in an anomalous situation in this regard. In order to establish that a particular edition of the newspaper, circulating via the post office, was seditious, the authorities were, in effect, obliged to tamper with the mails. This procedure was of dubious legality. The government could have protected itself against legal action in such instances by passing an indemnification law.

However, it could equally have avoided much of the confusion and extemporization apparent in its policy by the creation of a more appropriate device than the Protection of Person and Property (Ireland) act. Such an instrument was in preparation by Cowper and Forster in the spring of 1882. But neither man would remain in his post long enough to introduce what would ultimately become the Prevention of Crime Act. The eventual insertion of a press clause in the new Liberal coercion regime was a belated attempt to rectify the omissions of the 1881 model. That particular piece of legislation had, 'instead of eradicating *United Ireland*, in fact served to endow it with heroic and popular appeal'.[90]

Notes

1   Porter memo to Cabinet, 23 January, 1882, NAI, CSORP, 1888/26523.

2   Frank Hugh O'Donnell, *A History of the Irish Parliamentary Party* (London, 1910), 2 vols, vol. 2, 150–1.

3   Gladstone to Forster, 5 October 1881, H.C.G. Matthew, (ed.), *The Gladstone Diaries* (Oxford, 1990), 14 vols, vol. x, 140.

4   (21 May 1889, *Special Commission*, vol. 8, 88–9, 60321).

5   For example the advice of Andrew Marshall Porter, Solicitor General to the Under Secretary, 27 December 1881 regarding the issue of *United Ireland* of 24 December 1881 – 'The particular number in question is I think seditious in its tone.' NAI, CSORP, Police and Crime Division Reports, III, Compensation Cases, Crimes Act, 1882–3, Carton 6, 1881/46048.

6   A.V. Dicey, *Introduction to the Study of the Law of the Constitution* (London, 1902), 242.

7   Legg, *Newspapers and Nationalism*, 120.

8   Legg, *Newspapers and Nationalism*, 114.

9   W.E. Gladstone, *Gleanings from Past Years* (London, 1879), 16.

10   *United Ireland*, 10 December 1881.

11   *United Ireland*, 11 February 1882.

12   Dicey, *Introduction to the Study of the Law of the Constitution*, 235–6.

13   Dicey, *Introduction to the Study of the Law of the Constitution*, 242. This is rather at odds with the claim of another authority on the subject, William Blake Odgers, that, 'our press has been, ever since the passing of Fox's Libel Act … the freest in the world' (William Blake Odgers, *A Digest of the law of libel and slander*, (London, 1905), 18).

14   Lyons, *Charles Stewart Parnell*, 170.

15   For a time after the arrest of O'Brien the DMP was in some confusion as to who was actually responsible for editing the newspaper. A report from Mallon to the police commissioner on 20 October 1881 is highly speculative, suggesting that O'Connor had taken charge but admitting that 'it would be better that further inquiry be made to clear up this point' (Mallon to Talbot, 20 October 1881, NAI, CSORP, 1881/35864, Police and Crime Division Reports, III, Compensation Cases, Crimes Act, 1882–3, Carton 6, 1881–35775).

16   Warwick Haller, *William O'Brien and the Irish Land War*, 59.

17   O'Brien, *Recollections*, 379.

18   *United Ireland*, 12 November 1881.

19 While Gill is mentioned by O'Brien as having assisted in the editing of the newspaper (23 May, 1889, Special Commission, vol. 8, 180, 71800), Gill himself modestly made no reference to his contribution in an obituary tribute to O'Brien in 1928 in *Studies*. In a letter to Parnell in August 1881 Gill did write of the pending debut of *United Ireland*, 'How anxious I am to see the first number, and yet how sad it will make me when I see how little I have done for it!' (Gill to Parnell, 11 August 1881, T.P. Gill papers, NLI, MS 13478).

20 All biographical material from Dictionary of Irish Biography – http://dib.cambridge.org. (18 September 2013)

21 30 April 1889, Special Commission, vol. 7, 161, 60,238.

22 John Devoy, *Recollections of an Irish Rebel* (Shannon, 1969), 369–70.

23 One of whom was Chester Ives, correspondent of the *New York Herald* (21 October 1881, Mallon to Captain Talbot, NAI, CSORP, Police and Crime Division Reports, III, Compensation Cases, Crimes Act, 1882–3, Carton 6, 1881/35864).

24 Mallon to Captain Talbot, 21 October 1881, NAI, CSORP, Police and Crime Division Reports, III, Compensation Cases, Crimes Act, 1882–3, Carton 6, 1881/35864.

25 Anderson, Sir Robert – *Sidelights on the Home Rule Movement* (London, 1906), 144. Anderson makes the intriguing claim that it was O'Keeffe who wrote the body of the infamous *Times* facsimile letter published on 18 April 1887, atop Parnell's signature, which, Anderson theorizes, was genuine. In a preface to the 1907 edition of his book he claims to have had this verified but doesn't elaborate.

26 *United Ireland*, 18 February 1882.

27 Mallon to Talbot, 24 October 1881, NAI, CSORP, Police and Crime Division Reports, III, Compensation Cases, Crimes Act, 1882–3, Carton 6, 1881/36371.

28 A personality clash may well have been the reason for this. A fortnight later Mallon informed his superior that 'I have to report that from all the information I can gather Mr. Cowan MP could not bring the people connected with "United Ireland" to adopt his style of writing, consequently no protégé of his would take the acting editorship of the paper' (Mallon to Talbot, 8 November 1881, NAI, CSORP, Police and Crime Division Reports, III, Compensation Cases, Crimes Act, 1882–3, Carton 6, 1881/38894).

29 Ladies Land League leader, Anna Parnell suggested in her, often vitriolic, critique of Parnellism, *Tale of a Great Sham,* that the government facilitated the free passage of material from the prisoners to the outside world in the hope that they would, in the process, incriminate themselves. There is no evidence in the surviving files of the chief secretary's office that this was the case where *United Ireland* and O'Brien were concerned but it is not an entirely implausible scenario (Anna Parnell, *Tale of a Great Sham*, ed. Dana Hearne (Dublin, 1986), 85).

30 21 May 1889, *Special Commission*, vol. 8, 104, 70827.

31 William O'Brien, *Recollections* (London, 1905), 377.

32 Dictionary of Irish Biography – http://dib.cambridge.org/viewReadPage. do?articleId=a2531. The Irish newspapers included the *United Irishman* (1875–8) – not to be confused with Rossa's publication of the same name – and the *Nationalist*.

33 John Denvir, *Life Story of an Old Rebel* (Dublin, 1910), 219.

34 *United Ireland*, 29 October 1881. As more arrests followed, this column was filled with the names of those arrested and those who had succeeded in escaping arrest.

35 *United Ireland*, 5 November 1881. Thoms Directory (1881) lists one Thomas Edwards as the owner of that address but they are 'furnished lodgings' so Smallhorne may have been a paying lodger. The following week, 12 November, only one of twenty letters is traceable, coming from Land League offices in Cork.

36 *United Ireland*, 5 November 1881.

37 *United Ireland*, 12 November 1881.

38 *Pall Mall Gazette*, 24 April 1882.

39 *United Ireland*, 12 November 1881.

40 For example the attack on the house of Owen Curtin near Mallow, Co. Cork – *United Ireland*, 19 November 1881.

41 'The murder of men, the wounding of men, injuries to women, burning of houses, were spoken of in the columns of that press as being incidents in the warfare between the National League and the landlords.' Attorney general, 23 October 1888, *Special Commission*, vol. 1, 80.

42 21 May 1889 *Special Commission*, vol. 8, 104, 70830–31.

43 21 May 1889 *Special Commission*, vol. 8, 195, 70836.

44 22 May 1889 *Special Commission*, vol. 8, 154, 71460–1.

45 22 May 1889 *Special Commission*, vol. 8, 154, 71443.

46 HC Deb 22 February 1883, vol. 276, c627.

47 HC Deb 22 February 1883, vol. 276, c627.

48 William Moore Johnson, Irish attorney general, November 1881 – January 1883.

49 The received wisdom at this time – late November 1881 – prompted by DMP intelligence reports, was that *United Ireland* was on its last legs (Talbot to Forster, 24 November 1881, TNA, PRO, CAB 37/24, 1889, no. 21, 10.). On 10 December, Mallon wrote to Talbot that 'I believe they will throw up the sponge, and it is doubtful if another publication of the paper will issue' (Mallon to Talbot, 10 December 1881, TNA, PRO, CAB 37/24, 1889, no. 21, 10).

50 Diary entry, 2 December 1881, Moody and Hawkins, *Florence Arnold-Forster*, 328.

51 *United Ireland*, 18 February 1882.

52 30 April, 1889 Special Commission, vol. 7, 159, 60, 214.

53 *United Ireland*, 12 November 1881. 19 November 1881, *United Ireland* taking action

against Constable Cash for seizure, NAI, CSORP, 1881/40540 (file not found – reference from CSORP Index for 1881). 18 January, 1882, Intention to take action against chief secretary on behalf of the Irish Newspaper Publishing Company for seizures of *United Ireland*, NAI, CSORP, 1882/3037 (file not found – reference from CSORP Index for 1882. The newspaper also personalized the process by taking action against individual constables ('Irish National Newspaper Publishing Company Limited v McCormick', *United Ireland*, 28 January 1882).

54 *Public General Statutes Passed in the Forty-fourth and Forty-fifth Years of the Reign of Her Majesty, Queen Victoria, 1881,* 3.

55 *United Ireland*, 10 December 1881.

56 W.M. Johnson memo, 23 November 1881, NAI, CSORP, Police and Crime Division Reports, III, Compensation Cases, Crimes Act, 1882–3, Carton 6, 1881/40550.

57 *United Ireland*, 7 January 1882.

58 *Dictionary of Irish Biography*, http://dib.cambridge.org/viewReadPage. do?articleId=a6712. (20 September 2013)

59 W.M. Johnson memo, 25 November 1881, NAI, CSORP, Police and Crime Division Reports, III, Compensation Cases, Crimes Act, 1882–3, Carton 6, 1881/42170.

60 John Naish memo, 25 November, 1881, NAI, CSORP, Police and Crime Division Reports, III, Compensation Cases, Crimes Act, 1882–3, Carton 6, 1881/42170.

61 Mallon to Talbot, 1 December 1881, NAI-CSORP, Police and Crime Division Reports, III, Compensation Cases, Crimes Act, 1882–3, Carton 6, 1881/42170.

62 *United Ireland*, 10 December 1881.

63 W.M. Johnson memo, 9 December 1881, NAI, CSORP, Police and Crime Division Reports, III, Compensation Cases, Crimes Act, 1882–3, Carton 6, 1881/45112.

64 Mallon to Talbot, 14 December 1881, NAI, CSORP, Police and Crime Division Reports, III, Compensation Cases, Crimes Act, 1882–3, Carton 6, 1881/45113. The practice was to print on Wednesday and despatch copies to the country that night.

65 J.M. Naish, 15 December 1881, NAI, CSORP, Police and Crime Division Reports, III, Compensation Cases, Crimes Act, 1882–3, Carton 6, 1881/45113.

66 Mallon to Talbot, 14 December 1881, NAI, CSORP, Police and Crime Division Reports, III, Compensation Cases, Crimes Act, 1882–3, Carton 6, 1881/45113.

67 Mallon to Talbot, 16 December 1881, NAI, CSORP, Police and Crime Division Reports, III, Compensation Cases, Crimes Act, 1882–3, Carton 6, 1881/45114.

68 *United Ireland*, 24 December 1881.

69 *Freeman's Journal*, 17 December 1881.

70 *United Ireland*, 24 December 1881.

71 *United Ireland*, 24 December 1881. Distribution of *United Ireland* through the post

would raise further issues for the government. The newspaper's advice to its readers also indicates that it was far from being a mere commercial enterprise.

72 *United Ireland*, 24 December 1881.

73 *Times*, 16 December 1881.

74 *Times*, 24 December 1881.

75 *Times*, 24 December 1881.

76 *Times*, 24 December, 1881.

77 This was actually a series of amendments to the Peace Preservation (Ireland) Act of 1856.

78 *Public General Statutes Passed in the Thirty-third and Thirty-fourth Years of the Reign of Her Majesty, Queen Victoria* (London, 1870), 140–1.

79 *Public General Statutes Passed in the Thirty-eighth and Thirty-ninth Years of the Reign of Her Majesty, Queen Victoria* (London, 1875), 141.

80 *Times*, 24 December 1881. *United Ireland* commented acidly in response, 'Yes, a great many curious steps were feasible in those days; a packed jury was found to be a very Accommodating friend to English ministers, and it is scarcely surprising that they should be tempted now, in the face of that arch-fiend honesty, to sigh for those good old times when they could do precisely what they liked' (*United Ireland*, 31 December 1881).

81 Porter memo to Cabinet, 23 January 1882, NAI, CSORP, 1888/26523.

82 HC Deb. 9 February 1882, vol. 266, c441. The particular seizure to which he referred had taken place in Liverpool.

83 HC Deb. 9 February 1882 vol. 266, c442.

84 HC Deb. 9 February 1882 vol. 266, cc457–58.

85 Porter memo to Cabinet, 23 January 1882, NAI, CSORP, 1888/26523. He concluded with a wistful reference to the powers available under the 1870 Peace Preservation Act which, he opined, 'would have met the case, and relieved it of all difficulty'.

86 A.V. Dicey wrote in his *Introduction to the Study of the Law of the Constitution* that 'the unavowed object of a *Habeas Corpus* Suspension Act is to enable the government to do acts which, though politically expedient, may not be strictly legal … A Suspension Act would, in fact, fail of its main object, unless officials felt assured that, as long as they *bona fide*, and uninfluenced by malice or by corrupt motives, carried out the policy of which the Act was the visible sign, they would be protected from penalties for conduct which, though it might be technically a breach of law, was nothing more than the free exertion for the public good of that discretionary power which the suspension of the *Habeas Corpus* Act was intended to confer upon the executive. This assurance is derived from the expectation that, before the Suspension Act ceases to be in force, Parliament will pass an Act of Indemnity, protecting all persons who have acted, or have intended to act, under the powers given to the government by the statute' (Dicey, *Introduction to the Study of the Law of the Constitution*, 231).

87 Diary entry, 16 April 1882, Moody and Hawkins, *Florence Arnold-Forster,* 450.

88 Diary entry, 16 April 1882, Moody and Hawkins, *Florence Arnold-Forster,* 450.

89 A.V. Dicey, *Introduction to the Study of the Law of the Constitution* (London, 1902), 228.

90 Warwick-Haller, *William O'Brien,* 59.

CHAPTER THREE

Suppressing 'The Journalism of Murder' – 1882

'As for the recommendation to suppress the journalism of murder, that is already done. We do not know whether *United Ireland* ever went so far as to recommend assassination, but *United Ireland* has been suppressed. If therefore the recommendation is that all papers writing in the interest of the land agitation should be suppressed, we are very sure that English opinion will never tolerate a measure of the kind.'[1]

(*Daily News*, 13 April 1882)

'In the freedom of the Press and the freedom of public meetings we find all the elements of whatever permanent freedom there exists in this nation.'[2]

(John Bright, House of Commons, 30 March 1882)

Constructive suppression

On 6 January 1882 the lord lieutenant issued a formal directive that the police should, from that date 'seize and detain from time to time until further order all copies wherever exhibited of the newspapers entitled "United Ireland", "The Irish World" and "The United Irishman".[3] Given the difficulties the administration had been experiencing with the interdiction of *United Ireland* in particular, the injunction had a certain logic to it. But it contained no indication of the legal foundation for the decision or the statute upon which it was based. Up to that point seizures had proceeded only after a perusal of the relevant issue by the law officers and a judgment as to illegality but, as Marie Louise Legg has written, 'they needed to stop the newspapers' publication immediately and not just bolt the stable door after the horse had gone'.[4]

The lord lieutenant's January edict allowed the DMP and RIC *carte blanche* in their attempts to stifle the newspaper before its distribution. It was based upon a not entirely unreasonable assumption that all editions of the newspaper would contain treasonable or seditious material, until such time as *United Ireland* chose to moderate its editorial commentary. Politically the order could only have been made in the context of the suspension of due process and even from that perspective it was of doubtful legality. It was in keeping with the spirit of disconcerted extemporization being practised by Dublin Castle and described by O'Brien as 'the *reductio ad absurdum* of squalid unconstitutionality'.[5] It was duly followed by an indication from the solicitors representing the Irish Newspaper Publishing Company that the publishers of *United Ireland* intended to challenge the legality of the move in the courts.[6] The administration sought, quite literally, to put *United Ireland* out of circulation by whatever means it had at its disposal. Although the government's actions fell well short of forcing the outright suppression and closure of the newspaper they were, in effect, a form of pre-emptive censorship. While the administration could maintain it was respecting press freedom in not formally closing down *United Ireland* it was, constructively, making it virtually impossible for the newspaper to continue in operation.

In the House of Commons Edmund Dwyer Gray MP interrogated the government's right to, in effect, impose a blanket ban on the distribution of *United Ireland*:

Members were entitled to ask under what statute he seized *United Ireland*; under what Statute Government officials pursued boys in the street, and took property from them without paying them for it; under what statute hundreds and thousands of the copies of the paper were seized in England without any knowledge whatever as to whether the particular issue might contain seditious matter or not, but simply because it had the title *United Ireland*.[7]

The legitimacy or otherwise of government actions to close down *United Ireland* might, at some point, be tested in the courts. In the interim the Castle was making it difficult for the journal to function and relied on the principle of *sub judice* to deflect awkward parliamentary questions about its Irish press policies.

The newspaper's publishing and printing activities were concentrated on a business premises, 33 Lower Abbey St, to which the DMP had easy access. Although the police did not seize the presses (the *Irishman* continued to be printed on them each week[8]) the seizure of copies and type constituted a form of harassment that was difficult to circumvent without diversifying the operation. The staff of the newspaper could never be sure that the DMP would not arrive in numbers on a Wednesday evening as the paper was being printed for its all-important rural distribution and seize the entire print run. Without first ascertaining the presence of seditious material in that week's issue the move would have been of doubtful legality. But whereas that might have been of some propaganda value at a future date it would have been of little assistance in the short-term struggle for survival.

Part of the strategy of the DMP involved a form of quasi-illicit petty harassment of the, by then, largely voluntary staff of the newspaper. Mallon, in one of his reports to Talbot on 18 December 1881 warned the Police Commissioner that the newspaper, publication of which had moved to Liverpool and then to London, was returning to Dublin. Mallon had been tipped off, either by his informant, or a *complaisant* journalist, that Egan[9] had been advised that charges of sedition against *United Ireland* were far more likely to be brought in an English court than in Ireland, 'and that the vendors of same in Ireland could be arrested and brought to England for trial'. Hence printing of the newspaper in England had been abandoned as the continuation of publication there would facilitate such action by the authorities.

Mallon advised that if warrants were issued for the arrest of some of the Dublin printers, much as had been the pretext for the 15 December raid, 'the Police entrusted with the warrants should do just what they are not told to do. They ought through ignorant curiosity by the way of no harm take up some type here and some there taking good care not to put any back where they found it.'[10]

In addition to Egan in Paris the key figures in the survival of *United Ireland* from the time of the arrest of O'Brien up to the 'Kilmainham Treaty' were Liverpool printer John Denvir and various members of the Ladies Land League, most notably Hannah Lynch. Denvir was himself a journalist and former Fenian expelled from the organization in 1877 for his refusal to detach himself from the Home Rule movement. According to O'Brien's earliest biographer, Michael MacDonagh, Denvir made arrangements 'for the printing of the paper secretly in Liverpool, London, Paris, Derry and actually in Dublin, in its old office … though all the time police and spies were on his track'.[11] Denvir had first intervened when two of *United Ireland's* printers, Edward Donnelly and William McDonnell, both being sought by the DMP, arrived in Liverpool with stereotypes of one of the suppressed issues of the newspaper. Donnelly had escaped to England on the day James O'Connor was finally arrested (8 December) while McDonnell had managed to avoid a similar fate during the major raid on 15 December.[12] While Denvir's own machines were not big enough to produce the paper he persuaded a local Liverpool printer to do the job instead. Many of the printed copies were then brought to Dublin by Denvir's son and 'with help from Daniel Crilly and Eugene O'Sullivan of the *Nation* he distributed the paper himself'.[13]

Denvir continued to liaise with Egan in Paris for a number of weeks, taking advantage of the fact that the Protection of Person and Property act applied only in Ireland and that no English printer or publisher could be arbitrarily arrested without charge for producing the paper in England. However, the assertion made in his memoir, *Life Story of an Old Rebel*, that 'although illegal in Ireland there was nothing in the ordinary law to prevent the printing and circulation of *United Ireland* in Great Britain'[14] while technically accurate was only partly true. The seditious libel laws could be used to supply the absence of the PPP in England. It would have been less problematic to secure a conviction against the newspaper for seditious libel if the authorities brought an action in an English court. Denvir also acknowledged the fact that, although it was not illegal to print *United Ireland* in Liverpool or London 'the printers were perpetually harassed by the police to frighten them into giving up the job'.[15] On 24 February 1882, for example, Denvir was fined £22 at Liverpool Police Court for producing copies of *United Ireland* without the imprint required under the 1881 Newspaper Libel and Registration Act.[16] The penalty was insufficient to discourage the old Fenian from continuing to print.

Some highly imaginative stratagems were devised for getting the printed copies of the newspaper to Ireland on a weekly basis. The edition of 31 December, which carried an editorial on the banning of the Ladies Land League and the appointment of five new paramilitary Special Resident Magistrates – one of whom was the remarkable Clifford Lloyd – was packed in hampers and sent as dried fish. Another consignment was dispatched as 'woolen goods'. Still more copies were sent, in what can only have been a fit of self-conscious irony, in the name of British 'mercantile firms whose loyalty was unquestionable'.[17] Another consignment, seized at the North Wall in Dublin Port was, 'enclosed in a timber case and were made up in packages as if they were loaves of sugar'.[18]

The peregrinations of *United Ireland* became even more elaborate after the London printers finally succumbed to police and political pressure in January 1882 and discontinued publication. The edition of 28 January was printed in Paris. Copies were seized in Folkestone (34,000 on 27 January) and Dover (5,000 on 3 February) by a British police force that had clearly been forewarned. The legality of that seizure was raised by Thomas Sexton MP in the House of Commons on 20 February 1882 when he inquired of the home secretary 'by virtue of what Statute, or in the exercise of what legal authority the Government are entitled to confiscate private property, and to seize and retain an issue of a newspaper, without first having taken steps to ascertain or inquire if the issue in question contained illegal matter?' Harcourt's response made it apparent that the government had simply used *force majeure* rather than any statutory authority. He asserted that the seizure 'was done under the authority of the lords commissioners of the treasury. The lords commissioners of the treasury acted under proper legal advice; and if the legality of that is to be disputed, it must be a question in a Court of Law.'[19]

After the Dover/Folkestone seizures the strategy changed. The paper was set in type in Paris. Some copies were immediately printed off and sent to Ireland by post. Then, according to Denvir, 'the matrices from the type were brought over to me by carefully selected agents from Paris. From these, stereotype plates of the pages were cast'.[20] Again a Liverpool printer, other than Denvir, was used. He too quickly buckled under police pressure. In order to allow Denvir himself to print the paper it was reduced to four pages and Denvir was then able to make use of his own machines. By and large some copies of the paper reached Ireland each week, though it was often in such short supply that newsagents and street vendors, 'were reaping a rich harvest'[21] as copies changed hands for up to 2s 6d. Even at a mark-up of 2,900 per cent the fact that it managed to appear, despite the best efforts of the DMP and the RIC 'did perhaps more than anything else to keep heart in the people'.[22]

United Ireland and the Ladies Land League

With the proscription of the Land League the organization of the 'no rent' campaign fell to the Ladies Land League, founded in the US in 1880 by Fanny Parnell, but more closely identified with her more radical sister Anna Parnell. In her disillusioned diatribe against the Land League and her brother's policies, Tale of a Great Sham, Anna Parnell wrote of how, shortly after the Ladies League took over the 'no rent' campaign 'the Land League newspaper, United Ireland fell on our well-laden shoulders'.[23] The seizures, and the arrests of the editorial staff did not appear to discourage the distribution of the paper by members of the Ladies League but the arrest of the printers posed greater difficulties, 'for printing was not amongst our accomplishments'.[24] Anna Parnell offers at least one interesting explanation as to why the authorities found it difficult, despite seizing so many copies, to curb the paper's distribution. 'Oddly enough,' she claimed, 'the police were amongst the agents who helped to distribute the proscribed journal, for they used to supplement their incomes by selling the copies they were able to seize, as waste paper.'[25]

One of the most prominent, enterprising and tenacious members of the Ladies Land League, Hannah Lynch, seems to have made the survival of *United Ireland* a personal project. When James O'Connor was arrested under the Protection of Person and Property Act on 8 December 1881, according to Mallon 'he was instructing Miss Hannah Lynch in the duties of a sub-editor'.[26] The following week Mallon recorded that the main business of *United Ireland* was being performed by, among others, Hannah Lynch and her two sisters, Nannie and Virginia.[27] Lynch was present on 15 December for the most significant DMP raid on the Abbey Street premises. In *Unmanageable Revolutionaries*, Margaret Ward gives credit to Lynch for having engineered the publication of the newspaper in Paris, 'few other women had the necessary language skills or contacts'.[28] Lynch, who was only nineteen years old at the time of the establishment of the Ladies Land League in Ireland, 'had gone to convent school abroad and traveled extensively as a governess, an experience the women were to find very useful'.[29] According to Anna Parnell, Lynch was, on one occasion, personally responsible for the distribution of 30,000 copies of the journal around the country.[30]

Lynch was not the only member of the Ladies Land League to offer vital logistical assistance to *United Ireland*. John Denvir wrote about the involvement of 'the Misses Stritch', one of whom was Claire Stritch, joint honorary secretary of the organization.[31] They would travel to Paris each week and return with the matrices for the latest edition of the paper. Accentuating their act of rebellion, both were daughters of a Resident Magistrate. Joint Treasurer of the Ladies Land League, Kate Molony, provided much of the finance for the day-to-day running of the Abbey Street operation.[32] She also remonstrated with Mallon during the 15 December raid, demanding to see his warrant for the seizure of copies of the paper and, ever the honorary treasurer, insisting on indemnification for the property being confiscated.

As well as having to face harassment from the DMP the Ladies Land League stalwarts who kept *United Ireland* in circulation were subjected to condescending comments from the *Freeman's Journal*, and patronizing attitudes from at least some of their male counterparts. On 10 December 1881 Mallon reported to Talbot that 'The women of the L[adies] L[eague] meant to carry on the publication of U[nited] I[reland], however, some of the gentlemen contributors who went into the office on business left it in disgust and cut their connection instantly.'

Anna Parnell's experience of the Land War may have left her embittered and unalterably opposed to the policies of her older brother, but her involvement with *United Ireland* 'was the pleasantest part of all the work of the Ladies Land League; it was something that could, at any rate, be done, and did not seem so painfully like trying to make ropes of sea sand, as so much of our other tasks did'.[33]

The government and the newsagents

In taking the steps it did to contain or check the supply of copies of *United Ireland* the government was transgressing against one of the prevailing principles of Victorian economic life, the right of a merchant or manufacturer to profit from the investment of his capital without intervention. While the Liberal government might have been encumbered by a half-hearted regard for freedom of the press, the right to the free movement of goods and the entitlement to the profits derived from that free movement was axiomatic. As was, in this instance at least, the right to redress in the event of any gratuitous government interference in the conduct of legitimate trade.

Weighed against the property rights of newsagents was pressure from the likes of Resident Magistrate T.D. Fitzgerald, based in Carrick on Shannon, Co. Leitrim. He wrote to the under secretary, Thomas H. Burke, in December 1881, forwarding a marked copy of *United Ireland* whose 'direct tendency is to manifestly stir up the worst passion of the people and to incite them to additional opposition to all law, human and divine … its success in these directions is every day becoming the more apparent'.[34]

The DMP and the RIC were on the alert for copies of *United Ireland*, thousands of which made their way from Paris, London or Liverpool, past the ports or through the post, and were being displayed on shop counters around the country. These were seized when required and when it was practicable, but there were anomalies. In some instances issues of successive weeks of *United Ireland* or the *Irish World* were displayed side by side. A risible situation sometimes arose where copies from certain dates were confiscated and other editions left for sale where policemen had no specific instructions to seize that particular issue.[35]

In some instances newsagents resisted confiscation attempts. Ladies Land League member, Mary Ann Hurley, received a summons for abusive behaviour towards the police. She was recorded as having called them 'ruffians, perjurers, robbers and puppies'.[36] Her tirade resulted from an RIC raid on her father's shop in search of *United Ireland*. In late December 1881 the RIC entered the shop of a W.B. Massey in Cork and demanded all copies of *United Ireland* on the premises. Massey refused to comply and a scuffle ensued during which the newsagent tore up his copies of the paper and prevented police from going behind the shop counter to search for more. The police abandoned the attempt to seize the papers and left the premises.[37] Massey subsequently lodged a claim for compensation for a second, more successful, seizure on the part of the RIC.[38]

United Ireland had its own rubric for circumventing interference with sales agents. In its issue of 24 December, 1881 it asked readers to form clubs 'wherever an open sale in the shop of our local agent may be found impracticable'. The clubs would subscribe 3s 4d and get one copy a week for three months, post free. Then, 'arrangements should be made locally by which each copy shall pass from hand to hand, until the paper shall reach every corner of the island'.[39] Newsagents who were primarily motivated by their political committment to stock *United Ireland*, would, doubtless, have approved. Those incentivized by respect for the bottom line might have been aghast at the potential loss of revenue and this further challenge to the profit motive.

As the policy of seizure became more widespread the trickle of compensation claims from newsagents to the chief secretary's office began to swell.[40] To what extent the claims made by newsagents against the government were the genuine demands of out-of-pocket retailers is difficult to say. They might equally have been designed (by the agents and the newspaper) to discourage further seizures. But the chief secretary's files contain a number of letters from aggrieved newsagents pointing out that copies of *United Ireland* were, as a matter of course, purchased in advance by retailers. Thus seizures involved a loss of revenue to the newsagent rather than the newspaper. The inclination of the Castle was, at first, to resist all such claims. When, on 1 April 1882, John Fay, a Navan, Co. Meath newsagent applied for compensation for sixty-one newspapers (worth just over 5/-), taken by the RIC on 15 and 30 December, the law officer, John Naish recommended that the application be denied.[41] Yet two months later, when a similar claim was made by Mary Barry of Great George's Street in Cork, the atmosphere, in the wake of *United Ireland's* denunciation of the Phoenix Park murders, had changed. The latter seizure had taken place on 13 April 1882. Mary Barry had written to the new chief secretary, George

Otto Trevelyan, highlighting her plight and the inherent inconsistency in the RIC execution of its seizure orders.

> The same week this seizure was made in Cork the Dublin newsvenders [*sic*] were selling the same issue with impunity and that the previous week I got safely delivered the same amount of papers without any attempt at seizure.[42]

Even more zealous than the constables who raided Barry's premises was the policeman who, 'entered the house of Mr Patrick Kavanagh, Michael Street, Waterford, and, finding Mrs Kavanagh engaged in reading "United Ireland," attempted to take it from her, and in the attempt threw her down, put his knees on her stomach and tore her clothes, while he searched her in a most insulting manner'.[43] He was charged with aggravated assault but the Waterford magistrates only fined him a guinea as, according to the chief secretary, in response to a parliamentary question from Edmund Leamy MP, 'they believed he only did it in what he considered the discharge of his duty'.[44] Mary Barry eventually received some reparation. Naish recommended that compensation be 'discreetly paid'.[45] The Crown solicitor for Cork visited her shop and, 'without saying exactly from where [he] came'[46] paid her 10/- for the 120 papers she had lost.

Just as vulnerable to the majesty of the law were the street news-vendors or newsboys, of Dublin and Cork in particular. They were invariably searched if seen leaving 33 Lower Abbey St by the watching policemen. One had two copies (his entire supply) taken from him in Crampton Court in Dublin. When the DMP refused to give him a receipt for the appropriated copies, sympathetic onlookers passed the hat around for the young vendor.[47]

A *United Ireland* cartoon of 11 February celebrated the resourcefulness of these Artful Dodgers and the alleged heavy-handedness of the DMP. The drawing was of a ragged newsboy being grabbed by one of five burly policemen. The apprehending constable has lost his helmet in the chase. A second policeman holds a rifle and bayonet to the newsboy's head while a third holds aloft in triumph a copy of *United Ireland*. The caption reads 'British Burglars in Ireland'. The accompanying dialogue went as follows

> Burglar Bumskull (wroth and helmetless) : – Ha, my eyes! This
> infernal little rebel has a lot of that rascally *United Ireland* with
> him, I should think. Take *that*, and *that*, and *that*, and may the
> d----l stifle you for a viper
> Burglar Boobyhead (posing as a conquering hero):- Hurrah for
> the R.I.C.! Bless my sowl, [*sic*] we've captured a copy! Down
> with the Land League!
> Chorus of Burglars: – This glorious day we've won our pay –
> Three cheers for fearless Forster.[48]

According to Anna Parnell the newsboys were often highly successful in distributing the newspaper, and making a tidy profit in the process. She wrote that 'in Dublin the small newspaper boys used to hide it under their uniform of rags, and sometimes got as much as a shilling for it'.[49]

The Dublin Metropolitan Police and *United Ireland*

The fact that *United Ireland*'s arrival on the scene pre-dated the wave of 'suspect' arrests in October, 1881, by only a few months, might account for the Dublin Metropolitan Police's imperfect state of knowledge about the survival strategy employed by the newspaper. Superintendent John Mallon, the officer in charge of the detective unit, 'G' Division, the 'eyes and ears' of the Castle, was quite tentative in some of his early assessments of the effects of the PPP arrests on *United Ireland*. He was unable to say, definitively, who was editing the paper. He initially relied on information from the *New York Herald* correspondent, Chester Ives, from 'a Press man'[50] – who may also have been Ives – and from the observation of detectives placed outside the *United Ireland* premises in 33 Lower Abbey St. But within days the quality of the intelligence he was passing on to his superiors had greatly improved. By 24 October he was able to inform the police commissioner of the visit of Cowen to Lower Abbey St. On the same day he was also aware that William O'Donovan, a 'noted Fenian',[51] had taken a hand in the editorial process.

Mallon was also aware of the new chain of command within days of its establishment. On 8 November, he informed Talbot that 'Patrick Egan, Treasurer of the Land League is the nominal proprietor and all the current expenses are paid by him through the agency of some person in London who of course has some round about way of sending the money to Dublin.'[52]

He also told the DMP commissioner that circulation of *United Ireland* had halved due to their production difficulties and, remarkably, that 'the project of starting it as a daily paper on the 1st January has been almost abandoned'.[53] This would have been good news to Edmund Dwyer Gray had he been apprised of the fact. Later that month Mallon was in no doubt whatever as to the identity of the acting editor. James Bryce Killen, he informed Talbot 'appears to be the only responsible person in the office of *United Ireland* at present'. He described Killen as, 'an inveterate tippler'.[54] As one reads his reports it becomes clear that Mallon was no longer relying exclusively on the observations of his sentinels or on gossip gleaned by an American journalist with whom he was exchanging information. The assumption has to be that one of the many volunteers who kept *United Ireland* in operation from October 1881 to April 1882 was also working for Mallon.

This is confirmed at around the time of the major raid on the *United Ireland* premises on 15 December 1881. In the days beforehand Mallon had written a detailed report naming the printer, Edward Donnelly – 'a quiet inoffensive man [who] never identified himself with a political movement of any kind' – business manager Francis O'Keefe, his brother Arthur – a clerk who made occasional journalistic contributions – and another printer Thomas Noonan, as being vital to the maintenance of the newspaper. James O'Connor had been back in Dublin and 'may come to look after the business now and again' but the others were considered vital to its continued operation. 'Should the government deem it advisable to arrest these persons it would, I think, cripple the publication.'[55] Arrests warrants were issued but when Mallon and his detectives came to execute them none of the prime movers was on the premises. Some days later, on 15 December, there was a more comprehensive raid (see above) prompted by information that 'the manuscript' of that week's issue was to be found in the office. For the first time Mallon, notoriously protective of his informants, is unambiguous as to the source of this information. It came from 'my informant who is employed in the establishment'.[56] This is the only specific reference to Mallon's source within *United Ireland*. The DMP spy is not identified by name. All we know is that the informant was male, in which case the leaks were not coming from one of the many members of the Ladies Land League who had, largely, assumed control of the newspaper in early December.

The Liberal government and the Provincial Press

The apparent preoccupation of the Liberal government with *United Ireland* often worked to the advantage of the expanding cohort of militantly nationalist regional (mostly weekly) newspapers. Only in the case of *United Ireland* did the Liberals involve themselves in a sustained campaign of attempted suppression.

The parallel struggle with the Irish regional press was largely peripheral from the moment of the introduction of the Protection of Person and Property Act in 1881. Having conferred upon itself the capacity to imprison 'suspects' without charge the Gladstone government was not obliged to confront directly any issues of the curtailment of the freedom of the regional press. The incarceration of nationalist editors and proprietors of local newspapers became largely submerged in the wider strategy of wholesale arrests. Those jailed included Timothy Harrington of the *Kerry Sentinel*, Patrick Cahill of the *Leinster Leader* and Luke Hayden of the *Roscommon Messenger*.[57] While the influence they wielded through their weekly publications was undoubtedly a major consideration in the decisions to detain them the Liberals were able to avoid the accusation that they were directly suppressing press freedom by reference to the leadership positions they had all taken up in local Land League activities.

In 1866 there were 104 provincial newspapers in circulation in Ireland.[58] Many of those were Tory/Unionist or Liberal/Whig in their politics. Papers like the *Clare Journal*, founded in 1776, the *Mayo Constitution*, founded in 1805, or the *Carlow Sentinel*, which continued in operation from 1831 to 1920, were impervious to the rise of nationalist sentiment in the 1880s, other than as vociferous opponents of the activities of the Land League and the Irish National League. By 1892 there were 128 provincial newspapers and, apart from the numerical increase, the landscape had been transformed.[59] Between 1880 and 1892 more than thirty new journals began weekly or bi-weekly publication. Twenty of those were avowedly nationalist in their politics. In addition to the newcomers many better-established papers had, in the same period, switched their allegiance to nationalism. In 1882 the venerable *Waterford Daily Mail* (established in 1823), owned by Joseph Fisher, changed its affiliation from Conservative to 'National'. It was followed in 1883 by the *Tuam Herald*, owned by Richard J. Kelly, which switched from 'Liberal' to 'National'.[60]

Only four regional newspaper proprietors were prosecuted under the 1882 Crimes Act.[61] The cases were taken under section 7 of the act, which dealt with the punishment of intimidation or incitement to intimidate. (The introduction of the Prevention of Crime (Ireland), 1882 Act will be discussed in more detail in chapter four.) Edward Walsh, editor of the *New Ross Standard* and the *Wexford People* made his first appearance in court on 29 December 1882 charged with the publication of an illegal notice describing a number of men as 'land grabbers'. He was sentenced to fourteen days in jail. This was increased to five weeks in order to allow him to appeal. The sentence was subsequently confirmed on appeal but reduced to fourteen days.[62]

John MacPhilpin, editor of the *Tuam News*, faced three counts of intimidation on 1 January 1883. The charges related to the publication of articles against three Galway landlords written by correspondents from the Loughrea district. His counsel argued, unsuccessfully, that a newspaper editor could only be prosecuted under section 13 of the Crimes Act, which related to the conduct of the press. MacPhilpin was sentenced to a month in jail, without hard labour, on one of the three counts and to fourteen days on one of the other charges. The magistrates refused to increase the sentence to allow for an appeal.[63]

On 1 December 1883, John Callanan of the *Western News* was jailed for fourteen days for publishing an article in which detrimental reference was made to a Galway shepherd, John Crehan, who had taken the land of an evicted shepherd.[64] The previous year an employee of Callanan, Edward Barrett, had been jailed for seven days and four weeks, respectively, for reporting on two illegal Land League meetings. On that occasion Callanan had testified that Barrett had attended the meeting, as a reporter, on his instructions. The magistrates had stated at the time that they 'did not recognise the rights of the Press representatives more than any others at such meetings'.[65]

But the case involving a local news editor charged under the 1882 Crimes Act that attracted most attention was that of Edward Harrington of the *Kerry Sentinel*. The prosecution more closely resembled cases later conducted under the Tory government's 1887 Crimes Act than it did the considerably less energetic pursuit of regional editors by the Liberals. This was partly because of the unique nature of the case and partly because of the prominence in the nationalist movement of the owner of the *Sentinel*, Timothy Harrington MP and its editor, his brother Edward.

In May 1883 a number of printed threatening notices were posted around the town of Tralee purporting to have emanated from the Invincibles. They read:

> Any person or persons acting contrary to the orders of his superior officers will, as sure as he has breath in his body, meet with a worse death than Lord Cavendish and Burke got. As we intend to make history, we must remove all tyrants … Death to landlords, agents and bailiffs. By order of the Tralee Invincibles. God save Ireland from informers.[66]

In its edition of 22 May the *Kerry Sentinel* reported on the placarding and published the text of the notices. Based on the suspicion that the notices had been printed on its own presses, the premises of the *Kerry Sentinel* were raided on the same day by a force of thirty members of the RIC. All copies of the newspaper were seized. On Friday 1 June a larger force of constables returned and searched the premises again. On this occasion the print run of the paper and its entire plant was taken away. As the press clause of the 1882 Crimes Act did not specifically provide for any such penalty, the authority cited for such a dramatic confiscation of private property was section 14 of the same act. This permitted the police, under warrant from the lord lieutenant, to seize 'any arms, ammunition, papers, documents, instruments, or articles suspected to be used or to be intended to be used for the purpose of or in connexion with any secret society or secret association existing for criminal purposes'.[67] No explanation was offered as to why the search warrant proffered by the RIC had been made out six weeks before the appearance of the threatening posters.

An incensed *United Ireland* contrasted the treatment of the *Sentinel* with its own experience under the Gladstone administration:

> The Government seized *United Ireland* it is true, at various times, but at least they did not pick our pockets, rifle our drawers, abstract our ledgers, plunder our library, or cart off our machines and type.[68]

O'Brien accused the administration of indulging in blatant opportunism in an attempt to rid itself of a newspaper that ranked just below *United Ireland* in terms of its provocative commentary. He described the poster as 'a brutal joke' which had offered the government 'a chance, too good to be lost, of crushing a hated opponent'.

Edward Harrington and his foreman printer, James Brosnan, were arraigned on 4 June 1883, charged with printing illegal notices. As Timothy Harrington had been in London when the offending notices were posted he was not subject to indictment. Unlike the other local newspaper editors prosecuted by the Gladstone administration both men were tried under section 9 of the Crimes Act. This covered the offence of membership of, or taking part in, 'the operations of an unlawful association'.[69] On the second day of the trial two apprentice printers, Robert Fitzgerald and Maurice Kean, admitted to the court that they had been responsible for printing the (spurious) notices without the knowledge of the foreman or editor. In passing judgment, however, the magistrates rejected the acceptance of responsibility by Fitzgerald and Kean while accepting the culpability of their contributions to the offence. Harrington and Brosnan were jailed for six months, the two apprentices, who had pleaded guilty, for two months each.[70]

An appeal to County Court judge, O'Connor Morris elicited no sympathy. He too refused to accept the evidence of Fitzgerald and Kean and the sentence on Harrington was allowed to stand. As regards Brosnan, however, he found 'no evidence on which I could act that he was connected with the printing and publishing of this notice'.[71] At the conclusion of the original trial in Tralee the Crown had indicated its willingness to return the plant to its owner, Timothy Harrington. In doing so it avoided an action from Harrington for the return of his presses. He was in court when the announcement was made and characterized the original seizure as 'gross and violent robbery, perpetrated under the sanction of the Crown'.[72]

The six-month sentence on Harrington was the longest imposed on a newspaper editor under the terms of the 1882 Crimes Act. Under the much more rigorous regime of the 1887 Crimes act only three editors, P.A. McHugh of the *Sligo Champion*, John Powell of the *Midland Tribune*, and Edward Harrington himself, received similar sentences.

Feigning silence?

Did government action against the paper affect the management and the editorial policy of *United Ireland*? Clearly the administration had some success in hampering the actual production of the newspaper. In addition *United Ireland* opted for discretion in some of its British editions. Issues destined for the British market often bore little resemblance to those printed in the UK but intended for Ireland.[73] There was an acute awareness that administration concerns over the reliability of Irish juries in cases of seditious libel would not apply to their English equivalents.

United Ireland may also have been prepared to modify its editorial line in the expectation that the Castle would, in turn, modify its own regime of suppression. Just before the significant 15 December raid on the newspaper's premises Mallon recorded that his informant within the building was of the opinion that the edition of 17 December would be moderate in tone because 'they got a hint from Kilmainham, to the effect that if the paper could be kept afloat for two or three weeks hence, all danger of suppression would be over for a time'.[74] This would suggest that the actions being taken by the Castle were beginning to pay dividends. However, the term 'moderation' was relative when applied to *United Ireland*. The administration can only have hoped to reduce the stridency of the newspaper's commentary to the level of that emanating from the *Nation*. *United Ireland* was not about to become a weekly *Freeman's Journal*. Its very economic survival depended upon it reflecting a level of anger among the elements of Irish society from which it drew its readership. Neither was the newspaper likely to amend radically its polemical approach while it was being coerced by the government into so doing. But did the journal, for its own purposes, modify its advocacy of the 'No Rent Manifesto' and its opposition to the Land Courts, and curtail the worst excesses of 'Incidents of the Campaign' in the face of a determined government crusade of constructive suppression? And, if so, was this a policy of temporary and simulated moderation? Was *United Ireland*, in effect, feigning silence?

The *Times* commented on 27 January 1882 that '*United Ireland* is fighting hard, but is evidently getting the worst of it in the struggle with the authorities. Its strength is greatly impaired, and its tone is that rather of a spiteful but feeble vixen than of the daring outlaw'.[75] The following day, though not directly in response, *United Ireland* was anxious to scotch rumours of its incipient demise. 'We still exist, our colours still flying, our courage unabated, and our determination as firm as ever.'[76] In conjunction with this defiance, however, the newspaper tacitly conceded that the government was making some impact on its distribution. It announced a doubling of its cover price and suggested a new mechanism for circulating the paper. English readers were asked to buy as many copies as possible and post them to friends in Ireland.

United Ireland also conceded that, in the course of a seizure at the City of Dublin Steampacket company in North Wall the previous week, a quarter of the print run (the police estimate was 10,000 copies) had been captured by the authorities, although claiming that 'the stolen papers were replaced the next day by a new consignment'.[77] The following week 400 copies were seized in the Great Northern Railway terminus in Belfast and 1,000 copies in a house near Temple Bar in Dublin. The Folkestone seizure was estimated to have been of an entire print run of over 30,000 copies.[78] The 23 January edition of the paper was only four pages long. In some instances different editions were printed in London and Paris. The 28 January edition, quoted above, had to go to press earlier than usual with the result that many of the Land League notices had to be held over. Nonetheless, police and newspaper reports suggest that, despite official efforts, the newspaper *was* getting into the hands of those who wanted to read it.[79] The Dublin Correspondent of the London *Standard* commented that 'Notwithstanding all the endeavours of the authorities the U[nited] I[reland] is still selling most freely (with a tax by the newsvendors) throughout the country. This evening, copies, dated the 28th January, were to be purchased in all the principal streets, of course under cover.'[80]

Police activities in Ireland were mirrored by similar actions in England. Some operations were conducted in collaboration with the DMP. Irish detectives were, for example, involved in a move made by Liverpool police. A local printer's premises was raided and he was forced to give up 3,000 copies of the newspaper. The printer had only agreed to undertake the publication after being indemnified against any consequences. Those could be severe as the paper was published without carrying any imprint, the formal penalty for which was £5 per copy printed.[81]

Creative *United Ireland* survival stratagems continued into 1882. These included sending copies of the paper in parcels labelled, no doubt with conscious irony, 'the *Times*'.[82] When it was announced that the newspaper would be published in Paris, Scotland Yard had, according to *United Ireland* itself, dispatched two detectives to the French capital 'to see to what destination the parcels would be directed. To give them occupation and instruction, parcels were dispatched to eighteen different parts of France, Belgium, Holland and Germany with highly Hibernian addresses. That is *the wrong parcels*.' The paper gloated, 'the detectives' hands were too full telegraphing to police agents all over the Continent to observe how the genuine parcels were sent or where they were bound for'.[83] According to the paper this resulted in concerted police activity in Dover, Newhaven, Folkestone, Southampton and other ports. Ships 'had their cargoes pulled asunder and every traveller had his luggage rigorously overhauled'. This allowed *United Ireland* to turn the significant Folkestone reverse of 27 January into a minor triumph. 'If Mr. Forster thinks the result a satisfactory return for the employment of hundreds of men day and night at every port and every railway station in the kingdom, he is a meek and easily satisfied man.'[84]

Despite *United Ireland's* claims to have still been in wide circulation during the early months of 1882 there are dozens of reports in Police and Chief Secretary's files of police seizures. Most were in small numbers in rural Ireland. While it must be observed that Superintendent Mallon had a vested interest in claiming success in the police interception efforts in mid-February 1882 he insisted that, where Dublin was concerned 'it does not appear to be much in circulation here'.[85]

By April 1882 there was a perception, expressed within Dublin Castle and extending to the *Times*,[86] that *United Ireland* had begun to modify its more strident rhetoric. In the last public speech of his life, at Creggs, Co. Roscommon in October 1891, Parnell appeared to confirm the opinion expressed by the *Times* almost a decade before. He claimed, albeit in a highly adversarial context, that O'Brien had approached him in Kilmainham asking to be permitted to release an edition of the newspaper in April 1882 'without any reference to the "No Rent Manifesto", or to the incidents of the campaign or the struggle against rents', in order to save the paper from irreparable damage arising out of increasingly successful British attempts at suppression. Parnell, who acquiesced in the plan, described this, in 1891, as 'that white flag from the walls of Kilmainham'.[87]

The 8 April edition of *United Ireland* seemed to signal a change in direction. 'Incidents of the Campaign' had become the more innocuous 'The Pulse of the Country'. In addition a significant amount of column inches was devoted to the Poor Law Guardian elections and to the emerging policy of using those local polls to 'blood' aspiring 'reliable' nationalist politicians while, simultaneously, 'purging the Poor Law Boards' of landlord influence. An editorial heralded the fact that the disposition of a sum of £1.25 million had, as a result of these nationalist local election successes 'been taken from the garrison and taken possession of by the people' after a series of nationalist electoral victories.[88]

In the same issue the paper was also ostentatiously unwilling to publish the entire contents of a letter from a 'Cork County Farmer'. This related to the levying of an increased local tax, the so-called 'cess' tax, on areas where agrarian outrage was leading to compensation claims from victims, many of them landlords. *United Ireland* had been critical of this development,[89] seeing it as a punitive imposition on the many on account of the depredations of the few. The correspondent was reinforcing suspicions of a raft of spurious claims. He alleged that a local landlord had been awarded £25 for the theft of a greyhound, alleging that it was an agrarian crime with a political motive. The Grand Jury had subsequently increased the award to £100 and ordered that the amount be levied from three town-lands with the result that inhabitants of those localities would be forced to pay 8s in the £1 in the next 'cess'.

United Ireland did print 'Cork County Farmer's' allegation that, 'Every broken down Emergency man or hanger-on now has only to set fire to his haystack, or do some other job of the kind and he can make a fortune out of the poor farmer's pockets.' But that was as far as the paper was prepared to go. It commented that 'there is a good deal in our correspondent's letter which Mr. Forster would be glad to see us print, but which would never see the light if we printed it. The question of the assessment of Grand Jury tax is one the farmers are entitled to discuss for themselves, but which we are prohibited from discussing for them.'[90] The paper, although it had described the practice as 'appropriation'[91] and although it had been accused by the London *Standard* of advocating non-payment of the tax, had actually stopped short of so doing.

The tone of the issue can be taken as a signal to the authorities that, in the future, *United Ireland* would remain within the bounds of legality in its editorial commentary. There was a sense in which *United Ireland* was, in any case, becoming its own lead story. There is a certain circularity about the paper's content in the early months of 1882 as the government seizures provided copy for both the news pages and the editorial columns. The paper's continued existence, its resourcefulness in overcoming obstacles to circulation, and the focus on the issue of freedom of the press may have allowed *United Ireland* to resile from its redundant advocacy of the 'No Rent Manifesto' and its futile denunciations of the Land Courts. This, in turn, allowed the government to end the debilitating weekly fishing expeditions for outlawed copies of the paper, to obviate the risk of further claims from angry newsagents, and to mollify the radical wing of the Liberal party on the issue of abuse of freedom of expression.

A hint from Mallon brought about a close inspection of the *United Ireland* issue of 8 April 1882.[92] There was a division of opinion over whether to continue the inclusion of the paper under the terms of the lord lieutenant's order of 6 January. Attorney general Johnson took a hard-line approach. He was suspicious of the implied overture from the newspaper. 'It is quite possible that harmless papers or at least comparatively harmless ones will be published in order to avoid seizure [of future issues].'[93] Johnson appears to have been overruled by under secretary Burke. His signature is appended to notes from Samuel Lee Anderson to the DMP commissioner and the inspector general of the RIC, advising both not to seize that week's issue and 'in future not to seize this paper without instructions, but to obtain a copy of each issue as published and submit it for instructions'.[94] It was a return to the more measured policy of late 1881. Whether or not *United Ireland* had intended to concede ground in its 8 April edition, Dublin Castle had decided that the newspaper had shown sufficient evidence of a 'firm purpose of amendment' to be given the benefit of the doubt in the future.

Three days later the solicitor general, A.M. Porter, felt confident enough to write that:

> 'United Ireland' is greatly subdued in its tone: and although still very objectionable, is not on the face of it, distinctly treasonable: nor does it in terms advocate 'No rent' doctrine. I

> think the action of the Govt. should be carefully re-considered
> as regards this paper ... I think the time has come when
> another conference should be held on the subject. Meanwhile
> I cannot say that I see sufficient reason for seizing this paper.[95]

At least one representative of the retail sector, albeit one with privileged access to political information, must have sensed that government policy was about to change. On the same day Porter offered his revised opinion, the Chief Secretary's office received a letter from the Dublin branch of W.H. Smith's business over the signature of his Dublin manager, Charles Eason. Although the Middle Abbey street premises – to be taken over by Eason himself in 1886 – was owned by a leading Tory politician with no great affection for Ireland,[96] Eason had managed to distance the business from its owner's politics. As a consequence *United Ireland* was viewed by him, dispassionately, as a purely commercial commodity. His letter read:

> Sir, we are informed on what appears to be good authority that
> the prohibition of the sale of *United Ireland* has been removed.
> We shall feel obliged by your informing us if this is not correct
> as we are likely to have applications for it and would have to
> supply it if obtainable lawfully.[97]

When asked by Samuel Lee Anderson how to respond to Eason –Anderson himself suggested 'an evasive answer'[98] – Porter replied, 'I think the best course is to reply that although the last issue has not been seized, it will depend upon the character of future issues of the paper whether it will or will not be necessary to interfere with it.'[99]

The *Times* exulted that *United Ireland's* teeth had finally been pulled. It wrote on 14 April that 'the ban on the publication of *United Ireland* appears to have been removed and the paper is now openly sold and cried in the streets. This week's number is as moderate in tone as the last.'[100] Four days later – O'Brien had been released from Kilmainham in the interim – the *Times* commented that 'it is argued from the release of Mr O'Brien on Saturday and the instructions of the police not to seize any more copies of *United Ireland* that the government are meditating an entire change of policy. But there is nothing in *United Ireland* at present to make it worth the trouble of seizing. It is much milder than the other "National" prints, which have not been seized.'[101] This was in stark contrast to the assessment of Patton, the Dublin correspondent of the newspaper in the 16 December edition of the paper. Then he had said of *United Ireland* that, 'there is no abatement in the tone of the paper; the spirit of the *Irish World* which it had taken for its model; breathes throughout every page'.[102]

On 15 April 1882 O'Brien was released from Kilmainham to minister to his dying mother. She passed away a week later.[103] Prior to his final release he had been allowed out of Kilmainham on compassionate grounds on a regular basis in order to visit her. The authorities had additional reasons for letting him go in mid-April. Never a particularly healthy individual, O'Brien did not prosper physically in Kilmainham, in contrast to Parnell, who managed regular exercise and a small weight gain. The authorities received regular missives from fellow inmate and future MP, Dr Joseph Kenny, about his state of health.[104] Arising out of his bereavement, the deteriorating state of his own health and the suggestion that it was communications from within Kilmainham that led to the modification in the *United Ireland* line detected by Porter, the Castle concluded that O'Brien did not pose as much of a threat as he had done in October.

Such sentiments would have been reinforced by an extraordinary memo from Mallon, which belied the normally sensible advice and intelligence passed on by one of the DMP's great assets during this period. In March 1882, Mallon had been consulted on the advisability of releasing O'Brien on compassionate grounds. Mallon wrote: 'I think it would be imprudent to release him just now. It is likely that *United Ireland* will be discontinued and, if so, O'Brien will have saved his reputation by being in prison. If the publication is discontinued O'Brien will remain in the country until he sees the last of his mother, after he could go to France or Italy, perhaps to Egypt, and if his health recovers sufficiently he'd break with the Land League and resume his employment on the literary staff of the Freeman's Journal.'[105] It was a bizarre series of *non sequiturs* based either on faulty intelligence or wishful thinking and would prove to be utterly erroneous. The advice had been sought by under secretary Burke; it was only acted upon in the sense that O'Brien's incarceration continued for another six weeks.

At the time of O'Brien's discharge from Kilmainham there was already an inexorable movement towards a *rapprochement* between Parnell and the

Liberal government. Parnell had been released on compassionate grounds to attend the funeral of his nephew in Paris and had set in train – on parallel tracks involving the simultaneous intercession of Captain O'Shea and Justin McCarthy – the process that would lead to the Kilmainham Treaty and the informal end of the increasingly inchoate conflict that was the Land War. O'Brien's release and the easing of the suppression campaign against *United Ireland* must be seen in that context. He had contributed to the improving atmosphere himself by including in the paper, while still in prison, details of Parnell's thinking on future land legislation, including provision for arrears and tenant purchase.[106]

However, if there was any expectation on the part of the administration that O'Brien's journalism would remain circumspect after his release it was promptly dashed by his first 'post-Kilmainham' leader. In the edition of 22 April 1882 the editorial loudly proclaimed that 'we want a few weeks fair play, while we are repairing the ravages which an unexampled series of persecutions have made in our property. After that we will demand no forbearance either from our readers or from our foes.' He couldn't resist reminding the government of at least one of the consequences of their attempts to silence his paper. 'Brutally as the Liberal Government may have plundered us in other respects they have at least saved us the expense of advertising ourselves.'[107] The attorney general, when he had studied that week's edition of the journal, wrote on 24 April: 'I think it expressly probable that *United Ireland* will be as illegal a publication very soon as it was and I think a hint might be given to Mr. O'Brien to take care of himself.'[108] When Forster had signed the warrant for O'Brien's discharge, it had carried the customary rider 'release with usual warning'.[109] If the authorities chose to do so O'Brien could be re-arrested at any time under the terms of the PPP act. However, events in Phoenix Park on 6 May 1882 would make that piece of legislation redundant. It would be superseded by an arguably more draconian enactment of coercion legislation in the form of the Prevention of Crime (Ireland) Act.

Not long after O'Brien's release, Parnell too was discharged on foot of his celebrated letter of 28 April to O'Shea (actually written in Kilmainham with the Captain at hand on 29 April) which promised action on agrarian crime in return for arrears legislation and the *hors d'oeuvre*[110] of co-operation with the Liberals in future legislative measures. The unacknowledged 'Kilmainham

Treaty' was greeted with dismay by many of Parnell's supporters. Healy wrote that 'we felt that the Chief had lowered the flag, and had tried to deceive alike his countrymen and the British'.[111] There was some awareness at the time of Parnell's release that it was based on a deal that might have to be defended and justified to the Land League foot-soldiers, but full knowledge of the details of the accord did not emerge until the debate in the House of Commons of 15 May. There, Forster, who had retained a copy of the 28 April letter to O'Shea, embarrassed the Irish leader into reading the full text of the document after Parnell had attempted to read a redacted version to the House, *sans l'hors d'oeuvre*. In *United Ireland* of 6 May, therefore, O'Brien, whatever inside knowledge or misgivings he might have had about the 'Treaty' was not required to defend the details of the understanding. The editorial headline that week was an exultant 'Coercion gives up the ghost'.[112]

O'Brien might have faced a dilemma of his own in the weeks ahead as fuller details emerged of the nature of the *rapprochement* between Parnell and Gladstone. *United Ireland* had been lacerating the Liberals mercilessly since its establishment in August 1881. Gladstone himself had been subjected to almost as much abuse as the, now departed, Forster. In addition O'Brien was, at heart, a committed agrarianist. Although he could undoubtedly have done so with some *élan*, he might well have had personal qualms in propagandizing on behalf of a party leadership that was already re-directing the attention of the national movement away from the land struggle. In his memoirs O'Brien, retrospectively, lauded this burgeoning alliance between Parnell and the Liberals and dismissed criticisms of the end of the 'no rent' campaign and the effective reversal of previous policy in the tacit acceptance of the Land Commission. He rationalized that 'Parnell's positive genius had resorted to a General Rent Strike not as a vague revolutionary fetish, but as a conditional act of reprisal, which had now accomplished its practical purpose'.[113]

He contrasted the 'shattered reputation' of O'Connell in the wake of his release from Richmond prison in 1844 (conveniently ignoring the tumultuous procession which had greeted the Liberator's release) which left the champion of repeal, 'without a hope for the future of the policy for which he had been imprisoned', with that of Parnell, who had 'quitted Kilmainham as a potentate who had sealed the fate of the Minister who had imprisoned him, and as the ally of the Prime Minister'.[114]

In the *United Ireland* issue of 20 May a front-page letter (this one was signed, by a Paul O'Byrne, 4 Duke St, Dublin) posed the question: 'Sir, I cannot understand what the so-called Kilmainham Treaty means; is it an Irish party that was to be solely devoted to Irish nationality or subservient to the Whigs?.' The editorial response was somewhat Jesuitical:

> There was no 'Treaty of Kilmainham' other than there is whenever an Irish member proposes a great healing measure that is distasteful to the Government and when the Government has the courage to accept it in the teeth of former professions and to discard the hateful Minister who impeded it … if our correspondent imagines that the Irish party are shackled by any engagement whatever – much less by any obligation to condone the most atrocious Coercion code ever attempted to be fastened upon Ireland – we venture to prophesy that the next few weeks struggle will amply disabuse him.[115]

But O'Brien was not obliged to defend Parnell against allegations of 'surrender' or that he had 'enfeoffed himself to the Liberals at a moment when the No Rent strike had only to get a free rein to be insuppressible.'[116] He was not required to fill the role of journalistic enforcer of silence, on this occasion at least. The Phoenix Park murders and the consequent introduction by the home secretary, Sir William Harcourt, of the draconian Crimes Act – already being prepared by Forster before his resignation but rejected by the cabinet in April – meant that the *hors d'oeuvre* was, *pro tem* at least, returned uneaten. The Kilmainham Treaty may have led to the temporary retirement of John Dillon, the disillusionment of Davitt and the end of the tense love affair between the *Irish World* and Parnell, but it did not require any literary or philosophical gyrations on the part of O'Brien. Once the required period of abasement for the actions of the Invincibles had passed, O'Brien was free to resume his anti-Liberal phillipics with liberal abandon.

The Invincible effect
In its edition of 6 May 1882 *United Ireland* permitted itself to revel in a hint from Gladstone of a possible re-organization of the Castle administrative structures. In writing that 'the rats in the Castle cellars had better beware of

rat-traps; the vermin are going to have a bad time of it',[117] O'Brien may have fallen victim to what he once euphemistically described himself as his 'excess of emphasis'.[118] The phrase, and its unfortunate timing, was thrown back at him in the course of his evidence to the *Times* commission in 1889. There he acknowledged 'that sentence is a rough commentary upon Mr. Gladstone's words, and upon the strength of that paragraph I have been again and again accused of inciting to [*sic*] the Phoenix Park murders'.[119]

A few days after the brutal assassinations of Lord Frederick Cavendish and Thomas H. Burke, the phrase came back to haunt *United Ireland*. On 12 May the Conservative MP, Sir Walter Barttelot, was first into the fray when he referred to the editorial in a parliamentary question to the Irish solicitor general.[120] Neither was it just British politicians accusing *United Ireland* of having provoked the murders. In an interview with John Devoy's *Irish Nation* in New York, the Fenian chief, John O'Leary, angry at Parnell's suggestion that Fenians were responsible for the outrage, laid some of the blame at the door of *United Ireland* for what he described as a policy of incitement.[121]

The suggestion that O'Brien's splenetic language had, in any way, provoked the ferocious Phoenix Park attack was, of course, palpably absurd. Whatever peripheral influence the vitriol of *United Ireland* might have had upon the philosophy of the Invincibles, the reference in question, first appearing as it did a day before the murders, had none. However, the unwelcome attention it had aroused may have influenced O'Brien's judgment in his coverage of the outrage in the 13 May edition of his newspaper. In place of the usual front-page cartoon there was a large black-bordered space filled by the words – 'In token of abhorrence and shame for the stain cast upon the character of our nation for manliness and hospitality by the assassination of Lord Frederick Cavendish, Chief Secretary for Ireland, and of Mr. Thomas Burke, Under Secretary, in the Phoenix Park, 6th May 1882.'[122] Editorially O'Brien remarked that 'if the murderers had set to themselves the mission of doing more than centuries of British rule could do to break down barriers between the people and the officers of justice, they could not have better succeeded. It is the simple truth to say that the assassins would have run a more instant risk of being lynched in Dublin than in London.'[123] There were some who, while not openly critical of O'Brien's dismayed reaction, took issue with its submissive tone. The acerbic Joseph Biggar described the

United Ireland response as 'worthy of a *Times* leading article on the blowing to pieces of a Russian Grand Duke'.[124]

The Castle, which had actually taken a phlegmatic attitude towards the 'rats' reference on 6 May – Johnson had written that 'the coincidence of the ostensible date of the publication with the two dreadful murders gives the passage a significance which it would not otherwise possess'[125] – was somewhat ambiguous about O'Brien's apparently fulsome revulsion at the crime. In the same memo Johnson, who had the *United Ireland* of 13 May to hand, noted sceptically that 'in literal terms it professes abhorrence of these crimes. On the genuineness of these professions I offer no opinion other than the paper should not be interfered with.'[126] Johnson may well have already seen the comments in *United Ireland's* stable-mate, the *Irishman*, for which O'Brien also had editorial responsibility. They reeked of ambiguity. Referring to the gold standard seven hundred years of 'bloody strife' and 'the rapacity of the invaders' the *Irishman* opined that 'without excusing crime of any character or for any purpose, we hold that aggression is always followed by retaliation, and that repression is invariably the cause of outrage'.[127]

Courtesy of the campaign against the Crimes Act, O'Brien would rapidly recover his aplomb and his sense of injustice. He continued to wage war on Gladstone's government until its parliamentary defeat in late 1885. As we shall see, there were significant battles ahead but, arguably, the newspaper's finest achievement during the 1881–5 period was its very capacity for survival. It was its own best advertisement, something the paper acknowledged in a mocking expression of gratitude to Forster in February 1882:

> It was he who first opened the eyes of the public, or indeed our own, to the full merits of our paper. We were really modest enough to imagine that the British Empire might exist beside us. We at least supposed that the British Empire had power to strangle us if it put forth its brute strength. Mr.Forster has undeceived us on both these points.[128]

Of course, concurrent with its fight for survival, the journal pre-figured the less endearing traits that would characterize some of its own future repressive campaigns. It vilified, propagandized and deluded its readership and was anything but forceful in its deprecation of violence and outrage until the surgical knives were wielded in Phoenix Park. Margaret O'Callaghan has underscored its contribution to the facilitation of the transition 'from the clear politics of land to the more sophisticated Home Rule rhetoric of the National League … *United Ireland* constructed a unified nationalist voice out of the images and exclusions, the hootings and groanings, hissings and booings and heckling of the former on-circuit performers.' [129]

One of the principal 'exclusions' appeared to be the segregation of the Irish nationalist press when it came to the notion of freedom of expression. *United Ireland* regularly drew attention to the literary excesses of the Unionist press and the failure of the Castle to take retaliatory action against alleged instances of incitement emanating from the likes of the *Daily Express* or the *Dublin Evening Mail*.[130] It also highlighted what it saw as the hypocrisy of the advocacy of freedom of the press in England and disregard for the abuse of the same freedoms in Ireland.

The Liberals had come to power in 1880 with the announced intention of governing Ireland without recourse to special legislation. The message in the Queen's speech of 21 May 1880 was of a 'desire to avoid the evils of exceptional legislation in abridgement of liberty'.[131] Six months later Forster was still opposed to the suspension of *habeas corpus*. Gladstone's secretary, Edward Hamilton wrote in his diary that the chief secretary believed it would 'weaken the law of the land, be a bad precedent, and a temptation to rely on despotic power rather than on law'.[132] Those earnest intentions rapidly withered on the vine and had derived in the first place from a philosophy that strove to be different to that of the 'Beaconsfieldism' of the Tories. As Margaret O'Callaghan has noted 'the commitment to the maintenance of the ordinary law was a response to Liberal sensitivities, not a response to conditions in Ireland'.[133]

As it transpired, Liberal allegiance to freedom of the press had, almost inevitably, suffered the same fate as Liberal devotion to due process. Assailed by the violence of Ribbon-Fenianism in Ireland, Gladstone's administration had reverted to the default position of every British government faced with a similar set of circumstances. Confronted by the violent language of newspapers like *United Ireland*, the *Irish World* and the *United Irishman*, themselves perceived to be abusing freedom of expression, the government responded in kind. Florence Arnold-Forster was speaking for her adoptive father when she wrote in her diary in November 1881: 'one thing is certain, murder is not discouraged by the present leaders of the agitation – witness their organ *United Ireland* in which every fresh cruelty committed against an unhappy man – whether landlord or bailiff – or farmer, is entered under the heading – "Incidents of the Campaign" or "Spirit of the Country".[134]

If the government had expected *United Ireland,* after the arrest of its editor, to fade away obligingly, then its disappointment must have been as immediate as it was sustained. The newspaper defied logic and expectation and continued as it had begun. That very defiance became a threat to the Castle just as it boosted the morale of the Land League foot-soldiers. To the government *United Ireland* might have been both fallacious and mendacious in its misrepresentation of the success of the Land Courts. It was certainly viewed as seditious in its prosecution of the 'No Rent Manifesto'. O'Brien's phraseology in the first edition of the newspaper is interesting. His hopes for the journal, as expressed on the opening page, were that it would become a 'weekly Monster meeting'. Presumably this was predicated on his intention to be provocative and his ambition to attract a large readership. He may not have been conscious of an inherent irony. The monster meetings of the Repeal era of the 1840s were not known for the quality of their dialogue. They were tendentious harangues delivered, without mediation, by the leadership to an eagerly receptive faithful. In that sense at least, by the effective end of the Land War in May 1882, O'Brien could afford to be pleased with his handiwork.

Notes

1   *Daily News*, 13 April 1882.

2   HC Deb. 30 March 1882, vol. 268, c322.

3   6 January 1882, NAI, CSORP, Police and Crime Division Reports, III, Compensation Cases, Crimes Act, 1882–3, Carton 6, 1881/45842.

4   Legg, *Newspapers and Nationalism,* 161.

5   O'Brien, *Recollections*, 379.

6   McGough to chief secretary, 18 January 1882, NAI, CSORP, 1882/3037 (file not found). This was only one of a number of similar threats that, ultimately, did not materialize. As late as 8 March 1882 O'Brien was making applications to the authorities for copies of *United Ireland* to be sent to Kilmainham Gaol in order to expedite the case. On 19 March T.H. Burke referred to O'Brien's continued preparations for the case in a note to Forster.

7   HC Deb, 13 February 1882, vol. 266, c612.

8   In the absence of any specific reference in police files to the *Irishman* it must be assumed that its continued publication was of more value to the Castle, for low-level intelligence purposes, than its suppression.

9   He may even have been tipped off by Mallon himself. For many years after Egan's precipitate departure from Dublin to the USA at the time of the Invincible arrests in 1883 there were persistent rumours that the Land League Treasurer had been one of Mallon's informers. The suggestion was that Mallon had forewarned Egan that he was about to be arrested for complicity in the Phoenix Park murders in token of gratitude for information received since 1879 (McCracken, Donal – *Inspector Mallon: Buying Irish Patriotism for a Five-pound Note* (Dublin, 2009) 117).

10 Mallon to Talbot, 18 December 1881, NAI, CSORP, Police and Crime Division Reports, III, Compensation Cases, Crimes Act, 1882–3, Carton 6, 1881/564.

11 MacDonagh, *O'Brien*, 57. The only printing location MacDonagh omitted was Manchester.

12 *United Ireland*, 7 January 1882.

13 John Denvir, *Life Story of an Old Rebel* (Dublin, 1910), 211. There is no indication if T.D. Sullivan was aware that any of his employees were spending their spare time distributing a 'rival' weekly paper.

14 Denvir, *Life Story of an Old Rebel*, 212.

15 Denvir, *Life Story of an Old Rebel*, 213.

16 *Daily News*, 25 February 1882.

17 Denvir, *Life Story of an Old Rebel*, 214.

18 *Pall Mall Gazette*, 23 January 1882.

19 HC Deb. 20 February 1882, vol. 266, cc1097–8.

20 John Denvir, *Life Story of an Old Rebel*, 216.

21 John Denvir, *Life Story of an Old Rebel*, 215.

22 John Denvir, *Life Story of an Old Rebel*, 215.

23 Parnell, *Tale of a Great Sham*, 122.

24 Parnell, *Tale of a Great Sham*, 122.

25 Parnell, *Tale of a Great Sham*, 122.

26 Mallon to Talbot, 8 December 1881, NAI, CSORP, Police and Crime Division Reports, III, Compensation Cases, Crimes Act, 1882–3, Carton 6, 1881/41270.

27 Mallon to Talbot, 14 December 1881, NAI, CSORP, Police and Crime Division Reports, III, Compensation Cases, Crimes Act, 1882–3, Carton 6, 1881/45113.

28 Margaret Ward, *Unmanageable Revolutionaries : Women and Irish Nationalism* (London-East Haven, Ct.,1989),

29 Margaret Ward, *Unmanageable Revolutionaries*, 16.

30 Patricia Groves, *Petticoat Rebellion: The Anna Parnell Story* (Dublin, 2009), 164.

31 Patricia Groves, *Petticoat Rebellion*, 164.

32 Mallon to Talbot, 14 December, 1881, NAI, CSORP, Police and Crime Division Reports, III, Compensation Cases, Crimes Act, 1882–3, Carton 6, 1881/45113.

33 Parnell, *Tale of a Great Sham*, 123.

34 Fitzgerald to Burke, 5 December 1881, NAI, CSORP, 1881/43157.

35 *United Ireland*, 7 January 1881.

36 Ward, *Unmanageable Revolutionaries*, 28.

37 *United Ireland*, 7 January 1881.

38 8 April, 1882, NAI, CSORP. 1882/21783.

39 *United Ireland*, 24 December 1881.

40 NAI, CSORP, 1881/45266. CSORP, 1882/28798. CSORP, 1882/21783.

    United Ireland, 7 January 1882. *United Ireland*, 28 January 1882.

41 Fay to Inspector F.Purcell, 1 April 1882, NAI, CSORP, 1882/28798.

42 Barry to Trevelyan, 30 May 1882, NAI, CSORP, 1882/28798.

43 Edmund Leamy question to the chief secretary. HC Deb, 24 April 1882, vol. 268, cc1265–6.

44 Response of W.E. Forster, HC Deb, 24 April 1882, vol. 268, cc1266.

45 Naish memo, 17 June 1882, NAI, CSORP, 1882/27066.

46 Memo of W.V. Gregg, 29 June 1882, NAI, CSORP, 1882/28798.

47 *United Ireland*, 28 January 1882.

48 *United Ireland*, 11 February 1882.

49 Parnell, *Tale of a Great Sham*, 122.

50 Mallon to Talbot, 21 October 1881, NAI, CSORP, Police and Crime Division Reports, III, Compensation Cases, Crimes Act, 1882–3, Carton 6, 1881/35944.

51 Mallon to Talbot, 24 October 1881, NAI-CSORP, Police and Crime Division Reports, III, Compensation Cases, Crimes Act, 1882–3, Carton 6, 1881/36371.

52 Mallon to Talbot, 1 December, 1881, NAI, CSORP, Police and Crime Division Reports, III, Compensation Cases, Crimes Act, 1882–3, Carton 6, 1881/42170.

53 Mallon to Talbot, 8 November 1881, NAI, CSORP, Police and Crime Division Reports, III, Compensation Cases, Crimes Act, 1882–3, Carton 6, 1881/38894.

54 It should be pointed out that this particular piece of information appears to have come from the observations of Inspector Thomas Kavanagh (Mallon to Talbot, 25 November 1881, NAI, CSORP, Police and Crime Division Reports, III, Compensation Cases, Crimes Act, 1882–3, Carton 6, 1881/42170).

55 Mallon to Talbot, 1 December 1881, NAI, CSORP, Police and Crime Division Reports, III, Compensation Cases, Crimes Act, 1882–3, Carton 6, 1881/42170. Just a week beforehand Talbot had informed Forster, presumably based on information from Mallon that, 'in the opinion of the leading members of the conspiracy, *United Ireland* newspaper has failed to do the work intended. A new paper, to be called New Ireland, is probably to be published by Egan and Co. from Paris early in December or January next.' Talbot to Forster, 24 November 1881, TNA, PRO, CAB 37/24, 1889, no. 21, 10. *Copies of Secret Official Reports made by the Officers of the Dublin Metropolitan Police between December, 1880 and March, 1883 on the Subject of Secret Societies and the Nationalist Movement in Ireland.*

56 Mallon to Talbot, 14 December 1881, NAI, CSORP, Police and Crime Division Reports, III, Compensation Cases, Crimes Act, 1882–3, Carton 6, 1881/45113.

57 *United Ireland*, 27 May 1882. Coverage of their releases. All served longer terms in detention, without trial, than had William O'Brien.

58 Legg, *Newspapers and Nationalism*, 77.

59 Legg, *Newspapers and Nationalism*, 125.

60 Legg, *Newspapers and Nationalism*, 128. Kelly had been prosecuted in 1882 for the publication of a letter written by the American journalist James Redpath, 'encouraging divers ill-disposed persons to murder certain other persons, to wit, divers landlords' (*Freeman's Journal*, 16 August 1882). Kelly repudiated the sentiments espoused by Redpath and agreed to give any undertaking required by the court to avoid a custodial sentence. In this regard he was almost unique amongst avowedly nationalist editors in his singular lack of defiance.

61 TNA, PRO, CO 903/2 Miscellaneous notes series No. IV, 7–10. Only the cases of Edward Walsh, John MacPhilpin and John Callanan are cited. The prosecution of Edward Harrington, which also took place under the Crimes Act, is ignored. In addition William O'Brien was prosecuted for seditious libel and Edmund Dwyer Gray for contempt. Four reporters, Edward Barrett, Nicholas Barrett, Thomas Cunningham and James McDermott were jailed for attending proclaimed meetings. Three printers, James Brosnan, Robert Fitzgerald and Maurice Kean were tried along with Edward Harrington, of the *Kerry Sentinel* in 1883.

62 *Freeman's Journal*, 30 December 1882. TNA, PRO, CO 903/2 Miscellaneous notes series No. IV, 9. Only sentences of four weeks or more could be appealed to a higher court.

63 *Freeman's Journal*, 2 January 1883. TNA, PRO, CO 903/2 Miscellaneous notes series No. IV, 9–10.

64 *Freeman's Journal*, 4 December 1883. TNA, PRO, CO 903/2 Miscellaneous notes series No. IV, 7.

65 *Freeman's Journal*, 30 December 1882

66 *United Ireland*, 2 June 1883.

67 *Public General Statutes passed in the Forty-fifth and Forty-sixth Years of the Reign of Queen Victoria* (London, 1882), 61.

68 *United Ireland*, 2 June 1883.

69 *Public General Statutes passed in the Forty-fifth and Forty-sixth Years of the Reign of Queen Victoria*, 59.

70 *Freeman's Journal*, 6 June 1883.

71 *Freeman's Journal*, 11 July 1883.

72 *Freeman's Journal*, 6 June 1883.

73 Sir Robert Anderson wrote to T.H. Burke on 26 December 1881 that the London edition of *United Ireland* 'has scarcely anything in common with the Dublin paper save the name and the advertisements. I do not think the London paper, taken as a whole, affords sufficient grounds for a prosecution ... I do not think the London impression will be sent to Ireland when the Dublin imp. [*sic*] is so much more "advanced" in tone' (Anderson to Burke, 26 December 1881, NAI, CSORP, Police and Crime Division Reports, III, Compensation Cases, Crimes Act, 1882–3, Carton 6, 1881/46048).

74 Mallon to Talbot, 14 December 1881, NAI, CSORP, Police and Crime Division Reports, III, Compensation Cases, Crimes Act, 1882–3, Carton 6, 1881/45113.

75 *Times*, 27 January 1882.

76 *United Ireland*, 28 January 1882.

77 *United Ireland*, 28 January 1882.

78 *United Ireland*, 4 February 1882.

79 *Times*, 27 January 1882. Johnson memo 18 January 1882, NAI, CSORP, 1882/4305. Anonymous letter 25 January 1881, NAI, CSORP, 1882/4305.

80 *The Standard*, 30 January 1882.

81 *United Ireland*, 11 February 1882. Though in the case of the prosecution of Denvir, (cited above) the fine for releasing 800 copies without an imprint was £22.

82 *United Ireland*, 7 January 1882.

83 *United Ireland*, 18 February 1882.

84 *United Ireland*, 18 February 1882.

85 Mallon to Talbot, 11 February 1882, NAI, CSORP, 1882/8710.

86 *Times*, 14 & 18 April 1882. See fn.69 & 70.

87 *Freeman's Journal*, 28 September 1891.

88 *United Ireland*, 8 April 1882.

89 *United Ireland*, 28 January 1882.

90 *United Ireland*, 8 April 1882.

91 *United Ireland*, 28 January 1882.

92 Mallon to Talbot, 8 April 1882, NAI, CSORP, Police and Crime Division Reports, III, Compensation Cases, Crimes Act, 1882–3, Carton 6, 1882/16912.

93 W.H. Johnson memo, 8 April 1882, NAI, CSORP, Police and Crime Division Reports, III, Compensation Cases, Crimes Act, 1882–3, Carton 6, 1882/16912.

94 Memo of Samuel Lee Anderson, 8 April 1882, NAI, CSORP, Police and Crime Division Reports, III, Compensation Cases, Crimes Act, 1882–3, Carton 6, 17681/1882.

95 A.M. Porter, memo of 11 April 1882, NAI, CSORP, Police and Crime Division Reports, III, Compensation Cases, Crimes Act, 1882–3, Carton 6, 1882/unnumbered.

96 L.M. Cullen, *Eason and Son: A History* (Dublin, 1989), 130. Smith believed that the Liberal policy of coercion, having brought 'temporary security' was responsible for a recovery in his Irish firm's accounts in 1882 (Cullen, *Eason*, 133).

97 Charles Eason to Forster, 11 April 1882, NAI, CSORP, 1882/17524.

98 Anderson to Porter, 14 April 1882, NAI, CSORP, 1882/17524.

99 Porter to Anderson, 15 April 1882, NAI, CSORP, 1882/17524.

100 *Times*, 14 April 1882. The reference is to the editions of 1 & 8 April 1882.

101 *Times*, 18 April 1882. There had actually been an application for attachment against the *Freeman's Journal* in February made by the Land Commission for comments in the paper on a case conducted in Limerick (*United Ireland*, 11 February).

102 *Times*, 16 December 1881.

103 Mallon report, 22 April, 1882, NAI, CSORP, 1882/19234,

104 Dr Kenny journal, 22 December 1881, CSORP, 1882/19234. 11 January 1882, NAI, CSORP, 1882/19234.

105 Mallon memo, 7 March 1882, NAI, CSORP, 1882/19234.

106 *United Ireland*, 8 April 1882.

107 *United Ireland*, 22 April 1882.

108 W.H. Johnson memo, 24 April 1882, NAI, CSORP, Police and Crime Division Reports, III, Compensation Cases, Crimes Act, 1882–3, Carton 6, 1882/18924.

109 Appended note of W.E. Forster, 14 April 1882, NAI, CSORP, 1882/19234.

110 So described by Gladstone in his missive to Forster of 30 April 1882, after he had seen the letter brought by O'Shea from Kilmainham (Gladstone papers, BL, Add. Mss. 44160).

111 T.M. Healy, *Letters and leaders of my day* (New York, 1929), 162.

112 *United Ireland*, 6 May 1882.

113 O'Brien, *Recollections*, 419–20. O'Brien's positivity about the efficacy of the Kilmainham Treaty, viewed from a 1905 perspective, was, of course, coloured by the fact that he had, in 1903, fallen out with some of the 1882 sceptics and opponents of the accord, like Dillon, over the Wyndham land purchase scheme.

114 O'Brien, *Recollections*, 420.

115 *United Ireland*, 20 May 1882.

116 O'Brien, *Recollections*, 416.

117 *United Ireland*, 6 May 1882.

118 O'Brien, *Recollections*, 360.

119 21 May 1889, *Special Commission*, vol. 8, 106.

120 *Times*, 12 May 1882.

121 *Irish Nation*, 20 May 1882. Cited in William O'Brien and Desmond Ryan, eds. *Devoy's Post Bag* 2 vols, (Dublin, 1953), vol. 2, 222.

122 *United Ireland*, 13 May 1882.

123 *United Ireland*, 13 May 1882.

124 O'Brien, *Recollections*, 429.

125 W.H. Johnson memo, 11 May 1882, NAI, CSORP, Police and Crime Division Reports, III, Compensation Cases, Crimes Act, 1882–3, Carton 6, 1882/unnumbered.

126 W.H. Johnson memo, 11 May 1882, NAI, CSORP, Police and Crime Division Reports, III, Compensation Cases, Crimes Act, 1882–3, Carton 6, 1882/unnumbered.

127 *The Irishman*, 13 May 1882.

128 *United Ireland*, 18 February 1882.

129 Margaret O'Callaghan, *British High Politics and a Nationalist Ireland: Criminality, Land and the Law under Forster and Balfour* (Cork, 1994), 80.

130 *United Ireland*, 31 December 1881. *United Ireland*, 22 April 1882.

131 HL Deb, 20 May 1880, vol. 252, c66.

132 Dudley Bahlman, *The Diary of Sir Edward Walter Hamilton* (Oxford, 1972), 73.

133 Margaret O'Callaghan, *British High Politics and a Nationalist Ireland: Criminality*, 23.

134 Diary entry, 21 November 1881, Moody and Hawkins, *Florence Arnold-Forster*, 318–19.

CHAPTER FOUR

'Accusing Spirits': United Ireland and Seditious Libel – May 1882–January 1883

'The new organ of the national movement, *United Ireland*, under Mr. William O'Brien's direction, assailed the Spencer regime with unsparing vituperation. In a relentless spirit of hostility and with great ability every act of the executive was mercilessly criticised, every fault exposed, and every measure directed against free speech or fair trial denounced.'[1]

(Michael Davitt, *The Fall of Feudalism in Ireland*)

'*Attorney General:* The only objection that you had then to rebellion was that it was hopeless?

William O'Brien: In the circumstances of the time unquestionably, that was my own feeling.'[2]

(Evidence of William O'Brien to the *Times* commission, 23 May 1889)

'A desperate struggle for liberty of speech in Ireland'

While the unofficial compact that became known as the Kilmainham Treaty contained no specific guarantee that the repressive regime instituted by the Protection of Person and Property (Ireland) Act would be relieved or allowed to lapse, there was an assumption that a diminution in agrarian crime, implicit in Parnell's side of the bargain, would lead to an easing of coercion. In the wake of the Phoenix Park murders any such eventuality was politically untenable. In place of a gradual relaxation, coercive provisions, *de trop* in April 1882, had become *de rigeur* again in May. A template prepared for an increasingly isolated and uncompromising Forster and Cowper, became the consensus response of the Liberals to the murder of Cavendish and Burke. While the new chief secretary, George Otto Trevelyan, was fighting the by-election required by his elevation to Cabinet, the Prevention of Crime (Ireland) Bill, 1882, was introduced into the House of Commons by home secretary, William Vernon Harcourt, within days of the interment of the victims of the Phoenix Park assassinations.

The struggle that followed the Phoenix Park murders continued until the fall of Gladstone's government, and its ultimate expression, in press terms, was a highly personalized and envenomed clash between O'Brien and the two men at the apex of the Irish administration, the lord lieutenant, Earl Spencer and the chief secretary, George Otto Trevelyan. T.P. O'Connor wrote that 'Lord Spencer stuck with his Coercion Act and Mr O'Brien with his pen, and thus Mr O'Brien advanced to be one of the most powerful and popular figures in the country … he wielded almost as much power as Parnell himself.'[3] O'Connor's contemporary, the baleful Richard Pigott, loftily noted that O'Brien's crusade 'is about the safest form in which Land League rancour can manifest itself, since the parties assailed could not deign to notice it.'[4]

In the latter half of 1882 and beyond, O'Brien chose to cast Spencer and Trevelyan as the villains of the piece. This is not to suggest that he ignored the supporting players in Dublin Castle, but he reserved his most caustic comments for the lord lieutenant and the chief secretary. O'Brien was not politically naive enough to believe that the political interests of Gladstone's government and of the ascendant cabal in the 'permanent' administration in Dublin Castle absolutely coincided. But he nonetheless chose to underscore their mutuality. This was primarily for the benefit of a largely undiscerning audience that sought *bêtes noires* and expected to see their enemies clearly identified and anathemized. Of course both Spencer and Trevelyan were caught in the classic Liberal dilemma. Both men were aware, in the words of J.L. Hammond, that 'a government drawn into a quarrel with the Irish people would be unable to enforce respect for the law because its methods for obtaining justice would spread mistrust, and those methods would absorb all its energies to the neglect of reform'.[5] Neither, however, could do very much about extracting themselves and their administration from a cycle of suspicion that had already undermined and de-legitimized Forster's mission.

O'Brien subsequently acknowledged the dichotomy between the Liberal peer, his radical colleague and the unionist elite that dominated the Dublin Castle administration and the Irish civil service. In his *Times* commission evidence he was questioned about the vilification of Spencer and Trevelyan and, although disclaiming personal responsibility[6] for writing some of the more vituperative passages, he acknowledged, with regret, that 'unhappily we did hold Earl Spencer and Mr Trevelyan responsible for the acts of their subordinates in Ireland. As to Earl Spencer and Mr Trevelyan we were wrong, absolutely wrong. I am sorry there was an imputation of the kind. As to his subordinates we were absolutely, and in every particular, right.'[7]

Whatever their philosophical misgivings, Spencer and Trevelyan, in the political actions they took, were as rigorous in restricting intimidatory press commentary as their predecessors had been. In his evidence to the *Times* commission O'Brien spoke of this period as 'a desperate struggle for liberty of speech in Ireland'.[8] Because of the prosecution of the editors of a number of local newspapers O'Brien claimed, as it clearly suited him to do before the commission, that 'there was, practically speaking, no other paper left for public opinion except *United Ireland*; the consequence of course was I had to write far more fiercely than under any [other] circumstances I would have done'.[9]

While O'Brien was, by his own lights, conducting a struggle for the maintenance of free speech, he was simultaneously engaged in a political three-card trick. As his biographer Joseph V. O'Brien has observed, with the abandonment of the organisation and values of the Land League by Parnell and its replacement with the more centrally controlled Irish National League, 'it was left to William O'Brien to preserve the façade of advanced nationalism in the pages of *United Ireland*.[10] To an extent this became manifest in the 'lonely duel between Mr O'Brien and Earl Spencer which lasted with scarce an interruption for three of the fiercest years in Irish history',[11] as T.P. O'Connor put it just after the contest ended.

The Prevention of Crime (Ireland) Bill, 1882

The proposals for renewed coercion legislation extant in April 1882 reflected the disillusioned belligerence and pessimism of Forster's last weeks in office.[12] Its provisions were draconian and their actual introduction could only have been contemplated against the backdrop of the savagery of the Invincibles. Under the terms of the Bill, in response to the perceived unreliability of Irish juries, a special commission court could 'from time to time' be established at the behest of the lord lieutenant to try cases of serious crime. However, in a departure later deprecated by the Irish judiciary, in certain cases the jury could be dispensed with entirely and guilt or innocence established by the unanimous vote of three presiding judges. In the event that the traditional route of trial by jury was adopted, at the behest of the attorney general the jurors could be taken from a number of special jury panels based in seven counties and seven towns or cities around the country.[13] Special jurors were chosen from a greatly restricted pool consisting of ratepayers with a valuation of more than £20. The unspoken assumption was that such 'metropolitan' jurors – with a disproportionate representation of Protestants – shared the interests of the Castle elite in suppressing rural criminality.

Additional clauses covered the crimes of intimidation, incitement to intimidation, riot, unlawful association, illegal assembly, and the finding of persons and/or strangers at night under suspicious circumstances in 'proclaimed' districts. The legislation also conferred enhanced powers of search and arrest on the police and levied any legitimated payments for compensation for injury against the district in which the offence occurred.[14] This became known colloquially as the 'Blood Tax'.

The *Nation* described the proposed legislation as 'one of the most despotic measures ever introduced'.[15] The newspaper pointed out that over the previous half-century Ireland had been under coercion rule for thirty-five years and described the measure as being levied 'not against criminals, but against a whole people'.[16] The *Freeman's Journal*, while highly critical of the Bill, was also conscious that the Phoenix Park assassinations continued to resonate. It concluded its editorial with the pious but futile aspiration that 'the best hope is that its main arbitrary provisions will not in practice be largely put in force'.[17] The *Times*, on the other hand, had few difficulties with the legislation. While acknowledging that it was 'a remarkable departure in criminal jurisprudence',[18] the newspaper endorsed the Forster/Harcourt Bill with enthusiasm.

Unlike the Protection of Person and Property (Ireland) Act there was specific provision in the legislation covering journals whose content was deemed to 'contain matter inciting to the commission of crime'. In many respects the newspaper section – clause 10 as introduced, clause 13 as finally enacted – reads like the legislative realization of an attempt by Forster to address the legal concerns of the Castle law officers at the course adopted by the Irish executive in the repression of *United Ireland* and other newspapers prior to the Kilmainham Treaty. The Crimes Bill removed any ambiguity whatever, for the three-year duration of its operation, surrounding the power of the lord lieutenant to order the seizure of newspapers.[19] As introduced by Harcourt the first section of the Press clause read,

> Where, after the passing of this act, any newspaper wherever printed, is circulated or attempted to be circulated in Ireland, and any copy of such newspaper appears to the Lord Lieutenant to contain matter inciting to the commission of crime, that newspaper shall, when found in Ireland, be forfeited to Her Majesty, and any constable duly authorized by the Lord Lieutenant may seize the same.[20]

After minor amendment the words, 'inciting to the commission of crime' would become, 'inciting to the commission of treason or of any act of violence or intimidation'.[21]

From the point of view of the nationalist press, however, the regime could have been much worse. On 17 April 1882, Forster had circulated a memorandum seeking the contributions of the law office in the formulation of the new coercion bill he would not get to deliver. In response, Porter, the solicitor general, recommended that 'the Press clauses of the Act of 1870 … should be reintroduced, with some modifications'.[22] In his reply John Naish, the law adviser, sought a simple re-enactment of the press clause (section

30) of the 1870 Act without amendment.[23] The newspaper provisions of the 1870 Act, discussed elsewhere, provided for the confiscation of plant as well as newspapers in the case of repeat offences. When it came to the drafting of the 1882 Crimes Bill the government decided not to revert to the conferring of such radical powers.

As originally formulated, however, there was an additional obligation placed on a newspaper once it had first been penalized with the forfeiture of an entire print run. It would subsequently be obliged to post a security bond 'not exceeding £200, not to print or publish any newspaper containing any matter inciting to the commission of treason or any act of violence or intimidation'.[24] In the event of a further infraction, that surety, in addition to any copies of the offending issue, would be subject to forfeiture. This stipulation, in effect a recognizance or guarantee of future good conduct, was a variation of the concept of 'caution money' often exacted by continental governments from their newspapers as an earnest of good behaviour.

Spencer had serious doubts about this element of the legislation from the outset. On 13 May he wrote to Gladstone that 'I do not feel certain about the necessity of caution money for a newspaper.'[25] Ultimately, before the legislation got to Committee stage, the government decided to abandon the provision entirely. Spencer wrote to Gladstone on 29 May 1882, indicating that the potential requirement for recognizances had been deemed too onerous. 'This is a very strong and arbitrary power. It w[oul]d simply shut up a struggling local paper, the proprietor of which often lives from hand to mouth and c[oul]d not find £200.'[26] To many of his colleagues on the Liberal benches, not to mention in the executive branch of the Irish government, that was a consummation devoutly to be wished.

As far as the seizure of offending newspapers was concerned, the bill, as originally conceived and as finally enacted, meant that the lord lieutenant was to be judge and jury as to the treasonable or intimidatory intent of national, international and provincial newspapers found circulating in Ireland. Conviction of an editor for incitement to intimidation was to be left to a court of summary jurisdiction. Cases of criminal libel were not affected.

Oddly, given the experience of the already lengthy government battle with *United Ireland*, the legislation didn't address a number of key issues. Although the doubts over the legality of seizures were eliminated, the ambiguity over the status of the opening of posted packages of newspapers remained. While the Post Office had been instructed, under warrant, to seize certain newspapers sent through the mails,[27] there remained a level of uncertainty over the precise legality of opening newspapers in order to establish their seditious content.[28] On a practical level no legal provision was made for any preview of editorial content to determine whether it contained matter deemed to constitute incitement. Although itself a basic tenet of freedom of expression, this prolonged the anomalous situation whereby a publisher could distribute copies of his newspaper, or, as in the case of *United Ireland*, the entire print run, before it could be deemed illegal and have any copies seized. In the House of Lords debate on the bill, the Marquess of Lansdowne suggested that the press clause was so feeble that 'the only power which it gave to the Executive was that of seizing a particular issue of a particular paper, after the issue containing the criminal matter had been put in circulation. To his mind, that was very like locking the door after the horse was stolen.'[29]

But the newspaper provisions were sufficiently onerous to attract considerable adverse comment, not merely among the nationalist press, but in liberal British journals as well. On studying Harcourt's original proposals the *Freeman's Journal* observed that 'the Press clauses are even more oppressive than he stated'. It argued that the definition of a 'crime', to which newspapers might be alleged to have incited, was so broad under the terms of the bill 'that we doubt if any single publication of any single newspaper might not be held thus to offend'. But despite these conclusions the *Journal* counselled the Irish Party members not to obstruct the bill. 'They must discuss it moderately, and seek to amend it reasonably.'[30] However, the newspaper also warned 'let England and the English people reflect for a moment with what feelings they would receive proposals for their country such as they now prepare for Ireland'.[31]

United Ireland, unsurprisingly, referred to the newspaper clauses as a continuation of the press regime of Forster. This was to be achieved by means of 'provisions copied from the procedure which crushed the Russian Press'. It claimed a sort of vindication with the appearance in the legislation of the seizure provision.

> This clause, it will be seen, is a confession, that Mr. Forster, in doing exactly what is here described, and worse with *United*

Ireland, acted without any legal authority at all: else why take the authority now after it has been exercised in a much more brutal form?[32]

The newspaper decided, with tangible irony, to take the recognizance provision as 'a personal compliment'.[33]

United Ireland was joined in opposition to the press clauses by the liberal London newspaper, the *Daily News*.

> We confess that we regard with much apprehension the probable or possible effect of interfering with the right of public meeting and the freedom of the press in Ireland. It is not that we look upon these privileges as ends in themselves, or that we think their maintenance more important than the primary duties of Government but it shows to us that the cabinet would do well carefully to consider whether the enterprises of desperate men plotting in private are in any way frustrated by curtailing the opportunities of advised or inadvised speaking or writing. Secret societies are not, as Mr. Cowen said, to be put down by the use of the gag.[34]

One of the arguments made in liberal British newspapers and in the House of Commons against a highly specific and punitive attack on press freedom in the Crimes Bill was that editors were also subject to clause 7 of the legislation. This made it an offence to use intimidation or to incite any other person to intimidate by 'any word spoken or act done in order to and calculated to put any person in fear of any injury or danger to himself'.[35]

The furore over the introduction of the Crimes Bill allowed *United Ireland* to bury a story that was a source of embarrassment to the Irish Parliamentary party in general and Parnell in particular. In a debate on the still-unacknowledged Kilmainham Treaty, Parnell had been caught red-handed by Forster attempting to read a redacted version of his letter to Captain O'Shea of 28 April, 1882. This was the only textual evidence of the negotiations that had been going on for some time between the Irish leader and Joseph Chamberlain, mediated by O'Shea. When Parnell had read to the House a version of the letter without the infamous *hors d'oeuvre* of promised co-operation between the Irish party and the Liberals, Forster had forced him to consume the dish cold and read a copy of the unexpurgated version given to him by O'Shea a few days before his resignation as chief secretary. *United Ireland* was able to relegate the Commons debate on the subject to page seven, the last news section in the journal and a page often reserved for inconsequential material. The parliamentary report was carried under the thoroughly misleading headline, 'Mr. Forster's malignity raises a question that recoils on him.'[36]

The following week, in a satirical column in which the main points of the Crimes Bill were addressed through the prism of humour the newspaper suggested an alternative Press clause to the government:

> That all editors of National newspapers shall be forthwith tarred
> and feathered, their presses broken, and their type smashed;
> and that all publications found on their premises shall be burnt
> by the common hangman.[37]

In the same issue the newspaper also announced the release from custody of the editors of the *Leinster Leader* and the *Roscommon Messenger*. Both had served longer periods of incarceration than O'Brien under the terms of the Protection of Person and Property (Ireland) Act.

As an earnest of its intention not to be intimidated by the Crimes Bill *United Ireland* announced, in its edition of 17 June, that the paper would increase in size by sixteen columns (going from forty to fifty-six) and that its new presses were capable of producing 1,000 copies per hour. O'Brien, also announced, simultaneously, a move into the domestic sphere. The *Shamrock*, the weekly literary magazine, acquired from Pigott in 1881, was to be expanded. O'Brien's announcement of this development was positively Messianic and assumed the appearance of a moral crusade. The *Shamrock* would drive a wedge into English literary colonization of the Irish imagination.

> Who has not been deploring, time out of mind,' O'Brien
> inquired, 'the moral havoc wrought among our youth by the
> filthy cheap literature of England? What father, mother or priest
> has not shuddered to think of the poison instilled into pure

young Irish hearts by tales that propose no nobler ambition than those of juvenile thieves, and inspire no higher emotions than the nastiness of unwholesome intrigue?[38]

Rebellion by the judges of the Supreme Court of Judicature in Ireland, leading to the resignation of Exchequer Court judge Baron Fitzgerald,[39] ensured that although provision for three-judge courts remained part of the final legislation, it was never put into practice. Thirteen members of the Supreme Court met and delivered their own judgment on this aspect of the legislation, contending that such a development, 'would seriously impair public confidence in the judicial office, and thereby permanently injure the administration of justice in Ireland'. As the *Freeman's Journal* enthused, 'they decline to become judge and jury at the mandate of the Viceroy of the hour and the Government of the day'.[40]

The Commons' Debate

The debate on the Crimes bill was characterized by the clash of the contending forces of filibuster and cloture. Despite Irish efforts to prolong and obstruct discussion it was the Speaker's guillotine that ensured its passage within a conscionable period of time and the safe Liberal majority (bolstered by the vestigial revulsion for the Phoenix Park murders) that guaranteed its integrity.

There were amendments, and even an embarrassing defeat in a late division. But it was, by and large, the government itself that dictated any changes to the legislation.

Introduced by Harcourt, the home secretary, it was endorsed by Trevelyan, on 18 May 1882 in a Commons speech. In reference to the suppression of newspapers Trevelyan suggested, without overtly stating, that the legislation was designed to put on a statutory basis powers which the law officers had advised were already available under the common law. Such advice, at least according to the chief secretary, had been the basis for newspaper seizures already made. He maintained that the Bill was 'effectively framed against crime, and not against liberty'. By way of justification for any action taken against the press in Ireland, the chief secretary, while citing *United Ireland* as a paper 'which cannot be said to always keep within bounds' professed himself more concerned with the penetration of the 'atrocious sentiments' of Irish-American newspapers than he was with the potential for incitement of the native species:

> It is not to what is written in Ireland, but to what is read in Ireland, that we must look, if we are to judge of the necessity of making the law, not more severe, but more certain. Let anyone read the *Irish World*, let anyone read the atrocious sentiments in the *United Irishman* of Mr. O'Donovan Rossa, and he will allow that not only must such papers not be allowed to circulate in excited times through an ardent population, but that some means should be found to frame a law by which such pestilent wickedness shall not be published on Irish soil.[41]

In response Thomas Sexton drew the attention of the House to the anomaly of seditious publications in England escaping the attentions of the authorities while Irish newspapers, 'which advocated the cause of Irish liberty and not assassination', were vulnerable to seizure. He quoted from an anti-monarchist pamphlet freely available in London newsagents advocating the slaughter of the Royal Family.[42] This included the blood-curdling threat, 'Only your extinction can cure our misery … by the just and righteous vengeance of an insulted, outraged people – slaying you, and striding over your rotten carcasses as a justifiable reparation to an outraged nation.'[43] In this context, it was anomalous, Sexton suggested, that the newspaper clause of the Crimes bill applied only to Ireland.

Charles Russell, later to become lord chief justice, highlighted the philosophical weakness in the government's advocacy of arbitrary newspaper seizure:

> He desired that persons publishing matter that was treasonable, seditious, or calculated to disturb the peace should be punished by Constitutional means, and that these exceptional measures should not be resorted to. There was no proof that in this regard the ordinary law had failed.[44]

Russell was, of course, being disingenuous. There was ample anecdotal evidence that Irish juries were now disinclined to punish anything brought before them resembling political criminality.[45] Russell, however, warned the government – whose legislation he generally supported – against any attempt to restrict the free expression of opinion in Ireland:

> Even though the expression of that opinion should be irregular, riotous, and bordering on sedition, he maintained it was much better that that should be allowed than that there should be a repression and keeping down of anything like honest opinion and outspoken criticism. To use a trite illustration, it was very much like sitting on the safety-valve of a steam engine to prevent an explosion.[46]

Russell's submission, that the government should habitually have recourse to the 'ordinary law', was addressed by the solicitor general, Andrew Marshal Porter:

> 'Deal with them by the ordinary law,' say some of our friends— that is to say, by trial by jury, which has failed in the manner I have described in connection with every other kind of agrarian offence. Now, I ask, under these circumstances, what would be the use of these prosecutions? Their effect would be simply to give a stimulus to the circulation of particular papers, and to give them greater publicity and notoriety ... we are not attempting to gag or stifle any free discussion; we are aiming simply and strictly at crime alone. Are we, then, to wait until it is decided whether the publications I have alluded to are criminal or not? Are we to wait until the whole thing is done, and then institute a prosecution which will lead, perhaps, to a verdict of triumphant acquittal?[47]

Porter's diatribe took no cogniscance of the fact that the legislation, as framed, still required the government to wait until it was decided whether publications were criminal or not. It simply removed the need for a jury to give its subsequent *imprimatur* to any such decision.

The revised Clause 10 of the Crimes Bill was debated in Committee on 19 June. The debate took place against the background of the government

prosecution of the expatriate German anarchist weekly *Freiheit* for advocating regicide.[48] An attempt was made Lewis Llewellyn Dillwyn, radical
MP for Swansea, to confine the power of the lord lieutenant to ordering
the seizure of foreign newspapers only. This was resisted by Harcourt who
pointed out that:

> One of the intentions of this clause was to make it quite clear
> that the lord lieutenant's power to seize newspapers was legal;
> and if the power were confined to foreign newspapers, the Irish
> Government would have no remedy against Irish newspapers,
> except they proceeded before a jury. The hypothesis on which
> they had all along proceeded was that that was no remedy at
> all. If this Amendment were adopted, Irish newspapers would
> have the power to reprint the objectionable part of a foreign
> newspaper, and thus do all the mischief which it was the object
> of the clause to prevent.[49]

When Dillwyn invoked the *Freiheit* prosecution in making his case Harcourt
responded,

> The prosecution of the *Freiheit* was brought before an English
> jury; but if the case of an Irish newspaper were brought before
> an Irish jury, there would be no chance of a verdict being
> obtained against the paper. It was upon that hypothesis the
> Government had proceeded in the previous clauses, and it
> was upon that hypothesis they were proceeding now. If the
> only remedy possessed against objectionable Irish newspapers
> was that of proceeding before an Irish jury there would be no
> remedy at all.[50]

As on previous occasions Irish speakers challenged the home secretary to
quote from an Irish newspaper, in the words of T.P. O'Connor, 'any matter
which would come fairly within the scope of this clause'.[51] O'Connor also
rejected the notion, 'that the Jury Law had broken down with regard to
newspaper prosecutions in Ireland' though he resorted to citing, yet again,
the prosecutions of Pigott and Sullivan for seditious libel in 1868 as an
example of the even-handedness of Irish juries. That verdict had come three
years before the changes in the law that finally based qualification for jury
duty on rateable valuation of property. Lord O'Hagan's Law, as it was styled,

had exponentially increased the number of nationalist jurors and constituted 'a genuine attempt to end the packing of juries'.[52] The convictions of either Sullivan or Pigott would have been far less likely (outside a commission court) under 1882 conditions.

In his speech Trevelyan referred to the rigours of the 1870 Peace Preservation (Ireland) Act which, despite its 'extremely stringent clauses' in relation to the press, 'had not actually been put into operation'. Trevelyan expressed the opinion of the government that such severe measures were actually unnecessary and, 'the Irish Executive had come to the conclusion that the power contained in this clause was sufficient for the purpose in view'.[53] It was, after all, 'a power that he had practically been exercising for the past year or 18 months'.[54]

Goaded by the Irish challenges to quote a single seditious item from an Irish newspaper Harcourt rose again and produced an extract from the *Clare Journal* of 13 April, 1882 in which a death threat had been issued against a supplier of cars to the RIC. The home secretary gave no context for the quotation, which promised that the intended victim would 'die the death of Bailey, the informer of Dublin'.[55] Harcourt's production of the, undoubtedly venomous, extract was considerably devalued when the Whiggish MP, Captain William O'Shea, member for the county, intervened to point out that the *Clare Journal* was a Conservative newspaper which had, he presumed, been quoting a posted threatening notice as an item of news.[56] When O'Shea suggested that such material could be dealt with under the intimidation clauses of the Bill (see above) Harcourt responded that it would be, 'a very insufficient remedy to send the person who published a newspaper to prison for six months, and allow the publication of the newspaper to continue'.[57] Dillwyn's amendment was finally defeated by 143–33 and the clause, as amended by the government itself, was allowed to stand.[58]

The Prevention of Crime (Ireland) Act, 1882, limited in duration to three years, replaced the Protection of Person and Property (Ireland) Act as the coercion legislation *du jour*. The *Freeman's Journal*, of 12 July described it, sarcastically, as 'this latest essay in the art of Liberal government',[59] while urging the population to respond with dignity and moderation. On the same day the *Times* led the charge in support of the legislation by observing that 'it comes to the rescue of a timid and easily terrorised people'.[60] The *Daily News*, however, was less enthusiastic:

Further means for staying the plague of outrage and murder are urgently needed; and there might have been no reluctance to give them had they not been mixed up with the concession of powers which can only be used for repression of opinion. It has always been pointed out that utterance of even disloyal sentiments may prove a safety-valve for the letting off of angry feelings which are only driven to secret propagandism when open expression is prohibited.[61]

In *United Ireland* O'Brien railed against clause 13, while promising that, 'their iniquitous Press law will not be allowed to remain a dead letter, if they suppose that the mere menace of it will affright Irish Pressmen from telling them unpleasant truths to their beards'.[62] O'Brien also highlighted the fact that, under the legislation, courts of summary jurisdiction could send journalists to jail for six months. 'Any newspaper editor in Ireland may be degraded for the next three years, if he hurts the sensibilities of any pair of hired magistrates in any corner of the country.' O'Brien, giving full vent to his nationalism and his pietism – as had Tim Healy on a number of occasions during the Commons debate – highlighted, by way of contrast to the potential fate of Irish newspapers, the untrammelled publication of the atheistic weekly, *Freethinker*,[63] 'not the only nor the worst pestilential growth of the Press allowed to fatten under the aegis of the Government which is engaged framing laws to put a summary end to every Irish newspaper that shall be found a month hence advocating too loyally the sacred cause of charity and freedom'.

From the Phoenix Park to 'Accusing Spirits' – May–December 1882

After the passage of the Crimes Act and the effective collapse of the 'no rent' campaign, *United Ireland*, chastened by the Phoenix Park murders, rendered more cautious by the press clause, and/or called to heel by Parnell himself, caused no particular problems for Dublin Castle. It was sufficiently aggressive in tone to continue its vital function of guarding Parnell's left flank while not pushing its rhetoric beyond the point of no return and provoking the sort of seizures provided for under the terms of the new legislation. Coincidentally the Post Office was issued with an official instruction to cease all seizures of the paper on the same day as Cavendish and Burke were murdered.[64]

Hostilities between *United Ireland* and the Castle virtually ceased during the summer of 1882. The truce is reflected in the weekly instructions from the law officers to the DMP as to how to deal with the latest copy of the newspaper. Through June and July, notwithstanding the criticism levelled by the newspaper at the Crimes Bill, no action was advised.[65] The administration might well have felt it prudent to avoid a resumption of any appearance of newspaper suppression while the bill, complete with punitive press clause, was being debated. But in fact the instruction of 22 July was accompanied by an observation from the solicitor general that 'so far as I can judge (without reading every line of the paper) it is much altered in character; and cannot be said to transgress beyond the limits of lawful discussion of public matters.'[66]

However, an indication that *United Ireland*, despite the suspected softening of its aggressive tone, was still a concern to the security apparatus of the Castle, came in September 1882. Samuel Lee Anderson had requested a copy of the registration of *United Ireland* as a newspaper.[67] In a memo to his superior, Edward Jenkinson, Anderson explained that 'many of the most seditious newspapers fail to comply with the provisions of the "Newspaper Libel and Registration Act" and are liable to heavy penalties.'[68] He hoped to use this piece of legislation to harass *United Ireland*. The act in question – its full title was *An Act to amend the Law of Newspaper Libel, and to provide for the Registration of Newspaper Proprietors* – had been passed in 1881. The Act extended privilege – immunity from libel proceedings – to the 'fair and accurate' reporting of lawfully convened public meetings, allowed magistrates, with the agreement of the accused, to deal with insignificant libels summarily by means of a fine not exceeding fifty pounds, and established a register of the proprietors of newspapers. The penalty for failure to register was a fine not exceeding twenty-five pounds.[69]

To pursue the newspaper under the terms of the 1881 Act would have been of nuisance value alone, but Jenkinson expressed an interest in Anderson's idea and questioned his subordinate as to 'what procedure should be followed in such cases. Who should prosecute in the event of a prosecution being decided on?'[70] However, Anderson had failed to notice section 18 of the act. This exempted joint stock companies from the registration process.[71]

The solicitor general pointed this out and advised that, as a consequence, the act did not apply to *United Ireland*.[72] Determined not to be undone on a technicality Anderson applied to the Registrar of Companies to confirm that the newspaper was, in fact, owned by a joint stock company.[73] His dogged exploration of this opportunity to discommode *United Ireland*, commencing in September 1882, at a time when the journal's editorial content was largely unexceptionable, suggests an undiminished animus that played a major part in the subsequent decision to prosecute O'Brien for criminal libel.

This came about when *United Ireland* doffed its sackcloth and ashes and returned to the offensive. The context for the journal's rediscovery of its vituperative soul was the first significant trial under the aegis of the Crimes act, conducted in the commission court in Dublin. The first capital trial was that of a young Clare man, Francis Hynes. He was accused of having murdered a neighbour, John Doloughty, on Sunday, 9 July 1882. Doloughty, who worked for a farmer with whom the Hynes family was in dispute, was shot as he was returning to his home near Knockaneane after Mass in Ennis. He survived for just over twenty-four hours. While still lying at the scene of the crime, in answer to a question from a local resident magistrate, Captain Hugh McTiernan, he had identified Francis Hynes as his killer. Some doubts were cast on the 'dying declaration' of the victim, his widow gave evidence that no animosity had existed between the two men, and there was also considerable concern at what were seen as prosecution efforts to 'pack' the commission court jury with Protestant jurors. Of the forty-nine empanelled jurors the Hynes defence team had challenged eleven, the prosecution had asked that a further twenty-six stand aside, leading to the allegation, made by Thomas Sexton MP in the House of Commons that, 'there was [no] other reason except that those gentlemen were Catholics and Liberals in politics for their being cast aside'.[74] Hynes was found guilty in a two-day trial (11–12 August) and sentenced to be hanged in Limerick Jail by the commission court judge Justice James Lawson.

However, the death sentence was given an entirely different complexion by the personal intervention of O'Brien himself. The *United Ireland* editor's living quarters were in a modest room in the Imperial Hotel. It was in that establishment that the jury was sequestered on the night of 11 August. In the course of the night O'Brien's sleep was interrupted by an incursion into his room by an extremely inebriated member of the jury. It subsequently emerged that a number of the jurors had spent the evening mingling with members of the public in the billiard room of the Imperial Hotel and were the worse for drink. O'Brien drew the attention of the readers of the *Freeman's Journal* to this fact in a letter to the newspaper published on 14 August. He concluded by observing that 'I leave the public to judge the loathsomeness of such a scene upon the night when these men held the issues of life and death for a young man in the flower of youth'.[75]

The response of Mr Justice Lawson was swift and rancorous. Edmund Dwyer Gray, proprietor of the *Freeman*, was peremptorily summoned to a sitting of Lawson's court at which he was charged with contempt. In seeking a custodial sentence against Gray, Porter told the commission court 'if one paper was permitted to act in this way so should other papers, and where would it end? Such a thing was intolerable, and the article referred to, if it stood alone, would warrant the censure of the Court'.[76] Lawson sentenced an astonished Gray, MP, former lord mayor and serving High Sheriff of Dublin, to three months in jail.[77] Hearing of the debacle in New York Michael Davitt wrote in his diary, 'glorious blunder by Castle. No place like prison to inculcate hatred of British rule. Gray and *Freeman* will improve. Bravo idiot Lawson'.[78]

Despite the risk that the incarceration of its proprietor would see the editorial line of the *Freeman's Journal* becoming more extreme, the government did not seem too concerned at the outcome of the contempt case. On 17 August Gladstone informed the House of Commons emphatically that 'we do not see clearly that it is in our power to act for the liberation of Mr. Gray'.[79] After Gray was released, having served half his three-month sentence, Spencer wrote to the Prime Minister of his satisfaction with how the case had been handled. 'With the exception of unfortunate errors of speech on the whole Judge Lawson has done his work with ability and in a way deserves the thanks of good men'.[80] The *Daily Express* held that the jail term had 'undoubtedly produced a salutary effect, which it may be hoped will be permanent'.[81]

On 15 September Samuel Lee Anderson drew the attention of the new under secretary, R.G. Hamilton, to an article in the 16 September issue of *United Ireland* entitled 'A Deed Without Name'. This was an editorial diatribe against the hanging of Francis Hynes on 11 September that highlighted, once again, the activities of the allegedly packed jury and condemned the behaviour of Justice Lawson in the 'grotesque mockery of a trial'. The leader concluded that 'Earl Spencer is responsible for his death.'[82] Hamilton alerted Trevelyan and Spencer, describing the article as 'very bad', while adding that 'it does not contain any direct incitement to crime and I do not recommend a prosecution'. The chief secretary and the lord lieutenant concurred.[83]

Challenging alleged miscarriages of justice now became, for *United Ireland*, the crusade that nullification of the Land Courts and dissemination of the 'No Rent Manifesto' had once been. If O'Brien, as perceived by the Castle itself, had ever been pulling his punches, he abandoned that policy in the autumn and winter of 1882.

On 7 October 1882 *United Ireland* finally controverted any notion in official circles that it had modified its outlook. Two editorials in that issue once again attacked Lawson and the practice, whose existence was resolutely denied by the law officers in Dublin Castle, of jury packing. The occasion for the attack on Lawson, described by the paper as 'a ranting partisan in a judicial burlesque',[84] was his decision, at the end of the commission term, to release Gray from Richmond prison after serving half his sentence. Lawson gave as his reason for the display of clemency the fact that 'a considerable change for the better has taken place in the tone of the paper.'[85] This *United Ireland* described as 'a parting shaft of malice' from the judge.

The second phillipic, entitled 'The Bloody Assizes', was a condemnation of the inaugural manifestation of the commission court brought into being by the Crimes act. The court's first term had seen three men, Francis Hynes, Michael Walsh[86] and Patrick Walsh[87] sentenced to death. In its denunciation of the verdict in the case of Michael Walsh *United Ireland* bypassed Lawson and took issue with a jury, 'shamefully concocted, its partisanship was as indecent, and the evidence was evidence upon which an English jury would not hang a dog'.[88] O'Brien equated the approach of the administration to the sentiments once expressed in the unionist newspaper the *Daily Express*. Its editor G.V. Patton had editorialized, 'we must, to convict murderers, secure by hook or crook, by law or challenge, metropolitan, Protestant and loyal juries'.[89]

For its part the *Express* responded by contending that the 'Bloody Assizes' article was 'one of the worst that have yet appeared in that notorious print'.[90] Superintendent Mallon, in his weekly despatch of the newspaper to the law officers, drew the attention of his superiors to the two editorials. Edward

Jenkinson, assistant under secretary for police and crime, sought the attorney general's opinion. Johnson's response was unequivocal. 'In my opinion the two articles referred to are scandalous libels on the administration of justice and as such the publisher is indictable for the publication.'[91] The significance of the missive is immediately apparent. In the past the administration had baulked at a prosecution of *United Ireland* for seditious libel because of the necessity to prosecute in a Queen's Bench court before an ordinary jury. Johnson was of the opinion that, in this instance, the authorities could have recourse to the commission court, a special jury and an enhanced possibility of securing a conviction.

It was only the intervention of Spencer that prevented a prosecution. The lord lieutenant suggested that the article was 'bad, but then not incitement to crime or actually intimidation'. In response Hamilton advised Trevelyan, Johnson and Jenkinson that:

> It is evidently not H[is] E[xcellency's] desire to prosecute in this case. It might be well, however, to watch narrowly the articles in this paper for the next few weeks and have all the steps necessary to be taken for seizing it.[92]

'Accusing Spirits'

The executions of Hynes, and the two Walshes were quickly followed by the infamous Maamtrasna trial[93] which led to the hanging of Myles Joyce, Patrick Joyce and Patrick Casey. There is little doubt that the former was innocent.[94] In December Michael Flynn, Patrick Higgins and Thomas Higgins were executed for the murders of Joseph and John Huddy on the Mayo/Galway border. The victims were bailiffs in the employ of Lord Ardilaun whose bodies had been deposited in Lough Mask.

The frequency of capital sentences emanating from the commission court gave rise to a nationalist 'revenger' narrative. This held that the Castle, baulked of success in identifying the Phoenix Park murderers, had allied itself with the unionist population of Dublin and was avenging itself on innocent men 'framed' for a variety of agrarian murders. In fact the frequency of hangings was a direct reflection of the incidence of homicides in rural Ireland in the latter years of the land war. The impression of a plethora of executions was augmented by the concentration of the murder trials in Dublin. Although there were justifiable doubts about the guilt of some of those hanged during the operative period of the Crimes act, only in the case of Myles Joyce was there a clear case of innocence accompanied by blatant abuse of procedure.[95] There was in fact an equally tenable unionist counter-narrative, based on the re-emergence of the Invincibles, in which the very justice system itself was under threat from extreme nationalists. In November 1882 members of the Invincibles made unsuccessful attempts on the lives of Justice Lawson and Denis Field, a juror in the trial of Michael Walsh who had attracted press attention when he was seen to pass a note from the jury box to Norris Goddard, leading light of the landlord organization the Property Defence Association.

It was in this poisonous atmosphere that O'Brien wrote an editorial in the 23 December edition of the paper entitled 'Accusing Spirits'. It was a powerful Zola-esque phillipic in which he accused the authorities of judicial murder. The piece began with quotes from Francis Hynes, Patrick Walsh, Michael Walsh, Patrick Higgins, Myles Joyce, Thomas Higgins and Michael Flynn in which all pleaded their innocence of the offences for which they had just been sentenced to death or for which they were about to be hanged. [96] In the latter instance O'Brien invoked the Catholicism of the victims, insisting that, 'if the protestation on their lips were a lie they knew they were stepping into an eternity of torment'. He observed tartly that it was,

> Better, in any case, that a garrulous peasant should be kicked into eternity by Mr. Marwood[97] than that the detective police should acknowledge itself baffled, and cream-faced loyalists go about in terror of their lives. Our attachment to the elementary principles of justice impels us to deliberately say that, both as to the tribunal and as to the evidence, the proceedings against these men bear an indelible taint of foul play.[98]

O'Brien went on to allege that 'packed juries and bribed witnesses were the all-sufficient implements of justice … when the art of trying a man consists in picking out of the panel twelve of his deadly enemies, and then production of evidence means chiefly the getting at the worst side of the veriest villain in the community and humbly consulting his prepossessions as to the reward and the little precautions necessary to make the bed of the informer a bed of velvet, verdicts of guilty and hangings may be had in any desired quantity'. Describing the commission court sessions in Green Street as a 'White Terror' O'Brien went to the core of the rationale behind the juridical provisions of the Crimes act. He highlighted,

> [The] ghastly pretence that it is all done to save the sacred right of trial by jury in Ireland; that it is necessary to pack juries that we may have juries at all; that it is better to convict upon paid swearing than to adopt drumhead ideas of evidence. Out upon the imposture! If the trials of the last few months are trials by jury, such as Englishmen bled to maintain, we solemnly declare that the sooner we have the tribunal of the three judges, or the rough and ready justice of the court-martials, the better for public decency and for the accused themselves.[99]

O'Brien's diatribe against alleged jury-packing by the Crown in recent capital cases, as well as the widespread use of informers to secure convictions, would have been more convincing had it not been for his prior coverage of the Maamtrasna case. In the 18 November issue of *United Ireland* the editor had pointed out that a majority of the jurors in those trials were Roman Catholic. The following week he had written that 'we believe that the public are satisfied that a disgusting butchery has been avenged upon convincing evidence by juries comparatively fairly chosen'.[100] O'Brien's relative detachment in the Maamtrasna case may be attributable to the fact that the murders had been particularly savage and, apparently, non-political in nature.

The reaction of the Castle to the 'Accusing Spirits' editorial was swift. On the official publication day of the newspaper an order was issued for the seizure of all copies of *United Ireland* under section 13 of the Crimes act on the basis that it contained 'matter inciting to the commission of acts of violence and intimidation'.[101] O'Brien was summoned to appear before the Metropolitan Police court. The summons accused him of publishing,

> A false, seditious and malicious libel, contained in an article entitled 'Accusing Spirits' for the purpose and with the intent of bringing the Government of the country and the

administration of the law into hatred and contempt and in order to excite hostility against the same, and for the further purpose of disturbing the peace of the country and raising discontent and disaffection among the Queen's subjects. [102]

Unfortunately there is no surviving documentation to indicate exactly why the Castle found this article, in particular, offensive enough to provoke it into such an extreme course of action. In choosing to indict O'Brien the authorities ran the risk of repeating the mistake made in the prosecution of Parnell and the Land League leaders in 1880. Gladstone's secretary, Edward Hamilton, had pointed out at the time – and the logic applied equally to O'Brien in 1882 – that 'a state trial of that kind leads to a disagreeable dilemma. If it succeeds, those prosecuted become martyrs. If it fails they become heroes.'[103] Prosecutions of this sort were generally undertaken to embolden the supporters of the administration or to appear to be taking positive and punitive action.

Allegations of jury packing were almost routine in nationalist newspapers. Indeed, as T.P. O'Connor pointed out at the time, O'Brien's comments 'were such as are to be found in every English journal with regard to every case in which there is the slightest doubt of the … sufficiency of the evidence, or of the conduct of the jury or the judge. In the despotic *regime* which it suited the Government to establish in Ireland at this period, it was held that no such criticism was permissible.'[104] There was, however, an added element of latent paranoia. The murder attempts on Lawson and Field made the authorities particularly sensitive to the possibility of incitement to murder. The controversial 'Castle rats' reference made by *United Ireland* a week before the Phoenix Park murders (see above), had given rise to provocation allegations. These were to be reinforced in 1883 by the (spurious)[105] evidence of the informer James Carey that, in the words of Samuel Lee Anderson, 'it was the public attention thus drawn to Mr. Burke that led him to be selected for assassination.'[106] The decision to invoke the powers of seizure under section 13 of the Crimes Act and to prosecute O'Brien separately for seditious libel might simply have been an attempt to discourage newspapers from directing public attention to the activities of certain members of the judiciary or the Crown prosecution service. However, if that was indeed the case *United Ireland* inquired in its issue of 30 December 1882, why the administration took no action against the unionist *Daily Express,* when it reprinted the 'Accusing Spirits' editorial in full and followed it up with 'an article on its own account on the pending prosecution of Mr. O'Brien of a character which, to say the least of it, the jurymen who subscribe to the *Express* will not deem milk-and-waterish'.[107] O'Brien was, of course, being deliberately disingenuous, there was little likelihood of *Express* readers being provoked into a breach of the peace on reading the *United Ireland* editorial.

An alluring inducement to prosecute O'Brien, despite the inherent risk, was undoubtedly the looming Mallow by-election. In the summer of 1882 it became known that the attorney general, William Moore Johnson, was to be raised to the bench. This meant vacating his seat in the borough of Mallow. O'Brien, a native of the area, became the (reluctant) nationalist candidate. Opposing him as Liberal candidate was law adviser John Naish. Parnellites found it extremely difficult to win borough seats. These anomalous constituencies had small electorates (in some instances fewer than 300 voters) drawn from the wealthier members of the community and generally unmoved by the issues that had given rise to the creation of the Land League. The odds were stacked against O'Brien. Even Parnell expected his man to be defeated, while contending to O'Brien that 'you will get the least bad beating of anyone I know'.[108] In fact O'Brien's candidacy quickly began to prove highly popular with local voters and this prompted the administration to postpone the elevation of Johnson to the bench in order to defer the by-election. Johnson's appointment was finally confirmed on the day O'Brien appeared at the Police Magistrate's court in Dublin. The *United Ireland* editor accused the attorney general of taking 'measures to remove the Nationalist candidate safely out of fighting distance'.[109]

If the Castle hoped to distract O'Brien's focus with a lengthy legal battle, or inspire the Liberal voters of Mallow to reject his candidacy, they were to be disappointed. As O'Brien put it himself in his autobiography *Evening Memories,* 'the prosecution in Green Street doubled the majority in Mallow which broke for ever the power of Dublin Castle to corrupt the Irish boroughs'.[110] Conspiracy theorists can question the timing of the prosecution of O'Brien but there was nothing irregular in the speed with which the case proceeded. Much of the delay, which meant O'Brien's court appearances coincided with the most active part of the Mallow campaign, were prompted by an appeal to the Queen's Bench division made on behalf of the defence. A rapid conclusion of the prosecution would have been more to the liking of the Castle as it was confident of securing a conviction, with the potential inconvenience for O'Brien's candidacy that might have flowed from incarceration.

'The greater the truth, the greater the libel'

O'Brien stood accused of a crime which had proved useful to many previous governments in the suppression of dissent. As defined by legal scholars the offence involved the use of words designed 'to bring into hatred or contempt or to excite disaffection against the person of her Majesty, her heirs or successors, or the government and constitution of the United Kingdom as by law established, or either House of Parliament, or the administration of justice'.[111] O'Brien was specifically charged with 'inciting to the commission of acts of violence and intimidation'.[112]

Like that other useful legal standby, a charge of conspiracy, it was notoriously difficult to offer a defence against seditious libel. This made it a convenient net with which to go fishing for a conviction. In civil cases the defendant in a libel action could argue that the words complained of were true. If this was established satisfactorily defamation could not be proven against a publisher or editor. However, in the case of criminal libel, 'the defendant must be prepared to go further and prove not only that the words complained of are true, but also that their publication is for the public benefit'.[113] So truth was not a defence against an indictment for seditious libel. Furthermore, it was the counter-intuitive axiom in such a proceeding that 'the greater the truth the greater the libel'. Inherent in this apparent paradox was the idea that seditious libel constituted a breach of the peace. Therefore the more accurate the comments the more incendiary they were, and the more likely they were to cause such a breach. The American legal historian, Leonard W. Levy, has described seditious libel, in an American context, as 'an accordion-like concept, expandable or contractable at the whim of judges'.[114] A.V. Dicey, in his *Introduction to the Study of the Law and the Constitution* wrote that 'any one will see at once that the legal definition of a seditious libel might easily be so used as to check a great deal of what is ordinarily considered allowable discussion, and would, if rigidly enforced, be inconsistent with prevailing forms of political agitation'. Dicey went on to note:

The times when persons in power wish to check the excesses of public writers are times at which a large body of opinion or sentiment is hostile to the executive. But under these circumstances it must, from the nature of things, be at least an even chance that the jury called upon to find a publisher guilty of printing seditious libels may sympathise with the language which the officers of the Crown deem worthy of punishment, and hence may hold censures which are prosecuted as libels to be fair and laudable criticism of official errors.[115]

So it would prove to be in the case of O'Brien.

The *United Ireland* editor was outwardly defiant in the face of prosecution. He claimed to welcome 'as a perfect Godsend, the opportunity which Dublin Castle proposes to offer, to test once for all the fairness and honesty of the process yclept "trial by jury" in a Green-street courthouse.'[116] He revealed the thrust of his defence in the same editorial, pointing out that he had not accused juries of sending innocent men to the gallows. His criticism was of the manner of their empanellment, 'What we did charge and do charge is that where a certain limited class of men alone is selected, belonging to a particular religion, to the almost entire exclusion of jurors professing the religion of the vast body of the people of Ireland, such trial is not a trial by "peers".'[117]

O'Brien was not unconscious of the irony that as part of the state's retribution for his allegations of 'packing', he himself might face a partisan jury. 'We now demand,' he wrote, 'that the jurors, who are put in the box to try the issue between the Crown and ourselves, shall "stand indifferent" to both. But if the attorney general exercise his right of unlimited challenge, his picking and packing, then, indeed, better for decency sake, and for brevity, that Mr. William O'Brien should be triced up in a twinkling by the summary methods of Crimes Act R.M.'s.'[118]

O'Brien's first appearance in the case was in a court of summary jurisdiction, the Dublin Metropolitan Police court. He was defended by the former MP, and *Nation* editor and proprietor, Alexander Martin Sullivan, now a highly successful Queen's counsel. Sullivan himself had been jailed in 1868 for seditious libel arising out of an editorial on the execution of Allen, Larkin and O'Brien in Manchester. His principal antagonists in the *United*

Ireland trial were James Murphy QC, who had played a significant role in the Maamtrasna case and, in a further irony, Peter O'Brien, notorious in nationalist circles as 'Peter the Packer' for his alleged expertise in dictating the composition of juries. Murphy's task was to establish that 'Accusing Spirits', in his own words, 'may be reasonably termed as of a seditious character, that a jury may come to that conclusion, and that it is a case to submit to a jury to say whether or not they will arrive at that conclusion'.[119]

Murphy anticipated an attempt by Sullivan to justify the libel on the basis of the truth of the matter contained in the article. This defence was posited on the 1881 Newspaper Libel and Registration Act as well as 6 & 7 Victoria, chap. 96, known colloquially as Lord Campbell's Act (1843). The latter measure had introduced the concept of truth as a justification of a criminal defamatory libel, provided it was 'for the public benefit that the said matters charged should be published'.[120] Murphy pointed out to the Magistrate, C.J. O'Donel [*sic*] that a magistrate's court was not the place to make such a defence. Murphy contended that 'the magistrate had no jurisdiction to receive evidence of the truth of the libel, inasmuch as his function is merely to determine whether there is such a case against the accused as ought to be sent for trial'.[121] The prosecution, according to its lead counsel, only had to establish that O'Brien was responsible for publication and that the article could reasonably bear the interpretation imputed to it by the Crown. Murphy then went on to produce evidence that O'Brien was editor of *United Ireland* at the time of publication and submitted that there was only one interpretation of the contents of the article.

Sullivan, on O'Brien's behalf, accepted that a ruling in an 1870 case (*Queen v Duffy*)[122] meant that 'a seditious libel was outside the purview of Lord Campbell's Act' which clearly referred only to defamatory libel[123] and excluded sedition, obscenity or blasphemy. However, Sullivan went on to argue that the Newspaper Libel and Registration Act of 1881, which amended the law 'affecting civil actions and criminal prosecutions for newspaper libel'[124] superceded the *Queen v Duffy* judgment and offered such protection to a publisher or editor as, in its provisions, it made no reference limiting its application to defamatory libel only. Sullivan maintained that the 1881 Act was remedial legislation and had extended the remit of Lord Campbell's Act in that 'the restrictive words were omitted and the amending remedial provisions were extended to all criminal libels'. He went on to remind the magistrate of the 'well-established doctrine that a penal statute was to be interpreted as strictly, a remedial statute as liberally, as language would allow'.[125] Sullivan also accused the Crown of seeking to insert words to narrow the application of the 1881 Act. He reminded the magistrate that section 4 of that act provided, specifically, for a court of summary jurisdiction to 'receive evidence as to the publication being for the public benefit, and as to the matters charged in the libel being true'.[126]

Sullivan may have been angling for relief under section 5 of the 1881 legislation. This allowed a magistrate, assuming the defendant was prepared to forgo a jury trial, to decide that the libel was of a 'trivial character' and impose a fine of no more than fifty pounds. A magistrate's fine could be represented by O'Brien as a virtual dismissal of the Crown case and might be less hazardous than an appearance before a higher court with a predominantly unionist jury. He may also have been seeking to delay the entire process by ensuring it became bogged down in the lower court and thus failed to make it into the approaching session of the commission court. In a *United Ireland* editorial O'Brien, while complaining disingenuously that 'the Crown shirks the proof of the truth of the charges made in this journal', also noted that the newspaper was prepared to present 'three hundred witnesses' in O'Donel's court. [127] All were prepared to justify O'Brien's jury packing allegations.

In his judgment, O'Donel himself invoked section 5 of the 1881 act in ruling against Sullivan. He asked 'was it to be supposed for a moment that the section in the act of 1881, enabling a magistrate to dismiss a charge of libel, could by any interpretation include seditious libel, which the courts, both in England and Ireland, had held to be excluded from the operation of Campbell's Act ... He could not hold that that was meant to include a solemn charge of seditious or blasphemous libel.'[128] When Sullivan announced that he would apply to the Queen's Bench court for a ruling on the matter the case was adjourned until 22 January.

The coverage of the affair in the *Freeman's Journal* on 2 January 1883 was significant in that the newspaper, avowedly at least, made the editorial decision to forego its right of privilege to publish a full account of a legally constituted public meeting. In an editorial on the magistrate's court proceedings, in the edition of 2 January, the *Journal* acknowledged that it had not carried a report of a speech O'Brien had made to the voters of

Mallow at a lawfully convened election meeting on 31 December. O'Brien's address had included a lengthy *apologia* for the 'Accusing Spirits' editorial. Any doubt as to the existence of such privilege had been banished by Section two of the 1881 Newspaper Libel and Registration Act. This provided that, 'any report published in any newspaper of the proceedings of a public meeting shall be privileged if such meeting was lawfully convened for a lawful purpose'.[129] The decision not to report O'Brien's words was made because the *Journal*, 'being merely independent journalists, were afraid to publish yesterday [1 January]', and were only doing so today because the text of the speech had been published in the *Daily Express*, 'which may be considered in some sort the organ of Dublin Castle at present … now that it has our contemporary's imprimatur, we presume that its reproduction has the sanction of the powers that be'.[130]

According to the *Express* report of his Mallow speech O'Brien had claimed that,

> It won't be quite so easy as the Crown lawyers may think to say who is the prosecutor and who is the accused (great cheering) … from beginning to end of that article there was no pretence to pass judgment on the guilt or innocence of any particular person, and not one word of assumption that these men's dying declaration was true. What I charged there, and what I charge here, is that these men did not get a fair trial according to the laws of England, such as would justify the public conscience in disregarding their protestations of innocence (cheers); that in plain English juries were systematically packed from a class alien to the prisoners in politics and creed; that they who were the presiding judges betrayed a violence of partiality that I will not characterise further, and that the evidence was procured by a dangerous and demoralised system of offering enormous bribes to persons who were themselves supposed to be steeped in abominable crimes.[131]

Having now repeated the alleged libel on a public platform (for which, unlike Timothy Harrington, then being prosecuted for a similar offence, he was never subsequently tried) he went on to describe the jurors in the seven cases covered by the editorial as 'men whose prejudices ran bitterly against the prisoners, at a time when panic and vengefulness gave those prejudices an irresistible influence'. He charged that 'in the heart of a Catholic city and county, a ring of Protestant landlord dependents in Dublin have got practical mastery over the lives of their Catholic fellow countrymen (cheers)'.

The *Journal,* apparently liberated by the decision of its unionist daily counterpart to publish O'Brien's speech, carried an extensive extract in its editorial comment on the magistrate's court trial. It concluded, 'Mr. O'Brien himself acknowledges that if he cannot substantiate the charges made, he deserves punishment for making them. The Crown officials say that he must not be permitted the opportunity of substantiating or endeavouring to substantiate them. This, according to their contention, is the law. We presume they would also say that it is justice. We say nothing on the former question, which will be decided by the Queen's Bench. As to the latter, the public will form its own opinion.'[132]

Either the *Journal* was genuinely fearful of being dragged into a seditious libel case of its own or, post the incarceration of Gray for contempt in August 1882, it was making an ironic point to the Castle at the expense of the unionist *Daily Express*. O'Brien himself had already demonstrated the irony of the publication of the offending 'Accusing Spirits' article in full in the *Express*[133] without any legal consequences, despite the fact that it was knowingly reprinting an alleged libel. The *Journal* also carried the full text of 'Accusing Spirits' but only as court reportage in its edition of 2 January. The text had been read out in court by Murphy and clearly the *Journal* had more confidence in the robust nature of the traditional privilege afforded to the accurate reporting of court proceedings than the more recently fashioned statutory privilege for the coverage of legal public assemblies offered by the 1881 Act.

United Ireland's editorial comment on the outcome of the initial Magistrate's court trial was an admixture of misinterpretation and misinformation. O'Brien suggested that it was 'settled law' that,

> Truth cannot be pleaded as answer to a charge of seditious
> libel. The Crown has simply to allege that certain words or
> writings are false, and the only issues then left the jury to try
> are – Did the defendant print the article, and is it calculated to

stir up and excite and so forth? We trust it may not be held to be seditious libel if we are bold enough to assert that this is a pretty state of things.[134]

In making this assertion O'Brien ignored a significant piece of legislation passed in 1792 at the behest of the great Whig politician Charles James Fox and, as a consequence, known as Fox's Libel Act. This was 'An Act to remove doubts respecting the Functions of Juries in cases of Libel'[135] which restored the right of a jury to decide whether or not a libel had occurred. Increasingly, in the latter half of the eighteenth century, this right had been assumed by the judiciary. Whatever about the composition of a commission court jury it was not required to take direction from a judge as to whether or not a seditious libel had occurred.

United Ireland pointed out that Sullivan's invocation of the 1881 Newspaper Libel and Registration Act had been the first occasion on which the act had been deployed in such a manner. In spite of O'Donel's clear familiarity with the details of the new legislation the newspaper suggested he had ruled against it out of ignorance of the law. 'Yet with a fluency and grasp which do high credit to his attainments, he rolled off a decision on the point adverse to the defendant, and in the teeth of Mr. Sullivan's reading of the Statute. The government are to be congratulated on having such magistrates.'[136] The newspaper expressed little optimism that it would get a fair hearing of its *mandamus* application before the Queen's Bench court.

Casting further forward, to the inevitable commission court proceedings that would follow the expected Queen's Bench setback, O'Brien was just as pessimistic:

> Out of a panel of two hundred, specially called in Crimes Act fashion, it would indeed be surprising if they cannot find twelve subscribers to the *Daily Express*, their own kept organ, which discounted his conviction and discussed his 'punishment' in advance. They have their unlimited right of challenge, and nothing could be more simple. But, in truth, the exercise is needless; for the Crimes Act fixes the jurors qualification at a sufficiently lofty altitude to shut out almost every one save

landlords and Castle shopkeepers. Fair trial it is, then, hopeless to expect.[137]

The Queen's Bench court, presided over by lord chief justice of Ireland, George Augustus May, and, doubtless to the chagrin of O'Brien, Mr Justice James Lawson, heard the *ex parte* application, on Monday, 15 January 1883. O'Brien's counsel, J.F. Taylor, reiterated Sullivan's contention in regard to the supercession of the 1881 Act over the decision arrived at in the Duffy case in 1870. After a hearing enlivened by a series of intemperate interventions from Justice Lawson, the lord chief justice rejected the contention that the 1881 Newspaper Libel and Registration Act included seditious libel within its ambit in the manner suggested by Taylor. Therefore Lord Campbell's Act, and the superior court interpretation provided by the Duffy case, still applied. Hence a magistrate's court could not be required to hear evidence in justification of a libel that would not later be admissible in the trial court. The magistrate's function was merely to refer the matter to a grand jury that would decide whether or not to issue an indictment or 'true bill'.[138] May ruled that 'the magistrate was right in refusing to admit the evidence at the preliminary inquiry, and that the application must be refused'.[139]

It was a measured judgment and in its denial of O'Brien's right to present evidence of the truth of his allegations, and the accruing 'public benefit' before the commission court, it didn't augur well for his forthcoming trial. But May's was not the last word. That went to the dyspeptic Justice Lawson who derided O'Brien's case, maintaining that 'a more unfounded application never was brought before a court of justice'.[140]

In response *United Ireland* was suitably scathing where Lawson was concerned, before referring to a more salient aspect of the judgment, the fact that the newspaper would not, as anticipated, be permitted to justify 'Accusing Spirits' before the commission court jury. O'Brien editorialized:

> So that what is now established in Ireland is this:- a Government and its officials may commit any atrocity they fancy in a country, but no individual in the country may raise a protest. No matter what the Crown and government do, they are to be held sacred from the scrutiny of the people. It is only necessary to be a Crown official to have licence to commit any scandal,

with impunity from comment ... If we offer to prove the truth of what we say, we aggravate our offence; for the greater the truth the greater the libel. The one grand offence, in short against the Government in Ireland today is the Truth.[141]

In the same edition of the paper *United Ireland* carried a report of the executions of Patrick and Thomas Higgins for the Lough Mask murders. The last of the 'Accusing Spirits' had met their fates at the end of a hangman's rope.

So concluded O'Brien's attempt to test the efficacy of the 1881 Newspaper Libel and Registration Act insofar as it related to seditious libel. On Monday 22 January he returned to the Police Court for the formality of the referral of his case to the grand jury and thence, assuming the finding of a 'true bill', to the commission court. But not before another bravura performance on the part of A.M. Sullivan. O'Brien's counsel played to the gallery both within and outside the courtroom. He pointed out that a case of seditious libel had not come before an English court for half a century and that, quoting the cases of Bismarck and Pitt, politicians who felt they had been libelled had recourse to civil actions on their own behalf rather than resort to the use of the criminal law. After a stirring conclusion, in which O'Brien was represented as 'avowing all he has written, ready to justify it, but forbidden, and with a clear conscience and unstained honour' – a closing which attracted a round of applause from the gallery – the magistrate did not bother to seek a response from prosecuting counsel. He returned the case for trial and bailed O'Brien for the sum of £100.[142] When the defendant was leaving the court he was informed by the Crown solicitor for Dublin city that, under the terms of the Crimes act, he would be facing a special jury at the commission court.

O'Donel had dispatched O'Brien to the commission court to face Justice Harrison and a special jury on 9 February 1883. In the interim two notable events occurred: O'Brien became MP for Mallow, defeating John Naish by 161 to 89 votes, and the preliminaries began in the trials of the Invincibles.[143]

The commission of oyer and terminer for the city and county of Dublin – to bestow upon it its full title – opened on 5 February 1883. O'Brien's case was first to be heard by the city grand jury, whose twenty-three members would decide whether to find a 'true bill' or 'no bill' – i.e. to send O'Brien for trial or dismiss the case. In his attempt to explain the meaning of sedition to the Dublin jury, Justice Harrison, perhaps unconscious of the status within nationalism of the defendant in the precedent to which he referred, quoted from the charge of Mr Justice Fitzgerald in the case of *R v Pigott*, 1868.

> Sedition is a crime against society, nearly allied to treason, which it too frequently precedes, only by a short interval. It is a comprehensive term and embraces all those practices, whether by deed, by word, or by writing, which are calculated and intended to disturb the tranquility of the State and lead the Queen's subjects to resist or subvert the established Government of the Empire. [144]

Harrison continued his charge to the grand jury by quoting further comments made by Fitzgerald in relation to the rights of journalists. Fitzgerald had pointed out that 'a journalist representing a free Press may canvass and censure the acts of the government and of the State. It is open to him to discuss every act of public policy'. This right extended to discussion and criticism of the administration of the law. 'I say the public Press may – nay it is invited – to canvass the proceedings of courts of justice, for like every human tribunal, courts of justice are fallible and liable to error.'[145]

Moving away from the Fitzgerald judgment, Harrison, highlighted the limits of the freedoms enjoyed by the newspaper journalist and editor in exercising his right of expression:

> He may point out that there has been error in the administration of justice, or misconduct on the part of a particular judge, yet he ought not to use language that carries into the public mind contempt for the administration of justice or for the laws of the land …When a public writer exceeds the due limit that I have marked out, and uses his power and his privileges to create discontent or disaffection, or bring the laws into contempt, he becomes guilty of what the law calls sedition.[146]

Harrison then went on to read extracts from the 'Accusing Spirits' article to the grand jurors and advised them they were being asked to decide if the article did indeed constitute seditious libel, and whether it had been published with the intention of bringing the law of the land into contempt. The indecisiveness of the grand jury must have offered some encouragement to O'Brien. It took two days of discussion to agree to a 'true bill', and only thirteen of the jurors voted to send the *United Ireland* editor to trial.

Two days later O'Brien was back in Green street courthouse indicted as 'a wicked, seditious and ill-disposed person … devising and intending to stir up, and excite discontent and sedition among Her Majesty's subjects'.[147] The prosecution team included, once again, James Murphy and Peter O'Brien, but on this occasion was led by the newly appointed attorney general, A.M. Porter. Sullivan, once again defending, seized the moral high ground by announcing, before the jury was sworn, that his client did not intend to challenge any of the jurors. The Crown requested ten jurors to 'stand aside'. This was a right reserved to the Crown and did not, technically, equate to a challenge. Theoretically, if a jury was not empanelled from among the remaining special jurors those who had been asked to stand by might find themselves included. But in reality being asked to 'stand aside' amounted to a challenge. After the case had concluded *United Ireland* maintained that only two of the members of the jury were Roman Catholic.[148]

Before reading 'Accusing Spirits' to the jury Porter reminded them to put aside any prior knowledge they might have had of O'Brien or his newspaper and focus entirely on the editorial at issue. He pointed out that the crime of seditious libel was unusual in other jurisdictions:

> But in estimating the effect and the intent of any seditious publication, you cannot omit the consideration of the circumstances of the time and of the place where the publication occurs. It may be a comparatively harmless thing for a man to fling lighted matches about him in the middle of the Fifteen acres, but if he does the same thing in a powder magazine, the consequences are very different, and the act is on his part extremely different.[149]

As regards any idealistic notions the jurors might have had of freedom of the press Porter pointed out that 'the Press has no special liberty – no special indulgence. Its liberty is quite within the limits of the law; and if it transcends those limits, it has no more right to complain of being interfered with than a pickpocket would of interference with his personal liberty if he were interfered with in the course of exercising his pursuits.'[150] The only evidence presented by the Crown (three witnesses) was designed to establish that O'Brien was the editor of *United Ireland*.

In his address to the jury – the only defence O'Brien was permitted by law to offer – Sullivan reminded the jurors of their unique position in a case of seditious libel. Not only were they required to be judges of fact, but of law as well. This was due to the 'clarification' offered by Fox's Libel Act of 1792. It was, therefore, left up to a jury to apply the law in such a way as not to 'limit or punish honest indignation against flagrant wrong-doing'. Warming to his theme Sullivan pared down his argument to its essentials:

> What we impeach in our article is the mal-administration of the law – not the administration of the law – by certain subordinate officials under the cover and cloak of calling themselves the Crown. No doubt it is true that the public journalists must not go beyond certain points. The point and the limits which juries and constitutional judges have frequently drawn is this – namely to give a large latitude not merely to strength of expression, but I believe I am correct in saying that some of the most eminent jurists, go far beyond that, and hold that no jury ought to, and no jury ever will, weigh nicely a burst of honest indignation and anger against wrong if it be expressed *bona fide* for the purpose of calling attention to the wrong and not for the purpose of exciting contempt towards the government.[151]

Sullivan referred to O'Brien's particular concerns about the Hynes case and about the composition of juries. Porter had attempted to convey the impression that jury packing was a relic of bygone age. He had also suggested that O'Brien's comments concerning commission juries placed individual members of those, and future, juries in personal jeopardy. Porter's speech was made against the background of the recent Invincible attack on Field. Sullivan took his opposite number to task.

Never did I admire the forensic ability of the Attorney General more than I did today when he wanted to make you think that it was the jurors in the box that were accused in this case. What is accused is not the jurors, but the men who manage the jury panel, who prick and mark the list that will come into court, and when some men, some honoured and upright citizens of this metropolis, are insulted by a Crown subordinate telling them to stand by.[152]

To loud applause Sullivan concluded his virtuoso performance with the observation that in 'Accusing Spirits' O'Brien 'wrote this down for an honest public good, intending to cure the hateful system, and not for the miserable purpose charged in this indictment ... he will take from your hands in unquestioning confidence the verdict you award him, and he will leave your act, and he will his own, to the judgment of the generations of Irishmen that will follow upon you and to the accountability we all will have to render to the judgment seat of God'.[153]

The following morning, 10 February, the trial resumed. Porter made his address to the jury, which was then given direction by Justice Harrison. The twelve men, eight from the city itself and four from the Dublin suburbs of Blackrock, Bray, Foxrock and Killiney, retired to consider their verdict at 12.15pm. Fifty minutes later they returned and the foreman informed the judge dolefully that 'there is not the least chance of our agreeing'.[154] When Harrison pointed out that they did not appear to have given the matter much consideration, the foreman responded that they had gone into the case thoroughly. Harrison had no option but to dismiss the jury and inform O'Brien that he would be given ten days notice of any future trial. No such trial ever occurred and the seditious libel charges were never again laid against O'Brien.

The government had been unable to obtain a verdict against their journalistic nemesis, even in a commission court operating under the aegis of the Crimes Act. This can be interpreted as either a vindication of the *United Ireland* editor, or an endorsement of the fairness of the commission court regime and an example of the futility of jury packing. Many years later O'Brien noted, with some relish, that the verdict in the 'Accusing

Spirits' trial shattered 'the last defence of the jury-packers for the selection of Protestants and the exclusion of Catholics, for one of the two Catholics admitted among the twelve held out fanatically for a conviction while one of the ten "loyal Protestants" (the late Alderman Gregg) was so horrified by the proven justification of the worst charges in *United Ireland* that it was he who really baulked the Crown Prosecutors of their prey, and he left the jury box (as the Lord Lieutenant left Ireland two years afterwards) a steadfast Home Ruler for the remainder of his life'.[155]

One of the first to wish O'Brien well on his delivery was Parnell himself. His telegram read 'I congratulate you most heartily on your virtual acquittal, which is of the utmost importance to the cause of freedom of speech and writing in Ireland'.[156] The chief secretary's office papers are virtually silent on the entire matter, merely noting that O'Brien had stood trial and that 'the jury, being unable to agree, were discharged next day without verdict'.[157] O'Brien was, understandably, considerably less subdued in *United Ireland*. The result was treated as an acquittal. He began an editorial entitled 'A Virtual Verdict' with the allegation that the jury 'was as well and truly packed as the jury that convicted O'Connell or the jury that convicted Mitchel. Only two Catholics were suffered to be sworn.' In spite of this alleged manipulation he insisted that 'the Crown at this moment stands in the damaging position of having appealed to the people of Mallow and been beaten, of having appealed to the Dublin Grand Jury and had their bill all but cast back in their teeth, and of having appealed to a special jury of their own choosing, which special jury declined to say the Crown had given any answer to the terrible indictment contained in that article'.[158]

In conclusion he returned to the substance of the claims he had made in 'Accusing Spirits':

> Have the 'Accusing Spirits' been laid? Does anybody, outside the official ring, if even inside it, believe that the men tried for their lives in Green-street in a fit of frenzy last autumn were tried by juries 'indifferently chosen', by judges as calm-minded as Mr. Justice Harrison, or upon evidence that was not smirched with suspicion. If the Crown had responded to direct charges by honest investigation they might have removed a horrible stigma from these trials; as they have chosen to reply only

with repression, and abortive repression, the only conclusion ordinary people can come to is that things have been done in Green-street which will not bear the light in the nineteenth century.[159]

Having signally failed to enforce silence on *United Ireland* by special legislation or special juries, having had to cover its tracks with a new coercion act to formalize, *pro tem*, the legality of newspaper seizures, the administration appeared to have almost given up the ghost. Copies of the paper were still supplied to the law officers by Mallon on a weekly basis. Articles were adjudged by them to be seditious libels 'of a very bad character',[160] 'a direct incitement to the commission of acts of violence', [161] or 'vile and scurrilous',[162] but no further action was taken. The standard line was that it was not 'advisable to prosecute'.[163]

Arguably, as will be maintained in the next chapter, the authorities did not need to adopt such a direct approach to their *United Ireland* 'problem' in 1883–4. Instead the Castle was, inadvertently, offered an alternative and more circuitous option via the vitriolic pen of T.M. Healy. The resulting campaign would give rise to far greater concerns on the part of O'Brien than even those engendered by the 'Accusing Spirits' trials.

Notes

1   Davitt, *Fall of Feudalism in Ireland*, 380–1.

2   23 May 1889, *Special Commission*, vol.8, 183, 71838.

3   T.P. O'Connor, *Memoirs of an Old Parliamentarian*, (New York, 1929), 2 vols, vol. 1, 142.

4   Richard Pigott, *Personal Recollections of an Irish Nationalist Journalist* (Dublin & London, 1882), 445.

5   J.L. Hammond, *Gladstone and the Irish Nation* (London, 1938), 325.

6   As indicated elsewhere O'Brien later blamed Healy for most of the more vitriolic criticism. However, when certain passages were read to him, accusing Spencer, for example, of 'subsidising red-handed murderers' (23 May 1889, Special Commission, vol. 8, 192, 71940) he accepted that he had written them himself.

7   23 May 1889 *Special Commission*, vol. 8, 190, 71924.

8   21 May 1889 *Special Commission*, vol. 8, 112, 70864.

9   21 May 1889 *Special Commission*, vol. 8, 112, 70867.

10 O'Brien, *William O'Brien and the Course of Irish Politics*, 23.

11   T.P. O'Connor, *The Parnell Movement* (London, 1886), 509.

12   Forster was in favour of the restoration of the more punitive elements of the 1870 Peace preservation act (Virginia Crossman, *Politics, Law and Order in Nineteenth Century Ireland* (Dublin, 1996), 143).

13   The counties were Antrim, Cork, Dublin, Galway, Kilkenny, Limerick and Waterford; the towns and cities (or more correctly the 'County of the City of …') were Carrickfergus, Cork, Dublin, Galway, Kilkenny, Limerick and Waterford (*Public General Statutes passed in the Forty-fifth and Forty-sixth Years of the Reign of Her Majesty Queen Victoria,* (London, 1882), 73).

14   *Freeman's Journal*, 16 May 1882. The legislation as finally enacted is contained in *Public General Statutes passed in the Forty-fifth and Forty-sixth Years of the Reign of Her Majesty Queen Victoria*, 54–75.

15   *Nation*, 20 May 1882.

16   *Nation*, 27 May 1882.

17   *Freeman's Journal*, 16 May 1882.

18   *Times*, 18 May 1882.

19   *Public General Statutes passed in the Forty-fifth and Forty-sixth Years of the Reign of Her Majesty Queen Victoria*, 60.

20   *Freeman's Journal*, 16 May 1882

21   *Public General Statutes passed in the Forty-fifth and Forty-sixth Years of the Reign of Her Majesty Queen Victoria*, 60.

22   Porter to Forster, 22 April 1882, TNA, PRO, CAB 37/7, 1882, no. 9, 6.

23   Naish to Forster, 26 April 1882, TNA, PRO, CAB 37/7, 1882, no. 9, 11. Naish also recommended 'that the question of granting an indemnity for the seizure of *United Ireland*, the *Irish World*, and O'Donovan Rossa's *United Irishman*, should be considered'.

24   *Freeman's Journal*, 16 May 1882.

25   Spencer to Gladstone, 13 May 1882, Althorp papers, Add.Mss 76854 f.14.

26   Spencer to Gladstone, 29 May 1882, Althorp papers, Add.Mss 76854 f.29.

27   The warrants were renewed every four months. 15 February 1884, NAI, CSORP, 1884/2989. 14 June 1884, NAI, CSORP, 1884/14543. 24 November 1884, NAI, CSORP, 1884–25808.

28   Law officers in Ireland and Britain had disagreed in the 1860s over whether the Post Office Acts allowed for the opening of a suspect newspaper as opposed to a letter. Irish law officers contended that the Common Law (based on precedent) could be invoked where statute law did not cover all eventualities. When Harcourt, in 1882, received similarly contradictory advice he advocated seizure, suggesting that the newspapers concerned would not take legal action (TNA, PRO, HO 144/102, A20387. Legg, *Newspapers and Nationalism*, 112).

29   HL Deb. 10 July 1882, vol. 271, c1898.

30   *Freeman's Journal*, 16 May 1882.

31   *Freeman's Journal*, 19 May 1882.

32   *United Ireland*, 20 May 1882.

33   *United Ireland*, 20 May 1882.

34   *Daily News*, 24 May 1882.

35   *Public General Statutes passed in the Forty-fifth and Forty-sixth Years of the Reign of Her Majesty Queen Victoria*, 58.

36   *United Ireland*, 20 May 1882.

37   *United Ireland*, 27 May 1882.

38   *United Ireland*, 17 June 1882.

39   William E.Vaughan, *Murder Trials in Ireland, 1836–1914* (Dublin, 2009), 262–3. R.B. McDowell, *The Irish Administration* (London, 1964), 109. Fitzgerald, who had been appointed a law lord in June, 1882, resigned his seat on the Exchequer bench in July after the Crimes Act legislation was published and the government refused to delete the clauses relating to three-judge courts. (*United Ireland*, 3 June 1882. 29 July 1882.)

40   *Freeman's Journal*, 19 May 1882.

41   HC Deb. 18 May 1882, vol. 269, cc1014–15.

42   HC Deb. 18 May 1882, vol. 269, cc1046.

43   HC Deb. 18 May 1882, vol. 269, cc1046.

44   HC Deb. 23 May 1882, vol. 269, c1472.

45   Crossman, *Politics, law and order in Nineteenth Century Ireland*, 129.

46   HC Deb. 23 May 1882, vol. 269, c1472.

47   HC Deb. 23 May 1882, vol. 269. c1502.

48   The *Freiheit* editor Johann Most was found guilty and sentenced to sixteen months hard labour.

49   HC Deb. 19 June 1882, vol. 270, cc1689–90.

50   HC Deb. 19 June 1882, vol. 270, c1690.

51   HC Deb. 19 June 1882, vol. 270, c1690.

52   McEldowney, John F. 'The case of the Queen v McKenna (1869) and jury packing in Ireland'. Cited in William E.Vaughan, *Murder Trials in Ireland*, 127.

53   HC Deb. 19 June 1882, vol. 270, c1694.

54   HC Deb. 19 June 1882, vol. 270, c1702.

55   HC Deb. 19 June 1882, vol. 270, c1695.

56   HC Deb. 19 June 1882, vol. 270, c1696. Parnell later referred to the newspaper as 'a

landlord journal' and pointed out that its printing of the notice was by way of illustration of what a 'heinous institution' the Land League was (c1704). A number of Irish members had also claimed that the most enthusiastic and consistent citation of the excesses of the *United Irishman* was in the Unionist Dublin *Daily Express* rather than *United Ireland*.

57 HC Deb. 19 June 1882, vol. 270, c1697.

58 Tim Healy suggested that the £200 security bond proposal had merely been 'ballast', included in the legislation in order that it could be deleted as a concession to radical sensibilities (c1705). Dillwyn had already acknowledged that his principal objection to the press clause had already been removed with the withdrawal of the security bond proposal (c1705).

59 *Freeman's Journal*, 12 July 1882.

60 *Times*, 12 July 1882.

61 *Daily News*, 5 July 1882.

62 *United Ireland*, 24 June 1882.

63 The editor of which, George W. Foote, was convicted of blasphemous libel and jailed for a year in 1883.

64 Samuel Lee Anderson to Gustavus Cornwall, 6 May 1882, NAI, CSORP, Police and Crime Division Reports, III, Compensation Cases, Crimes Act, 1882–3, Carton 6, 1882, unnumbered.

65 3,10,17, 24 June.15, 22 July 1882, NAI, CSORP, 1882/3337.

66 A.M.Porter memo, 21 July 1882, NAI, CSORP, 1882/3337.

67 Anderson to Wyatt – 15 September 1882 – NAI-CSORP – Police and Crime Division Reports, III, Compensation Cases, Crimes Act, 1882–3 – Carton 6, 1882 – unnumbered.

68 Anderson to Jenkinson, 1 January 1883, NAI, CSORP, Police and Crime Division Reports, III, Compensation Cases, Crimes Act, 1882–3, Carton 6, 1883 – unnumbered.

69 *Public General Statutes passed in the Forty-fourth and Forty-fifth Years of the Reign of Her Majesty Queen Victoria* (London, 1881), 365–9.

70 Jenkinson to Anderson, 2 January 1883, NAI, CSORP, Police and Crime Division Reports, III, Compensation Cases, Crimes Act, 1882–3, Carton 6, 1883 – unnumbered.

71 *Public General Statutes passed in the Forty-fourth and Forty-fifth Years of the Reign of Her Majesty Queen Victoria*, 369.

72 Memo of A.M.Porter – 2 January 1883, NAI, CSORP, Police and Crime Division Reports, III, Compensation Cases, Crimes Act, 1882–3, Carton 6, 1883 – unnumbered.

73 Anderson to Registrar of Companies, 5 January 1883, NAI, CSORP, Police and Crime Division Reports, III, Compensation Cases, Crimes Act, 1882–3, Carton 6, 1883 –

unnumbered.

74 HC Deb. 17 August 1882, vol. 273, cc1990–1.

75 *Freeman's Journal*, 14 August 1882.

76 HC Deb. 17 August 1882, vol. 273, cc1988. Quoted from the court proceedings by Thomas Sexton, MP.

77 Dungan, *The Captain and the King*, 150–1.

78 Davitt diary entry, 16 August 1882, Davitt papers, TCD, MS9535.

79 HC Deb. 17 August 1882, vol. 273, c1981.

80 Spencer to Gladstone, 2 October 1882, BL, Add.Mss 76856 f.131.

81 *Daily Express*, 2 October 1882.

82 *United Ireland*, 16 September 1882. Spencer had declined a number of appeals for clemency for Hynes.

83 Anderson to Hamilton, Hamilton to Trevelyan, 15 September 1882, NAI, CSORP, Police and Crime Division Reports, III, Compensation Cases, Crimes Act, 1882–3, Carton 6, 1882/38380.

84 *United Ireland*, 7 October 1882.

85 *United Ireland*, 7 October 1882.

86 An 18 year old convicted of the murder of Constable Kavanagh of Letterfrack.

87 Convicted of the murder of Martin Lydon.

88 *United Ireland*, 7 October 1882.

89 *United Ireland*, 7 October 1882.

90 *Daily Express*, 6 October 1882 (although the issue of *United Ireland* was dated 7 October it would have been on sale from 5 October).

91 Attorney general Johnson to Edward Jenkinson, 10 October 1882, NAI, CSORP, Police and Crime Division Reports, III, Compensation Cases, Crimes Act, 1882–3, Carton 6, 1882/41142.

92 Spencer minute, Hamilton note, 11 October, NAI, CSORP, Police and Crime Division Reports, III, Compensation Cases, Crimes Act, 1882–3, Carton 6, 1882/41142.

93 Arising out of the murders of five members of the family of John Joyce in Maamtrasna, on the border between Galway and Mayo, on 17 August 1882.

94 Dungan, *Conspiracy*, 127–70.

95 On the part of Crown Prosecutor George Bolton (Dungan, *Conspiracy*, 159–66).

96 Had he postponed the publication of the article by a couple of weeks he could have added the capital sentences on Sylvester Poff and James Barrett in Kerry.

97 Official hangman, 1872–83.

98 *United Ireland*, 23 December 1882.

99   *United Ireland*, 23 December 1882.

100 *United Ireland*, 25 November 1882.

101 Order for the Forfeiture of Newspapers Under Section 13, 23 December, 1882, NAI, CSORP, Police and Crime Division Reports, III, Compensation Cases, Crimes Act, 1882–3, Carton 6, 1882/47393.

102 *United Ireland*, 30 December 1882.

103 Dudley W.R. Bahlman, *The Diary of Sir Edward Walter Hamilton* (Oxford, 1972), 65.

104 T.P. O'Connor, *The Parnell Movement* (London, 1886), 509.

105 The earliest the reference could have been read in *United Ireland* was Thursday 4 May 1882. At that point, as Carey was well aware, the Invincibles had already chosen Burke as their target and reconnoitred Phoenix Park to advance their plan of assassination.

106 Samuel Lee Anderson to Attorney General, 7 February 1884, NAI, CSORP, Police and Crime Division Reports, III, Compensation Cases, Crimes Act, 1882–3, Carton 6, 1884/3443.

107 *United Ireland*, 30 December 1882.

108 O'Brien, *Recollections*, 482.

109 *United Ireland*, 30 December 1882.

110 O'Brien, *Evening Memories*, 16.

111 Hugh Fraser, *Principles and Practice of the Law of Libel and Slander with Suggestions on the Conduct of a Civil Action* (London, 1897), 195.

112 Order for the Forfeiture of Newspapers under Section 13 of the Prevention of Crime (Ireland) Act, 1882, 23 December 1882, NAI, CSORP, Police and Crime Division Reports, III, Compensation Cases, Crimes Act, 1882–3, Carton 6, 1882/47393.

113 Fraser, *Principles and Practice of the Law of Libel and Slander*, 185–6.

114 Leonard W. Levy, *Emergence of a Free Press.* (Oxford, 1985), 8.

115 A.V. Dicey, *Introduction to the Study of the Law of the Constitution* (London, 1902), 243.

116 *United Ireland*, 30 December 1882.

117 *United Ireland*, 30 December 1882.

118 *United Ireland*, 30 December 1882.

119 *United Ireland*, 6 January 1883.

120 *A Collection of the Public General Statutes passed in the Sixth and Seventh year of the Reign of Her Majesty Queen Victoria* (Dublin, 1843), 714.

121 *Freeman's Journal,* 2 January 1883. This was based on precedent cases, notably *Labouchere v Lawson*, 1879.

122 The Duffy in question was Charles Gavan Duffy.

123 Defamatory libel against an individual, in certain circumstances, could involve criminal

rather than civil proceedings. For example, in section four of Lord Campbell's Act, it stated that 'if any person shall maliciously publish any defamatory libel, every such person, being convicted thereof, shall be liable to Fine or imprisonment or both' (*Public General Statutes*, 1843, 714).

124 *Public General Statutes passed in the Forty-fourth and Forty-fifth Years of the Reign of Her Majesty Queen Victoria*, 365.

125 *Freeman's Journal*, 2 January 1883.

126 *Public General Statutes passed in the Forty-fourth and Forty-fifth Years of the Reign of Her Majesty Queen Victoria*, 367.

127 *United Ireland*, 6 January 1883.

128 *Freeman's Journal*, 2 January 1883.

129 *Public General Statutes passed in the Forty-fourth and Forty-fifth Years of the Reign of Her Majesty Queen Victoria*, 366.

130 *Freeman's Journal*, 2 January 1883.

131 *Daily Express*, 1 January 1883.

132 *Freeman's Journal*, 2 January 1883.

133 *United Ireland*, 30 December 1882.

134 *United Ireland*, 6 January 1883.

135 Fraser, *Principles and Practice of the Laws of Libel and Slander*, 241.

136 *United Ireland*, 6 January 1883.

137 *United Ireland*, 6 January 1883.

138 *Daily Express*, 16 January 1883. The case would become a textbook example, like *R v Duffy* before it, of how 'a defendant is not allowed to set up as a defence upon the trial of an indictment or information for the publication of a blasphemous, seditious or obscene libel that such words are true, and that it is for the public benefit that they should be published'. Fraser, *Principles and Practice of the Laws of Libel and Slander*, 197.

139 William Green & Richard Manders, *Law Reports (Ireland) Digest of cases, vols I–XX inclusive* (Dublin, 1890), 685 (*Ex parte* O'Brien 1883, 12 L.R.Ir.29).

140 *Daily Express*, 16 January 1883.

141 *United Ireland*, 20 January 1883.

142 *United Ireland*, 27 January 1883.

143 Although the Crown was, at that point, far from establishing a cogent and *prima facie* case against all the men subsequently convicted of involvement in the Phoenix Park murders.

144 *Freeman's Journal*, 6 February 1883.

145 *United Ireland*, 10 February 1883.

146 *United Ireland*, 10 February 1883.

147 *Freeman's Journal*, 10 February 1883.

148 *United Ireland*, 17 February 1883.

149 *Freeman's Journal*, 10 February 1883.

150 *Freeman's Journal*, 10 February 1883.

151 *Freeman's Journal*, 10 February 1883.

152 *Freeman's Journal*, 10 February 1883.

153 *Freeman's Journal*, 10 February 1883.

154 *Daily Express*, 12 February 1883.

155 O'Brien, *Evening Memories*, 16–17.

156 *United Ireland*, 17 February 1883.

157 Murphy (solicitor) to under secretary, 10 February 1883, NAI, CSORP, Police and Crime Division Reports, III, Compensation Cases, Crimes Act, 1882, Carton 6, 1883/133.

158 *United Ireland*, 17 February 1883.

159 *United Ireland*, 17 February 1883.

160 Memo of John Naish, 7 June 1883, NAI, CSORP, 1883/28833.

161 Samuel Lee Anderson to attorney general, 9 August 1883, NAI, CSORP, 1883/ 28833.

162 Memo, 6 December 1883, NAI, CSORP, 1883/28833.

163 Edward Jenkinson memo, 10 June 1883, NAI, CSORP, 1883/28833.

CHAPTER FIVE

'The Continuation of War by Other Means' – United Ireland and the Dublin Castle 'Scandals', 1883–5

'The figures that one after the other thrust at us in the dark were cloaked as private litigants; but their daggers bore the official Castle mark.'[1]

(*United Ireland*, 9 August 1884)

United Ireland and 'The Kept Court'

The failure to secure the conviction of O'Brien in February 1883 meant the administration had been baulked, yet again, in its object of silencing or modifying the commentary of the Parnellite newspaper. Mandated weekly perusal of the journal was institutionalized in May 1883 when Edward Jenkinson, Assistant Under Secretary for Police and Crime, instructed his deputy, Samuel Lee Anderson, to send an early copy to the Attorney General for analysis on a weekly basis.[2] However, although action against *United Ireland* was occasionally contemplated, none was taken.[3] Typical of

165

the regular assessments of the newspaper's editorial copy was a series of minutes relating to the issue of 9 June 1883, and to an article entitled 'The Kept Court'. The latter was one of O'Brien's weekly phillipics against the Dublin Castle administration.

The various marginal comments in the relevant file reveal a level of official reluctance to take O'Brien through the courts again, for his journalism at least. Dublin Castle clearly wished to avoid affording O'Brien another opportunity to generate even more favourable publicity, and then report it as news. Anderson, in submitting this particular issue of *United Ireland* had drawn the attention of the solicitor general to the article. John Naish, recently defeated by O'Brien in the Mallow by-election, noted in the file that the article did not render the newspaper liable to prosecution under the Crimes Act but added that 'it is however a seditious libel of a very bad character'. In doing so he left open the possibility of another indictment on that charge. He recommended that the article be submitted to the Attorney General, A.M. Porter. Porter, in a minute for the lord lieutenant in the same file, wrote that 'I have no doubt that this article is a seditious libel: but it is not worse than things that are said without authoritative reproof in the House of Commons: and I doubt the prudence of a prosecution.'[4]

The administration had clearly become more circumspect in the prosecution of seditious libel since the collapse of the 'Accusing Spirits' case. Did that newly discovered circumspection result, in 1884, in a proxy campaign against the newspaper driven by circumstance and happenstance? Was it the case, in the absence of a viable alternative and in the wake of previous tactical failures, that surrogacy became an alternative course of action?

In August 1883, an intemperate article by T.M. Healy set in motion a chain of events that could have jeopardized the financial viability of the Parnellite newspaper. The government found itself in a position to take advantage of the situation and pursue a 'virtual' or vicarious action against O'Brien and *United Ireland*. Its, often reluctant, agents were Crown prosecutor, George Bolton, RIC director of detectives, James Ellis French, and Gustavus C. Cornwall, secretary of the General Post Office (GPO). According to O'Brien, and other nationalist commentators like Healy and Harrington, a confluence of interests, deriving from a clear imperative to protect the reputation of the administration, drove forward a *de facto* strategy of vicarious suppression.

All three surrogates were of considerable significance in the Irish government but it was Bolton who carried most weight. A native of Tipperary, and Crown prosecutor for that county, Bolton was, in reality, a much more substantial figure than his job description might suggest. Under the aegis of the Crimes Act he had conducted prosecutions in places far removed from his own bailiwick. He played a part in bringing the Invincibles to justice, though the real credit for that achievement was shared by his colleague John Adye Curran and Superintendent John Mallon of the Dublin Metropolitan Police 'G' Division. He would become notorious in 1884 when his conduct of the 1882 Maamtrasna case was highlighted by Kerry journalist and MP Timothy Harrington. Harrington accused him of suborning two 'approvers' (Timothy Casey and Anthony Philbin) to commit perjury leading to the execution of Myles Joyce.[5]

One of the earliest references to Bolton in *United Ireland* came in the issue of 10 February 1883. He was described as 'a very special pet in the inner circle of the Castle, and a chief proficient in securing the evidence of informers'.[6] O'Brien noted his involvement in the Maamtrasna and Huddy murder cases[7] (see above) and gloated over Bolton's discomfiture as a consequence of an adverse finding made against him in a recent lawsuit. Bolton's wife had died the previous March and he had failed to overturn her will, in which he was not a beneficiary. Sophia Bolton was a woman of some means who was considerably older than her husband. The couple (he was a widower, she a widow) married in 1869 and in 1878 Sophia Bolton sued her husband for fraud. George Bolton had himself drawn up their marriage settlement. However, he had not done so as per Sophia Bolton's instructions. Instead he fraudulently settled most of her fortune (£90,000) on himself. An English court had ordered him to pay her the sum of £30,000. This information had re-entered the public domain in the course of the probate action and was seized upon with glee by *United Ireland*. The paper delighted in informing its readers that Bolton had 'been guilty of adultery and of immoral intimacy with several women … It is needless to say the English jury scouted Mr. Bolton's claim to have set the will aside.'[8] As both court actions were a matter of public record the risk of a libel suit was negligible once O'Brien adhered strictly to the known facts of the case. Bolton, wisely, opted not to sue for defamation.

On 23 April 1883 *United Ireland*, warming to its self-appointed role as a watchdog of public morals, published details of a lawsuit for criminal conversation taken against Richard Wingfield, the Registrar of Petty Sessions Clerks. The sixty-year-old public servant had alienated the affections of the wife of an ex-policeman named Kinsella and had abandoned his own family in order to establish a domicile with Mrs Kinsella. Her husband had sued Wingfield and had been awarded £400 in damages. *United Ireland* inquired 'whether the firm and gentle Spencer will retain the profligate in his service at the Castle?'[9]

In the context of the newspaper's regular and strident phillipics against the policies of Spencer and Trevelyan and its weekly excoriation of 'nominal Home Rulers', like the MPs, The O'Donoghue, Richard O'Shaughnessy and James McCoan, the treatment of Bolton and Wingfield was relatively mild and can hardly be said to constitute a campaign against moral laxity in Dublin Castle. But an obscure reference published on 25 August arising, ironically, out of the bile of Tim Healy against the *Freeman's Journal*, inaugurated, by default, just such a moral crusade.

The *Freeman*, in an editorial comment, had disparaged the parliamentary tactics of Healy in August 1883. Healy, in the process of attacking the riot-control activities of an RIC Inspector called Cameron, pointed out to the House of Commons, sanctimoniously and gratuitously, that Cameron had lived with his wife in advance of their marriage. The politically impious Irish MP was castigated in the House for his display of prurience and moral superiority. The *Times* was first into the fray to condemn this breach of parliamentary etiquette. Healy was anything but contrite. According to his biographer, Frank Callanan, he 'dismissed the pretended incivility of public allusion to personal matters as a self protective device of a privileged caste, shielding the ruling class in Ireland from the exposure of their larger political depravity'.[10] The censure of the *Times* was meat and drink to Healy, but when that was followed by criticism from the *Freeman's Journal* he was incensed. Adopting a wounded '*et tu Brute*' approach Healy used his ready access to the columns of *United Ireland* to retaliate. On 25 August he wrote:

> The impartiality of the *Freeman* alone enables it to attack its friends, and while, as a general rule, none of its excellent articles on other topics are quoted in the English Press, any

censures on Irish representatives are eagerly telegraphed all over the Kingdom.[11]

After accusing the *Freeman* of, in effect, 'letting the side down' he went on to ridicule the deprecation by Dwyer Gray's newspaper of such 'attacks on private character'. He concluded, writing anonymously and in the third person, in a welter of bravado. He issued a threat:

> If the House of Commons wants to make rules to stop such questions as Mr. Healy's it is open for it to devote its valuable time to the attempt, but it will not do so until the life and adventures, and what is called the 'private character' of various Crown employees in Ireland, from Corry Connellan to Detective Director and County Inspector James Ellis French, are fully laid bare to the universe.[12]

Connellan was an Inspector of Prisons against whom there were outstanding allegations of sodomy. He had not been charged with any offence but had left Ireland hurriedly in 1868. He was in receipt of a government pension of more than £400 per annum.[13] French was a Corkman who had trained as an engineer but joined the RIC and rose quickly through the ranks. He would later claim to have been instrumental in the training of RIC constables in shorthand and assigning them to record the platform speeches at Land League meetings.[14] To the initiated the *United Ireland* article was a blatant allegation that French too was guilty of the crime of sodomy. Chance had led Healy to ignite 'an issue that touched a curious edge of rabid class resentment among conservative Catholic nationalists'[15] (among whom he was numbered). It was also the first salvo in a bitter struggle that could have bankrupted *United Ireland*, led to the insolvency and even the incarceration of its editor and ended its usefulness as the battering ram of constitutional nationalism.

O'Brien, in his autobiographical *Evening Memories* (1920), admitted that he had paid no attention to the paragraph at the time of its insertion and that French was completely unknown to him. He went on to affirm, however, that the offending paragraph was the *casus belli* 'on the strength of which Dublin Castle formed and carried on for several years a conspiracy, which is not too strongly characterised as a loathsome one, for the destruction of *United Ireland* and myself'.[16] O'Brien, hardly an impartial source, clearly took the view in 1920, as he had done in 1883–4, that the Castle establishment used the James Ellis French lawsuit, and others that were to follow, to achieve a goal which had heretofore eluded them in a series of police and court actions – the permanent closure of *United Ireland*.

According to O'Brien himself, Healy's attack on French only came to his attention when a writ for £5,000 in damages arrived at the offices of *United Ireland* from the RIC Director of Detectives. This is somewhat unlikely as French held back from instituting proceedings until October 1883 (seven weeks after the original libel) and, in the interim, *United Ireland,* whether via Healy or the editor himself is uncertain, made one veiled and one overt reference to him. But when, on receipt of the writ, O'Brien made inquiries of Healy, he was told that the latter's information in relation to the RIC official had come from 'a District Inspector of Constabulary at Charleville, and there could be no rational doubt that his information was well-founded'.[17] The informant was, in fact, RIC District Inspector Thomas Murphy (then of Monaghan),[18] who had told Healy of French's consenting homosexual involvement with certain young officers and his sexual harassment of others.

While O'Brien himself may have backed into a confrontation that had the potential to destroy both his newspaper and his own career, he was quick to assume ownership of the controversy by allowing the wilful aggravation of the libel on French in the 13 October issue of *United Ireland*. In the previous edition of the paper there had been an obscure reference to an allegation that 'an official intimately connected with the detection of crime in Dublin has been suspended from his functions under circumstances that are likely to create a profound sensation when revealed'. The following week in the column that unleashed most of the newspaper's weekly contumely, 'The Week's Work', the newspaper was confident enough to identify the mysterious official and announce that he had 'fled the Castle nest … carrying with him, it is believed, considerable sums of Secret Service money'. O'Brien added triumphantly that 'we take credit to ourselves for having rid the country of James Ellis French. A filthier wretch was not in the hire of the Castle, and a number of inconvenient questions will have to be answered in February next, when Parliament meets.'[19]

Unfortunately for O'Brien he had been misinformed, a fact he was forced to acknowledge the following week in the same issue in which *United Ireland* announced that French was suing the newspaper for defamation. Once again O'Brien, with an audacity bordering on the reckless, aggravated the original libel by promising the reading public 'such an exposure as will surprise persons who do not know as much about this ex-official and his class as we do'. Tempting fate, *United Ireland* wondered why charges of criminal libel had not been laid at the door of the newspaper, before concluding that the attorney general 'would not give his ex-underling the necessary *fiat* lest it might be supposed to lend any appearance of Castle sanction to a proceeding which certainly would not shed luster [*sic*] on Cork-hill'.[20]

The case was first mentioned in the Queen's Bench division on Saturday, 2 November 1883. Presiding over the court were the editor's irascible namesake, Justice William O'Brien[21] and Justice Lawson. O'Brien sought to reduce legal expenses and any potential award by having the case heard before the Dublin County Recorder. His counsel read a statement on his behalf making it clear that O'Brien's defence would be one of justification. The imputations were 'true in substance and in fact'. O'Brien added that 'I do not believe the plaintiff will dare to bring his case to trial before a jury'.[22] O'Brien's application failed. Lawson observed that 'it is destitute of all foundation and perfectly untenable'. [23]

O'Brien then proceeded regularly, in the columns of *United Ireland*, to taunt French for procrastination. In keeping with his assertion in the Queen's Bench court that the director of detectives would not dare press his suit because *United Ireland* was in a position to justify its allegations, he wrote on 1 December 1883 that 'unless we see some further signs of animation in Mr. James Ellis French very soon we shall be obliged to publish an interesting biography of him in weekly instalments'.[24] The explanation forthcoming from Dublin Castle for French's tardiness was that he was on sick leave, largely brought about by the spurious charges being made against him.

O'Brien, renewing his allegation of a Castle-inspired conspiracy to destroy *United Ireland*, further claimed that French had only sued the newspaper because he had been given no alternative by the Castle authorities and that his action was being financed from the Secret Service fund.[25] The Castle official or officials who had threatened French with dismissal, unless he took an action against *United Ireland*, were never definitively identified by O'Brien. Spencer and Trevelyan, among others, were accused by the newspaper of having coerced French into the libel court.[26] However, O'Brien himself, under House of Commons privilege, would merely assert in the chamber that Government support of French amounted to 'an attitude of benevolent neutrality while a private individual had to bring him to justice'.[27] Trevelyan, vehemently denying the charge of coercion, claimed not to have spoken to French 'between the time this article appeared in the *United Ireland* and the time when he actually brought his action against the editor of that paper'.[28]

In his memoirs O'Brien reiterated the allegation that 'French was informed that he would be summarily dismissed unless he brought an action for libel against *United Ireland* and to make the threat the more effective he was suspended from duty until he had successfully prosecuted his suit'.[29] But, writing in 1920, in the context of more than thirty years of a Liberal/ Nationalist alliance, he exonerated Spencer and Trevelyan of complicity. 'Earl Spencer, as it turned out, had the probity of a Stoic and the greatness of a Statesman; his Chief Secretary, Mr. Trevelyan, had the charm of a cultured gentleman. It is now clear enough that their profound ignorance of Irish affairs was imposed upon by the mad ex-Indian officers, roguish lawyers, and scurvy *agens* [sic] *provocateurs* who had control of the machinery of Law and Justice in Dublin Castle'.[30] O'Brien's penitent retraction bears out the comment of Sophie O'Brien of her husband that 'he had no enemy but the enemy of Ireland. And if the enemy became a friend, he was ready to shake hands heartily and forget the past'.[31]

French, Cornwall and Bolton v *United Ireland*

O'Brien's bullish and provocative approach towards French's suit and his positive encouragement of a swift resolution of the case might tend to suggest that *United Ireland* had compelling and definitive evidence against French. In fact nothing could have been further from the truth.

In 1920 in *Evening Memories* O'Brien revealed the hazards into which he was steering himself and his newspaper. He acknowledged that, when he had taunted French to pursue his case more vigorously, he had no solid evidence to advance in justification of the claims made in his newspaper:

A number of youthful District Inspectors and Cadets had been summoned to the Castle and with whatever reluctance made any further doubt impossible by their revelations; matters were in this posture when the solitary compromising sentence in *United Ireland* changed the half-convicted criminal into the protagonist of Dublin Castle against a hated foe … In the meantime the official investigation was dropped by those who alone could have induced the witnesses of his guilt to break silence, and the burden was thrown upon those who (it was calculated) must absolutely fail to do so.[32]

The still-supportive Inspector Murphy was asked to approach some of French's RIC accusers but 'the young officers … naturally refused to open their lips to the Castle's enemies'.[33] In a letter to the *Freeman's Journal* on 16 February 1900, at a time when he was at loggerheads with Healy, O'Brien deprecated the lack of assistance from the instigators of the libel, claiming that 'the unmasking and conviction of French and the crew behind him was accomplished without the slightest assistance in the way of evidence either from Mr. Murphy or Mr. Healy who had involved me in this hell of litigation in fighting out his own private battle with the *Freeman*'.[34]

However, O'Brien, in the event that his monumental bluff in the columns of *United Ireland* did not dissuade French from pursuing his libel action, set about obtaining the evidence he would need to prove justification of the newspaper's assertions. Private detectives were engaged, but at least one London-based detective employed by O'Brien, allegedly intimidated by 'two of French's minions [was] … threatened with a prosecution for felony unless he consented immediately to quit Dublin. This the unfortunate Englishman precipitately did.'[35]

O'Brien opted to fight fire with fire. At the instigation of the London solicitor George Lewis, who would later brief Parnell's counsel at the *Times* commission, *United Ireland* engaged the services of a London private detective, Meiklejohn,[36] whose own credentials were questionable. Meiklejohn had been dismissed from the Metropolitan Police detective force and sentenced to two years in jail for blackmail.[37] His sojourn in prison had not affected his professional capabilities, however, and it was Meiklejohn who hunted down the witnesses who were to prove crucial in the defence of justification advanced by *United Ireland*. In the course of his investigation he also discovered that French was not the only prominent Dublin Castle official vulnerable to charges of sodomy.

It became increasingly apparent that French was highly reluctant to pursue the case and it can reasonably be inferred that he was coming under some pressure from senior government associates to meet the challenges of O'Brien in court. O'Brien's solicitor P.A. Chance (of the legal firm of Chance and Miley) was told by French's lawyer that the detective director 'would have taken no notice whatever of the charge made against him if the Government had not compelled him to do so'.[38]

O'Brien regularly restated his claim that French had been under investigation by Castle officials prior to the initial *United Ireland* exposure, his homosexual activities (still criminal in 1883) having become impossible to ignore. He further alleged that the inquiry had been shelved in favour of using French as a reluctant bludgeon with which to pummel *United Ireland*. In the House of Commons on 17 June 1884 Trevelyan gave some credence to this charge when he acknowledged that French had been on 'sick leave' since 6 August 1883, more than two weeks prior to Healy's original libel. O'Brien claimed that French had actually been suspended while accusations against him by the young RIC constables were being investigated. Trevelyan went on to state that, on seeing the offending article, the RIC Inspector General, Colonel Bruce 'called Mr. French's attention to it, asking what steps he intended to take to repel so foul an imputation on his character?' While denying that French had been 'forced or asked to take this action' Trevelyan acknowledged that 'we may imagine that this was the original intention of the Inspector General'.[39] Bruce himself, in an 1884 memo, put the date of this meeting at 7 September, professed himself unaware of any inquiry into the conduct of the Detective Director being made by any member of the Irish government and asserted that he did not follow up the allegations 'as the matter was to become subject for trial in the Law Courts'.[40]

Subsequent to his first court appearance on 2 November 1883 French appeared to be as averse to pursuing the action to an early conclusion as he had been to set the process in motion.[41] The plaintiff's statement of claim was not served until 23 November. The action then hung fire for a further five months until *United Ireland* entered a motion for dismissal for want of prosecution. In the interim the RIC Assistant Inspector General, R.F.

Fanning, had written to French on 18 March 1884 'expressing dissatisfaction at the delay that had taken place, and … asking why Mr. French had not brought his case to trial'.[42] This was followed on 4 April by a letter from Inspector General Bruce insisting that 'there should be no further delay, and calling upon Mr. French to proceed to trial at the earliest day'.[43]

On the basis of evidence adduced by the plaintiff's counsel, that he was too ill to proceed, the application was adjourned for a month. But on 17 May 1884 the patience of the Queen's Bench court ran out and the action was dismissed for want of prosecution.[44] Thanks to the evidence gathered by the enterprising Meiklejohn there is little doubt that if French had pressed his case he would have lost. But by then *United Ireland* was engaged in two even graver 'life or death' struggles, one element of which O'Brien himself had initiated, and another which had been visited upon him by a careless sub-editor.

In the course of questioning a number of young men who admitted to having had homosexual relationships with French, Meiklejohn had unearthed another potential source of embarrassment to the Irish administration. Secretary of the GPO since 1840, Gustavus C. Cornwall, a married man of apparently impeccable reputation, was cited by a number of those questioned by the London detective as being an active homosexual. On the basis that Meiklejohn's witnesses were prepared to testify should Cornwall sue for libel, O'Brien inaugurated a new campaign with a pejorative reference to the GPO secretary. In the edition of 10 May 1884, in a piece clearly written in the context of the ongoing allegations against French, Cornwall was reported as having stated to acquaintances that the Irish climate had got the better of him and that he was about to emigrate. *United Ireland* suggested that an (unnamed) military man would 'find it hard to bear the pangs of separation' should Cornwall be forced to leave the country. The paper added that 'Mr. Cornwall's discovery of the unsuitability of our humid climate to an official of his tastes, dates from certain researches we were compelled to make into the heroic past of Mr. James Ellis French.' O'Brien even taunted Cornwall that should he object to the manner of his representation in the newspaper, he 'has his legal remedy. He will find in the Four Courts a talented and learned bar and highly sympathetic judges.'[45] Neither the gibe nor the libel was sufficient to attract a writ from the GPO secretary.

It was not until O'Brien repeated the allegation of undefined 'felonious practices' in the House of Commons on 19 May 1884 – while also making similar but unrelated charges against George Bolton – that Cornwall responded with a writ. *United Ireland* offered Cornwall 'our most heartfelt thanks. Having failed to force Mr. James Ellis French to tackle this journal in the Law Courts, Mr. Trevelyan now puts forward as the Castle's fitting champion the wretched man who is to be the nominal plaintiff in this action.'[46] Reinforcing O'Brien's claims that the libel writs were part of an orchestrated strategy to destroy *United Ireland*, within a week the newspaper had also received a writ for defamation from George Bolton.

The *United Ireland* campaign against Bolton was, as already noted, unrelated to that against French and Cornwall. Bolton, in his capacity as an efficient and ruthless Crown prosecutor, was an obvious political target for the newspaper. His achilles heel was his dishonourable treatment of his late wife. This arose out of a fraud perpetrated upon her that had been the subject of a civil court action. In previous sorties *United Ireland* had been careful to restrict itself to commentary, damaging to Bolton, but related to matters already in the public domain. However, by including Bolton in his 'felonious practices' indictment in the House of Commons, O'Brien risked serious consequences, outside of the privilege of the House, should *United Ireland*, in the phraseology of its reportage or commentary, enable the heterosexual Bolton to reasonably infer that he too was being accused of sodomy. This, as it transpired, is exactly what occurred.

In *Evening Memories*, written in 1920, O'Brien blamed 'a slipshod sub-editor' who 'published the Notice of Motion under a sub-heading, "A Precious Trio", which was not, of course, covered by Parliamentary privilege, and the slim Mr. George Bolton promptly pounced upon the sub-heading as charging him with the particular form of guilt in respect of which the two previous actions for libel had been instituted against *United Ireland*'.[47] The law in this case was clear. In instances 'where the libel complained of is an article or paragraph preceded by a title, it is not sufficient to prove the truth of the facts stated in the article or paragraph: the title itself must be justified, or the plaintiff will succeed'.[48]

However, in his own editorial commentary O'Brien had, in all likelihood, done as much damage as any sub-editor by failing to make distinctions between his allegations against Bolton and those against French and

Cornwall. In the *United Ireland* edition of 24 May, in an excoriation of Spencer for shielding all three men, O'Brien concluded that 'even an English Lord Lieutenant cannot afford to identify himself with *unclean beasts* [my italics] who insist upon bringing their profligacy out of the lupinar into the daylight'.[49] Such rhetoric offered Bolton a clear opportunity to exact some measure of revenge on the irksome *United Ireland* editor. Whether or not he was under any form of governmental duress to do so Bolton would have been aware that his action, should it prove successful, would greatly enhance his somewhat battered personal reputation with his employers.

On 30 May 1884 Bolton sought damages of £30,000 on the basis that he had been defamed by association. The claim was for a multiple of that of French who was, in essence, suing for a similar libel. Where Bolton also differed from Cornwall and French was that he adroitly insisted that as *United Ireland* was distributed throughout the country, the action should proceed in Belfast. Logic suggested that this would prove hugely detrimental to O'Brien's cause. A civil action before a largely unionist jury in Belfast was unlikely to go the way of the editor of the country's leading nationalist weekly newspaper, irrespective of the flawed credentials of the plaintiff. Just as worrying for O'Brien, who had only recently survived a charge of seditious libel, was the possibility of a prosecution for criminal libel,[50] which, according to Frank Callanan in his biography of Healy, 'was widely rumoured'.[51]

On 17 June 1884 Bolton sought an attachment for contempt based on the continued coverage of the case in *United Ireland* subsequent to the presentation of the libel writ.[52] In 7 June issue of his newspaper O'Brien had acknowledged that he never intended to associate Bolton with the 'crimes' of which he accused French and Cornwall. Nonetheless O'Brien, never content to leave well enough alone, added that *United Ireland* had, nonetheless 'designated Mr. Bolton as forger, an adulterer, a swindler, a bankrupt, a defrauder of his own wife, a suborner of false testimony, a withholder of true affidavits, as base an all-round member of society as could be produced outside Dublin Castle circles ... [But] this journal has never by word or hint imputed to Mr. Bolton the unmentionable abominations which we have undertaken to bring home to Messrs French and Cornwall. We have not, and never pretended to have, a tittle of evidence that his tastes and theirs were alike.'[53]

177

The Queen's Bench court, presided over by Lord Chief Justice Morris, Justice James Lawson and Justice William O'Brien, agreed with Bolton that O'Brien, in attempting, half-heartedly, to mitigate the libel had treated the court with contempt. In a gratuitous but characteristic comment Lawson remarked that 'there was a most terrible vilification of the character of the plaintiff'.[54] This prompted O'Brien to refer in print to 'the astounding recklessness, indecency and savagery with which his spite against this journal broke loose'[55] and accuse Lawson of having fatally prejudiced any future jury against the defendant.

United Ireland was fined £500 by the Queen's Bench court. The *Freeman's Journal* immediately established an indemnity fund to pay the fine. O'Brien's application for a change of venue, of the libel action proper, was refused. In the light of O'Brien's previous condemnation of egregious jury-packing Bolton's affidavit is highly ironic. This pointed out that 'the paper *United Ireland* had an extensive circulation amongst the class of persons in Dublin from which jurors were selected, and had a strong influence upon their minds and feelings. For all these reasons he believed a fair trial could not be had in Dublin.'[56] A *United Ireland* libel trial in front of a Belfast Unionist jury promised to be, as O'Brien put it himself many years later, 'equivalent to laying the venue against an early Christian in the Colosseum'.[57]

On 2 July 1884 the *Cornwall v O'Brien* case came before Justice O'Brien and a special jury in the *Nisi Prius* court. The defence, once again, was one of justification. Many years later O'Brien acknowledged, in the event that Cornwall was actually acting as a proxy for the government in its struggle against *United Ireland* 'they had hit upon a champion more doughty than the grovelling Detective Inspector. Cornwall was an aristocrat of quite a ducal presence and with nerves of steel, and he pressed on the trial with the haughty confidence of one who felt that the witnesses whose silence the Government could have without difficulty broken down could have no conceivable motive for destroying themselves to oblige the Government's enemies.'[58]

Newspapers like the *Times* chose to shield its readers from most of the evidence that followed. Coverage by the *Freeman's Journal*, despite a claim to be conflicted because of the explicit nature of the testimony, was detailed. *The Nation* did 'not consider it necessary to republish any portion of it in our columns'.[59] In the style of the muckraking but still prurient twentieth-century tabloid the *Freeman* contended that its salacious coverage was dictated by a demand for the truth that 'left the public journalist no choice but to report the case at considerable length'.[60] Unsurprisingly treatment of the proceedings in *United Ireland* itself, was more extensive still.

If indeed the Castle had sought to employ the eminently respectable GPO secretary as an artillery piece to blast the Parnellite newspaper out of existence those tactics quickly came unstuck. Cornwall, magisterially, denied all the charges made against him. He sought 'rather to pontificate than to make the excuses of a criminal'.[61] Cornwall's defence crumbled, however, when three men, under duress from Meiklejohn and O'Brien's solicitors Chance and Miley, reluctantly testified against him. Malcolm Johnston, was a twenty-one-year-old Dubliner, Alfred McKernan, from Pembroke Road, was a bank official in his mid twenties and George Taylor, the oldest of the three, at thirty-three years of age, was a B & I shipping clerk.

In *Evening Memories* O'Brien recalled how, up to their actual appearance in court, the defence team was uncertain as to whether the three men would testify. 'In one of those sudden gusts of infantile fretfulness which are apt to sweep over persons of their peculiar mentality,' he wrote in 1920, 'the three essential witnesses, as they sat in a waiting room adjoining the Court had refused point-blank to be examined and proposed to walk away. Had they persisted, there was no legal coercion, much less private inducement, to detain them.'[62] A further change of heart, however, saw all three agree to go through with their testimony. O'Brien attributes the conquest of their reluctance to a 'febrile change as unaccountable as the previous outburst' – as if some native volatility inherent in their very sexuality, rather than threats of exposure from his legal team, as alleged in the subsequent criminal trials, had prompted a change of mind. But, 'before the first of them had been half-heard, the crisis was over. Once begun, the evidence not only rained, it poured.'[63]

Based on direct testimony of assignations in a range of locations, including Cornwall's house and the Botanical Gardens in Glasnevin, the jury (whose impartiality had been questioned by the *Freeman's Journal* – given that at least five of its members were Protestant)[64] found in favour of O'Brien. The following day the *Freeman's Journal* depicted the *United Ireland* editor as a latter-day Savonarola who had taken on 'a moral leprosy'.[65] The main nationalist daily newspaper accused the government of having wilfully refused to take action against men of whose crimes it must have been aware, 'for these crimes belong almost exclusively to the official classes'. The *Journal* added pointedly, 'nor will anyone believe that the Government which detected the Phoenix Park murderers could not have detected French and Cornwall'.[66]

The *Journal* might have been less inclined to wrap a cloak of sanctimony around O'Brien had it been privy to information then circulating that was reported to Spencer at around the time of the collapse of Cornwall's libel action. A week after O'Brien's acquittal Spencer wrote to the lord chancellor, Sir Edward Sullivan, seeking an investigation of a rumour that a 'Mr.Boyle' had 'bolted on account of complicity in the French and Cornwall case and that he paid O'Brien £2,000 to keep his name out of the case'.[67] The lord lieutenant sought a report from the DMP and the exposure of O'Brien if the rumour could be substantiated.[68] Sullivan responded quickly. He spoke to Hamilton who gave complete credence to the rumour and confirmed that Harrel, the DMP commissioner 'is quite alive to the information and getting at the matter. He thinks a more substantial amount of money has passed'.[69] Clearly Harrel was unable to verify the story, which may well have been circulated maliciously, as no authenticated version of the rumour emerged into the public domain.[70]

The attitude of the *Nation* throughout the affair was supportive of O'Brien and *United Ireland* and the venerable nationalist newspaper took numerous opportunities to harangue the Castle on its own behalf. In the aftermath of Cornwall's unsuccessful lawsuit the *Nation* editorial asked 'How can the government of this country justify themselves for their conduct with regard to this case? There is no justification for them. The existence of the evil with which Mr. O'Brien set himself to grapple was well known to them ... why did they leave to a private individual the dreadful labour, the infinite risk, and the heavy cost of endeavouring to bring the culprits to justice? These questions they will have to answer to the country. Earl Spencer and Mr. Trevelyan are bound to meet them if they can; but so far it seems as if they had no defence to offer'.[71]

However, in 1905, the same year in which O'Brien published his first volume of memoirs, *Recollections* (it ends before the 'Scandals' episode) the long-time proprietor and editor of the *Nation*, T.D. Sullivan,[72] in his own autobiographical *Recollections of Troubled Times in Irish Politics* is vitriolic in his criticism of O'Brien's campaign of 'vague references to appalling enormities which it led the public to believe were being secretly practised in Dublin Castle'. Sullivan also attacked O'Brien personally, claiming that '*United Ireland*, under his management, soon became a costly luxury to the organisation. It was always in a state of volcanic eruption. Sensational charges, "revelations", and denunciations, blazed in its columns every week.' Sullivan goes on to question the significance of the *United Ireland* victory and excoriate O'Brien for his treatment of Spencer who 'was cartooned, libelled, and lampooned in savage fashion, but he never made those attacks the occasion of any interference with "the freedom of the Press".[73] Sullivan's attitude is in marked contrast to the editorial line of the *Nation*, two decades before. Then O'Brien had single-handedly 'broken up the infamous gang whose abominations were such as might bring the vengeance of God upon the land. He has routed, crushed and scattered the monsters of iniquity whose devilries were a peril to the community, and he has stayed the spread of a moral plague worse to human society than the ravages of fever, cholera or leprosy.'[74]

Sullivan's reference to Spencer's respect for the freedom of the press seems ironic given the administration's overt campaign against *United Ireland* in 1882 and the prosecution of O'Brien in 1883. It must, however be seen in the context of his own arrest in 1887 at the behest of a Conservative Chief Secretary, Arthur Balfour and his personal animosity towards the establishment of *United Ireland* as a weekly newspaper, effectively in competition with the *Nation* and with the other periodical under his control, the *Weekly News*.

In its first issue after the Cornwall verdict (12 July 1884), *United Ireland* itself was exultant. The newspaper used the same imagery as the *Freeman*:

> We attacked the propagators of the horrible English leprosy with a vivid consciousness that the only possible end could be ruin and unutterable disgrace on their part or on ours … By a train of circumstances little short of miraculous our enemies have been put under our feet. Justice has been vindicated in the teeth of those whose business it was to vindicate it.[75]

The collapse of Cornwall's case led, in short order, to his arrest as well as that of French and a number of other prominent Dublin citizens, including Captain Martin Kirwan of the Royal Dublin Fusiliers (cousin of Lord Oranmore) and Army doctor Albert de Fernandez. In the trials that followed, French was sent to prison for two years, but only after two juries had disagreed about his guilt. Cornwall was eventually acquitted of charges of buggery[76] and conspiracy after a retrial. A subsequent application on his part to have the libel case reopened was refused in the Common Pleas Division on 6 December 1884 by Mr Justice Murphy who, while acknowledging that Cornwall had not been found guilty of the crime of buggery, contended that he was guilty of crimes that were 'equally loathsome' and 'that a vile gang existed in the city, leagued together for the pursuit of unnatural depravity and vice, and that Cornwall was one of that gang'.[77] Because of the frequent references to the accused in the 'scandals' as having attended a variety of musical recitals and events the euphemism 'musical' began to be applied in Dublin to homosexual men. Tim Healy credits Joseph Biggar with coining the appellation. As he relates in the first volume of his autobiography, 'Biggar, one night, as we were going home from the House of Commons, queried, "Have you noticed that all those blackguards were musical?" To be "musical" was almost a capital offence with Joe.'[78] To be 'musical' in a Biggaresque sense of the word had actually carried the death penalty until 1861.

Bolton was somewhat more successful in his Belfast action against O'Brien. Despite the direction of Mr Justice Barry to the jury that it was his 'solemn conviction'[79] the editor had not intended to imply that Bolton was guilty of the offences imputed to French and Cornwall, the (entirely Protestant) jury found in favour of the plaintiff and awarded damages of £3,050. In his suit against *United Ireland* Bolton was awarded £500. O'Brien announced that, as he had no assets, he had no intention of honouring payment of the award made against him, in which case Bolton stood to gain only the £500 from *United Ireland*. This sum was covered by the *Freeman's* Indemnity Fund, so there was no threat to the financial stability of the newspaper.

In terms of his own private indebtedness (£60–70,000) the Belfast awards were a drop in the ocean for the Crown Prosecutor. In parallel with the Belfast case Bolton was also facing bankruptcy proceedings in the Dublin courts.

On this basis the Solicitor General announced in the House of Commons on 4 August that Bolton had been suspended from his duties. O'Brien would later assert that Bolton's 'trade was at an end. He was never permitted to pack a jury more.'[80] This was, palpably, not the case. It was not long before he was rehabilitated as Tipperary Crown Prosecutor. In fact O'Brien himself would encounter the redoubtable Bolton in court during the Plan of Campaign. In 1888 Bolton introduced Resident Magistrate William Henry Joyce to the *Times* solicitor Joseph Soames. Their partnership would drive the *Times* case against the Irish Party during the Parnellism and Crime Commission. Joyce regarded Bolton in 1888 'as perhaps the ablest criminologist at the disposal of the Irish government, and a man at all times *persona grata* in the law room at Dublin Castle'.[81]

United Ireland v Spencer and Trevelyan

After the three court verdicts *United Ireland* reiterated its allegation that the entire process had, from the outset, constituted 'one of the most unscrupulous plots ever concocted to slay this journal. French, Cornwall, Bolton, the judges of the Court of Queen's Bench, were simply so many algebraical expressions to represent the quenchless hate with which Earl Spencer's Government is pleased to pursue us'.[82] Spencer and Trevelyan, the newspaper contended, had created a virtuous circle for themselves. One in which the optimum result was the defeat and disappearance of *United Ireland* but which could, equally, encompass the prosecution of any or all of the Castle litigants should the desired outcome not eventuate.

Irish MPs conducted a sustained campaign of attrition against the Irish executive at Westminster while O'Brien and Healy waxed vitriolic against Spencer and Trevelyan in the columns of *United Ireland*. In the House of Commons, O'Brien accused the government of ignoring the behaviour of French even though they had damning evidence against him.[83] He also insisted that French had been employed 'as a kind of stalking-horse against him and *United Ireland*; and it was simply because this man had not the nerve and pluck to brazen the thing out, as Cornwall afterwards did, that he was dismissed'.[84] Trevelyan, in a speech that anticipated his disillusioned resignation later that year, insisted that the September inquiry into the conduct of French had been referred to the Irish attorney general,[85] who 'stated that nothing had transpired to establish *prima facie* proof of

French's guilt'.[86] He concluded that 'I think it was very hard that Members of the Government should have their names mixed up with these odious crimes, because some person employed under them in the thousand and one Departments of the Public Service had been accused or even eventually found guilty of such a crime.'[87]

It was due to a large measure of good fortune, Meiklejohn's investigative prowess and 'persuasive' personality, and (to a lesser extent) O'Brien's own management that *United Ireland* did not become the only victim of the Castle 'scandals'. O'Brien had taken on 'appalling risks which extended beyond *United Ireland* itself'.[88] In 1889 (three years after Spencer's enthusiastic support of Gladstone's Home Rule Bill) a somewhat chastened O'Brien told the *Times* commission that most of the highly personalized attacks made on the lord lieutenant, chief secretary and under secretary (Hamilton) were actually written by Healy.[89] This included the notorious gibe that Spencer should be further elevated within the peerage, and take the title of 'Duke of Sodom and Gomorrah'.[90]

United Ireland repeatedly impugned the reputations of Spencer and Trevelyan, alleging that they countenanced and covered up, initially, the activities of French and then knowingly extended the same protection to Cornwall. O'Brien had been emphatic in the issue of 1 March 1884 that 'we shall prove that his official superiors knew his character all along and supported him against us in his prosecution in order to break down a hated adversary'.[91] An editorial on the same subject the following week, 'A Castle Martyr', which suggested that French was about to be dispatched to a lunatic asylum at the instigation of the lord lieutenant, drew an apoplectic response from the Irish lord chancellor, Sir Edward Sullivan. While opposed to a prosecution on the grounds that, based on previous experience, 'a conviction cannot be currently calculated upon', Sullivan, who described the leader as 'simply atrocious', insisted that 'I have no doubt that it constitutes in law a highly seditious libel in all its parts, for which Mr. O'Brien can be indicted and prosecuted on the part of the Crown, containing as it does the express charge that the L[or]d Lieutenant is willfully shielding Mr. French.'[92] Although he contended that seizure of the plant of *United Ireland* was permissible under common law he advised against testing the law in this instance, 'as it might be suggested that an article personal to the L[or]d Lieutenant was made the pretext for taking such an extreme course.'[93]

However, after the abject failure of French or Cornwall to prevail over *United Ireland* any suggestion of punitive action against O'Brien's newspaper became more problematic, to the extent that the Executive involved itself in behind the scenes moves to ensure that the editor was not incarcerated for his failure to pay the £500 fine imposed by the Queen's Bench court for contempt on 17 June. In mid-July, as O'Brien continued to defy the Queen's Bench, Trevelyan expressed misgivings to the lord lieutenant about the possible arrest of the *United Ireland* editor. Spencer sought the advice of Sullivan, informing him that Trevelyan had maintained that any such action against O'Brien would appear vindictive and unjust.[94] The Lord Chancellor agreed with the chief secretary that 'O'Brien's possible arrest is the most awkward I ever came across. There cannot be the slightest doubt that his arrest now would give rise to every misconception, it could never be understood in England.'[95] Spencer accepted that 'if O'Brien goes to prison he will be looked on as a martyr',[96] and Sullivan set about quietly ensuring this did not happen. After a number of unofficial conversations with Justices O'Brien and Lawson, the Lord Chancellor ensured that the matter was quietly shelved and the need to confront O'Brien did not arise.[97]

If the Castle expected any sort of journalistic *quid pro quo* from O'Brien, it was not forthcoming. Instead, emboldened by his successful defiance of a Queen's Bench court ruling, the *United Ireland* editor continued his slash-and-burn approach to the executive. When, in November 1884, following his criminal court acquittal, Cornwall sought to renew his civil case against *United Ireland*, O'Brien published a scathing editorial claiming that only the impeachment of Spencer 'can satisfy the public mind'. He was compared unfavourably to a previous viceregal incumbent, the notorious Thomas Wentworth, 1st Earl of Strafford. Strafford, according to *United Ireland*, was 'guilty of more menial offences'.[98]

R.G. Hamilton, the under secretary, sought the opinion of Spencer as to what action to take. Having already failed to mend the ways of *United Ireland* by interning its staff without trial or prosecuting its editor for sedition, the administration was running out of options. Hamilton suggested seizure of both newspaper and plant. The latter was, of course, not provided for under the terms of the 1882 Crimes Act. Hamilton was aware that 'the House of Commons would expect the seizure to be followed by a prosecution'. This, he accepted, was not viable, 'for every means would be tried to secure a disagreement of the jury & such a result would be disastrous'. However, his logic was simple: 'What I had in mind was to leave to O'Brien to take such remedies as he saw fit.'[99] The strategy that Hamilton was proposing, all-out economic war, was spelt out in more detail by his private secretary, J.H. Davies in a note to Spencer's secretary, Courtney Boyle: 'The existence of a paper depends entirely on its commercial success and a few repeated seizures of its whole issue would undoubtedly seriously cripple it if indeed they did not altogether crush its power.'[100]

The option of scorching the earth around *United Ireland*, which had clearly failed in the winter of 1881/2, was rejected by Spencer. The lord lieutenant adopted a more measured and nuanced approach than some of his subordinates: 'On the whole we cannot take up this article for prosecution or seizure or both … if we ever have to proceed to extremities it w[oul]d be better to seize some occasion where the paper incites to some illegal act.'[101]

Hamilton made one further attempt to persuade Spencer of the wisdom of implementing a policy of arbitrary seizure. He reiterated the financial basis for what was essentially a procedure of dubious legality: 'If this were done two or three weeks in succession the circulation of the paper would be so impaired that probably they would be more careful in future.'[102]

However tempting was the notion of bleeding *United Ireland* dry of its subscriber income, the strategy was not pursued. The only alternative course of action proposed was to take the Castle's case to the London press. Henry Campbell Bannerman, chief secretary in succession to Trevelyan, argued that the extremism of *United Ireland* and, *ipso facto*, of the Irish party at Westminster, required a greater airing in British national newspapers. Hamilton agreed: 'The extreme party is very susceptible to ridicule and if some paper like the *Pall Mall*, which is distinctly in sympathy with much of their programme, were to treat the matter from this standpoint I think much good would be done.'[103] Spencer gave the scheme his *imprimatur* in late November but the *Pall Mall Gazette* did not co-operate. Unlike the *Times*, which made its columns available to the counter-narrative of the Salisbury administration in the late 1880s, Stead's paper declined the opportunity to censure or ridicule the fulminations of *United Ireland*.

'Othering' the Castle

Whether or not he actually wrote the swingeing attacks on Spencer and Trevelyan, as editor of *United Ireland* O'Brien was legally and morally responsible for them. In 1900, at a time of personal and political estrangement from Healy, O'Brien wrote to the *Freeman's Journal* to accuse the future governor general of Ireland of not accepting his own share of the responsibility for the *United Ireland* diatribes, and claimed that Healy 'went on hobnobbing with the statesmen whom he was anonymously attacking'.[104] Although O'Brien had resiled from this position by the time of the publication in 1920 of *Evening Memories* (where Healy's role is dealt with more graciously), the *Freeman* letter conveniently glosses over the fact that, whatever the origin of the invective, O'Brien took much of the credit for a sustained newspaper campaign seen in many nationalist quarters as an act of reprisal for the alleged miscarriages of justice that had characterized the Irish administration under the Crimes Act.

While O'Brien may have stumbled upon the 'Castle Scandals' via the spleen of Healy, he skilfully exploited the unsought opportunity to conduct a campaign of simultaneously blatant, and yet subtle, alienation. Taking a leaf from the colonist's handbook he practised, to appropriate a phrase used in a 'post-colonial' context, the dark art of 'othering'. This is defined as establishing one's own identity by stigmatizing an 'other'. Classically, it is a self-affirming device employed by the colonist. The colonized 'other' is denigrated and derided. This has the effect of undermining the colonized while aggrandizing the colonist. What O'Brien was doing, decades before the promulgation of post-colonial theory, was stigmatizing the government (embodied and actualized in the repetition of the phrase 'the Castle') and quarantining the administration behind a journalistic *cordon sanitaire*. The imagery used in *United Ireland* of 'unspeakable' crimes and 'abominations' and the application of responsibility for such alien felonies to those not directly accused of 'unnatural practices' (Spencer and Trevelyan) was designed to invite the contempt of 'decent' Irishmen and women and not simply the antipathy of those of a pietistic nature.

O'Brien was, very capably, inverting the conventional process of 'othering'. The government (Dublin Castle) was indicted, by association, with the 'felonies' of Cornwall and French. Sodomy – though O'Brien was pruriently careful never to give the 'unnatural practices' a name in editorial commentary – was referred to as 'The Garrison Crime'.[105] The guilt of Cornwall and French, when it was finally established, was equated with the guilt of an entire governing establishment. O'Brien had learnt the lesson of the Phoenix Park murders well. In that case the entire nationalist movement had been stigmatized by the actions of the Invincibles. The result was the creation of a political atmosphere conducive to the introduction of the draconian Crimes Act.

O'Brien made his intentions clear in an editorial after the failure of Cornwall's civil action against his newspaper. 'May we not cherish the dream that that same force of honest Irish indignation which has lashed the wretched Cornwall [will] sweep into the sea the whole fabric of English rule within which the dark brood of the Cornwalls and Frenches have had their birth and nurture.'[106] The reaction to the success of *United Ireland*, was, in certain quarters, exactly what O'Brien had sought. The Father Mathew Total Abstinence Association applauded the editor for his struggle against 'the further development among our youth of a terrible vice hitherto unknown in this Holy Ireland of ours'.[107] It was not much of a stretch to view the administration that presided over alien and 'unnatural' practices as, in itself, alien and unnatural, a parasitic growth that required excision.

In his study of homosexuality in Irish history, *Terrible Queer Creatures,* Brian Lacey has written that 'nationalist Ireland laid these crimes at the door of unionism, highlighting the connections of the protagonists with the administration and the army. Newspapers at the time spoke of "this vice" as a foreign import.'[108] The *Freeman's Journal* went further by insisting that 'despotic forms of government and odious vice have had in the history of the world an association so common as to be justifiably held as cause and effect'.[109]

Even unionist Ireland endorsed the notion of homosexuality as an exotic import. The *Dublin Evening Mail* while rejecting the *Freeman* thesis, laid the blame at the door of 'the discipline and training of English public schools … We should like to know at what schools most of the persons who figured in the late trial were educated, and regret that the question was not put to them.'[110] As for the Dublin correspondents of English newspapers O'Brien accused them of 'systematic distortion'[111] and of an extremely partial presentation of the Cornwall libel trial. Later he wrote that 'The Tory papers, which made a sickening parade of their virtuous determination to suppress the reports of the Cornwall trial, displayed their righteousness by publishing at length everything favourable to the prisoner, and rigidly suppressing the evidence against him.'[112]

On a more subtle level, however, O'Brien had chosen well the 'disease' that needed to be expunged. As one commentator has put it 'the heterosexual public through the ages has always associated homosexuality with its enemies'.[113] Part of the reason for this is a consequential sense of efficacy and empowerment. In his excoriation of Spencer and Trevelyan, as well as the RIC for its shielding of French in particular, O'Brien was suggesting not only the fatally flawed governance of a decadent British administration in Ireland but the debilitating nature of such an 'unmanly' form of decadence. Thus British governance in Ireland was simultaneously effete and pernicious. Many years later, in *Evening Memories*, O'Brien, writing in the context of the ineffectual case made against him by French, hinted at this notion when he wrote that 'providentially the cowardice of persons thus diseased is commonly as abject as their depravity'.[114]

The entire campaign was designed to reinforce the fundamentally 'alien' nature of British rule in Ireland. The garrison even imported its own vices, vices which were not native to Ireland and which would never thrive in purely Irish soil. O'Brien's suggestion, implied in much of his journalistic coverage of the affair, was that the Castle had been morally undermined and British rule rendered vulnerable to collapse, literally and metaphorically, at the hands of an ethically (and ethnically) superior Irish nation. It was a case of 're-othering' *par excellence*. The entire affair contributed to the resignation of an exhausted and disenchanted George Trevelyan on 22 October 1884.

For O'Brien's 're-othering' to have had a lasting effect the 'Dublin Scandals' (the preferred nomenclature of the English press as opposed to 'Castle Scandals' or 'Castle Abominations' of the Irish nationalist press) had to make some impact on the 'other'. If O'Brien wished to prick the moral conscience of Britain (the non-conformist conscience that would rise up against Parnell in late 1890) British public opinion was required to be challenged and to reassess its relationship with Ireland on the strength of its disillusionment with the manner in which Dublin Castle governed Ireland. As it happened, there was precious little interest in the affair and little evidence of penitence or breast-beating *saeva indignatio* on the part of the British press or public.

Coverage of the case in the main English newspapers was scant.[115] The *Times*, through its Dublin correspondent, G.V. Patton, reported on the *Cornwall v O'Brien* libel action in July 1884 but gave no sense of the dramatic and damaging testimony of Johnston, McKernan and Taylor. The justification of the allegations of *United Ireland* by the chief witnesses against Cornwall was cloaked in neutral language. 'The witness deposed to conduct on the part of the plaintiff which tended to justify the alleged libel,'[116] was how Patton represented the evidence of McKernan who had admitted to assignations with the GPO secretary. The report of the final day's proceedings and the actual verdict was dispatched in fewer than three hundred words. The only comment made by the *Times* is an aside from Patton on 12 July to the effect that 'the verdict in the Cornwall case has given a fruitful text to the Nationalist papers this week.'[117] After the arrests of Cornwall and French the *Times* opined that the charges against them had 'excited but little feeling even among the populace, the subject being one from which the public generally recoil'.[118] Throughout the court appearances that followed coverage was perfunctory and reference was made only to 'certain practices' when it came to identifying the charges against the various accused. The *Times*, on more than one occasion, referred to the 'composure' of Cornwall in the dock. The *Bolton v O'Brien* and the *Bolton v United Ireland* cases in Belfast were, on the other hand, dealt with in far greater detail.[119]

The *Times* Dublin correspondent actually advised the court, rather paradoxically for a journalist, to prohibit all publication of the details of the ongoing case until the close of the trial, in the interests of public morality. 'For curiosity would be exhausted and the interest in the proceedings gone by the time when the verdict is known.'[120] Patton was so anxious to prevent extensive coverage of the trials that he even suggested an Act of Parliament could be passed if the courts did not have authority, as the law stood, to prevent publicity.[121] O'Brien, a frequent critic of Patton in the pages of *United Ireland*, wrote that 'every day's report is in fact a gross and scandalous libel upon the defendant and his solicitor'.[122] Adding later that 'as long as Dr. Patton's Dublin letter remains the golden link between England and Ireland, the two people are as sure to loathe one another as O'Donovan Rossa could wish them'.[123]

The liberal *Daily News* was supplied with its Irish copy by the *Freeman's Journal* reporter Andrew Dunlop. Dunlop, a committed Unionist who had once worked for the *Daily Express*, was already living on borrowed time with the *Freeman*. The tone of his *Daily News* despatches had often been criticized by O'Brien in *United Ireland* and by the end of 1884, Edmund Dwyer Gray, under pressure from a number of sources, terminated his staff position.[124] In reporting *Cornwall v O'Brien* for the *Daily News* Andrew Dunlop dealt with the crucial evidence of the three chief witnesses against the GPO Secretary in fewer than 300 words, observing merely that 'they gave evidence in support of the charge made against the plaintiff ... the evidence is unfit for publication'.[125] When it came to Cornwall's actual trial Dunlop referred to, substantially, the same evidence as being 'considerably shaken on cross examination'.[126] The acquittal of Cornwall was reported, briefly, without comment.[127]

Coverage in the crusading Liberal *Pall Mall Gazette* was minimal, especially when seen in the context of some of the campaigns later conducted by its radical editor W.T. Stead. Stead had replaced John Morley as editor in the very week of Healy's initial libel. According to Stead, Ireland was the one subject Morley 'really cared about'.[128] Had Morley not been elected to Parliament, coverage of the 'scandals' might have been more copious and judgmental. Stead reserved his righteous indignation for his celebrated campaigns against child prostitution and the parlous state of the British navy.

Where does the *United Ireland* campaign sit in the context of the journalism of the 1880s? It was not until 1887 that Matthew Arnold, in an article in *Nineteenth Century* drew attention to what he described as 'a new journalism'. Although he disapproved of it, describing it as 'feather-brained', he acknowledged that it was 'full of ability, novelty, variety, sensation, sympathy, generous instincts'.[129] However, the existence of this new strain of journalism predates Arnold's 'discovery' and identification of the phenomenon. The so-called 'new journalism', with its emphasis on news over opinion, its elevation of the personal and its fetishization of the sensational, was well established by the time Arnold assailed its practice and the man he saw as its progenitor, W.T. Stead. Arguably, there was nothing particularly 'new' in the 'new journalism' of the 1880s either. Raymond Williams has maintained in *The Long Revolution* that it was simply a transfer of the ethos of the Sunday paper and of cheap 'penny dreadful' literature into the culture of the daily newspaper.[130] What distinguished it from the Sunday

191

journals was that, often taking its cue from the 'muckraking' tradition of the USA, some of the exponents of the 'new journalism' placed a premium on investigation. Henry Labouchere's *Truth* was a case in point. Labouchere's was the first journal that had a permanent staff of investigative journalists. Its proprietor had the protection of a large personal fortune that allowed *Truth* to withstand even a successful libel action.

In establishment quarters the onset of this 'new journalism' was often greeted with expressions of censorious dismay and overt antagonism. It must be remembered that 'in the early part of the nineteenth century British journalists had been the frequent objects of social opprobrium. Sir Walter Scott had once observed that 'nothing but a thorough-going blackguard ought to attempt the daily press'[131] as a profession. One of the prevailing tropes of the nineteenth century was of the journalist as blackmailer.[132] Proven instances of attempted extortion by newspapermen encouraged the opportune conviction that journalists who wrote for the popular press were a species of professional extortionist.

In the case of O'Brien and *United Ireland* there is much to link the newspaper with the rise of 'new journalism'. Like Stead and Labouchere, O'Brien placed a premium on campaigning and investigation. He saw little distinction between the private and the public, or the personal and the political, when issues of hypocrisy and accountability were involved. But in its bespoke advocacy and scathing partisanship *United Ireland* is closer to what Raymond Williams has dubbed the nineteenth century 'pauper press'. Newspapers of this ilk were radical, served a specific cause and were inherently unprofitable. They were subject to 'continual financial pressure met by persistent voluntary or ill-paid effort, not only by journalists but by collectors and sellers serving a cause rather than a commercial enterprise'.[133] Whatever about its financial position – perfectly sound from the middle of 1882 onwards – the improvisational nature of the entire *United Ireland* enterprise as well as its extreme partisanship reinforced the notion that it was well outside the pale of 'decent' society.

H.G. Cocks has illustrated in his monograph *Nameless Offences: Homosexual Desire in the Nineteenth Century* how the former Chartist, John Frost, attempted in 1856 to ignite a campaign against sexually abusive practices in the penal colony of Van Diemen's Land (Tasmania). He was scorned by the mainstream press who accused him of 'ridiculous pretensions'.

Cocks contends that, in part at least, O'Brien succeeded where Frost had failed because of the 'changed nature of the press and its relationship to investigative reporting'.[134] In addition O'Brien prevailed because of the support he commanded in the House of Commons, the sort of support which Frost lacked in Tasmania. However, he added that the explicit nature of the *United Ireland* charges, not to mention its untrammelled verbatim reportage from the court, meant that 'the similarity of O'Brien's work to the disreputable scandals raised in the lowest newspapers and to the tactics of the extortionist was not lost on the British press'.[135]

The exploitation by Trevelyan of *United Ireland's* employment of Meiklejohn played into the prevailing prejudice of the British establishment. The chief secretary was eager to emphasize the detective's conviction for blackmail. The inference was clear. Should he have failed to make the analogy sufficiently unambiguous Trevelyan added in a House of Commons speech on 17 June 1884 that Bolton's tardiness in bringing an action against *United Ireland* (despite their constant references to him as a convicted fraud and adulterer) was because 'although he was bitterly attacked in *United Ireland*, [he] had not been, attacked in such a manner as to make it absolutely necessary for him either to bring an action or retire from the society of decent mankind'.[136] Once again the inference was clear, *United Ireland* and its editor were outside the realms of 'decent mankind'. After O'Brien's vindication in the Cornwall libel suit Healy turned the tables on the government in the House of Commons by pointing to a letter written by French while on remand 'in which he said, referring to Government officials, that if he took a certain course he would "perhaps see some of them in the dock"'.[137] Healy, also pointedly, referred to government officials as, 'men of tainted character, of loathsome lives, men with whom no one in decent society, or with a shred of self-respect, would be seen'.[138]

Did the episode of the Dublin Castle 'scandals' constitute a co-ordinated effort on the part of the government to drive *United Ireland* into bankruptcy and silence? Was this the continuation of the failed policy of suppression by other means? Alternatively, was the entire episode merely the inevitable attempt by allegedly defamed individuals to defend their reputations when failure to do so would have invited the conclusion that the accusations made against them were genuine? Or was the motivation of the government simply the defence of the reputation of the administration in Ireland with any negative outcome for *United Ireland* an eminently desirable collateral consequence? On the basis of *cui bono* as well as considerable circumstantial evidence, it can reasonably be inferred that the Castle executive, at the very least, was proactively involved in the affair. It is more difficult to establish a pattern of specific and directed intervention that calculatedly exploited the three libel actions.

In the case of French it appears to have been the intervention of the authorities alone that prompted him to tiptoe reluctantly towards his own defence. With Cornwall the issue is less clear. Like French he could have taken action before he did. But his claim that it was only when O'Brien implicated him in the scandal during a House of Commons debate that he was forced to respond is given considerable credence by the timing of his writ. The question must be asked of the Dublin Castle affair, whether the government would have put much faith in French and Bolton as agents in a concerted attempt to suppress *United Ireland*. The latter sued and won his case on a technicality. Given his own reputation for chicanery and fraud, not even a Belfast unionist jury was prepared to take the opportunity to silence a profoundly irritating and effective nationalist Cassandra by awarding Bolton crippling damages against *United Ireland*. It is somewhat ironic that the individual who, at the outset, enjoyed the worst public reputation of the three, should have been the only one who caused any injury whatever to O'Brien.

French clearly had no stomach for the fight and had long been the subject of the kind of rumours that would have rendered it unlikely his employers would repose much confidence in his capacity to refute the allegations of the newspaper. However, it would be unsafe to assume that governmental knowledge of the guilt of French (acquired via the investigations of Bruce) constituted a disincentive to proceed with the director of detectives as a viable agent of the ruin of *United Ireland*. A cynical interpretation of what transpired is that the Castle administration would have (erroneously) assumed that the only evidence against French came from within the ranks of the RIC. Once *United Ireland* entered the fray that evidence evaporated. Having pleaded justification *United Ireland* would have to prove its case. The newspaper discovered, unsurprisingly, that RIC constables who were prepared to testify against French at an internal disciplinary hearing would withhold that evidence if it served to facilitate the case of the leading nationalist tribune.

Cornwall, on the other hand, was a far more credible candidate to spearhead the kind of Castle-inspired campaign of suppression alleged by O'Brien. He was, on the face of it, a more formidable opponent for *United Ireland* than French. There does not appear to have been any widespread knowledge of his sexual activities. His action progressed rapidly. The time that elapsed between the serving of the writ and the trial itself was a mere two months. In the defence of his reputation, and perhaps in the pursuit of a desired governmental objective, he was prepared to make a robust case before the Queen's Bench court. Even O'Brien acknowledged that he made a redoubtable and credible witness. *United Ireland* described how he 'delivered his answers with a majesty that seemed to fascinate the Court ... he left the witness-chair without a break in the superb chain of his perjuries'.[139]

It was O'Brien's thesis in *Evening Memories* that 'the verdict in the Cornwall case broke the neck of the Coercion Act of 1882–5'.[140] This assertion is repeated by his earliest biographer, Michael MacDonagh.[141] In neither instance is any attempt made to substantiate such a bold claim, and it has been dismissed by Frank Callanan as untenable.[142] If it was made in the context of the resignation of Trevelyan (to whom O'Brien makes amends in *Evening Memories*),[143] then it is exaggerated. Trevelyan's departure was prompted by a veritable *tsunami* of personal abuse and not just the relentless waves of adverse commentary inspired by the Castle 'scandals'.

However, O'Brien may have been referring to a destabilization of procedure rather than to any weakening of will on the part of the government in the prosecution of subsequent cases under the Crimes Act. The nature of the indictment of Cornwall had unforeseen consequences for the administration and the partiality shown towards the accused gives credence to O'Brien's conviction that the three libel actions were tactical elements in the Castle's overweening strategy designed to overcome *United Ireland* once and for all. Cornwall faced charges of buggery and felony after the evidence adduced against him in the libel trial by Taylor, McKernan and Johnston. He was acquitted of the former charge and then faced the felony charge in late October 1884, along with Martin Kirwan (see above). Once again he was acquitted. However, *United Ireland* pointedly asked why he had not been charged with the more easily proven crime of conspiracy. O'Brien alleged, in the issue of 3 November 1884, that the felony charge had been levied by the prosecution because the Crown was aware that it had insufficient evidence to make such a charge stick. The suggestion was that Cornwall had been rewarded for the stand he had taken against *United Ireland* by the entering of a feeble indictment against him.

The corollary of the Cornwall judgment emerged in early November at the Green Street commission court in the trial of the leading Fenian Patrick Neville Fitzgerald; he was being tried for his part in the so-called 'Tubbercurry conspiracy'. He was alleged, by two informers, to have been a Fenian recruiter. In its 15 November issue *United Ireland* reported his acquittal, and alleged that in its efforts to facilitate the release of Cornwall, the Crown had inadvertently guaranteed the liberty of Fitzgerald. Because the government was being closely monitored in the Cornwall case, according to O'Brien, it had felt obliged to try Fitzgerald on a charge of treason–felony rather than conspiracy. Furthermore its efforts to undermine the evidence of 'approvers' (Taylor, McKernan and Johnston) in the Cornwall/Kirwan case fatally (and permanently) weakened its own case against Fitzgerald, based as it was on approver evidence. 'It was their own adroit arrangements for shielding Cornwall and French from justice that ensured the acquittal of Fitzgerald', exulted O'Brien. He also obligingly pointed out that 'when the Crown were making their elaborate arrangements for safeguarding the Unspeakables, we warned them that they were creating precedents which would yet turn to their own confusion and destruction'.[144] In that sense the *United Ireland* campaign against the 'Unspeakables' might have had collateral benefits and the Castle campaign to silence the newspaper might well have resulted in unexpectedly detrimental consequences. O'Brien's thesis was that the seeds sown in the Cornwall indictment, and reaped in the Fitzgerald case, negated the effectiveness of the Crimes Act. However, it is just as likely that a decline in violent agrarian crime led to a reduction in the prosecution of treason–felony cases and a reduced need for the use of informer and 'approver' testimony.

There is no documentary proof confirming the existence of a co-ordinated government strategy to rid itself of *United Ireland* through the agency of three high-profile libel cases potentially ruinous to the Parnellite newspaper. Neither O'Brien's absolute conviction, nor the moral certainty of his nationalist contemporaries, constitutes evidence of such a conspiracy against the Castle. Clearly all three plaintiffs benefitted from the 'neutrality' of the Castle and were facilitated by the authorities in a variety of ways: but not in any illicit or unprecedented fashion. Neither can we assume, solely on the basis of *cui bono*, that such an activist strategy ever existed. But had French not faltered, had Cornwall prevailed, or had Bolton managed to extract a greater sum in damages from *United Ireland*, there would have been a silent beneficiary whose interests would have been well served by an outcome which its own policies had been unable to effect.

Towards a new Crimes Act

The 1881–2 period was one of frenetic actvity on both sides of the political–agrarian divide. In contrast, the 1883–4 period was one of relative stasis. The Land League was proscribed; the National League was slowly establishing a foothold; the land courts offered a potential solution to the rent issue; 'outrage' was on the decline; work was being done in the background on issues like arrears; and the first rumblings of Irish local government reform were being detected coming from the direction of Birmingham, as Joseph Chamberlain sought to enter the lists. The under secretary, Hamilton, was able to write to Lord Spencer, in November 1884 that 'the outrages are fewer in number at the present moment and of a mere trifling character than they have been since 1882'.[145]

The Land Commission was dealing with the grievances of tenants-at-will and the Crimes Act, in a markedly different fashion, with the effects of the grievances of landless labourers and disgruntled leaseholders. With electoral reform a priority for the Gladstone administration Ireland was no longer centre stage at Westminster. Not that a perusal of the pages of *United Ireland* during this period would have suggested quiescence or tranquility. Reading the newspaper during this time of relative lethargy one gets a sense of perpetual motion and excitement that was hardly a reflection of political reality. The campaigning journalism of O'Brien in *United Ireland* served a vital purpose. At a time of consolidation and transition it created an illusion of incessant activism. Often, however, the 'activity' was self-generated. The causes were frequently those of O'Brien himself, with *United Ireland*, rather than the House of Commons, as the platform through which to advance them. As his biographer, Joseph V. O'Brien, has remarked, 'the most aggressive face presented to British rule was O'Brien's long journalistic harangue against jury-packing and malpractice by Dublin Castle officials'.[146]

The highly personalized attacks on Spencer and Trevelyan clearly impacted on the members of the executive individually and collectively. This is clear from a series of memoranda circulated on a confidential basis in 1885, in the aftermath of the Cornwall/French controversies. It is also apparent from correspondence between members of the Dublin Castle executive through much of 1884.

The anathemization of *United Ireland* began with the lord lieutenant, but even Spencer's abhorrence of O'Brien's newspaper was tinged with an awareness of the necessity for caution. In August 1884, with the Irish party and the Tories in the throes of what Harcourt referred to as 'the Maamtrasna alliance', and with O'Brien fulminating against sodomy in high places on a weekly basis, Spencer wrote to Gladstone:

> I anticipate constant attacks upon the administration of the Law from the Parliamentary Party and the Class of O'Brien … attempts have been made to throw discredit on the Crown officials. This we must patiently meet but it will be a trying ordeal. "The United Ireland" [*sic*] is violent & abusive beyond all precedent. It heaps the grossest abuse on the Irish Executive & does immense harm. It is however impolitic (at all events at present) to touch it. [147]

Spencer permitted himself to hope that, as a result of the various libel cases in which *United Ireland* was engaged, that 'O'Brien … may disappear without our intervention.' But he was concerned about the effect of O'Brien's campaigning on Liberal opinion in Britain and he expected even more attacks as the renewal of the Crimes Act approached.

One particularly demoralizing result of the constant bombardment in the House of Commons and the nationalist press was the resignation of Trevelyan as chief secretary. Spencer had warned the Prime Minister of the rapid deterioration in Trevelyan's morale in mid-September, 1884:

> I have slowly come to the conclusion that in the public interest
> it is most desirable that Trevelyan should be relieved. He did
> admirably till the worry of Irish affairs in & out of the House
> of Commons affected his health and nerves ... he has become
> irritable at times to an excessive degree, though this phase
> passes away rapidly. While it is on him he may commit some
> grave error.[148]

With the 1882 Crimes act due for renewal in the middle of 1885, the Executive
bent its collective mind to improvement, amendment or replacement of
the waning coercion legislation. In a March memo Spencer analysed the
weaknesses and shortcomings of the regime. While acknowledging that 'the
condition of Ireland has greatly improved since 1882', he insisted 'it would
not be safe' to continue with no coercive legislation in place.[149]

Spencer, in a brief survey of 'the condition of the country', bemoaned
the inadequacy of the government's propaganda response to the narrative
promulgated by the National League: 'No antidote in the shape of counter-
meetings or opposing newspapers is found in any part of the south or west
of Ireland.' He went on to advocate a scaled-back Crimes act that would be
made applicable, as elements of permanent statute law, to the entire United
Kingdom. He admitted that 'I see great obstacles in this course, but it would
remove the reproach with all its attendant difficulties which exceptional
legislation brings on Ireland, without interfering with the liberty of the law-
abiding subject in England.'[150] Gladstone, despite the certainty of Radical
opposition, sought the advice of distinguished counsel Sir Henry James on
the practicalities of extending Irish coercion legislation to English statute
law. James studied the 1882 act and responded that 'substantially none of
the clauses ... can be properly made applicable to England in our opinion
... and a considerable number of Radicals would most determinedly oppose
any application of the clauses contained in the Irish Act to England.'[151]

Spencer's memo included an item by item assessment of the efficacy of
the act since its passage. This accepted, for example, that the clause providing
for non-jury trials of felonies had never been put into force and could be
dropped.[152] His evaluation of the press clause of the Crimes act, section 13,
was similarly downbeat:

> Except for American papers this has been of no use. For before
> an Irish paper can be seized its contents have to be considered
> and submitted to the law officers. While this is going on the
> paper is being circulated. If then seized the effect is not good.[153]

Spencer recommended that the section be dropped, 'as it is practically
useless'. He went on to suggest that there was a growing body of opinion
among law officers in England and Ireland that 'under the common law
papers containing treasonable matter or incitement to crime can be seized'.
However, he introduced two significant caveats. Such a procedure would
undoubtedly lead to a court action for recovery of the confiscated papers;
and no binding legal decision had ever issued from a court to that effect. It
was the lord lieutenant's view that 'to be relying on a power never judicially
established is an unsatisfactory course'.[154]

Spencer's definitive proposal, one previously advocated by the Irish law
officers at the time of the framing of the 1882 legislation, was to return to a
more effective and punitive press clause like that contained in the 1870 Peace
Preservation Act. The primary purpose was to constrain newspapers like
United Ireland. The assessment of their power and potential for fomenting
extreme disorder, even in the context of a period of relative inactivity, was
stark:

> Papers of the class of *United Ireland* operate in reality as a
> constant and powerful incentive to treason and violence in
> their worst forms ... The result of allowing these writings to go
> on unchecked will be gradually to bring the peasantry of large
> districts and the humbler classes in large towns into a frame
> of mind which will prepare them for any step, possibly to the
> extent of a rising.[155]

Spencer, long a victim of some of the more excessive vitriol emanating from
United Ireland, concluded with an evaluation that would be rejected by
the later Conservative administration of Arthur Balfour: 'Prosecuting the
editor, who, if arrested, gets a slight punishment, and whom it may be most
difficult to convict, is useless to check the evil, and will only aggravate it.'

The lord lieutenant was supported in Cabinet by the home secretary; however, Harcourt had already indicated to Spencer that he was unlikely to achieve a restoration of the more penal press clauses of the 1870 legislation. The lord lieutenant, in a letter to Harcourt in January 1885, had described Irish nationalist newspapers as 'a growing and increasing evil which if it is not checked will present us with nothing but discontent in Ireland'.[156] Harcourt's response was discouraging. The home secretary replied 'as to the press clauses I fear it is too late for you to ask for them now'.[157]

Spencer's appraisal of the press clause of the Crimes Act did not meet with much dissent from his advisers. Campbell Bannerman, the new chief secretary, was scathing in his estimation of the capacity of Irish juries to chastise newspaper editors. 'At present the government is paralysed in the presence of most noxious and scandalous publications, because any step taken would lead in one way or other to a jury trial.'[158] He sought summary powers as an alternative but despaired of getting any such legislation through the House of Commons.

The lord chancellor, Sir Edward Sullivan, agreed with 'cutting and pasting' the press section of the 1870 legislation. His assessment shows evidence of the scars from the barrage maintained by *United Ireland* over the previous twelve months:

> This press from week to week teems with the most atrocious and unfounded libels on the Irish Viceroy and his government, abounds in treasonable and seditious writing, but so carefully addressed to the law that a prosecution for treason–felony could scarcely be sustained. The productions of this dire press are extensively read though the provinces, and as there is no counteracting influence of any kind, they are, as a rule, believed by the lower orders of the people. Thus utter demoralization ensues, absolute treason is veiled under Home Rule, and the most determined attacks upon the maintenance of British law in Ireland are covered by the most horrible assaults upon the Viceregal authority.

Sullivan, much as would Balfour in the 1887 Crimes Act, called for the use of summary powers to deal with the nationalist press. He concluded with sentiments that would have been worthy of anything emanating from the subsequent battle waged by the Tories against the same opposition:

> I am certain that this dreadful press only exists by reason
> of its being allowed, and that apart from the fanaticism and
> wickedness by which it is conducted, it has no real support.
> I am sure that a vigorous and sustained effort under the law
> would destroy it.[159]

It is difficult to discern in the philosophy of Spencer in early 1885 the
steadfast supporter of Home Rule who would emerge in 1886. In their
assessment of his handling of the May 1882 crisis, A.B. Cooke and J.R.
Vincent have written of Spencer: 'His response to the crisis itself, and his
wise and temperate handling of events that followed, transformed him
from a loyal, almost unnoticed servant of his party into an embodiment of
traditional English patriotism.'[160]

In the longer term his dealings with Ireland – and those must have been
influenced in some fashion by his often outrageous treatment in the pages of
the nationalist press – transformed him into an unlikely proponent of Irish
devolution.

On this Damascene highway he was joined by an equally unlikely
fellow-traveller in Edward Jenkinson. The assistant under-secretary, whose
main responsibility was the curbing of political criminality, compiled a
fascinating report for his Liberal masters on the state of the country in 1885.
Avowedly an assessment of secret societies in Ireland and America it was,
essentially, a lengthy manifesto for Home Rule written many months before
the 'conversion' of Gladstone to the concept. Jenkinson's dossier bemoaned
the missed opportunity of 1883, 'when we were strong and had repressed all
outrage in Ireland' and accepted that repression was no longer an option. The
people of England would not for long consent to see Ireland ruled under a
despotic form of Government. Jenkinson was critical of government policy
on two principal counts, its inherent dishonesty and its failure to grapple
successfully with a militant nationalist press:

> It had the pretence of being a constitutional government, but we
> only kept the country in order by suspending the Constitution;
> and we were not honest, because, while we set our face against
> Home Rule, we gave free licence to the press, and allowed it to
> vilify and abuse our administration and to educate the people

to believe that Ireland never can be prosperous except it has a Parliament of its own.[161]

The Liberals, of course, never managed to introduce an alternative to their 1882 Crimes act. By the middle of 1885 they were out of office and by early 1886 when they returned to power, devolution rather than coercion was on Gladstone's agenda. However, in their consistent espousal of the corrective terms of the 1870 Prevention of Crime act (a piece of legislation whose press clauses were never actually strictly enforced) the Irish executive was clearly prepared to go to similar lengths as would their Tory counterparts during the approaching Salisbury/Balfour regime. That they would countenance such measures, without the egregious provocation of the Plan of Campaign with which to contend, is testimony to the impact of the cascade of abuse heaped on their heads by O'Brien's campaign of 'othering'.

Notes

1   *United Ireland*, 9 August 1884.

2   Samuel Lee Anderson to attorney general, 5 May 1883, NAI, CSORP, 1883/10982.

3   Samuel Lee Anderson to solicitor general, 5 May 1883, NAI, CSORP, 1883–13493 (as cited in Chapter 4. Naish suggested a *United Ireland* article, 'The Kept Court' was seditious. The attorney general agreed but 'doubted the prudence of a prosecution').

4   Samuel Lee Anderson to Solicitor General, 5 May, 1883, NAI, CSORP, 1883–13493.

5   Timothy Harrington, *The Maamtrasna Massacre: the Impeachment of the Trials* (Dublin, 1884). Summarized in Dungan, *Conspiracy*, 127–70. See also chapter 4 of this work.

6   *United Ireland*, 10 February 1883.

7   The *United Ireland* article appeared before Timothy Harrington exposed the trial testimonies of two informers and three witnesses as, at best, suspect. In the Maamtrasna case Harrington would allege that Bolton had been involved in a conspiracy to secure a tainted verdict against Myles Joyce.

8   *United Ireland*, 10 February 1883.

9   *United Ireland*, 28 April 1883.

10   Callanan, *T.M. Healy*, 89.

11   *United Ireland*, 25 August 1883.

12   *United Ireland*, 25 August 1883. In his autobiography, *Letters and Leaders of My Day*, Healy takes no responsibility whatever for the piece, merely commenting that, 'Important persons were accused by *United Ireland* of offences which cannot be specified' (Healy,

Letters and Leaders of My Day, 195).

13 HC Deb. 7 July 1884, vol. 290, cc228–9. 'Mr. Healy gave Notice that he would move the reduction of the Estimates by the sum of £436 11s. 4d., paid by Her Majesty's Government for the last 15 years to a man who fled from the country for an unnatural offence.'

14 *United Ireland*, 3 November 1884.

15 Callanan, *Healy*, 89.

16 O'Brien, *Evening Memories*, 18.

17 O'Brien, *Evening Memories*, 19.

18 Callanan, *Healy*, 90. Callanan adds that the episode ruined Murphy's career. He was transferred to Charleville, then Nenagh, then dismissed. He blamed Healy and O'Brien for his misfortune and, in the wake of the ongoing Liberal alliance attacked them as 'lickspittles' in a privately published pamphlet in 1894.

19 *United Ireland*, 13 October 1883.

20 *United Ireland*, 20 October 1883.

21 Whose support for Home Rule seems to have ended after his defeat in the Ennis by-election of 1879 by Lysaght Finigan.

22 *United Ireland*, 9 November 1883.

23 *United Ireland*, 9 November 1883.

24 *United Ireland*, 1 December 1883.

25 *United Ireland*, 1 December 1883.

26 *United Ireland*, 7 June 1884. HC Deb. 17 June 1884, vol. 289, c691.

27 HC Deb. 12 May 1884, vol. 288, cc13–14.

28 HC Deb. 17 June 1884, vol. 289, c696.

29 O'Brien, *Evening Memories*, 19.

30 O'Brien, *Evening Memories*, 19.

31 Sophie O'Brien to Mrs A.W. Bromage, 7 March 1952, O'Brien papers, NLI, MS 5924.

32 O'Brien, *Evening Memories*, 19.

33 O'Brien, *Evening Memories*, 20.

34 *Freeman's Journal*, 16 February 1900.

35 O'Brien, *Evening Memories*, 20.

36 H. Montgomery Hyde, *The Other Love: an Historical and Contemporary Survey of Homosexuality in Britain* (London, 1972), 147.

37 HC Deb. 17 June 1884, vol. 289, c695.

38 Chance and Miley, Solrs, letter to editor of *United Ireland*, 28 June 1884.

39   HC Deb. 17 June 1884, vol. 289, c700.

40   Memo from Col. Bruce in response to inquiry from T. Browning, Irish Office, made in preparation for a Parliamentary Question of O'Brien, 9 May 1884. NAI, CSORP, 1884/24345. In his book on William Henry Joyce, *The Prime Informer: A Suppressed Scandal* (London, 1971), Leon O'Broin alleges that Bruce 'was drinking so hard and so continually that he was quite unable to exercise any control whatsoever' (O'Broin, *The Prime Informer*, 26).

41   H. Montgomery Hyde puts his reluctance to proceed down to 'serious financial difficulties through speculation in real estate' (Montgomery Hyde, *The other love*, 148).

42   HC Deb. 17 June 1884, vol. 289, c703. Speech of Trevelyan on motion of Arthur O'Connor seconded by William O'Brien.

43   HC Deb. 17 June 1884, vol. 289, c703.

44   *United Ireland*, 9 August 1884.

45   *United Ireland*, 10 May 1884.

46   *United Ireland*, 24 May 1884.

47   O'Brien, *Evening Memories*, 24–5.

48   Hugh Fraser, *Principles and Practice of the Law of Libel and Slander*, 82.

49   *United Ireland*, 24 May 1884.

50   A misdemeanor punishable by fine or imprisonment where the words used tended to provoke a breach of the peace. The most common form of criminal libel during this period was seditious libel (more so than blasphemy or obscenity) though a defamatory publication could be the subject of criminal proceedings – Fraser – *Principles and Practice of the Law of Libel and Slander*, p183–4.

51   Callanan, *Healy*, 90.

52   The previous week O'Brien had barely survived a similar motion from Cornwall who complained of material published by *United Ireland* subsequent to his own writ.

53   *United Ireland*, 7 June 1884.

54   *United Ireland*, 21 June 1884. Lawson also suggested that O'Brien was 'as safe in Belfast as in Church – that is if he were ever in a church' (laughter).

55   *United Ireland*, 28 June 1884.

56   *United Ireland*, 21 June 1884.

57   O'Brien, *Evening Memories*, 25.

58   O'Brien, *Evening Memories*, 23.

59   *The Nation*, 12 July 1884.

60   *Freeman's Journal*, 8 July 1884.

61   O'Brien, *Evening Memories*, 28

62 O'Brien, *Evening Memories*, 30–1.

63 O'Brien, *Evening Memories*, 31

64 *Freeman's Journal*, 8 July 1884.

65 *Freeman's Journal*, 8 July 1884.

66 *Freeman's Journal*, 8 July 1884.

67 A search among the 'Officers of government and public departments' in Thom's directories from 1882–6 reveals only one 'Boyle' entered in 1882 whose entry has been deleted in 1884. He is Major E. Boyle, Gentleman Usher of the lord lieutenant's household. However, the search itself is based on an assumption that the 'Boyle' in question was another public servant and the correspondence is quite specific that the fugitive in question was a civilian.

68 Spencer to Sullivan, 17 July 1884, Althorp papers, BL, Add. Mss. 76975, f.27.

69 Sullivan to Spencer, 18 July 1884, Althorp papers, BL, Add. Mss. 76975, f.28.

70 'Boyle' is not identified but in a lengthy discourse on the entire affair the unionist journalist Michael J.F. McCarthy refers to a number of unnamed individuals who fled the country to avoid prosecution. 'Boyle' may well have been amongst them: 'Men of various trades and professions were implicated in the riot of infamy: a Protestant stockbroker who escaped from the country ; a young Protestant merchant who likewise fled. The stockbroker, after reading "United Ireland", asked his partner's advice. "If you are innocent," was the answer, "stand your ground; if you are guilty, fly!" A well-connected young priest also disappeared and his place knew him no more' (McCarthy, *The Irish Revolution*, 360).

71 *The Nation*, 12 July 1884.

72 He had taken over the running of the paper in 1876 when his brother A.M. Sullivan moved to England to pursue a distinguished career at the Bar (Dictionary of Irish Biography, Cambridge, 2009) http://dib.cambridge.org/viewReadPage.do?articleId=a8386 (21 September 2013).

73 T.D. Sullivan, *Recollections of Troubled Times in Irish Politics* (Dublin, 1905), 75.

74 *The Nation*, 12 July 1884.

75 *United Ireland*, 12 July 1884.

76 Cornwall was, bizarrely, tried under the Crimes Act. This allowed for the selection of a special jury, the composition of which was alleged by *United Ireland* to favour the defendant. The main witness against him had been rejected as unreliable by *United Ireland* in the civil case. It was this acquittal that led, in part, to the formulation by Henry Labouchere in 1885, of an amendment to the Criminal Law Act that made acts of 'gross indecency' between males, punishable by up to two years in jail.

77 *United Ireland*, 13 December 1884.

78 Healy, *Letters and Leaders*, vol. 1, 195.

79 *United Ireland*, 9 August 1884.

80 O'Brien, *Evening Memories*, 33.

81 O'Broin, Leon, *The Prime Informer: A Suppressed Scandal* (London, 1971), 50.

82 *United Ireland*, 9 August 1884.

83 HC Deb. 21 July 1884, vol. 290, c1804. 'They knew if they inquired further, and in earnest, they would come upon most horrible disclosures, and with the knowledge and in the belief that he (Mr. O'Brien) must almost inevitably fail where they could easily have succeeded, they stood neutral.'

84 HC Deb. 21 July 1884, vol. 290, c1807.

85 Trevelyan put the date of the inquiry at 5/6 September. Bruce mentioned 7 September (NAI, CSORP, 1884/24345). Both dates contradict O'Brien's claims that the investigation of French had already begun before the 25 August Healy libel.

86 HC Deb. 21 July 1884, vol. 290, c1814.

87 HC Deb. 21 July 1884, vol. 290, c.1816.

88 Callanan, *Healy*, 91.

89 23 May 1889, *Special Commission*, vol. 8, 190, 71924-6.

90 *United Ireland*, 30 August 1884.

91 *United Ireland*, 1 March 1884.

92 Sullivan to Spencer, 7 March 1884, Althorp papers, BL, Add. Mss. 76975. No folio number indicated.

93 Sullivan to Spencer, 7 March 1884, Althorp papers, BL, Add. Mss. 76975. No folio number indicated.

94 Spencer to Sullivan, 15 July 1884, Althorp papers, BL, Add. Mss. 76975, f.23.

95 Sullivan to Spencer, undated but clearly 16 July 1884, Althorp papers, Add. Mss. 76975, f.25.

96 Spencer to Sullivan, 17 July 1884, Althorp papers, BL, Add. Mss. 76975, f.27.

97 Sullivan to Spencer, 18 July 1884, Althorp papers, BL, Add. Mss. 76975, f.28. Sullivan to Spencer, 9 September 1884, Althorp papers, BL, Add. Mss. 76975. f.37.

98 *United Ireland*, 22 November 1884.

99 Hamilton to Spencer, 20 November 1884, Althorp papers, BL, Add. Mss. 77060, f.143.

100 J.H. Davies to Courtney Boyle, 22 November 1884, Althorp papers, BL, Add. Mss. 77060, f.145.

101 Spencer to Hamilton, 21 November 1884, Althorp papers, BL, Add. Mss. 77060, f.144.

102 Hamilton to Spencer, 25 November, Althorp papers, BL, Add. Mss. 77060, f.156.

103 Hamilton to Spencer, 23 November 1884, Althorp papers, BL, Add. Mss. 77060, f.146.

104 *Freeman's Journal,* 16 February 1900.

105 *United Ireland*, 9 August 1884.

106 *United Ireland*, 12 July 1884.

107 *United Ireland*, 19 July 1884. Thaddeus C. Breen, 'Loathsome, impure and revolting crimes: the Dublin Scandals of 1884', *Identity*, no. 2, July 1982, 9.

108 Brian Lacey, *Terrible Queer Creatures: Homosexuality in Irish History* (Dublin, 2008), 144.

109 *Freeman's Journal*, 8 July 1884.

110 *Dublin Evening Mail*, 8 July 1884.

111 *United Ireland*, 12 July 1884.

112 *United Ireland*, 23 August 1884.

113 Thaddeus C. Breen, 'Loathsome, impure and revolting crimes: the Dublin Scandals of 1884', *Identity*, no. 2, July 1982, 9.

114 O'Brien, *Evening Memories*, 21. O'Brien's hostility towards homosexuality was, of course, very much of its time and, no doubt, his expressions of revulsion had a moral as well as a tactical basis. However, it must be pointed out that his zeal might also have emanated from the denial of latent homosexual inclinations of his own. Among the papers of the assistant secretary of the Land League, P.J. Quinn, are two letters sent by O'Brien to the young Quinn, in 1882. Quinn had been imprisoned in Kilmainham along with O'Brien before being moved to Enniskillen. Both, as O'Brien's biographer Sally Warwick-Haller comments, read like love letters, notwithstanding the more florid epistolary style of the period. In the second note O'Brien wrote 'I cannot tell you how delightful your expressions of affection were to me. Believe me you did not read my note oftener than I did yours or devour it with more eagerness. If you had been a pretty girl murmuring out her love, it would not have been more pleasant than to discover how thoroughly we are united in affection.' Later O'Brien upbraids himself for 'falling into a passionate love-letter style' (O'Brien to Quinn, undated, 1882, NLI, MS 5930, ff.117–19. Warwick-Haller, *O'Brien*, 57).

115 Though Healy writes in his autobiography that he was told by the radical MP Joseph Cowen (himself a newspaper proprietor) that 'the verdict for O'Brien shook the Cabinet more than any previous event' (Healy, *Letters and Leaders*, 195).

116 *Times*, 5 July 1884.

117 *Times*, 12 July 1884.

118 *Times*, 16 July 1884.

119 *Times*, 31 July, 1 August, 4 August 1884.

120 *Times*, 7 August 1884.

121 *Times*, 8 August 1884.

122 *United Ireland*, 12 July 1884.

123 *United Ireland*, 13 September 1884.

124 Dunlop, Andrew, *Fifty Years of Irish Journalism* (Dublin, 1911), 251. Dunlop was retained as a casual employee throughout 1885 but sustained pressure resulted in his services being dispensed with entirely by the *Freeman* at the end of that year. In 1886 he moved to the more politically convivial surroundings of the *Irish Times*.

125 *Daily News*, 5 July 1884.

126 *Daily News*, 29 October 1884.

127 *Daily News*, 30 October 1884.

128 Frederic Whyte, *The Life of W.T. Stead* (London/New York, 1925), 2 vols, vol. 1, 82.

129 Matthew Arnold, 'Up to Easter', *Nineteenth Century* XXI (May 1887), 638.

130 Williams, *The Long Revolution*, 218–19.

131 Quoted in Mark Hampton, 'Journalists and the "Professional Ideal" in Britain: the Institute of Journalists, 1884–1907', *Historical Research*, vol. 72, no. 178 (June 1999), 183.

132 Ibid.

133 Williams, *The Long Revolution*, 210.

134 H.G. Cocks, *Nameless Offences: Homosexual Desire in the Nineteenth Century* (London, 2003), 139

135 Cocks, *Nameless Offences*, 142.

136 HC Deb. 17 June 1884, vol. 289, c697.

137 HC Deb. 04 November 1884, vol. 293, c915.

138 HC Deb. 04 November 1884, vol. 293, c917.

139 O'Brien, *Evening Memories*, 28–9.

140 O'Brien, *Evening Memories*, 33.

141 MacDonagh, *The Life of William O'Brien*, 80.

142 Callanan, *Healy*, 91. He refers to the claim as 'a considerable overstatement'.

143 O'Brien, *Evening Memories*, 19.

144 *United Ireland*, 15 November 1884.

145 Hamilton to Spencer, 20 November 1884, Althorp papers, BL, Add. Mss. 77060, f.143.

146 Joseph O'Brien, *William O'Brien and the Course of Irish Politics*, 25.

147 Spencer to Gladstone, 26 August 1884, Althorp papers, BL, Add. Mss. 76860, f.345.

148 Spencer to Gladstone, 20 September 1884, Althorp papers, BL, Add. Mss. 76860, f.354

149 Spencer memo, 23 March 1885, TNA, PRO, CAB 37/14, no. 19, 1.

150 Spencer memo, 23 March 1885, TNA, PRO, CAB 37/14, no. 19, 2.

151 Sir Henry James to Gladstone, 11 May 1885, Gladstone papers, BL,Add Mss 44219 ff.175–6. James was aided in his deliberations by the solicitor general.

152 Spencer memo, 23 March 1885, TNA, PRO, CAB 37/14, 1885, no. 20, 1.

153 Spencer memo, 23 March 1885, TNA, PRO, CAB 37/14, 1885, no. 20, 2–3.

154 Spencer memo, 23 March 1885, TNA, PRO, CAB 37/14, 1885, no. 20, 3.

155 Spencer memo, 23 March 1885, TNA, PRO, CAB 37/14, 1885, no. 20, 3.

156 Spencer to Harcourt, 19 January 1885, Althorp papers, BL, Add.Mss. 76933, f.207.

157 Harcourt to Spencer, 25 January 1885, Althorp papers, BL, Add.Mss. 76933, f.208.

158 Campbell Bannerman memo, 26 March 1885, TNA, PRO, CAB 37/14, 1885, no. 21, 1.

159 Edward Sullivan memo, 31 March 1885, TNA, PRO, CAB 37/14, 1885, no. 21, 3.

160 A.B. Cooke and J.R. Vincent, 'Lord Spencer on the Phoenix Park murders', *Irish Historical Studies*, vol. 18, no. 72 (September, 1973), 584.

161 TNA, PRO, CAB 37/23 1889, no. 13, Memo, Secret Societies in Ireland and America, April 1889. This reproduction of the memo, by the Balfour administration in Ireland, rather bizarrely and unnecessarily, reproduces all of Jenkinson's apologia for Home Rule.

CHAPTER SIX

Sisyphus Agonistes: Balfour, the Tories and the Limits of Censorship, 1886–1887

'There was no possible course open to the Irish Executive but to prosecute and punish those editors and proprietors of newspapers who disgraced the press by allowing their journals to become the organ and engine of a criminal conspiracy of the meanest and most cruel description.'[1]

    (*Press prosecutions in Ireland in the year 1889*, printed for the attention of the Cabinet)

'Life would not be worth living for a newspaper man if he were to make himself responsible for everything which is quoted in a paper as a matter of news.'[2]

    (William O'Brien, evidence before *Times* commission)

Prioritizing silence

The return to power of the Conservative party with a comfortable overall majority in the aftermath of the 'Home Rule' election of July 1886[3] removed the contentious issue of legislative devolution for Ireland from the parliamentary agenda. It also effectively ended the polemical 'truce' that had brought about a major modification of the anti-government rhetoric of newspapers like *United Ireland*. From early 1886, when it became clear that Gladstone intended to introduce a measure of Home Rule, O'Brien's newspaper had toned down its criticisms of the Liberal administration and increased the frequency of its positive coverage.[4] Gladstone progressed from being 'a shuffler as well as a tyrant'[5] to the status of 'Colossus'.[6]

Between 1887 and 1891, coinciding with the tenure as chief secretary of Arthur James Balfour, editorials relating to Home Rule, never particularly frequent up to that point, virtually disappeared from the pages of *United Ireland*. The only context in which the subject was raised was that of the oft-touted imminent collapse of the Salisbury administration, or the spate of by-election victories of what *United Ireland* described as 'Home Rule candidates' (Gladstonian Liberals) between 1888 and 1890. This 'flowing tide', to use Gladstone's own phrase, presented the Irish party with a dilemma. Where was the balance to be struck between catering to an increasingly restive rural population as the spectre of agricultural depression returned, and ensuring that an activist agrarian policy – vital to maintain the National League and the Irish Party's status at home and in the USA – did not embarrass and discommode the Grand Old Man and his party? This was especially so at a time when falling agricultural prices were putting even the judicially arbitrated rents of the 1881 Land Act beyond the reach of many tenants. As Conor Cruise O'Brien has remarked, 'the old question had to be answered in a new and unfamiliar political context: a context of alliance with an English party and respect for English public opinion'.[7] What was also added was a further novelty, in the form of frequent appeals to that same public opinion.

The 'indoor' and 'outdoor' strategy that was adopted by the League (insofar as it actually was a strategy) was relatively successful in dealing with both exigencies. However, it also managed to antagonize a Tory government that had resiled from the (largely chimerical) days of the Carnarvon ministry and the 'Maamtrasna alliance'. Coming to terms with the Irish nationalist press became central to Conservative policy under Salisbury. However, the Tories reversed the Liberal dynamic. While the strategy of dealing in a punitive fashion with the Irish press may have been a primary concern, the tactics were to take aim at the periphery. Hence the propensity to impeach local rather than national newspaper editors, like O'Brien. The Liberals, to whom the exercise of control of the Irish nationalist press had been more peripheral, had focused their attention on the 'centre', as exemplified by their struggle with *United Ireland*.

The Conservative administration found itself, between 1886 and 1891, dealing with a somewhat more disjointed and highly localized variation of the agrarian opposition endured by their Liberal predecessors in the first half of the decade. Salisbury's government was required to put out numerous small fires rather than deal with a national conflagration similar to the Land War. Their principal opposition was based in the perennially troublesome counties of Kerry and Clare and on the scattered estates of the Plan of Campaign. During the tenure of Arthur Balfour the government afforded itself the luxury of largely ignoring the 'centre' after an initial and barely successful foray against the *Nation*, and an inconclusive joust with *United Ireland*. Thus, while Balfour saw the struggle with the nationalist press as an integral part of his containment policy, that conflict was waged, by and large, against a number of isolated regional targets.

The relatively accommodating approach to Ireland of the newly-appointed Conservative chief secretary, Sir Michael Hicks Beach (July 1886–March 1887), who had occupied the same position under Disraeli, and the subsequent conciliation polices of the Balfour brothers in the late 1880s and early 1890s, can often mask the absolute nature of the philosophical *bouleversement* which characterized Conservative policies in Ireland from the accession of Balfour on 7 March 1887. In combining with the Liberal Unionists to defeat Gladstone's Government of Ireland Bill the Conservatives had 'carefully orchestrated a rhetorical onslaught on the notion of Home Rule for Ireland'.[8] Following the 'Home Rule crisis' the thrust of the policy of Salisbury and his nephew was 'to preserve the Empire against a violent and foreign-dominated conspiracy'.[9] The Salisbury government would have no truck with what Randolph Churchill described as 'trafficking with treason'.[10] The new administration conducted a campaign for 'the utter discrediting of "nationalism" in Ireland [which] … created a reality in which future constitutional bargaining with Nationalists was ideologically impossible'.[11]

The lead came from a prime minister who 'detested the Irish, and saw coercion as the proper expression of sacred union'.[12]

The Tories, once Balfour controlled the arsenal, took aim at agrarian dissent as expressed via intimidation or boycotting, or through incitement to either activity. Because the government viewed the Irish political leadership as being at the helm of an anarcho-nationalist criminal conspiracy, utilizing agrarian elements as its shock troops, it adopted an undifferentiated approach. As Margaret O'Callaghan has noted, 'the constitutional party, the cattle hougher, the back street assassin, the boycotter, they were all the same: criminal because they were nationalist'.[13] This aggressive methodology would have its apotheosis in the punitive clauses of the (permanent) 1887 Crimes act, the retributive response to the Plan of Campaign and the indictment of the Irish constitutional movement by the *Times* commission. The philosophical logic of the Salisbury administration *vis-à-vis* Ireland was captured by its helpmate, the *Times* newspaper, on 7 March 1887, in an editorial accompanying the first article in the series 'Parnellism and Crime'. This excoriated the Gladstonian Liberals for their compact with the Parnellites:

> Mr. Gladstone and his party are deliberately allying themselves with the paid agents of an organization whose ultimate aim is plunder and whose ultimate sanction is murder, to paralyse the House of Commons and to hand Ireland over to social and financial ruin.[14]

In taking on the agents of Irish constitutional nationalism, in an effort to discredit their *bona fides*, Balfour and Salisbury also found themselves engulfed in a conflict with the Irish nationalist press. This eclipsed anything experienced by Forster or Spencer from 1879 to 1883. While the Liberal struggle with Irish nationalist newspapers, as already suggested, might have been somewhat tangential to that administration's elemental clash with the Land League, Balfour's campaign against a determined coterie within the Irish nationalist press (many of them National League activists of long standing) played a pivotal role in the Conservative government's tussle with its Irish adversaries.

An essential adjunct of this campaign was the advantage afforded the authorities by their use of summary jurisdiction in the prosecution of editors. The Liberal government, in its 1882 Crimes Act, had legislated for the use of three-judge courts in the processing of certain criminal trials. This was deemed essential as a mechanism for bypassing the inevitable partisanship of predominantly nationalist juries. As we have seen, judicial opposition meant that, though enacted, the provision was never put into effect. The 1887 Crimes Act went a step further. In cases of intimidation – the offence was defined and designed to cover a multitude – offenders could be tried before two 'removable' resident magistrates in the absence of a jury.

Armed with his new powers Balfour immediately thrust at the centre. The intention was to seek exemplary punishment against two prominent national newspaper editors *pour encourager les autres*. But the new act, at least where the press was concerned, did not flourish in its early trials. It was tested in a rather unproductive clash with the *Nation* and *United Ireland* followed by an important, and inconclusive, action against Edward Walsh of the *Wexford People*. This unpromising debut was followed by a concurrent strategy involving the prosecution of provincial newspaper editors for the publication of the reports of meetings of 'suppressed' branches of the National League, and the filing of charges against news-vendors for selling journals in proscribed areas carrying such reports. An adaptation or tactical adjustment in 1889 saw the adoption of the more easily defensible policy of prosecutions in the case of overt intimidation of specified individuals.

The centrality of this rigorous press policy during the Balfour regime had much to do with the relative indifference of the activist chief secretary towards hallowed notions of newspaper freedom. While acknowledging his reluctance to embark on any blatant attack on the liberty of the press, Balfour clearly had no overweening attachment or affiliation to the concept. It was merely an irksome fact of life with which he had to contend. Accordingly Balfour did not indulge in any agonized hand-wringing when it came to vying with Irish nationalist newspapers. He merely continued probing to establish how far he could travel down the road of suppression.

Unlike Forster and Spencer in the early 1880s, Balfour had to deal in the House of Commons with a strengthening and cohesive opposition to his policies, especially those involving press controls. As the Irish attorney general, Dodgson Hamilton Madden, put it, when contrasting the situation in 1882 with that of 1887, 'the times were certainly different in some respects because the then chief secretary for Ireland had the support not only of the government but of the opposition'.[15] Balfour faced antagonism from a greatly enlarged Irish Party and the 200-odd Gladstonian Liberals. Neither could he depend on the support of the radical cohort among the Liberal Unionists. This was despite the fact that his methods were hardly any more extreme than those available to and availed of by the Liberals during and after the land war. They were merely applied with enhanced vigour.

Forced to opt for a minimalist policy of outlawing publication of National League branch notices in proclaimed areas Balfour was greatly assisted in his campaign by recalcitrant newspaper editors. These men were often members of the urban elites who dominated the leadership of the Irish National League. Were 'press prosecutions' little more than a mechanism for punishing these men for the leadership positions they adopted in their own localities and their advocacy of the Plan of Campaign? Whether this was the case or not most of the twenty editors or proprietors of national or local newspapers charged under the Crimes Act afforded the administration ample scope for prosecution by their persistent infringement of the law.

In his lengthy and exhaustive opening speech to the *Times* commission the attorney general, Sir Richard Webster, a reluctant advocate for the *Times* and, in reality, spokesman for the Tory government, made it clear that the Salisbury administration saw itself as facing the continuation of a nationalist conspiracy begun by the Land League, 'a concerted and preconceived conspiracy with definite objects, with definite aims'.[16] He included the organs of the nationalist press in that conspiracy. Singled out for mention were the *Irish World, Chicago Citizen, Boston Pilot, Freeman's Journal, United Ireland*, the *Irishman*, the *Nation*, the *Weekly News, Cork Daily Herald*, the *Kerry Sentinel*, the *Evening Telegraph* and the *Sligo Champion*.[17] No doubt the editors of, amongst other journals, the *Wexford People* and the *Roscommon Herald* – not to mention the irascible O'Donovan Rossa – would have felt chagrined at their exclusion from such a 'Roll of Honour'. Webster was merely reflecting the mindset of the chief secretary for Ireland who, early on in his battle with the National League, had identified newspaper reportage of the Plan of Campaign as a significant threat and as one of the main drivers of boycotting and threatening behaviour.[18] Accordingly Balfour chose to accept the gauntlet thrown down by nationalist editors in response to his strategy for dealing with widespread intimidation.

The Hicks Beach interlude

The government's first job in Ireland on assuming office, in pursuance of Salisbury's promise of 'twenty years of resolute government',[19] was the extirpation of Liberal influences in Dublin Castle. The Prime Minister did not help his cause by his choice of chief secretary. Salisbury's first Irish minister, Sir Michael Hicks Beach, had the misfortune, in common with many of his predecessors, of being a comparatively reasonable man. In addition he departed from Tory orthodoxy by nurturing the 'earnest and governmentally unpopular belief in the gravity of the renewed agricultural depression of late 1886'.[20] Hicks Beach's intention in acquiescing to a return to Dublin was, in his own words, to 'wipe away the effect of the introduction of the Home Rule bill not merely on the official mind but on the people at large'.[21] This he hoped to achieve with as little fuss as possible. In her study of the formation of Tory policy in the first year of the Salisbury administration Margaret O'Callaghan has written of the new chief secretary that 'Hicks Beach, in Ireland, still clung to the assumption that the game was the same as previously; that coercion would be used if and when serious crime seemed to warrant it, and that simultaneously the legitimate grievances of an oppressed tenantry would be appeased.'[22]

The normally merciless *United Ireland* did little worse during his tenure than accuse their new adversary of 'Hicks-Beachery',[23] an undefined crime based more upon his not being John Morley (his Liberal predecessor) than upon any particularly Satanic qualities of his own.[24] The newspaper defined his policy, enunciated in a speech in November 1886 in Bristol, as one of deadly stealth. 'The Irish tenantry are not to be coerced but drugged. The League is not to be openly fought but subjected to the process of slow poisoning.'[25] A few abatements and concessions would be made until the teeth of Irish opposition had been pulled. Or so, at least, it appeared.

One of Hicks Beach's first tasks on assuming office was to deal with agrarian mayhem in Kerry. The formidable Major General Sir Redvers Buller, scourge of the Zulu and holder of a Victoria Cross, was appointed to tackle the disorder with his customary vigour. However, he quickly 'went native'. Buller's disillusionment with some of the more egregious examples of predatory landlordism in the south-west of the country prompted him to disparage before the Cowper commission – then holding hearings into issues of land tenure – many of those whose interests he was supposed to be protecting. This drew an amused observation from *United Ireland*. 'It is clear that before the government suppresses the National League they will have first to suppress General Buller.'[26]

Not that either Buller, soon to be appointed under secretary, or his chief were opposed to the introduction of some element of coercion, but 'their shared view was one of acceptance of the existence of genuine hardship as a pre-condition of violence in the south-west [and] … a belief that the suppression of the National League was unwise and unnecessary.'[27] That philosophy would change radically when Salisbury finally got to grips with his Irish policy after the prorogation of Parliament in the winter of 1886, and appointed his nephew, Arthur Balfour, as his principal agent of change.

Even the Plan of Campaign, launched in response to the defeat of Parnell's 1886 Tenant Relief Bill, in a *United Ireland* article subtitled 'A Memo for the Country',[28] initially 'went unchallenged'.[29] Hicks Beach adopted a comparatively sanguine approach to this striking new development, although he described it a few months after its introduction as 'an effort by concerted action on the part of one class to deprive another class of rights to which the latter class is by law entitled'.[30] The 'Plan' spread quickly on what O'Brien described, with some hyperbole, as 'estates where the people were driven to the last pitch of desperation'.[31] The preliminary legal response to this new challenge was guarded. In December 1886 *United Ireland* published a leaked memo from the attorney general, Hugh Holmes, regarding the taking of Plan 'rents' on the Ponsonby estate in Cork. The Crown's leading law officer had, according to the newspaper, informed the local divisional commissioner, Captain Plunkett, that 'I do not see how any action can be taken by the executive.'[32]

Nonetheless, even before the departure of Hicks Beach from the Irish Office in March 1887, official concern at the steady progress of the Plan of Campaign, the re-emergence of boycotting as a weapon on Plan estates and the recrudescence of alleged incitement to intimidation on nationalist platforms and in the press, did prompt a number of measures aimed at re-asserting the authority of the Tory ministry.

The *Freeman's Journal* was able to announce on 3 December 1886 that 'The Plan of Campaign advances rapidly.'[33] Dublin Castle was paying particular attention to the speeches being made at mass meetings around the country designed to advance the cause of the Plan. Hicks Beach explained in a memo to the cabinet that 'at first Mr. Dillon seemed to be alone in taking it up, and his early speeches were moderate and harmless.'[34] Then, in a speech made on 21 November, Dillon gave the administration the opportunity it sought to test the legality of the Plan in a superior court. Dillon made a very violent speech, and simultaneously 'there was sufficient evidence available to support an indictment for conspiracy against both him and Mr. O'Brien.'[35] Partly in order to prevent Dillon and O'Brien re-offending while on bail (which was mandatory in such cases), an application was made to the Queen's Bench to place Dillon under the Rule of Bail. This obliged him, if the presiding judge found the Plan of Campaign to be an illegal conspiracy, to enter into recognizances to be of good behaviour.

It is clear from the cabinet memo that the authorities hoped for a repetition of a similar case involving Healy and Davitt in 1882. On that occasion Healy refused to enter into recognizances and was jailed. The Castle authorities hoped that Dillon would remove himself from the fray on a point of principle by a similar refusal.

Judges O'Brien and Johnson, in a Queen's Bench ruling on 14 December 1886, found Dillon to be a person of 'evil fame'. This was a pre-requisite to their ruling that the Plan of Campaign was a 'criminal conspiracy'. Dillon was given twelve days to enter into a personal security of £1,000 and two sureties of £500 each or go to prison for six months. In its consideration of the verdict the *Freeman's Journal* maintained that the result had been a 'foregone conclusion' and commented that 'Mr. Dillon has led, with others, an attack upon a conspiracy amongst a number of the worst landlords in Ireland to extract admittedly unjust rents.'[36] In a more acerbic reaction *United Ireland* held that 'Mr. Dillon was farcically prosecuted in the Queen's Bench in order to give Judge O'Brien a peg on which to hang a declaration reversing the Attorney General's unfortunate opinion.'[37]

Having obtained their Queen's Bench *imprimatur* the authorities struck forcibly at the organizers of the Plan in Loughrea, Co. Galway on 16 December 1886. There Dillon, Matt Harris and David Sheehy, all MPs, and William O'Brien – temporarily without a constituency – were arrested for collecting Plan 'rents' from tenants on the notorious Clanricarde estate[38] in what O'Brien described as 'Sir M. Hicks Beach's first whiff of grapeshot'.[39] A week later the Loughrea prosecution was abandoned, and, in effect, became a State trial for conspiracy in the Dublin police court, with a number of other 'conspirators' added to the docket. These proceedings Conor Cruise O'Brien characterizes as being akin to the trials of Parnell and others in January 1881, a mere pretext for 'demonstrating the inadequacy of the ordinary law'[40] and a prelude to the introduction of enhanced coercion legislation. However, William O'Brien, one of the traversers, claimed that the Crown was sufficiently interested in the proceedings to change the venue to Dublin County and attempt (unsuccessfully) to 'pack' the jury.[41] The Castle itself judged that the case would be heard there 'under as favourable circumstances as are possible in Ireland'.[42] The Crown discontinued the prosecution after the jury disagreed on its verdict on 24 February 1887.[43]

Prior to the resumption of the action against Dillon, O'Brien and their colleagues the Chief Secretary, in a memo to the Cabinet in January 1887, had pointed out the obvious Achilles heel of the original procedure. The case could not be dealt with summarily and it was 'hopeless with the present jury system to prosecute successfully crime of this kind in the counties in which agrarian agitation most prevails'.[44] Hence the metamorphosis of the 'Loughrea' case, the move to Dublin and the discovery that not even predominantly unionist juries could be relied upon to produce a verdict acceptable to the administration. The same memo ominously concluded that, in addition to the use of the crime of conspiracy, promotion of the Plan of Campaign could be punished by alternative means. Hicks Beach wrote that 'those who advocate it by speech or writing may be prosecuted for sedition, or for inciting others to join in a criminal combination'.[45] It would be Arthur Balfour who would follow through on the logic of the latter statement far more robustly than its original author.

To defeat the plan Hicks Beach foresaw the need to replicate some of the coercion legislation of previous governments. He observed that 'some summary remedy seems absolutely necessary to enable the Executive to effectually combat such a state of things as exists at present in Ireland'. This applied as much to 'words spoken or written in order to and calculated to incite persons to engage in a criminal conspiracy', as it did to the conspiracy itself.[46] His successor needed no persuasion on that count.

The inadequacies of common and statute law in dealing with the promotion of the Plan of Campaign, as mediated through the printed word, were illustrated in the January 1887 prosecution of Jasper Tully, editor of the *Roscommon Herald*. Tully was brought before a jury at the Sligo Winter Assizes on 3 January 1887. He was indicted for 'writing notices tending to incite unlawful meetings or combinations threatening violence' contrary to section 3, chapter 44, 1 & 2 William IV. This was an 1831 amendment to the so-called 'Whiteboy Acts' of the eighteenth century (15 & 16 George III), which threatened the publisher of any 'notice, letter or message exciting or tending to excite any riot, tumultuous or unlawful meeting or assembly, or unlawful combination or confederacy' with incarceration.[47]

More than half a century after its original passage, in the absence of special legislation, it was disinterred on an *ad hoc* basis by a government wishing to discourage newspapers from publicizing the activities of the more activist branches of the League. The option of a full-blown sedition trial – the more obvious vehicle for a press prosecution in the absence of coercion legislation – was not pursued. The experience of the Liberals with William O'Brien in the 1882 'Accusing Spirits' trial might have served as salutary discouragement. Were it not for the fact that a new coercion law was already in preparation at the time, the Tully prosecution might even be seen as a dry run, designed to establish if the 1831 legislation was still serviceable.

The case was heard before chief baron Palles and what *United Ireland* described as 'a jury well and truly packed. They were Protestants to a man, the Crown having ordered twenty-two Catholics to stand by.'[48] Tully had published five reports in the *Herald* starting on 17 April 1886 (barely a week after the introduction of the Home Rule bill) of National League meetings at which boycotting resolutions had been passed.

In his direction to the jury Palles expressed grave reservations about the appropriateness of the usage of the 1831 amendment. He held 'that the law of criminal libel has no application at all to these prosecutions under the Whiteboy Acts.'[49] The 'well and truly packed' jury voted 10–2 in Tully's favour before being dismissed, for being unable to reach a verdict, by the chief baron. The fact that the statute under which the *Herald* editor had been tried called for penalties of up to seven years in prison may have had an impact on the verdict. The potential sentence was clearly out of proportion with the nature of the alleged crime. This was something the government later conceded in the 1887 Crimes Act when sentences with a maximum tariff of six months (albeit in non-jury courts) were introduced.

Just as the failure of the Loughrea/ 'State' prosecutions hastened the onset of the 1887 Crimes Act, so did the exposure of the inadequacies of the 1831 legislation ensure that consideration of how to restrain press support for the widespread renewal of agrarian agitation became central to the context in which that legislation was framed.

Arthur James Balfour, with his own particular brand of languid enthusiasm and insouciant energy, happily took up the challenge of devising new ways to thwart the nationalist press.

'Mr Golfour' begins his round

Balfour assumed office on 7 March 1887 owing to a debilitating illness that forced the resignation of Hicks Beach. On the same day the *Times* newspaper published, to little fanfare other than a few blasts on its own trumpet, the first of its series of articles on 'Parnellism and Crime'. Balfour would later be a party to the use of that newspaper as a battering-ram in his war against the National League and the Irish Party.

In his seminal work on political violence in Ireland, Charles Townshend has noted that 'British rule in Ireland so often found itself paralysed because it could neither operate on English principles (because it did not have sufficient public co-operation) nor abandon English principles and govern by the direct application of force.'[50] This was undoubtedly the case through much of the nineteenth century. But the chief secretaryship of Arthur Balfour was exceptional in many respects. The imperturbable and eminently capable Balfour, a somewhat surprising choice for the position, was not prone to intellectual paralysis and saw no great need to rely on the co-operation of Irish nationalists in their own governance. Equally, however, he was willing to dispense concession as well as repression. Despite his authorship of a work entitled 'A defence of philosophic doubt',[51] Balfour's ministry was not noted for its dubiety.

United Ireland assumed they had got the measure of Lord Salisbury's nephew when they described him as 'a delicate lily of the aristocracy': 'He is a rickety and lackadaisical young man whom one could better imagine dining off the contemplation of a sunflower than tackling a problem in statesmanship which foiled Cromwell and broke Mr. Forster's stubborn heart.'[52]

Given his well-known passion for the game of golf *United Ireland* took to describing the new chief secretary dismissively as 'Mr Golfour'.[53] An equally sceptical, though somewhat less acerbic, *Freeman's Journal,* noting Balfour's 'aristocratic languor', was highly critical of the appointment: 'This young gentleman has three qualifications for the post. He is the nephew of Lord Salisbury; he has no reputation for statesmanship to injure; and he knows nothing of Ireland.'[54]

The *Pall Mall Gazette* exhibited concern for Balfour's life and health. While insisting that the appointment was an unashamed example of nepotism Stead's newspaper suggested that it was 'nepotism not of the patronizing but of the murderous order'.[55]

What no one seemed anxious to highlight was the fact that, as one of his biographers has demonstrated, Balfour had certain useful qualifications for the job in hand. He had, for example, 'displayed resolution in dealing with crofters' disturbances at the Scottish Office'.[56] The new chief secretary, soon to lead 'one of the most controversial Irish administrations of the century',[57] came to Dublin wielding his 'carrot and stick' policy of physical and moral force unionism. 'Cool and disdainful',[58] his resolve, in the execution of an extremely difficult portfolio, quickly impressed a number of prominent Castle functionaries frustrated by the apparent pusillanimity of his predecessors. Among these was the young Crown attorney Edward Carson and his more senior colleague Peter O'Brien. The latter referred to Balfour as 'a fearless chief'.[59] The admiration was reciprocated.

Balfour shared his uncle's view that 'severity had to precede conciliation'.[60] Accordingly his Crimes bill, introduced three weeks after his accession to the Cabinet, demonstrated the sort of 'resolution' that was to distinguish his regime. According to Margaret O'Callaghan it unnecessarily 'provoked a confrontation between "all" of nationalist Ireland and the "forces of law and order"'.[61] Essentially Balfour's bill was a compromise between the proposed three-judge courts of the 1882 Crimes act and the modified suspension of *habeas corpus* implicit in Forster's Protection of Person and Property Act of the previous year. There was very little that was new under the sun when it came to 'special' legislation for Ireland. In cases of boycotting, intimidation and – where the press was concerned – incitement to either, jury trials would be replaced by decisions made in courts of summary jurisdiction (petty sessions, assizes) by two resident magistrates. *United Ireland* noted, wryly, that this signalled an acceptance of the failure of the practice of jury 'packing': 'They purpose [*sic*] destroying trial by jury because they have failed to corrupt it.'[62] However, unlike the two main Liberal coercion acts of the 1880s, the 1887 law was intended as a piece of permanent legislation.

The nationalist press was a clear barrier to the enforcement of 'physical-force unionism' and dismissive of the efficacy of its moral-force accessory. Accordingly Balfour's crusade to undercut the growing influence of the nationalist press, particularly in rural Ireland, was at the core of his ministry. In December 1887 he wrote to his uncle that press prosecutions were 'a necessary element in the policy of suppressing the League' and that 'it will be a very serious matter to allow the newspapers to win.'[63] In parallel with his endeavours to silence the subversive noise from the platform Balfour also sought to silence the dissentient narrative emanating from the printing presses.

However, where the nationalist press was concerned, Balfour was clear on the potential snares awaiting him. He would have to deal with press solidarity, editorial defiance of the law, some highly imaginative legal challenges, in addition to the inevitable judicial and juridical frustrations. But he would also have to contend with the intense scrutiny of the British press, polity and public. As L.P. Curtis has argued, 'English public opinion was more articulate and sensitive on this subject than on any other; and fear of offending this force affected Government policy to a large degree.'[64]

Balfour was conscious of the need to deflect potential criticism from British champions of press freedom in his framing of new legislation. His intent was to avoid drawing unnecessary attention to his plans to curtail the nationalist press by the simple omission of any dedicated press clauses. Shortly before Balfour's own elevation to Cabinet status Major General Buller had been withdrawn from his Kerry eyrie and temporarily promoted to the vacant position of under secretary. Less than a week after assuming office Balfour wrote to his new deputy about his plans to inhibit the activities of the nationalist press in the new Crimes act: 'I hope we shall be able to hit the papers in our bill sufficiently hard without introducing them *eo nomine*. Public opinion is sensitive about phrases though callous about things. I am afraid of the freedom of the press.'[65]

In the context of regimes of coercion legislation, stretching back to the 1870 amendment to the Peace Preservation (Ireland) Act, Balfour's press proposals for his 1887 bill might have seemed modest enough. The powers vested in the executive under the 1870 act, viewed with a certain nostalgia by some Castle functionaries, were, as already noted, particularly draconian.[66] The 1881 Protection of Person and Property Act had no dedicated press clause but in regions where *habeas corpus* had been suspended that was no obstacle to dealing summarily with obnoxious editors. The focus in that legislation was on those manning the 'engines' and using the 'implements' rather than on the plant itself. The (now expired) 1882 Crimes Act did have a press clause, section 13, but as already noted, this amounted to little more than a retrospective papering over of cracks that had become evident relating to the issue of seizure.

Where Balfour's proposals were different was in the complete absence of any specific reference to the press, and in his circumvention of the problem of securing guilty verdicts against newspaper sedition under the ordinary law, by recourse to summary jurisdiction. Balfour would have been made aware that there was ample precedent for the summary (i.e. non-jury) prosecution of newspaper editors for intimidation or incitement to intimidation under previous coercion legislation. But he hoped to go further. The chief secretary proposed to exceed the severity of the 1882 Crimes Act 'change of venue' provisions by legislating for the removal of trials to London subject to High Court and Privy Council approval.[67] He intended to include newspaper editors in this provision. In correspondence with Buller on 19 March 1887 he outlined his ambitious plans:

> We are all agreed I think that seditious libel should be punished summarily, and that if possible, it should also be punished under the clause providing a special tribunal and a change of venue to London. The former course we shall adopt and the only doubt about the expediency of adopting the latter arises from the complexity of the Law of Sedition, and the apparent difficulty of getting even an English jury to convict under it.[68]

What is clear from this communication is that Balfour was prepared to make an attempt to stifle editorial commentary, as opposed to simply inhibiting the capacity for press incitement by the publication of boycotting notices. Balfour resented what he saw as the 'lies' purveyed by nationalist newspapers in their editorial columns. His proposal sought to deter some of the more egregious propagandists by eliminating the protection afforded them by a local jury trial. He was, however, persuaded by Hartington to abandon plans to move coercion trials to England,[69] and it was not found necessary to prosecute any newspaper for seditious libel while he was chief secretary. However, Balfour, despite his assertions that 'we do not propose to interfere with the liberty of the press',[70] clearly intended to challenge, in courts of summary jurisdiction, some of the more outrageous editorial assertions of nationalist newspaper editors.

By the time the legislation had passed he had, just as clearly, learned something about the limits of his powers. Ultimately he went no further in framing his legislation than to attempt to ensure that the more raucous elements of the National League did not benefit from the publicizing of, in particular, their boycotting activities. A month after his Crimes bill passed through the House of Commons – it was signed into law by the Queen on 18 July – Balfour was conceding to Buller that it had not been feasible to punish seditious libel through the agency of two resident magistrates ruling from the bench in an assize court:

> Newspapers are responsible for most of the mischief in Ireland; but I apprehend that a mischievous article is not therefore an article which ought to be prosecuted. There are, in the first place, legal difficulties in the way of getting a verdict, and, in the second place interference with the freedom of the press, is a cry which has more effect in England than almost any other; and it is, besides this, extremely difficult to prosecute a newspaper for an article of a general kind without laying yourself open to the accusation that you are using the Crimes Act to injure a political opponent.[71]

Under the new law offending newspaper editors would be tried before stipendiary resident magistrates at assize courts. Most of those magistrates held their positions at the pleasure of the Castle. They were characterized by the Irish nationalist press as 'removables' who were paid to do the bidding of the law officers. With the exception of the prosecution of the *Nation* and *United Ireland* in late 1887, all thirty-nine 'press prosecutions' under the Criminal Law and Procedure (Ireland) Act, 1887, up to January 1891, were conducted under the aegis of just such sessional courts. 'Law, evidence, convictions, and sentences are manufactured wholesale at the Castle and retailed at the petty sessions', railed *United Ireland* shortly after the passage of the act. [72] In the debate on the bill Parnell referred to the magistrates as 'creatures' of the executive.[73] The *Kerry Sentinel* was caustic in its assessment of their judicial neutrality, calling them 'a contemptible pack of parasites who are only hungering to show their soulless servility'.[74]

Furthermore, as *United Ireland* pointed out, Balfour reassured the House that the universality of access to the normal appeal process would mitigate any potential injustice inherent in the absence of juries.[75] This guarantee was subsequently nullified in a number of entirely predictable manoeuvres undertaken by magistrates unwilling to be reversed by a higher court. These included the imposition of a single sentence, or cumulative sentences, of fewer then four weeks in duration. Such terms of imprisonment eliminated the right of appeal. The newspaper pointed out the anomaly that, 'every man sentenced in England to imprisonment without the option of a fine has the absolute right of appeal'.[76]

Creating a new 'Castle press'?

One of the traditional methods used by the Castle to exercise a degree of control or influence on newspapers was the placing of advertisements. This amounted to thousands of pounds a year and at the turn of the nineteenth century was, for some journals, the difference between solvency and bankruptcy. By the late 1880s it was not such a significant factor in the survival of newspapers but it did impact on their profitability. However, there is little doubt that government advertising was still used in the 1880s to incentivize, coax or pressurize politically *complaisant* newspapers. Just as the Land League could jeopardize the viability of an economically vulnerable regional nationalist newspaper by withdrawing its advertising so could the Castle maintain a subtle whip-hand on marginal unionist journals. Only moderate nationalist newspapers (like the *Freeman's Journal*) were favoured with government advertising revenues.

The *Nation* sought to test the waters in September 1886. An application was made to the chief secretary's office for official advertisements to be placed with the paper.[77] The application was *apropos* a promise from the administration that, where appropriate, advertisements would be placed in nationalist weekly newspapers. This followed a parliamentary question from J.J. Clancy MP. Clancy had requested a full list of newspapers, daily and weekly, in which the government placed official notices. William Jackson, secretary to the Treasury, while claiming to the derisive jeers of Irish party members that the government 'never take into account the politics of a newspaper in giving out their advertisements'[78] responded with a listing of a dozen favoured papers.[79] When Clancy pointed out that only two were nationalist, Jackson promised to look into the matter.[80] On foot of the exchange in the House of Commons the under secretary's office, on 10 September, requested a report from Superintendent Mallon on 'what are the leading nationalist weekly newspapers published in Dublin?' Mallon responded on 20 September: 'The *Freeman's Journal* of course has the largest circulation.[81] Next to it commercially is the *Nation*. It has a Farmer's column and would be a good medium of advertisement similar to the one in question. I don't know if *United Ireland* cares much for government patronage.'

The opinion of government departments as to the value of placing advertisements in the *Nation* was canvassed. David Harrel, the DMP commissioner responded that his department's advertising amounted to about £70 per annum and was usually placed in dailies, mostly the *Freeman*, *Irish Times* and *Daily Express*, with occasional recourse to the two evening papers the *Mail* and *Telegraph*. By early October Hamilton and Hicks Beach had decided not to deviate from standard procedure. In a note to the chief secretary, Hamilton wrote 'I see no reason for departing from the usual practice.'[82]

There followed what can only have been a mischievous application from *United Ireland* for government advertising. It clearly did not arise from any inclination to publicize the edicts and directives of the new Tory administration and was certainly not based on financial need. In the period since the Home Rule crisis of April–June the paper had been selling more than 100,000 copies a week. A communication from Westminster to

Hamilton informed the under secretary of the application and inquired 'is it in your view desirable that we should do so; either on account of its circulation amongst people who ought to be reached or on account of any trouble to you which a refusal might produce?'[83] Hamilton saw 'no reason so far as the Irish government is concerned for adding this paper to the list'.[84] When a further inquiry from the Inspector of Fisheries sought instructions on another request from the newspaper for advertising Hamilton was equally emphatic. It was left to Hicks Beach to exercise a modicum of diplomacy. He responded that 'I think it enough to advertise ... in the local newspapers of largest circulation amongst those interested, irrespective of politics. In this case "United Ireland" would not be included.'[85]

United Ireland returned to the issue on a regular basis. In January 1888 it reproduced a memo allegedly sent by Balfour on the distribution of government money for advertising in the public press. The memo noted that:

> The advocacy of particular political opinions is not in itself a sufficient reason for giving or withholding Government advertisements, but 1) The benefit of the doubt should always be given in favour of papers accepting law and order. 2) The fact that a particular paper is boycotted is a strong ground for giving it Government advertisements and a conclusive ground for not withdrawing them if already given. 3) No Government advertisements under any circumstances be given to any newspaper that violates the law.

Describing the memo as 'a shabbier attack on the National Press, if possible, than the imprisonment of editors, newsagents and printers' and 'an outrageous attempt out of the public rates to subsidise bankrupt and scurrilous Coercion rags', *United Ireland* proceeded to parse the memo:

> 'The benefit of the doubt' is a very neat way of suggesting that all public advertisements are to be withheld from National newspapers, and that journals 'supporting law and order' – *id est*, the savage coercion administration – are to have a monopoly. If a paper is boycotted – that is to say, if a paper

is hated and shunned by the public, it is a 'strong ground' for filling its columns with advertisements, which the public will never read, paid for out of the pockets of that same public, and intended for their information.[86]

Assuming the memo was genuine – and there was no serious challenge to its authenticity from the Castle – it was clear that despite the promise from William Jackson to J.J. Clancy in September 1886, no significant change was envisaged. It is equally apparent that exchequer funds were actually being used as a form of subsidy for sympathetic newspapers. While the *Daily Express* and the *Evening Mail* were perfectly capable of nipping the hand that fed them, the time-honoured policy of effective subsidy goes some way towards clarifying a journalistic conundrum: how did the predominantly nationalist city of Dublin manage to support three unionist daily newspapers?

The elusive press provisions of the Criminal Law and Procedure (Ireland) Act, 1887

When introducing the Criminal Law and Procedure (Ireland) Act, 1887 on its first and second readings (the latter coinciding with the publication of the *Times* 'facsimile' letter on 18 April 1887) Balfour, given licence by the absence of any explicit press clauses, or even a single mention of the word, drew precious little attention to the implications of the legislation for Irish nationalist newspapers. In tabling the bill on 28 March 1887 he merely drew attention to the fact that in framing its own equivalent in 1882, the Liberals had appropriated for themselves certain extraordinary powers now omitted in his own bill. These included 'certain laws relating to strangers, and certain clauses dealing with the Press'.[87] He, rather disingenuously, expressed the belief that 'by giving magistrates power of summary jurisdiction for inciting to these offences we may be able to deal with that class of cases, and prevent the Press from being sharers in these crimes'.[88] In response to criticisms from Gladstone on the occasion of the second reading he observed that 'we bring in a Bill which, whatever else may be said of it, is not open to the charge that it interferes with personal liberty, or with the freedom of the Press, to the same extent as the Act which the right hon. Gentleman passed in 1870 did'.[89]

As far as the Irish nationalist press was concerned the operative elements of Balfour's bill were section 2.2, which related to the use of violence and intimidation, section 2.4, which rendered liable to prosecution 'any person who shall incite any other person to commit any of the offences herein-before mentioned', and section 7, which enjoined against promoting the objects of an illegal association.[90] However, by the time of its passage, having weathered a turbulent and highly personalized Commons debate, Balfour was disposed to make haste slowly in the deployment of the Crimes act against the press. He wrote to Buller in this spirit of *festina lente* shortly after his bill became law:

> Of course I do not mean by this that we are to allow the last sub-section in Clause 2 to remain a dead letter. But I think it ought to be applied with more caution than almost any other portion of Bill, and I should like very much to lay down, in concert with you, the precise principles on which we mean to proceed in the future with such matters[91]

The radical MP and journalist Henry Labouchere took issue, in the Commons debate, with Balfour's assertion, 'that his Bill would not affect the Press'. He contended that:

> If the Bill were passed the Press would be at the mercy of the Government, and the Press of Ireland would be subject to such an Act as had never yet been passed in the most despotic Government in the world. Even in Russia a newspaper had three warnings before it was suppressed.

Labouchere also inquired how the government proposed to distinguish between English and Irish newspapers, and deal with any potential 'incitement to boycott' published in an English newspaper that also circulated in Ireland.[92] Labouchere's defence of press freedom was rather more spirited than that of Parnell. The Irish leader's sole intervention in relation to the press provisions came in his speech in opposition to the bill on 1 April. Drawing attention to Balfour's assertion that 'we do not propose to interfere with the liberty of the Press', Parnell observed, 'oh, no, no; not directly. Everything is to be done indirectly in this Bill.'[93] He then alleged that the powers of the 1887 bill were similar to those invoked under Forster's Protection of Person and Property Act and would allow for the prosecution of employees of papers unconnected with editorial policy. Significantly, when Balfour responded he did not specifically deny the Irish party leader's allegation, choosing instead merely to point out, gratuitously, that the 1870 coercion legislation of the first Gladstone administration permitted 'the Government to confiscate the whole newspaper and plant'.[94] Parnell can have had no sense that he was partly correct but that the collateral victims of Balfour's putative policy would not be printers[95] and typesetters but humble news-vendors.

After the bill had passed into law, on the occasion of the consequential August 1887 debate on the proscription of the National League, Gladstone returned to the theme of the press provisions of the new legislation. He sought to expose the official mythology that the Irish press had emerged unscathed from the Crimes act: 'No Press Clauses! Not for the world would this Government have the odium of Press Clauses; but it is a new and ingenious invention to avoid the odium of Press Clauses.'[96] Balfour accepted the implied compliment to his ingenuity and declined to address the issue in his response to the Liberal leader.

Despite the paucity of discussion on the issue during the Crimes bill debate the Irish nationalist press was under no illusions as to what the legislation might mean, if pressed to its logical conclusion. A *Kerry Sentinel* editorial was typical:

> There is not a sentence of this article, which our readers are now perusing, but could be by pliant magistrates tortured into an offence against this measure when it becomes law under the excuse of its being aimed at disturbing 'the maintenance of law and order'.[97]

A constant refrain of the nationalist press following the passage of the 1887 Crimes act was that 'new offences' had been created under its terms. Newspaper editors could now go to prison for publishing reports they claimed had been explicitly legalized by the 1881 Newspaper Libel Act. Balfour always sought to contradict this contention. In the House of Commons on 6 June 1887 he noted of his legislation that 'it has been alleged that new offences are created by it. The Government do not admit that.'[98] In a discussion document produced for the Cabinet in early 1888 Balfour argued the point even more vigorously: 'The [press prosecutions] … have been restricted solely to cases of persons who persistently and defiantly took a most prominent and dangerous part in the working of illegal associations, by publishing notices, not as matters of public interest, but with a view to furthering … unlawful objects.'[99]

After the National League was suppressed as a 'dangerous association' in areas proscribed by the lord lieutenant the *Nation* announced that it intended to stymie Balfour, the inveterate golfer, by offering space in its columns to the reports of suppressed branches of the League.[100] The *Freeman's Journal* criticized the censorious elements of the legislation but decided against defiance of the law. An important aspect of Balfour's policy was to guard against just such a development.[101] The *Journal* took to heart the words of the chief secretary in a speech in Manchester in which he set out his intentions in relation to the Irish press: 'Mere abuse will be treated with contempt, but when it comes to open advocacy of crime … you have become criminals, and, as criminals I shall proceed against you.'[102]

Challenging the Crimes Act

Did the struggle between Balfour and nationalist newspapers that followed the imposition of the Crimes act have much to do with the advancement of the cause of press freedom? Or did the national and local press editors who defied the law do so, primarily, to tweak the lion's tail and advance the cause of agrarianism in general and the Plan of Campaign in particular? Was Balfour seeking to curtail the commentary and influence of the nationalist press in jailing editors? Or was he simply arresting prominent nationalist leaders, who also happened to be newspaper editors, while holding the press to account for the defiance of pre-existing laws on incitement?

Clearly it was of paramount importance for the noises emanating from the Irish nationalist journalists to be invocations of press freedom – this played to important constituencies in Britain which might otherwise be disinclined to support a continuation of the agrarian excesses of the land war era. It was equally an imperative of the Conservative government to deny such legitimacy to their nationalist press opponents. Balfour would always steadfastly maintain that he was not attempting to subvert press freedom. He was simply applying the same logic to the rogue press as he was to other rogues. Neither stance, of course, is entirely to be trusted or accepted at face value.

The nationalist position on press imprisonments was encapsulated in a *Cork Daily Herald* editorial after the incarceration of its editor, Alderman John Hooper, in December 1887: 'Alderman Hooper … has simply discharged his duty as a journalist – a duty which, thank God, but few journalists in Ireland to-day wish to shirk.'[103] It was a bald statement of doctrinal purity. Nationalist editors would go to jail to maintain freedom of expression in the Irish press. While this was true, up to a point, it was also an idealistic facade behind which lurked the frequent fellow-travellers of the ideologue, special pleading and reputation enhancement.

Balfour's own justification for the incarceration of Hooper, and many other nationalist editors, is best expressed in a memo to Cabinet written at a time when few members of the profession had actually been prosecuted. Balfour was not one who was much given to passionate public statements of self-exculpation or explanation. This expression of his philosophy was reserved solely for his government colleagues.

He argued that a newspaper publishing a fact about a crime or a 'criminal' society, as an item of news, with no ulterior motive, was not liable to prosecution: 'A newspaper, however, which deliberately devotes its columns to the publication of matter … avowedly with the intention of advancing and furthering the objects of a dangerous, illegal association, at once forfeits its position as an ordinary journal.' Irish journals, wrote Balfour, had absolute licence to criticize government policies or officials 'and this liberty, to which the freest press in the world is alone entitled, is at the present moment exercised in Ireland without let or hindrance to an extent and with a personal bitterness of vituperation which is certainly not exceeded, if indeed it can be approached, by the journals of any other nation.'[104]

By the end of August, 1887 Sir Joseph West Ridgeway had replaced Buller as under secretary[105] and the National League had been declared a 'dangerous association' by the House of Commons, thus making its activities liable for suppression in areas proscribed by the lord lieutenant. Even the unionist *Dublin Evening Mail*, a newspaper prone to 'angry myopia'[106] was unable to excite itself very much at the prospect of government action. It displayed little confidence in the resolve of the administration to curtail the activities of the League.[107] *United Ireland* issued instructions to branches in suppressed areas as to how to proceed in the event of suppression. Meetings should, at first, be held in public, then, if banned, in private houses. If dwellings were invaded by the RIC the suppressed branch should immediately amalgamate with the nearest unsuppressed branch and begin the process all over again. The newspaper assured its readers 'they will tire of it before the League'.[108]

However the Parnellite newspaper also counselled caution, pointing out how things had changed since the Land War. In the dying days of 1882 the Land League had the bulk of the forces of British politics ranged against it. In 1887, in contrast, the Liberal party was allied to the Irish party at Westminster, whatever its reservations about the National League or the Plan of Campaign. Gladstone had written of 'the rash and outrageous proceedings of the Government' and its 'cruel and oppressive policy' in Ireland.[109] *United Ireland* warned that 'All this entails responsibility. That alliance removes the element of desperation from our councils and replaces it by the element of restraint. It now lies upon every true man within his sphere to do his best to see that nothing is done in rashness or despair.'[110]

As threatened after the passage of the Crimes Act the *Nation,* once the lord lieutenant had proscribed the first National League branches – in Wexford as it happened – duly flouted the law by publishing reports of branch meetings there. It was joined in this action by *United Ireland*. In their respective issues of 1 October 1887 the two newspapers carried rather innocuous reports of meetings on Sunday 25 September of the Shelburne branch of the League, held at Ramsgrange, Co. Wexford, and the Carriganima branch in Co. Cork, among others.[111] This, according to the Crown, was done 'with the view of promoting the objects of the association' and was contrary to section 7 of the Criminal Law and Procedure (Ireland) Act, 1887.[112] In the subsequent court case Sullivan 'made no attempt to deny that publication was with this object'[113] and, in an editorial, claimed that Balfour's 'mandate was treated with the most perfect contempt on last Sunday by all the branches of the League, against which his proclamation was directed'.[114] *United Ireland* had not only wilfully flouted the law but had issued a provocative challenge to Dublin Castle to take action against it in an editorial entitled 'What are they going to do about it?'[115] Elsewhere the newspaper said of Balfour, 'If he does not prosecute the sooner he hands in his resignation the better for himself.'[116]

Summoned to appear before the divisional magistrate C.J. O'Donel [*sic*] at the Northern Divisional Police Court on 6 October, T.D. Sullivan, then Lord Mayor of Dublin, arrived for the hearing in full mayoral attire accompanied by the nationalist members of Dublin corporation in their own finery. According to Dublin journalist J.B. Hall 'the proceedings had an indescribably serio-comic aspect'.[117] The serio-comic virtually descended into out and out farce when Thomas Sexton MP and an RIC superintendent almost came to blows over Sexton's attempt to place the city sword and mace on a table in front of O'Donel's bench.[118] Sullivan was defended by Tim Healy. Edward Carson took the Crown brief, his participation indicating the importance placed on the outcome by the executive. O'Brien, also summoned, failed to make any appearance whatever for his own trial. The outcome was utterly disconcerting and potentially damaging for the Crown. O'Donel, a magistrate neither beloved of the Castle nor employed at the pleasure of the executive, dismissed the case on the grounds of the Crown's failure to produce evidence as to the nature of the proceedings at the proclaimed meeting. He held that the prosecution had failed to establish that the convocation that took place in Ramsgrange on 25 September, was actually an assembly of the Irish National League. Carson immediately asked for the magistrate to state a case to a higher court. Healy, anticipating a fairer hearing in the Exchequer Court, where Chief Baron Palles would preside, insisted on the case being stated to that court rather than to the Queen's Bench.[119] Pending the outcome of those proceedings the case against O'Brien and *United Ireland* was suspended. The *Daily Express* was critical of O'Donel, describing him as 'needlessly fastidious, not to say crochety', adding ominously that if O'Donel's judgment was allowed to stand 'the press clauses are, so far as we can see, unworkable'.[120]

United Ireland attacked the entire procedure, pointing out that 'there is not one sentence in the reports complained of to which any reasonable man could take exception as being anything but the open expression of political opinion and because newspapers published them as a matter of public interest they are guilty of crime forsooth, and their editors and proprietors liable to six months imprisonment, plank-bed, and association with foot-pads and corner-boys?'[121] Four columns to the right of this comment the journal carried another series of reports on the activities of suppressed branches. The *Nation* also repeated the offence for which its editor had been tried.[122]

The *Nation*, in addition, echoed a point made a few days earlier by the bi-weekly *Wexford People*, a journal soon to find itself in similar straits. Its editor, Edward Walsh, outlined two apparent anomalies in the proceedings being taken against Sullivan and O'Brien. The first was that the officers of the Ramsgrange branch, apparently, faced no charges themselves for organizing the 25 September meeting. Secondly, the unionist *Irish Times* had also carried a column entitled 'Meetings of the suppressed branches'. In this the paper had run the same report of the Ramsgrange meeting on Monday 26 September as was carried by both nationalist weeklies the following Saturday. [123]

The latter anomaly, mischievously and disingenuously pointed out repeatedly in the months ahead by the nationalist press, was not actually indicative of any legal inconsistency on the part of the administration. The *Irish Times, Dublin Evening Mail* and *Daily Express* often carried reports of suppressed National League branches, but clearly did not do so with the intention of 'promoting the objects of the association'.[124] In that sense the southern unionist papers afforded a useful cover for Balfour in his assertions that an item of news published 'with no ulterior object in view, is no more liable to prosecution in Ireland than it is in any other portion of the kingdom'.[125] The former anomaly, on the other hand, was never clearly addressed by the administration,[126] and reinforces the belief that one of the intentions of the Crimes Act legislation was not the prosecution of the small fry at officer level in local branch networks but of the rather more influential figures in the local press who were, almost on principle and as a visible act of defiance, obliged to continue coverage of National League activities.

Understandably the nationalist press gloated over the government's embarrassment in the Dublin Police court. The *Freeman's Journal* referred to the trial as a 'miserable fiasco' and added that 'the repression of the right of free publication must appear absurd in itself and disastrous in its consequences. It amounts to nothing more or less than driving under the surface the outward manifestations of discontent'.[127] The Dublin unionist papers were disgruntled at the Crown's handling of the case. The *Evening Mail* held Carson to be largely responsible for the fiasco while the *Express* insisted that O'Donel had been 'too fastidious' in his central ruling.[128]

English newspapers were equally scathing. The *Daily News* suggested that Balfour's attempts to confound the Irish press had already been defeated. 'The present advisers of the unfortunate Lord Lieutenant cannot even comprehend the details of their own wretched legislation … if the Irish executive retains any vestige of prudence, it will withdraw without further loss of reputation from a foolish and hopeless struggle.'[129] The *Times* bemoaned the fact that 'the omission to adduce evidence, which might have been easily obtained, has given a temporary appearance of triumph to the party of disorder'.[130] The *Standard* fulminated against 'the stupidity – there is no other word for it – of the officials to whom the management of the prosecution was left'.[131]

The consternation of the executive at the failure of their first tilt at the nationalist press was mitigated by the decision of the Exchequer court in the hearing of the 'case stated'. There, chief baron Palles, a judicial figure far less beloved of the Castle than even the Dublin divisional magistrate,[132] and Mr Justice Andrews reversed the police court ruling on the charges against Sullivan and remitted the case to that court to be reconsidered by O'Donel.[133] Anticipating a positive outcome in the Exchequer court, West Ridgeway had already written to Balfour hinting that on the grounds of expediency he was 'inclined to think that it will be better not to continue this particular prosecution but merely to say that the law having been now defined by the highest legal authorities any future infraction of it will be promptly punished'.[134] His suggestion was based on legal opinion tendered by the law officers.

Balfour, responding immediately, was not similarly minded. Although normally *ad idem* with the resolute West Ridgeway, the chief secretary's instincts on this occasion were to be much more aggressive than his subordinates. He would occasionally, in his campaign against the press, have to be persuaded by Salisbury to modify his belligerence.[135] In this instance he informed the under secretary that 'I confess my first inclination would be to go ahead …We have now got our weapon and we must use it with vigour.'[136] Balfour's opposition to the proposed *nolle prosequi* may have emanated from low expectations of the quality of the legal advice he was getting.[137] Salisbury had warned him of the pusillanimity of his law officers a few weeks before, when he wrote to his nephew 'you have the stupidest lot of lawyers in Ireland any Govt. [*sic*] was ever cursed with'.[138]

After the successful Exchequer court appeal ruling on 10 November 1887 West Ridgeway again urged the chief secretary to drop the cases against Sullivan and O'Brien. While accepting that both *United Ireland* and the *Nation* should be penalized in the event of repeat offences he advised against a return to O'Donel's court. His reasons were outlined in a letter to Balfour on the day of the favourable ruling of Baron Palles:

> a) We are winning, and can afford to be generous if we can do so without injury to the public interests. A semblance of generosity would have a good effect and somewhat disarm our opponents in England.
> b) Our object is to *deter*. If the papers in question cease the publication of the reports of suppressed branches we have gained our end. If they continue the publication we may at once prosecute. [139]

But where the continued prosecution of Sullivan was concerned Balfour's view prevailed and the case returned to the Dublin police court on 2 December. There O'Donel sentenced Sullivan to two months in prison.[140] Sullivan waived his right to appeal. However, the case against O'Brien was not pursued because, in the interim, he had become an inmate of Tullamore prison arising out of his appearance before the magistrates at Mitchelstown. The *Daily Express* heaved a sigh of relief and patted the administration on the back. 'The recent action of the government is all that can be desired.'[141]

Thereafter *United Ireland* was left entirely to its own devices, despite some egregious transgressions, as Dublin Castle concentrated its fire on the more fractious regional newspapers.

Notes

1   TNA, PRO, CO903/2. Miscellaneous Notes, Series ix, 9–14 – *Press prosecutions in Ireland in the Year 1889.*

2   22 May 1889, *Special Commission,* vol. 8, 165, 71571.

3   With 316 Tory seats in the House of Commons Salisbury was in a position to govern even without the support of the seventy-seven Liberal Unionists returned.

4   See Appendix 2 – Table 1 and Table 2.

5   *United Ireland*, 31 December 1881.

6   *United Ireland*, 17 April 1886.

7   O'Brien, *Parnell and his Party,* 199.

8   O'Callaghan, *British High Politics*, 107.

9   F.S.L. Lyons, 'Parnellism and Crime, 1887–90' in *Transactions of the Royal Historical Society*, fifth series, vol. 24, (1974), 138.

10 In his election address, on 19 June 1886, to the voters of South Paddington, quoted in an appendix to Winston Churchill's biography of his father, *Lord Randolph Churchill* (London, 1906) 2 vols, vol. 2, 492.

11 Margaret O'Callaghan, *British High Politics*, 113–14.

12 Edward Pearce, *Lines of Most Resistance: the Lords, the Tories and Ireland, 1886–1914* (London, 1999), 2.

13 Margaret O'Callaghan, *British High Politics*, 114.

14 *Times,* 7 March 1887.

15 *Belfast Newsletter*, 15 February 1890.

16 *The Special Commission on Parnellism and crime*, 11 vols, (London, 1890) vol. 1, 41.

17 *Special Commission*, vol. 1, 43.

18 Balfour to Buller, 13 March 1887, Balfour papers, BL, Add. Mss. 49826, f.29.

19 David Steele, *Lord Salisbury: a political biography*, (London, 2004), 200.

20 O'Callaghan, *British High Politics*, 132.

21 *Pall Mall Gazette*, 15 November 1886.

22 Margaret O'Callaghan, *British High Politics*, 109.

23 *United Ireland*, 28 August, 1886. The newspaper also gave him the unflattering nickname of 'Mickey the Botch', 29 January 1887.

24 *United Ireland* did make at least one ritual denunciation in which it described Hicks Beach as a 'vengeful and unsparing tyrant' – this was, ironically, in the course of an article alleging the existence of a government 'minute' in which the chief secretary agreed to a recommendation of the Attorney General, Hugh Holmes, *not* to prosecute *United Ireland* for the publication of a 'vindictive' speech (*United Ireland*, 2 October 1886). In *Evening Memories* O'Brien, albeit in 1920, described Hicks Beach as an, 'English gentleman of sensitive honour' (O'Brien, *Evening Memories,* 209).

25 *United Ireland*, 20 November 1886.

26 *United Ireland*, 27 November 1886.

27 O'Callaghan, *British High Politics*, 142.

28 *United Ireland*, 23 October 1886. In some analyses the Plan is seen as an undifferentiated response to ongoing agrarian issues and a renewal of the agricultural emergency of 1879. Others, like Phillip Bull, see it as 'a reactivation of land agitation to meet the necessities

of the nationalist movement' (Phillip Bull, *Land, politics and nationalism: a study of the Irish land question* (Dublin 1996), 104). Parnell's obvious disapproval would tend to add weight to the former interpretation.

29 Stephen Ball, *Policing the Land War: Official Responses to Political Protest and Agrarian Crime in Ireland, 1879–91*, Unpublished PhD thesis, Department of Historical and Cultural Studies, Goldsmith's College, London, 2000, 114.

30 13 January 1887, TNA, PRO, CAB 37/19, 1887 no. 1, Memo on Plan of Campaign, 1.

31 O'Brien, *Evening Memories*, 160.

32 *United Ireland*, 4 December 1886.

33 *Freeman's Journal*, 3 December 1886.

34 TNA, PRO, CAB 37/19 1887 No. 1, Memo on Plan of Campaign, 13 January 1887, 3.

35 TNA, PRO, CAB 37/19 1887 No. 1, Memo on Plan of Campaign, 13 January 1887, 3.

36 *Freeman's Journal*, 15 December 1886.

37 *United Ireland*, 24 December 1886.

38 *Freeman's Journal*, 17 December 1886.

39 O'Brien, *Evening Memories*, 192.

40 O'Brien, *Parnell and his party*, 207.

41 O'Brien, *Evening Memories*, 205–6.

42 TNA, PRO, CAB 37/19 1887, No. 1, Memo on Plan of Campaign, 13 January, 1887, 4.

43 *Freeman's Journal*, 25 February 1887.

44 TNA, PRO, CAB 37/19, 1887, No. 1, Memo on Plan of Campaign, 13 January 1887, 2.

45 13 January 1887, TNA, PRO, CAB 37/19, 1887, No. 1, Memo on Plan of Campaign, 1.

46 TNA, PRO, CAB 37/19, 1887, No.1, Memo on Plan of Campaign, 13 January 1887, 5.

47 In the original wording they would be 'transported beyond the seas' but, of course, by 1887 there was no such outlet available to the British government. The amendment was designed to rectify an anomaly in the original law whereby, in the words of Earl Stanley, then chief secretary 'a man who incited to these crimes was punishable with death, while he who committed them was only a misdemeanant' (HC Deb. 22 September 1831, vol. 7, cc487–8).

48 *United Ireland*, 8 January 1887.

49 *Freeman's Journal*, quoted in *Roscommon Herald*, 15 January 1887.

50 Charles Townshend, *Political Violence in Ireland: Government and Resistance since 1848* (Oxford, 1983), 96.

51 Arthur James Balfour, *A Defence of Philosophic Doubt; Being an Essay on the Foundations of Belief* (London, 1879).

52 *United Ireland*, 12 March 1887.

53 *United Ireland*, 27 September 1890.

54 *Freeman's Journal*, 7 March 1887.

55 *Pall Mall Gazette*, 7 March 1887.

56 Sydney H. Zebel, *Balfour, a Political Biography* (Cambridge, 1973), 63. According to Catherine B. Shannon, 'Balfour attributed the crofter no-rent campaign in the Highlands to the contagious example of Irish rural agitation' (Catherine B. Shannon, *Arthur J. Balfour and Ireland, 1874–1922* (Washington DC, 1988), 23).

57 R.J.Q. Adams, *Balfour, the Last Grandee* (London, 2007), 77.

58 Crossman, *Politics Law and Order*, 162.

59 Baron Peter O'Brien, *The Reminiscences of the Right. Hon. Lord O'Brien (of Kilfenora): Lord Chief Justice of Ireland* (Dublin, 1916), 71.

60 Shannon, *Arthur J. Balfour and Ireland*, 36.

61 O'Callaghan, *British High Politics*, 114.

62 *United Ireland*, 9 April 1887.

63 Balfour to Salisbury, 27 December 1887, British Library, Add. Mss. 49688 ff.186–9 [Copy].

64 Curtis, *Coercion and Conciliation*, 210.

65 Balfour to Buller, 13 March 1887, Balfour Papers, BL, Add. Mss. 49826, f.29.

66 *Public General Statutes passed in the Thirty-third & Thirty-fourth Years of the Reign of Her Majesty Queen Victoria* (London, 1870), 143.

67 Shannon, *Arthur J. Balfour and Ireland*, 37.

68 Balfour to Buller, 19 March 1887, Balfour Papers, BL, Add. Mss. 49826, f.33.

69 Adams, *Balfour*, 83.

70 HC Deb. 28 March 1887, vol. 312, c1651.

71 Balfour to Buller, 8 August 1887, Balfour Papers, BL, Add. Mss. 49826, f.149–52.

72 *United Ireland*, 1 October 1887.

73 HC Deb. 1 April 1887, vol. 313, c268.

74 *Kerry Sentinel*, 22 November 1887.

75 *United Ireland*, 28 June 1890.

76 *United Ireland*, 2 August, 1890

77 13 September 1886, Eugene O'Sullivan, *per pro* T.D. Sullivan, NAI, CSORP 1886/19605.

78 HC Deb. 10 September 1886, vol. 309, cc153.

79 *Northern Whig, Belfast Newsletter, Cork Constitution, Cork Examiner, Dublin Daily Express, Dublin Evening Mail, Freeman's Journal, Irish Times, Londonderry Sentinel, Tyrone Constitutional Waterford News* and *Galway Vindicator*. He could have added the *Dublin Daily Telegraph* had he been in a position to wait longer before answering

Clancy's question, first posed the previous day.

80   Clancy at first insisted that only one of the papers included on the list was nationalist. He quickly conceded that there were two. In fact there were three, the *Freeman's Journal*, Thomas Crosbie's *Cork Examiner* and Cornelius Redmond's *Waterford News*.

81   Mallon was presumably referring to the *Weekly Freeman*.

82   Hamilton to Hicks Beach, 6 October 1886, NAI, CSORP 1886/19605.

83   Civil Service commission to Hamilton, 26 October 1886, NAI, CSORP 1886/19605.

84   Hamilton to Lord Chancellor, 27 October 1886, NAI, CSORP 1886/19605.

85   Hicks Beach to Inspector of Fisheries, 5 November 1886, NAI, CSORP 1886/19605.

86   *United Ireland*, 14 January 1888.

87   HC Deb. 28 March 1887, vol. 312, c1656.

88   HC Deb. 28 March 1887, vol. 312, c1651.

89   HC Deb. 18 April 1887, vol. 313, c1222.

90   *Public General Statutes passed in the Fiftieth and Fifty-first Years of the Reign of Her Majesty, Queen Victoria, 1887* (London, 1887), 51–2.

91   Balfour to Buller, 8 August 1887, Balfour Papers, BL, Add. Mss. 49826, f.149–52.

92   HC Deb. 31 March 1887, vol. 313, c.100.

93   HC Deb. 1 April 1887, vol. 313, c266.

94   HC Deb. 1 April 1887, vol. 313, c275.

95   With the single exception of Patrick Corcoran of the *Cork Examiner*.

96   HC Deb. 25 August 1887, vol. 319, c1842.

97   *Kerry Sentinel*, 8 April 1887.

98   HC Deb. 7 June 1887, vol. 315, c1255.

99   TNA, PRO, CO 903/2, series no. vi, 3 (Undated – probably February 1888).

100 *The Nation*, 27 August 1887.

101 Balfour to Salisbury, 27 December 1887, BL, Add. Mss. 49688 ff. 186–9 [Copy].

102 Adams, *Balfour*, 85.

103 *Cork Daily Herald*, 21 December 1887.

104 TNA, PRO, CO 903/2, Series No. V, 3–11, February 1888.

105 Balfour had written to Londonderry, the Lord Lieutenant, of Ridgeway, a highly esteemed colonial civil servant that 'he is an Irishman by birth, which is a good thing; but has never lived in Ireland; which is not a bad thing' (Balfour to Londonderry, 12 August 1887, BL, Add. Mss. 49826, ff.159–60).

106 Patrick Maume, '"This Proteus of politics": the *Dublin Evening Mail* on Gladstone, 1868–1898' in Daly and Hoppen, *Gladstone: Ireland and Beyond* (Dublin, 2011), 103.

107 Quoted in *United Ireland*, 27 August 1887.

108 *United Ireland*, 3 September 1887.

109 Gladstone to Sullivan, 7 October, 1887, quoted in J.B. Hall, *Random Records of a Reporter* (Dublin, 1928), 232.

110 *United Ireland*, 27 August 1887.

111 *United Ireland*, 1 October 1887, *Nation*, 1 October 1887.

112 *Freeman's Journal*, 7 October 1887.

113 TNA PRO CO903/1/4, 5 'Press prosecutions in Ireland from the passing of the Criminal Law and Procedure Act up to the 31st March, 1890.'

114 *Nation*, 1 October 1887.

115 *United Ireland*, 1 October 1887.

116 *United Ireland*, 1 October 1887.

117 J.B.Hall, *Random Records*, 232

118 T.D.Sullivan, *Recollections*, 237.

119 *Freeman's Journal*, 7 October 1887.

120 *Daily Express*, 7 October 1887.

121 *United Ireland*, 8 October 1887.

122 T.D.Sullivan, *Recollections*, 238.

123 *Wexford People*, 5 October 1887.

124 Neither the Liberal or Tory administration was eager to confront the 'aggressive breaches of verbal decorum, like those of the populist nationalist journals' indulged in by unionist newspapers like the *Evening Mail* (Maume, 'This Proteus of politics' in *Gladstone: Ireland and beyond*, 120) although to have done so would have disarmed allegations of partiality and allowed for action against similar excesses in nationalist journals. However, to have challenged either would have jeopardized the official assertions that censorship of commentary was *ultra vires*.

125 See fn.110.

126 Other than to point out that many of the newspaper accounts were of fictional meetings (see below).

127 *Freeman's Journal*, 7 October 1887.

128 *Evening Mail*, 7 October 1887, *Daily Express*, 7 October 1887.

129 *Daily News*, 7 October 1887.

130 *Times*, 7 October 1887.

131 *Standard*, 7 October 1887.

132 Curtis, *Coercion and Conciliation*, 194.

133 *Freeman's Journal*, 11 November 1887.

134 West Ridgeway to Balfour, 7 November 1887, BL, Add. Mss. 49808 f.4–6.

135 For example, in relation to the prosecution of news-vendors. See below (Chapter 8).

136 Balfour to West Ridgeway, 8 November 1887, Add. Mss. 49808, f.7–10.

137 Curtis, *Coercion and Conciliation*, 209.

138 Salisbury to Balfour, 14 October 1887, cited in Robin Harcourt Williams, *The Salisbury–Balfour Correspondence, 1869–1892* (London, 1988), 212.

139 West Ridgeway to Balfour, 10 November 1887, BL, Add. Mss. 49808, ff.14–17.

140 As a first-class misdemeanant, thus guaranteeing him a less rigorous prison regime than that of a felon and rather less onerous than the norm for subsequent Crimes Act prisoners. In Richmond prison he occupied the same cell allocated to Edmund Dwyer Gray in 1882 but he was soon transferred to the more spartan Tullamore prison. TNA, PRO, CO 903/1/4, 5, 'Press prosecutions in Ireland from the passing of the Criminal Law and Procedure Act of 1887 up to the 31st March 1890.' and TNA, PRO, CO 903/2, 23 November 1887, 'Report on treatment of first class misdemeanants'.

141 *Daily Express*, 3 December 1887.

CHAPTER SEVEN

'Pigottism' and Crime –
Balfour and *United Ireland,*
1887–90

The prosecution of the *Nation* was the first and last case pursued to a conclusion by the Tories against any nationally circulated newspaper. In contrast to the prolonged struggle between the Liberal government and *United Ireland*, the Conservative administration declined to take the Parnellite journal to court after the initial inconclusive charges in October 1887. Beyond that first arraignment, and despite a number of clear opportunities and provocations, *United Ireland* appeared to lead a charmed life. The obvious question is, why, given its infinite capacity for inflicting propagandistic damage on the Balfour administration, was this the case?

By 1886, as O'Brien put it himself '*United Ireland* was now in the full tide and torrent of its power.' The high-water mark of its circulation – 125,000 – was 'reached with the number that presented a coloured portrait of Gladstone'.[1] From being a drain on the resources of the Land League in 1881–2 the newspaper was, apparently, channelling a generous proportion of its profits into the coffers of the National League by mid-decade. O'Brien mentions the sum of £2,000 as having been forwarded 'for the national funds' in 1886. This is largely confirmed by accounts for the Irish Newspaper and Publishing Company that show an excess of income over expenditure for the financial year – ending 31 August 1886 – of £1,943.[2] The newspaper also had as a fighting fund 'a considerable sum to our credit in the Hibernian Bank'.[3]

A further contrasting element, other than the paper's rude financial health, with the Liberal government era, was the question of editorship. William O'Brien had spent six months in Kilmainham prison from October 1881 to the end of April 1882 and was, from February 1883 to December 1885, the representative of the people of Mallow in the House of Commons. But those constraints, preventing him from devoting himself entirely to his newspaper, were eclipsed in the period 1887–91. His routine involvement with *United Ireland* during that period was heavily circumscribed by the regularity and duration of his incarcerations under the Tories, and the extent of his personal commitment to the Plan of Campaign. In effect, from the time of the passage of the 1887 Crimes Act, O'Brien ceased to have much day-to-day connection with *United Ireland*. His name continued to appear on the back page as the sole proprietor of the journal and, as he acknowledged to the *Times* commission in 1889, he was still responsible for its editorial content. But the editorship of the newspaper passed to barrister and journalist Matthias McDonnell Bodkin, described by O'Brien as 'a devoted friend, who during my now constant compulsory absences conducted the paper with a combined daring and wisdom that was never at fault in the perilous years of our mortal combat with Mr. Balfour'.[4]

Bodkin's apprenticeship, like that of O'Brien himself, had been served while writing for the *Freeman's Journal*. There he came under the tutelage of the editor John B. Gallagher, 'a Whig of the old school [who] never allowed his personal views to influence the conduct of the paper'.[5] Bodkin and O'Brien had first met when O'Brien had consulted the younger man, then a practising barrister, during his campaign against alleged miscarriages of justice in late 1882. Bodkin became a contributor and, after O'Brien's incarceration in late 1887, acting editor.[6] By his own acknowledgement Bodkin wrote virtually all the newspaper's editorials between September 1887 and December 1890, and during that period, '*United Ireland* was conducted in defiance of the laws of libel'.[7]

Just as the newspaper appeared to lead a charmed life during Balfour's tenure so too did Bodkin himself. There is no evidence in the recoverable files[8] of the Chief Secretary's Office that Dublin Castle was aware of who was responsible for the editing and leader-writing duties of *United Ireland* during O'Brien's long absences. Indeed the reverse is the case. In May 1888, more than six months after Bodkin had taken over the editorship, West Ridgeway wrote to Balfour noting that 'we are ready to prosecute *United Ireland* immediately an enquiry has shown us who are responsible for its publication.'[9] As late as June 1890, in response to an inquiry from West Ridgeway as to who actually was accountable for the output of the newspaper, Harrel, Dublin Metropolitan Police Commissioner, could do no better than assert that 'William O'Brien M.P. is proprietor and editor. John J. O'Shea is sub editor. James O'Connor is sub editor. Edward Donnelly is printer. I have no doubt that if it were decided to proceed against "United Ireland" evidence would be forthcoming to prove that the above named or at least some of them discharged the duties of the offices assigned to them.'[10] Just a few months before, O'Brien had written to the actual editor from France saying 'I hope the burden of *UI* [*sic*] has not yet broken your back. If all goes well I hope very soon to relieve you of a little portion of the load.'[11]

O'Brien was careful when giving evidence to the *Times* commission (see below), in response to a general question asking him to identify any of those who had collaborated with him in the production of the newspaper, not to make any reference whatever to Bodkin.[12] O'Connor, Healy, J.J. O'Shea, James Bryce Killen and T.P. Gill were all mentioned, but O'Brien scrupulously avoided crediting Bodkin with making any contribution to the editorial policies of the paper. When, on 15 December 1888, Bodkin published a scathing leader about the delinquencies of the *Times* commission, accompanied by a telling cartoon, the attorney general demanded that the presiding judges summon O'Brien to offer an explanation and an apology.[13] Bodkin sought leave from O'Brien to appear in his place as he felt that 'I should be allowed to take the defence of the article I had written on my own shoulders. I assured him that I had written it with the hope of proceedings and with a view to its defence.'[14] O'Brien refused the request and made an exculpatory speech before the Commisison in January 1889 which impressed the three presiding judges.[15]

O'Brien's refusal to allow Bodkin to plead may have been because he believed himself to have been a better advocate than the young part-time barrister. Alternatively we can credit his own explanation to Bodkin, who was informed that 'there are half a dozen Coercion summonses and warrants out against me at present. If I am caught first by the *Times* I will be treated as a first-class misdemeanant, which is luxury compared to the lot of a Coercion Court prisoner.'[16] However, it is just as likely that O'Brien was endeavouring to protect Bodkin from undue negative public attention.

Less well-recognized than the contribution to *United Ireland* of Bodkin was the editorial influence of John Dillon. This dated from as early as 1887, when Dillon was instructing Bodkin to deal with a perceived *faux pas* of Davitt's.[17] His advice on that occasion included the wording of a tentative disavowal of a speech by Davitt in which, in the context of the renewed agrarian campaign, the Land League founder had expressed reservations at his previous condemnation of 'moonlighting'. Dillon, after suggesting how Bodkin should distance the Plan of Campaign from Davitt's intemperate language, added a cautionary note, telling the acting editor that, 'you had better be very guarded & cautious in your references to Davitt'.[18]

The following year Dillon, along with Timothy Harrington, intervened directly in preventing the publication of an editorial written by a disillusioned O'Brien after Parnell's speech to the 80 Club in London in May 1888 in which he had disparaged the Plan of Campaign. O'Brien had written a leader that Bodkin was instructed to publish. It concluded, 'we cannot honestly endorse Mr. Parnell's reasoning; we loyally and finally bow to his authoritative judgment. He is the only man living who has the right or has the power to wound the Plan of Campaign in a fatal spot. May the new policy which he foreshadows prove to be as strong an armour for oppressed Irishmen and as redoubtable a terror for their foes.'[19] In an accompanying note Dillon credits Harrington with actually preventing the publication of O'Brien's leader. 'Had it been published,' wrote Dillon, 'it would have utterly ruined our movement and driven me and others out of public life.'[20] However, O'Brien's response to the interception of his diatribe was a telegram to Dillon rather than Harrington. It read simply, 'do as you desire?'[21] The two editorials actually published in the following issue of *United Ireland* were a polemic on the ongoing Carnarvon–Parnell controversy and a ritual obituary notice for the 1887 Crimes Act.[22]

Dillon's involvement in editorial decisions continued up to the cessation of Bodkin's own connection with the newspaper in December 1890. A number of pieces of correspondence of that year point to the influence wielded by Dillon. In these Bodkin is supplied with copy, instructed as to content and upbraided for the inclusion of articles that 'irritate O'Brien excessively and can not serve any object'.[23] In his memoir of his period as acting editor of *United Ireland* Bodkin makes no reference whatever to any participation on the part of Dillon in editorial decisions. But the frequency of the former's correspondence and its often peremptory tone suggest that Bodkin was circumscribed in exercising his editorial remit and answerable not just to O'Brien. It is notable that during Bodkin's tenure as O'Brien's deputy *United Ireland*'s praise of Dillon's speeches and actions became increasingly extravagant. Dillon virtually replaced Parnell as *primus inter pares* in the editorial columns of the newspaper. During a period in which the party leader ruled almost *in absentia* he was virtually supplanted by his most influential deputy in the panegyrics of the Parnellite newspaper.[24]

Just as Bodkin, not unexpectedly, extolled the virtues of the Irish Party leadership in the columns of *United Ireland*, so did he continue the O'Brien practice of excoriation of the 'enemy'. Into this category fell Tory ministers and politicians, unionist leaders and journalists, Castle functionaries, policemen and resident magistrates. Bodkin's rhetoric of animosity during the tenure of the Conservative administration was on a par with that of O'Brien's during the period of Liberal governance.

How *United Ireland* avoided a raft of personal libel suits during this period remains something of a mystery. It must be assumed that many of its 'victims' did not want to be seen to sue a journal of such 'ill-repute', while for others there was actually an element of cachet in being attacked in its columns. One of Balfour's most active, highly thought of[25] and, consequently, reviled resident magistrates was Lieutenant Colonel Alfred Turner, who had responsibility for the hotspots of Clare and Kerry. He was the subject of constant abuse in the columns of *United Ireland*. The Castle itself recorded eleven violent attacks on Turner in the newspaper, nine of those coming between 1888 and 1890.[26] Those gibes prompted Turner to observe to the chief secretary that 'the abuse of O'Brien and the like is … not unpleasing'.[27] Clearly nationalist excoriation did no harm to Turner's career prospects. In his autobiography, *Sixty years of a soldier's life*, Turner described *United*

Ireland as 'a most ably edited but terribly vituperative weekly'.[28] He actually found some of the 'epithets' hurled at him by the newspaper so colourful that he quoted them at length in his memoir.[29]

However when *United Ireland*, in editorials entitled 'The lie direct' and 'Ferocity and falsehood', accused Turner of lying under oath, the under secretary wrote to Balfour apprising him of the fact that 'Turner wishes to go for "United Ireland" which charged him in gross terms with perjury. The A.G. is considering the matter – favourably I hope'.[30] It is unclear whether Turner was awaiting permission from his superiors to pursue a private prosecution for libel or whether the law officers were adjudicating on whether the Crown itself should take a case of criminal libel on his behalf. The judgment of Peter O'Brien, newly promoted to the position of Attorney General, was that 'as Colonel Turner has effectively vindicated himself in public estimation from all libellous attacks I think it is better not to gratify libellers by bringing an action against them and enabling them to appeal to the disaffected portion of the public for sympathy'.[31] It was a legal opinion that encapsulates one of the main reasons why *United Ireland* was not subjected to more actions for defamation. Either a civil suit from Turner or a criminal prosecution on the part of the Crown would have experienced grave difficulties with an Irish jury. There is little doubt, unless the journal could prove its allegation, that Turner would have won damages in another jurisdiction.[32]

Subsequently *United Ireland* attempted to provoke Turner into instituting a personal lawsuit, inviting him to do so in the columns of the paper. It was clear from the heavy hints dropped by Bodkin in the columns of the journal that he believed he had evidence of sexual misconduct against the magistrate.[33] The paper was clearly hoping that Balfour would, as others in his position had done in the past, encourage private prosecutions for libel by some of his officials. Bodkin wrote in October 1888, 'we trust … that Colonel Turner's courage has been screwed to the sticking-point in his last interview with Mr. Balfour, and that the wretched Colonel is to be the scapegoat of his Chief's newest device to avenge his failure in intimidating the Press'.[34] The journal, however, was not to be favoured with a heterosexual re-run of the Castle 'scandals' of 1883–4, though its information against Turner was probably accurate enough. In a letter to Balfour in September, 1888 West Ridgeway admitted that Turner was vulnerable on that count, 'sometimes', he informed the Chief Secretary, 'there is a lady in the case'.[35]

In a subsequent missive the under secretary referred to the affair 'taking a nasty turn' and a 'discharged servant incident'.[36]

In a November 1890 memorandum, prepared for the cabinet, the Irish Office quantified the extent of the personalized and often libellous abuse of resident magistrates by *United Ireland*. Their research stretched back to 1882. It is noteworthy that far more of the pejorative coverage emanated from the 1887–90 period. The memo noted a total of sixty magistrates who had been 'attacked' in the columns of *United Ireland*, fifty-four of whom were still serving. During that period only twenty resident magistrates had escaped the attention of the newspaper, eleven of those were based in Antrim, Armagh, Down, Fermanagh and Derry. The other nine, the memo noted, 'owe their immunity to the fact that from one reason or other they have not had thrown upon them the duty of administering the [Crimes] Act'.[37]

A grand total of 137 abusive or negative references to resident magistrates was noted in the pages of *United Ireland* in the nine years covered by the survey. While fifteen cases were recorded under Liberal administrations (1882–5 and January to July 1886) 122 instances were recorded under the Conservatives. The bulk of those, 108, came in the wake of the passage of the 1887 Crimes Act.

The annual totals were as follows:

1882	3
1883	5
1884	4
1885	8
1886	1
1887	34
1888	39
1889	18
1890	25[38]

Not unexpectedly 1886, the year of Home Rule, was the twelve-month period during which *United Ireland* avoided almost completely any criticism of the magistracy. On the other hand the busiest year for contumely was 1888, the first full year of the operation of the Crimes Act. Interestingly only six of the 137 editorial items on magistrates carried by the newspaper referred to press-related prosecutions. One of those was from 1882 and half from 1887. Not all of the disparagement related to court cases. Magistrates were also criticized, for example, for their handling of public order incidents.[39] The most-abused magistrate was not, in fact, the aforementioned Alfred Turner, but his colleague Cecil Roche, based in Munster and dubbed by *United Ireland* 'the briefless barrister'.[40] He was subjected to a total of twenty-six personal attacks in the pages of the newspaper, was accused of 'low vices and foul tongued profanity'[41] and of avoiding his creditors.[42] Roche did not sue *United Ireland* either. According to West Ridgeway neither he, nor Turner, 'would care to have any old indiscretions raked up in cross examination'.[43] Neither did the Crown institute libel prosecutions in defence of its own stipendiaries. The memorandum outlining the extent of the 'attacks' is full of statistical and anecdotal information as well as extensive quotation. However, it offers no definitive explanation as to why, despite its many clear violations of the laws of libel, *United Ireland* was never held to account.

It was not as if these officials were unwilling to take legal action against other newspapers to defend their reputations. In at least two instances magistrates sued the much more 'respectable' *Freeman's Journal*. To a Victorian gentleman the *Journal* was a newspaper whose defamatory comments would inevitably come to the attention of one's peers. Vesey Fitzgerald RM, for example, won a case against the *Freeman's Journal* taken in Belfast, though the jury failed to agree on damages.[44] Another RM, Captain Stokes, successfully sued the *Journal* for publication of a speech by William O'Brien in which he claimed to have been libelled. No action, however, was taken against O'Brien for the speech itself. The contents of the speech had also been published by the unionist *Daily Express* and *Irish Times*, but no similar action was taken against either of those newspapers.[45]

In addition to the dozens of stipendiary magistrates who might have had legal claims against *United Ireland*, many other public and private citizens could have opted to sue the newspaper. The editor's namesake, Judge William O'Brien, was, for example, described as 'the most corrupt judge on the Irish Bench' and 'the ugliest man in Europe' in the same editorial.[46] While the latter claim may well have been justifiable as fair comment the former was certainly actionable. Captain William O'Shea was once called a 'furtive professional pimp and go-between'.[47] A Crown prosecutor in

Tipperary, Arnold Power was described by *United Ireland* as 'a pimp and a spy'[48] without any consequences. Unionist journalists and editors were regularly subjected to defamatory abuse but made no legal response.

In his memoir the barrister, attorney general, judge and lord chancellor, Peter O'Brien, with some pride, referred to himself as having 'the distinction of being the most abused man in Ireland'.[49] O'Brien was certainly vilified and, arguably, libelled by *United Ireland* on a regular basis. In September 1887, in the wake of the Mitchelstown killings, *United Ireland* alleged that it had in its possession a cipher telegram sent by O'Brien, then Solicitor General, to Edward Carson. The latter was Crown prosecutor in the Crimes Act trial of William O'Brien. The newspaper editor was being defended, over-vigorously in eyes of the Castle, by Timothy Harrington. The substance of the *United Ireland* story was that Peter O'Brien was making plans to have Harrington disbarred at the next Benchers meeting.[50] Both Carson and O'Brien denied the allegation.[51] In its edition of 15 October 1887 *United Ireland* invited Peter O'Brien to sue the newspaper for libel. 'The burden of proof will be upon us,' the journal claimed, adding invitingly that if the story was inaccurate 'nothing can save us … from ruin.'[52] O'Brien was very highly thought of by West Ridgeway. He wrote to Balfour in December 1887, in disparaging terms of O'Brien's senior colleague, then Attorney General, John Gibson (brother of Ashbourne), concluding that 'I shall be very glad indeed when he moves up and makes room for Mr. O'Brien.'[53]

It may be argued that, even in the nineteenth century, where the 'professionalisation' of journalism was still in its infancy, there was a reluctance on the part of members of the fourth estate to sue each other for libel. They had at their disposal, after all, and were not averse to using, the columns of their own publications to respond to everything from robust criticism to outright defamation. Nonetheless, journalists did sue other journalists for libel in the 1880s. William O'Brien himself, for example, took legal action against the unionist *Cork Constitution* in 1888 for an article in which it was alleged that 'the meanest and most criminal motives' were attributed to him by the newspaper.[54] In the course of the action O'Brien alleged that he had been accused of making his living from murder and violence.[55] He won his case and received damages. However, none of O'Brien's habitual targets in his own profession, most notably Dr G.V. Patton, editor of the *Daily Express* and Irish correspondent of the *Times*, ever sought damages for potentially libellous comments made about them in *United Ireland*. O'Brien on the other hand sought, and secured, at least one apology from Patton.[56] While it was not beneath O'Brien's dignity to seek a retraction from Patton it was, presumably, *infra dig* for his unionist rival to 'notice' *United Ireland's* vilification. The fictional Quintus Slide of Trollope's *Daily Banner* was far from being the only nineteenth-century journalist to be considered beneath contempt.

Clearly, as we shall see below, there was a marked disinclination on the part of the Crown to take on *United Ireland* for a variety of alleged infractions. In that context it was understandable that individual officials might have been even more reluctant to challenge the licence accorded O'Brien's publication. There also existed a certain Victorian bravado associated with displaying a capacity to tolerate whatever punishment, short of physical violence, was being doled out by one's enemies. As Peter O'Brien observed in his memoir (edited by his son), 'Newspaper abuse never yet intimidated anyone worth his salt.'[57]

There was, as has been pointed out in the case of Colonel Turner, also an element of kudos associated with being the target of a newspaper such as *United Ireland*. In William O'Brien's own lawsuit against the *Cork Constitution* the man who was responsible for the actual writing of the libel – later proved against the defendants – W.J. Ludgate, was questioned for the plaintiff by Tim Healy. In the course of his cross-examination Ludgate claimed that he was 'called a liar every day in the *Cork Herald*' and it was pointed out that he featured in a list of hostile journalists published by *United Ireland* under the title 'Brigade of Liars'. When asked by Healy if, as a consequence, he harboured ill-feeling towards either of the nationalist publications in question Ludgate replied that he treated such attacks as testimonials 'calculated to benefit me in the eyes of those who employ me.'[58]

An additional disincentive might have been that any plaintiff suing *United Ireland* in an Irish court would be unlikely to succeed in convincing a jury of the justice of his cause. But while that may have been the case in an action taken in Dublin, it was certainly not a hindrance to an action in Belfast or in Britain, where the paper was also published. However a clear deterrent was the lack of resources of O'Brien himself. The only successful suit against the *United Ireland* editor had been that of George Bolton in Belfast in 1884. The editor always claimed that he had never paid the damages owed, nor had he ever reimbursed Bolton's costs, as he had neither the means nor the inclination to do so. While the newspaper itself did have resources, as noted above, these could be rapidly dispersed by O'Brien to avoid distraint.

Matthias McDonnell Bodkin acknowledged in his memoir *Recollections of an Irish Judge* that '*United Ireland* in my time had not only immunity from libel actions, but stranger still it had immunity from coercion prosecutions.'[59] He failed to offer any explanation as to why this might have been the case. The understandable reluctance on the part of public officials to take on *United Ireland* in the civil courts was clearly matched at executive level in Dublin Castle. This disinclination was often noted by the journal itself and by other nationalist newspapers. At least one, the *Waterford News*, in 1890, contrasted this phenomenon with the government's enthusiasm for prosecuting the provincial press: 'The Balfourian government dares not enter the lists with *United Ireland* – evil deeds by stealth is their motto and they satisfy their revengeful cravings by slinking into a provincial town and striking a blow at the proprietor of a provincial journal.'[60]

In the early months of the operation of the Crimes Act there does appear to have been an intention on the part of the Conservatives to commence a struggle with *United Ireland* comparable to that of their Liberal predecessors. With O'Brien on bail, pending appeal after the Mitchelstown trial, the Castle became interested in who might replace him as editor. Balfour himself inquired of his subordinates in October 1887, 'if O'Brien's sentence is confirmed who will be responsible for *United Ireland* when he is in Gaol?'[61] In a follow-up communication to the DMP West Ridgeway urged the police to investigate the matter and identify O'Brien's successor.[62] In response the DMP commissioner, David Harrel, pointed out that the newspaper was distributed by Messrs Charles Eason and Son, and that 'I have no doubt that Mr. Eason or some person in his establishment may be relied on to prove as to the carrying on of the business of the paper.'[63]

In early January 1888, *United Ireland* itself clearly advertised the fact that the Castle was about to move against it. It flagged to its readers the warning that the chief secretary 'is going to seize *United Ireland* at headquarters. He has failed to break us down by attacking our newsagents and imprisoning our editor, so at last, at long last, he has nerved himself to walk into the lion's den in Lower Abbey-street.'[64] The reference to the 'newsagents' was to an alternative means of harassing *United Ireland* then being explored by

Balfour. This consisted of arresting newsagents in proscribed areas selling copies of the journal containing illegal National League branch notices. A number of newsagents were prosecuted in this way between November 1887 and March 1888. Whatever information, if any, *United Ireland* had obtained leading it to anticipate such a raid, turned out to be inaccurate. The offices of the journal were left untouched.

Not that the executive had given up on the idea of punitive action against the newspaper. In April 1888 West Ridgeway was inquiring of the chief secretary whether he believed '*United Ireland* should be proceeded against. That newspaper has, in its last number, intimidating notices.'[65] The following month the under secretary gave as his reason for seeking an extension of the Crimes Act to the city of Dublin that 'we cannot strike at *United Ireland* or the central League until that section has been extended'.[66] Balfour seemed to indicate his acquiescence in a letter of 19 May 1888 pronouncing himself inclined 'to proceed, at all events, against *United Ireland*'.[67] A hint as to why no action was actually taken is contained in the last line of Balfour's letter in which he urges West Ridgeway to 'hurry up the attorney general'.

The paper, as befitted a journal carrying reports of suppressed National League branches on a weekly basis, remained under close scrutiny throughout the most intense period of the Plan of Campaign and the operation of the Crimes Act.[68] While Balfour and West Ridgeway occasionally demanded action against *United Ireland* it would appear that the law officers required an especially high standard of evidence to persuade themselves to initiate a prosecution against the newspaper. The mere fact of the publication of notices of suppressed branches was deemed insufficient to merit prosecution in the case of the Parnellite weekly. Even in the context of a change of emphasis, from March 1888, in the nature of press prosecutions, the law office evinced a clear reluctance to take action against the nationalist weekly. A slight relaxation in the prosecutorial regime at that time meant that evidence of 'local injury' consequent on boycotting or intimidation, as opposed to the mere publication of reports of suppressed branches was, in future, required before the initiation of legal proceedings.[69]

However, despite the enforcement of this modified regime in the case of local newspapers, *United Ireland* still appeared to be exempt from prosecution. In June 1890, for example, a firearms attack on a tenant farmer in Clare, James Molony of Ballykinnacurra, forced him to give up his share of an 'evicted' farm he had taken along with three others. Details of the condemnation of Molony, issued by the suppressed local National League branch, had been carried in *United Ireland*. That alone might not have been sufficient to rouse the law office, but there were additional aggravating grounds for action. West Ridgeway wrote to the chief secretary about the case on 25 June 1890: 'Here is a case against *United Ireland* which it may be desirable to prosecute. *United Ireland* denounces and an attempt to murder follows. I would put the whole working staff of the newspaper into the dock if the A.G. [*sic*] thinks that a prosecution can be instituted.'[70]

Balfour immediately sought an interview with the attorney general but no action was taken. Shortly thereafter the other three partners in the joint enterprise handed back their shares to the landlord. This prompted West Ridgeway to write to Balfour that, despite his recommendation for the prosecution of *United Ireland*, 'its intimidation has now appeared to be successful.'[71] An appended note in the relevant file, initialled by Balfour, instructed the attorney general that 'this should be dealt with promptly'. More than a month later the file was still circulating among law office functionaries and nothing had been done. The file was then mislaid and, yet again, no action was taken against *United Ireland*. It is clear from the documentation on the case that the law officers were seeking, unnecessarily under the strict terms of the Crimes act, to establish a definite connection between the sanctions ordered by the National League against Molony, an attack that took place on him, and his decision to give up his share of the evicted farm. The reluctance of the law officers to prosecute is as apparent as the frustration of their political masters.

So, while there was little ambivalence over the prosecution of local newspaper editors under the Conservatives, there was a distinct lack of enthusiasm for confrontation where *United Ireland* was concerned. In his own memoir, written almost thirty years after the events in question, O'Brien offered a (rather obvious) explanation for the Tory reluctance to prosecute. Referring to Hicks Beach, O'Brien pointed out that he was given ample provocation but 'maybe his Dublin Castle advisers were rather disposed, from gruesome experiences of their own, to give him exaggerated fore-warnings against treading again the bitter Calvary of Forster and Spencer'.[72]

West Ridgeway appeared to give credence to O'Brien's 'vestigial memory' explanation. In one of his anti-*United Ireland* diatribes to Balfour, in

September 1888, based actually on a Bodkin editorial on the magistracy – 'Devils citing scripture' – the under secretary suggested that 'the law officers be instructed emphatically that the first opportunity is taken of prosecuting O'Brien for articles such as this. I say "emphatically" because there is decidedly an inclination in the Law Room to leave O'Brien alone and I do not think that it is based entirely on legal grounds. It would be a great coup to run him in on such a charge.'[73] The under secretary appeared to hold the denizens of the law office in some contempt. After the debacle of Pigott's *Times* commission evidence and suicide, he took a perverse pleasure in the 'dismay' of the Castle's legal establishment, referring to them in a letter to Balfour as 'our weak-kneed brethren in Dublin'.[74]

L.P. Curtis acknowledges this consistent lack of will on the part of the law officers (even Balfour's personal favourite, attorney general Peter O'Brien) ascribing it entirely to a simple reluctance to arraign (William) O'Brien, a reluctance that also extended to the prosecution of Dillon. 'The truth was these two men caused the administration almost as much trouble in prison as they did when free. The Irish law officers never enjoyed the prospect of prosecuting them.'[75] Given the amount of time O'Brien[76] spent in prison or on bail during the late 1880s it is difficult to accept that the Castle was not prepared to prosecute him, however reluctant they might have been to do so. But this could have been an unspoken factor in the failure to deal rigorously with *United Ireland*. The failure to identify Bodkin as *locum tenens* and to take legal action against *him* was another factor in allowing *United Ireland* untrammelled access to its radicalized readership.

A further complicating factor was that many of the reports being carried in *United Ireland*, and in local newspapers, of the activities of National League branches, were bogus. As early as December 1887, long before the Crimes act had definitively proved its effectiveness in suppressing the activities of the National League across most of the country, the RIC was reporting that meetings in proscribed districts, advertised in the nationalist press as having taken place, were actually fictional. An RIC Sergeant in Macroom, Co. Cork, outlined what was really happening: 'On Saturday evening the Secretary draws up a report of the meeting dated for the next day, Sunday, in which he gives a list of resolutions passed, &c., &c. … and the report duly appears in the newspaper.'[77]

The following year out of twenty-seven meetings reported to have taken place in Co. Kerry the RIC deemed twenty-two to have been bogus.[78] The practice continued into 1889. A Cabinet memo, circulated by Balfour, noted that 'imaginary proceedings of imaginary meetings are concocted by the Secretary and an account sent to the local newspapers, or *United Ireland*.'[79] However, it should be noted that in no instance was a case taken to court in order to expose such alleged fictions. It must also be borne in mind that it would have suited the local constabulary to claim that a high percentage of reported meetings were spurious.

Perhaps the conviction of the administration that a sizeable percentage of the reports of National League meetings carried in the paper were bogus might well have been tested in the courts. While prosecutions would probably have collapsed had cases been based on reports found to be false, the potential for the embarrassment of *United Ireland* and the implication that the health of the League at local level was based on such fictions, might have been worth the effort.

But did the reluctance to take on *United Ireland* begin and end in the Dublin Castle law office or did it actually extend all the way to the top? Was there an element of caution and restraint where Balfour was concerned as well? Was there a distinct unwillingness to become involved in a war on too many fronts simultaneously? A crucial indicator as to Balfour's strategy came in a memo to West Ridgeway written a year after the publication of the Crimes Act had emphatically demonstrated the new chief secretary's robust approach to public order issues. It signalled a potential change in tactics, one that tallied with the inherent caution of the law office.

This was written at a time when only half a dozen cases had been taken against newspaper editors, all but one of which were for the mere publication of the notices of suppressed branches of the National League.[80] The memo found Balfour in circumspect mode, possibly chastened by the difficulties encountered in the Sullivan case and the failure, on appeal, of the case taken in October 1887 against Edward Walsh of the *Wexford People*. He informed the under secretary that, with regard to future press prosecutions 'my inclination, at this moment, is to hold our hand, to watch events carefully; to take careful note of any illegal publication; (especially when it is of intimidatory character); and to watch how far impunity will conduce to increased violations of the 7th section'. He continued in prudent vein, while emphasizing that 'these observations I do not make dogmatically':

> Interest in the Irish controversy is, for the present, diminishing
> on this side of the Channel; and I am rather unwilling to revive
> it by a fight at what is after all the weakest point in our line
> of defence; i.e. – the press prosecutions. I think, if we went
> at anybody we should be obliged to go at *United Ireland,* and
> there would come to be a life and death struggle between that
> newspaper and the Government, having among its incidents
> repeated prosecutions, and, possibly, imprisonment of William
> O'Brien. This ... might have, among its other consequences,
> that of reviving the waning influence of the newspaper in
> question.[81]

So, while counselling a prudent approach, it is apparent that Balfour was
only advocating this policy because, as he perceived it at least, there was no
necessity to ratchet up the conflict with *United Ireland* into a 'life and death
struggle'. This would involve contending with O'Brien, a journalist with
a high degree of visibility among committed advocates of press freedom
in England (some of whom were in the ranks of the Liberal Unionists).
A similar sentiment dictated discretion when it came to the possibility,
mooted in 1888, of prosecuting T.P. O'Connor's *Star* newspaper in England
for criminal libel after it described the death of nationalist prisoner John
Mandeville in July 1888 as 'murder'.[82]

When the press campaign was later intensified the targets were vulnerable
local newspaper editors rather than the more celebrated and prominent
proprietors of *United Ireland* and the *Star.* The Parnellite newspaper itself
overtly acknowledged as much in 1890 when it wrote that '*United Ireland*
is exempted because an attack on *United Ireland* would inevitably attract
public attention.'[83]

Left unstated in Balfour's memo on that occasion was the possibility that
an over-vigorous approach to *United Ireland,* leading to, at worst, its closure,
would put pressure on the more moderate *Freeman's Journal* to issue a
challenge of its own to the administration by infringing the Crimes Act.
A few months before, in correspondence with the prime minister, Balfour
had mooted the possibility that any sign of weakness on the part of the

administration might prompt the *Journal*, already coming under just such pressure, to ape its nationalist rivals. Back then, in December 1887, he had noted that 'our proceedings have produced a violent attack by the partisans of the offending newspapers against the *Freeman's Journal* which has kept within the law – *not* I need hardly say through loyalty, but through fear'. He went on to predict that 'if we give up the battle the *Freeman* will of course go in heart and soul for the suppressed branches, and our difficulties will be greatly increased'.[84] However, the logic of his initial observation to Salisbury was that Gray's paper[85] might come under even more pressure to conform to nationalist newspaper 'orthodoxy' if the government came down too heavily on *United Ireland* in particular.

As noted by Marie-Louise Legg, behind every decision made during this period to prosecute a newspaper, however insignificant its circulation, was the recognition of another ineluctable reality, that to do so meant conferring on the 'victim' the status of nationalist martyr.[86] *United Ireland* often goaded the administration on this count: 'We are not insensible to all Mr. Balfour's delicate compliments. Still less are we insensible to splendid advertisements he has given us *gratis* – our order books forbid us to be that.'[87] Balfour would have been well aware of the role played by Liberal coercion policies in the growth in popularity of the Parnellite newspaper. While O'Brien was appearing on public platforms and making himself personally liable to prosecution for sedition there was no particular need to afford extra publicity to his newspaper by making him additionally accountable for its content.

In their separate memoirs O'Brien and Bodkin boast about the potential prison sentences, running into thousands of years, racked up by both men under the terms of the Crimes act. Yet neither served a single day in jail under the Conservative administration on foot of an article or editorial published in *United Ireland*. The government did not lack for provocation and, notwithstanding an ill-disposed Dublin divisional magistrate in O'Donel, did not lack for evidence to ensure a successful outcome had either man ever been brought to trial. But a fear of the reaction of the British press to any act of censure on a newspaper seen as the mouthpiece of Parnell – now under the protective wing of Gladstone – allied to a reluctance in the law office to revisit the scene of previous reverses, conspired to keep *United Ireland* out of the magistrates courts. Had the political will been there to 'proclaim' Dublin things might have been different. The under secretary was eager to take on just such a challenge. Writing to Balfour in May 1888, expressing, *inter alia*, misplaced confidence in the prospects of a successful consummation of the *Times* case against the Irish party, he went on to advocate a final *coup de grace*:

> If it is successful then I would suggest that advantage be taken of public feeling for a general advance all along the line, on our part. If we could strike at the N.L [*sic*] in Dublin and at *United Ireland* I really believe that we should finally triumph and the movement would be overcome.[88]

His optimism would soon sink in the quicksands of Pigottism.

Was it a mistake on the part of the authorities to leave well enough alone where *United Ireland* was concerned? Given the rigorous policies pursued by Balfour against local newspapers (see fn83) it might be assumed that little, if anything, was lost, by leaving *United Ireland* untouched. Indeed an appropriate sense of haughty disdain might have been conveyed by the Castle's inertia. The good fortune of the Parnellite journal, in largely avoiding prosecution, might have been seen as, or represented as, a statement of the irrelevance of the newspaper. However, given what we know of the thinking of the Castle on the subject, this was obviously not the case. The documentary evidence shows that the authorities were never very far from taking action. Neither would Irish nationalists, purchasing more than 100,000 copies of the paper each week, have given any credence to such an analysis.

It is difficult to see in any sustained struggle between the Tories and *United Ireland* any result other than a repetition of that which eventuated in the conflict between the newspaper and the Liberals. The nationalist journal would have been buffeted and perhaps temporarily chastened but would have survived and continued its provocative commentary. If the suspension of *habeas corpus* in 1881, and the incarceration without trial of most of its employees, did not result in the closure of the paper then it is difficult to see the less drastic use of summary jurisdiction inflicting any permanent damage. When the paper became largely irrelevant, at least as far as the Castle administration was concerned, after 1891, the damage was entirely self-inflicted.

An interesting but ultimately unhelpful hypothetical question is what might have happened had O'Brien stuck to his last and continued to edit the paper on a daily basis from 1887 to 1891? Would the Castle have succumbed to temptation, and any amount of healthy *prima facie* evidence, and opted for prosecution? The fact is that O'Brien, despite his prolonged absences, was at all times accountable and responsible for the output of his paper. He simply made himself more conveniently amenable to the law in a variety of other ways that proved less hazardous for the government.

In his study of violence in Irish nationalist politics under the Union, Charles Townshend sees much of the alienation of popular sentiment and resistance to the legal strictures of the British administration as 'not merely negative. It was rather the upholding of a different system of law or of social control.'[89] In this context *United Ireland* can be seen as the *Dublin Gazette* of this alternative Irish polity, this parallel legal system based on a substituted consent. Just as the population as a whole could do nothing to avoid the publication of the edicts of the lord lieutenant in the *Gazette*, other than to pay little or no attention to them, the Tory government chose to undermine the edicts of *United Ireland* by essentially ignoring it. The Castle's alternatives were limited.

'Pigottism' and crime – placing constitutionalists in a terrorist 'frame'

On 26 November 1884, at a time of relative inactivity on the part of Irish parliamentarians, the *Times* carried a full-page article quoting extensively from *United Ireland*. The article, and accompanying editorial were designed to influence opinion in regard to the decision to be taken on the renewal, then imminent, of the 1882 Crimes Act. The *Times* asked, before offering its exhibits, 'what chance there would be of coping successfully with sedition if that Act were not renewed and if Ireland were abandoned to the influence of writers and speakers like those whose utterances we reprint'. It then went on to quote from a number of *United Ireland* editorials of the previous four months beginning with one of 23 August, 1884 – 'A New Glory for Green-street' – which contrasted the jury verdicts in the cases of Myles Joyce and Gustavus Cornwall.

The *Times* then accused the Irish newspaper of being the inspiration behind political violence and of inciting further crimes through its inflammatory commentary. 'We know from the evidence of Carey how direct an influence the denunciations of "The Castle" had upon the minds of the men who planned the Phoenix Park murders, and the attacks on Lord Spencer published during the last four months exceed in violence and bitterness anything that was ever written against Mr. Forster and Mr. Burke.'[90]

The *Times* was, in essence, 'priming' its readership, enhancing the 'frame' in which Irish nationalism was equated with criminality. It was a dry run for the 'Parnellism and Crime' articles of the *Times*, which sputtered into life on 7 March 1887, before catching fire with the publication of the 'facsimile' letter on 18 April. The series was part of a unionist attempt to undermine the basis of moderate Irish nationalism by treating the very concept as oxymoronic. Irish parliamentarians were to be removed from a constitutional frame of reference and re-contextualized in an extremist frame. An acceptance of the *Times'* re-framing led inevitably to the conclusion that even Irish constitutional/parliamentary activity was a mere cloak for covert support of intimidation and violence, designed to secure the expropriation of the Irish landed class and secession from the United Kingdom. As Paul Bew has noted 'it tended to treat one of the greatest popular mass national movements Europe has known as a conspiracy'.[91]

While there was no direct involvement of the Salisbury government in the compilation of the 'Parnellism and Crime' series there was an element of pre-publication collaboration between the newspaper and the Home Office,[92] and a suspicious convergence of the publication of the 'facsimile' document and the second reading of Balfour's controversial Crimes Bill. Though there may not have been a verifiable *Times*/Tory conspiracy, there was a clear confluence of interest.

Both parties more than made up for any initial absence of co-ordination in the months following the appearance of the articles – inspired by the tireless fictional leg-work of Richard Pigott – which emanated from the pens of Irish journalist J. Woulfe Flanagan, a confidante of W.H. Smith,[93] and secret policeman Sir Robert Anderson. The participation of the Attorney General in *O'Donnell v Walter* and the *ex post facto* claim by Anderson that he had official approval for his penning of the 'Behind the Scenes in America' articles merely added to the aura of complicity, copper-fastened by the use made of Resident Magistrate William H. Joyce in compiling material for the newspaper to use in its prosecution of the case against the

Irish parliamentary party.[94] Four months before the formal hearings began West Ridgeway had reported to Balfour that Soames, the solicitor for the *Times*, had had a successful fishing expedition among the chief secretary's registered papers and police files. He told the chief secretary that Soames had 'made a great haul here of Land League papers' and was confident that 'the result is to make the "Times" case quite safe in the coming action'.[95]

United Ireland frequently alleged extensive collaboration between the government and the *Times* in the compilation of its case against the Irish party and the National League. In the wake of the ignominious collapse of Pigott, the journal alleged that 'all the vile agencies of officialdom were employed for the "Forger"'. Bodkin then advanced the names of some of the inhabitants of the newspaper's rogues' gallery, Bolton, Plunkett, Roche and Turner, as collaborators-in-chief. It alleged they had 'collected evidence and corrupted witnesses'.[96] Interestingly the name the newspaper missed was the far more significant William H. Joyce. It was only when Bodkin became privy to a cipher telegram addressed to the Galway Resident Magistrate, that the newspaper also identified the man they nicknamed William 'Hangman' Joyce, as having played a major part in the collusion.[97]

When indicting Irish nationalism in its various constitutional forms – 'without crime this conspiracy, this organisation, never could have succeeded'[98] – attorney general, Sir Richard Webster, in his 'Jekyll and Hyde role'[99] speaking on behalf of the Salisbury government via its proxy the *Times*, anathemized most of the leading Irish and American nationalist newspapers as 'approving of sedition and the commission of crimes, outrages, boycotting and intimidation'.[100] His list, which included the moderate nationalist *Freeman's Journal* omitted the most seditious journal of them all, O'Donovan Rossa's *United Irishman*.

Other than the close examination of William O'Brien regarding the editorial policies of *United Ireland* and the *Irishman*, as well as occasional references to the widespread importation of the *Irish World* during the early years of the land war, the historical role of nationalist newspapers in the alleged conspiracy, promised by Sir Richard Webster, was not extensively explored by the commission. However, contemporaneous events did bring both *United Ireland* and the *Kerry Sentinel* to the attention of Justices Hannen, Day and Smith. Indeed the *Times* commission, almost by default, became a potential weapon in the armoury of the state against two of the most egregiously offensive Irish nationalist journals.

The first transgression came from the *Kerry Sentinel*. On 14 November 1888, having listened to five days of Webster's indictment and a week of evidence, Edward Harrington – one of those named in the *Times* indictment – could contain himself no longer. In a *Sentinel* editorial he alleged that 'the Commission is the creature of the Government and "Times" conspirators, and there must be no blinking the fact that Irish members never had and never got the chance of having any confidence in its fairness'. He accused the three tribunal judges of manifest prejudice and also commented that other newspapers were unwilling to castigate the commission as he had done because of a fear of the contempt laws. Summoned before the commission on 21 November, Harrington refused to seek clemency or plead mitigation of any kind. Spurning the advice of his own counsel, he told the commission, unapologetically, 'I accept the responsibility of what appears in my paper.' He was fined £500.[101]

Not to be outdone by the 'success' of the upstart *Sentinel*, *United Ireland* was quickly into the fray. There may have been an element of solidarity in Bodkin's decision to assail the commission. Equally he may have been belatedly protecting his journal's vitriolic pre-eminence against a regional pretender. But in the 15 December 1888 edition of the newspaper he described the commission as a 'waste of time', while alleging that witnesses had been threatened and bribed to give testimony. The principal complaint of the leader was the reluctance on the part of the *Times* to come to grips with its own 'facsimile' allegations.[102] The editorial was clearly designed to provoke a reaction from the commission commensurate with that of its response to the *Kerry Sentinel*.

On 14 December the attorney general drew the attention of the commission to the 'flagrant' article, insisted that its effect would be to intimidate certain witnesses and demanded that proceedings should be taken against O'Brien.[103] Commission President, Justice Hannen, while registering his irritation at the frequency of what he called 'these interferences'[104], agreed to take steps to secure the appearance of O'Brien before the tribunal, after the Christmas recess, to answer for the comments of his paper.

In the interim Bodkin fanned the flames by editorializing on the summons in the next issue of *United Ireland*. 'Our comment on the evidence before the Commission, we are free to confess,' he maintained, 'was a contempt of the first water. For speaking the truth fearlessly we have no contrition, but if the Attorney General can suggest a line in our leader in which he has diverted from the strictest accuracy, we will tender an ample apology.'[105] He then proceeded to aggravate the contempt by questioning the independence of the commissioners and suggesting that they might be disposed to accomplish judicially what the government had been unable to achieve by means of executive power: 'The Attorney General might feel that if he succeeded in doing what the Exchequer division prevented his colleague, Mr. Balfour from doing, and gets Mr. O'Brien into jail for a month for contempt, the sitting of the Commission has not been altogether in vain – for his client and his colleagues.'[106]

According to his own account of what followed, Bodkin sought to persuade O'Brien to allow him to face the Commission himself, as *de facto* editor of *United Ireland* and as the actual writer of the offending article. 'I assured him that I had written it with the hope of proceedings and with a view to its defence.'[107] O'Brien, however, demurred: 'I urged in vain. It was impossible,' O'Brien said, 'that he could not allow anyone but himself to take the responsibility for *United Ireland.*' 'But, my dear boy,' he added, 'you have done me a personal service. There are half a dozen Coercion summonses and warrants out against me at present. If I am caught first by the *Times* I will be treated as a first-class misdemeanant, which is luxury compared to the lot of a Coercion Court prisoner.'[108]

O'Brien made his appearance before Justices Hannen, Day and Smith – all of whose integrity his newspaper had previously questioned[109] – on 15 January 1889. While he disavowed authorship of the original editorial he accepted responsibility and liability for its publication. He apologized to the bench, disclaiming any intention to impugn the conduct or integrity of the justices. He then went to the core of his argument, which was that the commission was, in reality, a quasi-political proceeding that 'differs from a Parliamentary Committee simply in its being conducted by judges'. Accordingly he reserved the right to comment critically on the *Times*' conduct of its case. He pointed, in particular, to the publication by the *Times* itself of a pamphlet consisting of the opening indictment of Irish constitutional nationalism by the attorney general. This, he claimed, had effectively been represented as a set of conclusions rather than a list of allegations.[110]

It was a subtle piece of misdirection and it worked admirably. O'Brien was treated far more leniently than had been the much more defiant and taciturn Harrington, who had made no defence whatever. To some extent O'Brien was pushing against an open door. The commission president had, a few days before the publication of the original *United Ireland* editorial, made his own annoyance clear at the leisurely pace at which the *Times* was conducting the case for the prosecution. On the previous 12 December he had delivered himself of a terse declaration from the bench. He concluded by observing that: 'It is to be remembered that rarely, if ever, can any legal investigation be exhaustive. Life is not long enough, and I do hope that we shall be allowed to entertain the hope that years of our lives will not be consumed in this inquiry.'[111]

The irritation and boredom of the justices, as well as the submissive nature of O'Brien's initial apology, persuaded the judge-commissioners to impose, and immediately remit, a lenient punishment. While acknowledging that *United Ireland* had overstepped the boundaries of fair comment, the justices, who may well have been taking advantage of a clear opportunity to demonstrate their independence, refused to afford satisfaction to any possible executive notions of 'censorship by Commission'.[112]

Not unnaturally *United Ireland* gloated at the outcome, hailing it as 'a victory of supreme importance for the liberty of the Press'.[113] Both Bodkin and O'Brien, in their memoirs, make exaggerated claims for the nature and the significance of this minor victory. Bodkin maintained that one of the effects of the ruling was that 'for very shame sake the *Times* was compelled to produce the forged letters, which were instantly exposed. The result was the collapse of the case, the disgrace of the *Times*, the suicide of the forger, Pigott, and the complete vindication of Parnell.'[114] It should be noted that Pigott did not actually make his disastrous appearance until six weeks later. O'Brien too viewed the event through a lens of his own devising. His account of his appearance before the Commission judges involved considerable special pleading, given the fulsome nature of his apology to the bench: 'Inexpressible was their disgust to find that I had nothing to withdraw, and nothing to apologise for, but on the contrary in response to Sir Richard Webster's horror-stricken citations, reiterated *United Ireland's* most militant sentiments in patches more purple still.'[115]

It had been mooted by Harrington that the government might seek to deploy 'contempt' as a silver bullet to be used against the Irish nationalist press, with the commissioners wielding the weapon. But if the use of the laws of contempt, solely a judicial prerogative, was ever envisaged as even a partial solution to the recalcitrance of the Irish nationalist press – and there is no evidence that this was the case – then the notion withered on the vine in the wake of the clemency afforded O'Brien for the transgression of *United Ireland*. The paper itself warned against any renewed effort to use the contempt laws for this purpose: 'The judges who exercise the law of contempt so savagely in Ireland would do well to mark the courtesy, good sense, and fair-play with which their English brethren have acknowledged the right to public opinion not to be bullied into silence.'[116]

In truth the only notable use of the contempt laws in order to, *ex post facto*, gag the press, had been the punishment meted out to Edmund Dwyer Gray in 1882 in the wake of the Hynes case, when the *Freeman's Journal* editor had been committed to Richmond prison for six weeks by Justice Lawson for publishing O'Brien's condemnation of the nocturnal antics of certain jury members in the case.

The *Times*, in making its case against the Irish party, to all intents and purposes, came to grief when Richard Pigott was eviscerated by Sir Charles Russell in his infamous cross-examination. However, in the course of the commission the newspaper did do the state some service in at least one other regard. To the delight of the Salisbury administration, and somewhat to the discomfiture of both parties, Parnell and O'Brien were among the 'defendants' in the *Times* action closely examined by the newspaper's counsel. A significant portion of their testimony, especially in the case of O'Brien, related to the founding, funding and fetishes of *United Ireland*.

As with much of his evidence Parnell was suitably vague on detail in his cross-examination. Where he was not imprecise he was often evasive. Paul Bew has described his performance at the Commission as being 'little short of ludicrous'.[117] When asked, for example, by Webster on 2 May 1889 about *United Ireland* and the No Rent Manifesto, Parnell contended that because of the administration's attempt to suppress the journal 'it could not be described as the Land League organ'[118] during the winter of 1881/2. The Irish leader would have been well aware that copies of the newspaper were reaching Ireland almost on a weekly basis and that its publication was in the hands of Land League treasurer Patrick Egan in Paris.

When challenged about some of the more extreme language used by the newspaper he took refuge in the editorial independence of O'Brien[119] and his status as 'a representative of the advanced section of the Land League'.[120] He was equally disingenuous when questioned about the policies of the *Irishman*. He dismissed all consideration of the significance of the newspaper by claiming that 'we paid no attention to the *Irishman*. It was a mere thing that was kept going for no particular purpose or object'.[121] When asked why an avowedly Fenian newspaper was not simply closed down Parnell claimed that the management by the Land League of Pigott's former journal, 'rendered the paper innocuous'.[122] But he was unable to say why the organization had allowed its continued publication.

The following day Parnell assured the Commission that the *Irishman* had continued in existence simply to provide employment for James O'Connor. He also expressed surprise that, contrary to his firmly expressed belief 'the paper had continued in existence after the end of 1882, when I have a distinct recollection of advising and requesting Mr. O'Brien to drop its publication'.[123] He was also forced to concede that he had never publicly remonstrated with O'Brien about editorial content in either *United Ireland* or the *Irishman* to which he personally objected. His explanation was that he had done so privately 'with regard to *United Ireland* paragraphs and articles [which] have often appeared of a stronger character than I could have approved'.[124]

Parnell also afforded the Commission an interesting insight into his relationship with the steward of *United Ireland*:

> If I had occasion to dissent radically from the conduct of the *United Ireland* newspaper, and if I considered that anything I objected to from time to time in the newspaper was anything more than a temporary aberration or a circumstance due to the excitement of the moment, and that it indicated a determination on Mr. O'Brien's part to carry out a definite policy so much in advance of mine ... I should undoubtedly have to consider whether the great advantage of the presence of a man of such

distinguished ability as a journalist and eloquence as a speaker, in the ranks of the party, would not be counterbalanced by the disadvantage of his extreme views.[125]

When he himself appeared three weeks later, O'Brien was so weakened physically by his various incarcerations that he was given permission to remain seated while he gave his evidence. He made no effort to conceal his former Fenian sympathies, telling the Commission that 'it is one of the things I am proudest of in my life. They trusted me without having taken an oath.'[126] He was also open about his ambiguous relationship with constitutionalism. He memorably characterized the Anglo-Irish connection as 'simply the relations of civil war, tempered by the scarcity of arms'.[127] When questioned about his attitude to military insurrection he proclaimed that 'if our people were an armed people, and if we had the remotest chance of coping with the power of England, I for one, without a moment's hesitation, would have risked my life in it'.[128]

However, he insisted that his instructions from Parnell before assuming the editorship of *United Ireland* were that, at all times, 'the paper was to be conducted within constitutional lines'.[129] As with Parnell before him he was vague as to the reasons for the retention of the *Irishman*. He also claimed not to have supervised it very closely and wondered aloud why, if the content of the *Irishman* was so repugnant, it had been allowed to continue publication on a weekly basis when *United Ireland* was being rigorously suppressed. He suggested this might have been because it was useful as a source of low-level intelligence for Dublin Castle: 'It used to be a joke with us that nobody in Ireland used to buy the *Irishman* except the Chief Secretary.'[130]

In addition to his studied elusiveness O'Brien was, at times, as disingenuous as Parnell had been before him. He disclaimed, for example, any editorial control of *United Ireland* while he was imprisoned in Kilmainham, from October 1881 to April 1882. This came about when he was challenged about the incendiary content of the 'Incidents of the Campaign' column. His disavowal directly contradicted the claim made in his autobiography, *Evening Memories*, that, 'the whole editing [was] done all the time from the unfortunate Chief Secretary's own grim jail of Kilmainham'.[131]

In the face of a number of provocative passages from both *United Ireland* and the *Irishman*, quoted to him under cross-examination by the Attorney

General, O'Brien repeatedly denied that there was ever any 'incitement to outrage' contained in the columns of the paper. He insisted that 'distinctly … it was advocating peaceful means'.[132] He was, however, consistently equivocal when asked whether he approved of some of the more blood-curdling Land League and National League branch resolutions that were reported verbatim in the newspaper.[133] He blithely offered the justification that, 'reports in *United Ireland* are simply clipped out from other papers. We had no real staff'.[134] Later he offered pressure of work as his excuse for missing some of the more inflammatory insertions: 'I was not able to attend to the minor news part of the paper so closely, owing, as I say, to having to write the entire paper myself, and to having to read every letter that came into the office as well'.[135]

In pecuniary terms the cost to the *Times* of the commission (in the region of £200,000[136]) was many multiples of the financial losses incurred by nationalist newspapermen in prosecuting their campaign against the Liberal and Conservative governments combined. However, other than causing O'Brien a few awkward moments when he gave his own evidence to the commission in May 1889, such as his forced repudiation of some of the *Irishman's* content,[137] and establishing that *United Ireland* frequently crossed a line between caustic commentary and virtual incitement – hardly a shocking or revelatory assertion – the *Times* legal team probably only served to further enhance the reputation of the nationalist weekly as an 'insurrection in print'.

As Margaret O'Callaghan has asserted in her seminal work, *British High Politics and a Nationalist Ireland*, the outcome of the deliberations of the commissioner-judges was something far less than the Parnellite moral victory that is often claimed.[138] The routing of Pigott has long tended to obscure the qualified nature of the exoneration of the Irish party from the charges laid against it by the *Times*. Indeed many Parnellites, O'Brien amongst them, might well have been somewhat discommoded by the effect of a totally clean bill of health from the commission on their radical credentials and pretensions. The commission report concluded that 'the respondents did enter into a conspiracy by a system of coercion and intimidation to promote an agrarian agitation against the payment of agricultural rents, for the purpose of impoverishing and expelling from the country the Irish landlords, who were styled the "English Garrison"'.[139] It was much as Parnell himself had expected but was also considered by West Ridgeway to be 'quite satisfactory'.[140] The under secretary had been one of the earliest sceptics when it came to the *bona fides* of the 'facsimile' letter and in November 1888 demonstrated his acuity by predicting that 'the result will be that we will be much as we are'.[141]

In his first memoir, *Recollections*, O'Brien had claimed, somewhat floridly, that 'the writings of *United Ireland* purported only to be to literature what a bugle-charge in the midst of the battle is to music. The bugle-charge, at least, was heard in every corner of the island, and set the heart's blood of the young and brave a-tingling in an entirely satisfactory manner'.[142] After such a public endorsement as the hostility of the *Times*, the 'bugle-charge' was heard even more loudly across nationalist Ireland.

Notes

1   O'Brien, *Evening Memories*, 168.

2   O'Brien papers, University College, Cork, UCC-WOB-PP-AA, f.81, Accounts for the Irish National Newspaper & Publishing Company.

3   O'Brien, *Evening Memories*, 168.

4   O'Brien, *Evening Memories*, 354.

5   Matthias McDonnell Bodkin, *Recollections of an Irish judge: Press, Bar and Parliament* (Dublin, 1914), 32.

6   Bodkin, *Recollections*, 149.

7   Bodkin, *Recollections*, 150.

8   Many potentially useful files are missing, though an indication as to their contents can be gleaned from the line entries in the relevant CSORP ledgers.

9   West Ridgeway to Balfour, 16 May 1888, British Library, Add.Mss 49808, f.144–9.

10   Harrel to West Ridgeway, 24 June 1890, NAI, CSORP, 1890/14986.

11   O'Brien to Bodkin, 9 April 1890, NLI, MSS 10702 F.S. Bourke Collection.

12   Evidence of William O'Brien, 23 May 1889, *Special Commission,* vol. 8, 181 [71813].

13   Statement by Sir Richard Webster, 14 December 1888 [*sic*] *Special Commission,* vol. 3, 405.

14   Bodkin, *Recollections*, 154.

15   Submission of William O'Brien, 15 January 1889, *Special Commission,,* vol. 3, 458–9. Ruling of Sir James Hannen, 16 January 1889, vol. 3, 511. Hannen referred to O'Brien's contribution as, 'a speech of great ability, which has certainly favourably impressed us'.

16   Bodkin, *Recollections*, 154.

17   Dillon to Bodkin, undated, 1887, NLI MS 10702, F.S. Bourke collection.

18   Dillon to Bodkin, undated, 1887, NLI MS 10702, F.S. Bourke collection.

19   O'Brien to Dillon, 10 May 1888, John Dillon papers, TCD, MSS 6736, f14.

20   Dillon memo, 9 May 1888, John Dillon papers, TCD, MSS 6736, f13.

21   O'Brien to Dillon, 10 May 1888, John Dillon papers, TCD, MSS 6736, f14.

22   *United Ireland*, 12 May 1888

23   Dillon to Bodkin, three notes, 16 June 1890, Monday [undated], Saturday [undated], 13 November 1890, NLI MS 10702, F.S. Bourke collection.

24   For example, 19 May 1888, 23 June 1888, 22 September 1888, 29 September 1888, 9 March 1889, 29 June 1889.

25   West Ridgeway to Balfour, 3 June 1888, British Library, Add. Mss 49808, f.153. 'I have always been of the opinion that Turner was the only DM who worked the Act with real energy.'

26   TNA, PRO, CO 903/2, Miscellaneous Notes, Series No. XL, 'Resident Magistrates in Ireland who have been attacked in columns of *United Ireland*'.

27   Turner to Balfour, 16 April 1888, British Library, Add. Mss 49820, ff.39–40.

28   Alfred E. Turner, *Sixty Years of a Soldier's Life* (London, 1912), 225–6.

29   Turner, *Sixty years of a Soldier's Life*, 243–4.

30   West Ridgeway to Balfour, 10 May 1888, British Library, Add. Mss 49808 f.130. The allegation of perjury was made in the *United Ireland* issue of 28 April 1888.

31   O'Brien to West Ridgeway, 1 June 1888, NAI, CSORP, 1888/9773.

32   Just that year in a comparable English case, *Roberts v. Owen and others* (1888), in finding for the plaintiff the Judge had noted that 'A newspaper may comment on the evidence given by any particular witness in any inquiry on a matter of public interest; but may not go the length of declaring such evidence to be "maliciously or recklessly false." The plaintiff was awarded £250 in damages (William Blake Odgers, *A Digest of the Law of Libel and Slander*, (London, 1905), 200).

33   *United Ireland*, 3 November 1888.

34   *United Ireland*, 27 October 1888

35   West Ridgeway to Balfour, 24 September 1888, British Library, Add.Mss 49808, f.230–3.

36   Ridgeway to Balfour, 5 October 1888, British Library, Add. Mss. 49809, ff.1–4.

37   TNA, PRO, CO 903/2, 3, Miscellaneous Notes, Series No. XL, 'Resident Magistrates in Ireland who have been attacked in columns of *United Ireland*'.

38   TNA, PRO, CO 903/2, 2–32, Miscellaneous Notes, Series No. XL, 'Resident Magistrates in Ireland who have been attacked in columns of *United Ireland*'.

39   *United Ireland*, 17 September, 1887 – Captain Plunkett at Mitchelstown, also accused of

perjury and described as 'the champion liar of the force', *United Ireland*, 14 April 1888 – Turner at Ennis.

40   *United Ireland*, 30 June 1888.

41   *United Ireland*, 17 December 1887.

42   *United Ireland*, 8 November 1890.

43   West Ridgeway to Balfour, 29 September 1888, British Library, Add. Mss. 49808, ff.234–5.

44   Fitzgerald had approached West Ridgeway seeking indemnification in the event of losing his case. Although acknowledging that such a procedure would be illegal the under secretary informed Balfour that the RM, 'went away satisfied that Government would help him'. West Ridgeway to Balfour, 18 February 1889, British Library, Add. Mss. 49809, ff.79–82.

45   *United Ireland*, 13 April 1888.

46   *United Ireland*, 27 October 1888.

47   *United Ireland*, 3 November 1888.

48   *United Ireland*, 30 March 1888.

49   O'Brien, *Reminiscences*, 78.

50   *United Ireland*, 8 October 1887.

51   O'Brien, *Reminiscences*, 75.

52   *United Ireland*, 15 October 1887.

53   West Ridgeway to Balfour, 10 December 1887, Add. Mss. 49808, ff.25–7.

54   Canon Keller to William O'Brien, 27 March 1888, O'Brien papers, UCC, WOB-PP-AB, f.20.

55   *United Ireland*, 4 August 1888.

56   *United Ireland*, 4 August 1888.

57   O'Brien, *Reminiscences*, 79.

58   *United Ireland*, 4 August 1888.

59   Bodkin, *Recollections*, 150–1. Bodkin even went so far as draw the attention of the executive to its own dereliction. In one issue of *United Ireland* he wrote that 'we presume we should be grateful to the brave Mr. Balfour for the immunity from prosecution which he kindly permits us' (*United Ireland*, 21 September 1889).

60   *Waterford News*, 14 June 1890.

61   Balfour, memo, 25 October 1887, NAI, CSORP 1887/18986.

62   West Ridgeway, marginal note, 26 October 1887, NAI, CSORP 1887/18986.

63   Harrel to West Ridgeway, 7 November 1887, NAI, CSORP 1887/18986.

64   *United Ireland*, 7 January 1888.

65 West Ridgeway to Balfour, 10 April 1888, BL, Add. Mss. 49808, ff.101–2.

66 West Ridgeway to Balfour, 16 May 1888, BL, Add. Mss 49808, ff.144–9.

67 Balfour to West Ridgeway, 19 May 1888, BL, Add. Mss. 49826, ff.516–8.

68 Alleged National League meetings reported in *United Ireland*, 27 July 1887, NAI, CSORP, 1887/15710 (missing file), NAI, CSORP 1890/3008.

69 Balfour to West Ridgeway, 13 March 1888, BL, Add. Mss. 49826, ff.377–85.

70 West Ridgeway to Balfour, 25 June 1890, NAI, CSORP 1890/14986.

71 West Ridgeway to Balfour, 21 July 1890, NAI, CSORP 1890/14986.

72 O'Brien, *Evening Memories*, 169.

73 West Ridgeway to Balfour, 29 September 1888, BL, Add. Mss. 49808, ff.234–5.

74 West Ridgeway to Balfour, 4 March 1889, BL, Add. Mss. 49287.

75 Curtis, *Coercion and Conciliation*, 204.

76 A man described by West Ridgeway as 'the meanest and most malignant reptile crawling'. West Ridgeway to Balfour, 29 September 1888, BL, Add. Mss. 49808, ff.234–5.

77 TNA, PRO, CO 903/2, series 1, 13, memo (undated but after 24 December 1887), 'Bogus reports of Irish National League meetings'. There are similar RIC claims in TNA, PRO, CO 903/2, series no. iv, 25 and TNA, PRO, CO 903/2, series no. vi, 19, and numerous other Cabinet and CSORP files.

78 Curtis, *Coercion and Conciliation*, fn.220.

79 20 February 1889, TNA, PRO, CAB 37/23, 1889, no. 5, 'Political condition of Ireland, January, 1889'.

80 The exception was the prosecution of P.A. McHugh, editor of the *Sligo Champion*, for intimidation of tenants in two articles.

81 Balfour to West Ridgeway, 13 March 1888, BL, Add. Mss. 49826 – ff.377–85.

82 Mandeville, jailed with O'Brien, had died some time after being released from jail, where he had experienced an exceptionally harsh prison regime. When the idea of prosecuting O'Connor was put to him by the chief secretary, West Ridgeway indicated his approval, writing to Balfour that 'I think the prosecution of the "Star" very desirable' (West Ridgeway to Balfour, 13 July 1888, BL, Add.Mss 49808 ff.183–4). When wiser counsels prevailed in London, the under secretary expressed regret that 'the prosecution against the "Star" has fallen through' (West Ridgeway to Balfour, 14 July 1888, BL, Add. Mss 49808 ff.185–6).

83 *United Ireland*, 16 August 1890. Among the local newspaper editors jailed, largely for the publication of illegal or intimidatory notices were Edward Walsh (*Wexford People*), Edward Harrington (*Kerry Sentinel*), John Hooper (*Cork Daily Herald*), P.A. McHugh (*Sligo Champion*), John Powell (*Midland Tribune*), P.J. Conlan (*Carlow Nationalist*), John O'Mahoney (*Tipperary Nationalist*), John McEnery (*Limerick Leader*), Jasper Tully

(*Roscommon Herald*).

84   Balfour to Salisbury, 27 December 1887, BL, Add. Mss. 49688, ff.186–9.

85   Shortly to be owned by Edmund Dwyer Gray Jr. after the death of his father on 27 March 1888.

86   Legg, *Newspapers and nationalism*, 113.

87   *United Ireland*, 7 January 1888.

88   West Ridgeway to Balfour, 15 May 1888, BL, Add. Mss 49808, ff.142–3.

89   Townshend – *Political Violence in Ireland*, 5.

90   *Times*, 26 November 1884.

91   Paul Bew, *Charles Stewart Parnell* (Dublin, 1980), 106.

92   F.S.L. Lyons, 'Parnellism and Crime, 1887–90' in *Transactions of the Royal Historical Society*, fifth series, vol. 24 (1974), 126.

93   Maurice Walsh, 'The leader writer: James Woulfe Flanagan', in Kevin Rafter, ed., *Irish Journalism before Independence: More a Disease than a Profession* (Dublin, 2011), 63.

94   See Leon O'Broin, *The Prime Informer*, and T.W. Moody, 'The Times versus Parnell and Co, 1887–90', in *Historical Studies* (London, 1968), 159–65.

95   West Ridgeway to Balfour, 15 May 1888, BL, Add. Mss. 49808 ff.142–3.

96   *United Ireland*, 16 March 1889.

97   *United Ireland*, 17 August 1889.

98   Opening address of the attorney general, Sir Richard Webster, 22 October 1888, *Special Commission*, vol. 1, 41. The full list was *Irish World, Chicago Citizen, Boston Pilot, Freeman's Journal, United Ireland, Irishman, Nation, Weekly News, Cork Daily Herald, Kerry Sentinel, Evening Telegraph* and *Sligo Champion*.

99   F.S.L. Lyons, 'Parnellism and Crime, 1887–90' in *Transactions of the Royal Historical Society*, fifth series, vol. 24 (1974), 133.

100   Opening address of the Attorney general, Sir Richard Webster, 22 October 1888, *Special Commission*, vol. 1, 43.

101   22 November 1888, *Special Commission*, vol. 2, 227.

102   *United Ireland*, 15 December 1888.

103   14 December 1888, *Special Commission*, vol. 3, 405.

104   His annoyance had been exacerbated by a demand from counsel for the Irish party seeking the appearance of the Warden of Merton College for remarks published in the *Times* that were allegedly prejudicial to the inquiry. The Warden had, according to counsel, compared Davitt and Dillon to the Whitechapel murderer.

105   *United Ireland*, 22 December 1888.

106   *United Ireland*, 22 December 1888

107 Bodkin, *Recollections*, 154.

108 Bodkin, *Recollections*, 154.

109 TNA PRO CO903/2, series xi, 'English judges condemned as partial in *United Ireland*'.

110 15 December 1888, *Special Commission*, vol. 3. 458–9.

111 12 December 1888, *Times* Commission, vol. 3, 308.

112 16 December 1888, *Special Commission*, vol. 3. 511.

113 *United Ireland*, 19 January 1889.

114 Bodkin, *Recollections*, 154.

115 O'Brien, *Evening Memories*, 415.

116 *United Ireland*, 19 January 1889.

117 Bew, *Parnell*, 107.

118 Special Commission, 2 May 1889, vol. 7, 159, 60214.

119 'Mr O'Brien managed the paper. Mr O'Brien would not allow or would not occupy his post for a single hour if the paper was to be managed by anybody besides himself.' *Special Commission*, 2 May 1889, vol. 7, 164, 60282.

120 *Special Commission*, 2 May 1889, vol. 7, 163, 60266.

121 *Special Commission*, 2 May 1889, vol. 7, 165, 60321.

122 *Special Commission*, 2 May 1889, vol. 7, 166, 60332.

123 *Special Commission*, 3 May 1889, vol. 7, 206, 60468.

124 *Special Commission*, 3 May 1889, vol. 7, 205, 60463.

125 *Special Commission*, 3 May 1889, vol. 7, 206, 60478.

126 *Special Commission*, 21 May 1889, vol. 8, 72, 70579.

127 *Special Commission*, 23 May 1889, vol. 8, 182, 71832.

128 *Special Commission*, 23 May 1889, vol. 8, 182, 71836.

129 *Special Commission*, 21 May 1889, vol. 8, 88, 70734.

130 *Special Commission*, 21 May 1889, vol. 8, 91, 70759.

131 O'Brien, *Evening Memories*, 15.

132 *Special Commission*, 23 May 1889, 175, 71711.

133 *Special Commission*, 22 May 1889, vol. 8, 130, 71120-71125 – 165, 71559–71566.

134 *Special Commission*, 22 May 1889, vol. 8, 130, 71130.

135 *Special Commission*, 22 May 1889, vol. 8, 153, 71443.

136 *History of the Times: the Twentieth Century Test, 1884–1912* (London, 1947), 89.

137 *Special Commission*, 22 May 1889, vol. 8, 151, 71416.

138 O'Callaghan, *British High Politics*, 119.

139 *A Popular and Complete Edition of the Parnell Commission Report* (London, 1890), 146.

140 West Ridgeway to Balfour, 16 February 1890, Add.Mss. 49810, ff.231–2. *United Ireland* characterized the report as a vindication, taking as its cue the apoplectic response of the *Daily Express* (United Ireland, 22 February 1890).

141 West Ridgeway to Balfour, 9 November 1888, BL, Add. Mss. 49809, ff.13–16.

142 O'Brien, *Recollections*, 423.

CHAPTER EIGHT

Quis Custodet Ipsos Custodes

'The Land League, it will be remembered, was still an infant institution when Mr. Patrick Egan proposed to exclude from it the representative of one of the Dublin newspapers – the *Daily Express*. There were, however, more prudent men in the organisation than Mr. Patrick Egan.'[1]

(Irish Loyal and Patriotic Union, *The Real Dangers of Home Rule*)

Una duce una voce

Despite its own travails, it is unsafe to assume that *United Ireland* and its regional contemporaries campaigned diligently to preserve freedom of expression whenever their commercial or political rivals were threatened. On the contrary, Irish nationalist newspapers were often as keen to 'enforce silence' as they were to display collegiality in defence of the right of free comment on matters of political controversy.

United Ireland, while stridently laying claim to martyr status in its fight to retain its own entitlement to a regime of unfettered commentary, adopted a contradictory approach when it came to its political opponents and even some erstwhile allies. This practice far exceeded normal journalistic sniping. The Parnellite newspaper went well beyond the cut and thrust of commercial rivalry to, in effect, endanger the personal safety of others in a climate of heightened tension. While clearly lacking any capacity to 'enforce silence' by legal means, newspapers like *United Ireland* strove to achieve similar results by means of subtle, or occasionally blatant intimidation. *United Ireland* seemed to see as its task the excoriation of both unionist newspapers and individual journalists as well as the thorough policing of Parnellite orthodoxy amongst the nationalist press. Ironically this intimidatory partisanship reached its apotheosis on the nationalist side, not with anti-unionist diatribes during the Home Rule crisis of 1886, or the Plan of Campaign, but with the discordant invective of the Parnellite split. As the Irish party sundered, the journal was ultimately reduced to the status of purveyor of malevolent propaganda. By then O'Brien had disowned his creation, while Bodkin and Healy were involved in an equally disreputable publishing enterprise. However, *United Ireland* was already a competent propagandist long before it was driven to extremes by the bile of the *National Press*.

The butt of *United Ireland's* scorn depended on prevailing Parnellite convention. While Unionist journalists like G. V. Patton and Andrew Dunlop were predictable targets, O'Brien and Bodkin were also known to focus their vitriol on previously lionized nationalist newspaper editors, like the unruly James Daly of the *Connaught Telegraph* and John MacPhilpin, editor of the *Tuam News*. Similarly, the American journalist and socialist Henry George was alternately feted and disparaged as he became a surrogate for Michael Davitt,[2] with whom the newspaper was frequently at odds, but whose iconic status generally protected him from overt attack.

Because *United Ireland*, in addition to its primary role as a delivery vehicle for Parnellite propaganda, had a secondary function – that of Parnell's hagiographer[3] – an element in its pursuit of the likes of James Daly, John O'Connor Power, Frank Hugh O'Donnell and Patrick Ford was to neutralize their challenges to the Irish leader's perceived infallibility or pre-eminence. Whereas the excoriation and targeting of individual members of the unionist press left them open to potential and actual violence, the victimization of nationalist journalists and editors was more in the nature of ritual humiliation. Such attacks were intended to act as a disincentive to any deviation from Parnellite principles.

Notwithstanding the fact that *United Ireland* was largely preaching to the converted, its approach and that of other less prominent Irish local newspapers is consistent with the concept, enunciated by Jurgen Habermas, of 'tutelage'. In his critique of twentieth-century media the German philosopher asserts that 'tutelage' amounts to an attempt to bludgeon or suborn a readership, to 'deprive it of the opportunity … to disagree'.[4] *United Ireland* can be accused of having hectored its readers almost as much as it did its political opponents. An alternative, more charitable, analysis, however, might characterize it as an early progenitor of the practice of 'framing', i.e. 'an attempt to promote a particular … causal interpretation [or] moral evaluation'.[5] This involves the use of coded language to influence and/or set up expectations in a readership or audience. However, there was very little code used by *United Ireland*, which tended to favour robust and direct rather than oblique language.

Mr Parnell's Rottweiler

While most modern newspapers are identified, or identify themselves, with either a broad or clearly defined political philosophy, it is generally assumed that where 'straight' news rather than editorial comment is concerned, reportage should be factual and objective. This was not necessarily the case with their nineteenth-century counterparts. In an era before commercialization really took hold, reporting of news events often directed the reader towards certain conclusions, rather than merely setting out undisputed facts.

The veteran Irish correspondent of the *Daily News*, Andrew Dunlop, who wrote a number of pamphlets for the Irish Loyal and Patriotic Union,[6] parted company with his employer in 1889, when it was suggested to him that 'I should write in a tone favourable to Home Rule.' Dunlop refused to do so. Prior to his departure Dunlop claimed that 'when the paper became a Home Rule organ I simply sent the news, and did not "tone" my correspondence one way or the other'.[7] However, Dunlop's objection to the editorial directions from London, dictated by, among others Arnold Morley and Henry Labouchere, had nothing to do with any misgivings about the unwarranted primacy of comment over fact in reportage. His difficulty lay simply in his personal opposition to Home Rule. His attitude towards the issue of subjectivity in the transmission of news reports was unambiguous.

'I contend,' he wrote in his memoir, 'that the toning is not only justifiable, but commendable, when it helps to point out the true significance of the events recorded.'[8]

Dunlop was not unique in wearing his political heart on his journalistic sleeve. Most journalists sought and secured positions on newspapers whose political allegiance was compatible with their own. If that allegiance changed they were expected to adapt or, more commonly, to seek more congenial employment elsewhere.[9] An obvious case in point was James O'Connor, an employee of the avowedly Fenian *Irishman*, who remained in his position after the Parnellite takeover of the newspaper.

But increasingly, as newspapers began to tap into a mass market, and journalistic practice became more standardized, reporters, in some instances, were no longer expected to 'tone' their reportage. Those still required to do so in a manner that conflicted with their personal beliefs needed to be capable, rather like members of the legal profession, of adopting the appropriate 'slant' required by their employer. The noted Fenian, William O'Donovan, for example, wrote leaders for the unionist *Irish Times*.[10] The cartoonist Thomas Fitzpatrick, who worked primarily for the *Freeman's Journal*, briefly supplied material to *The Union*, a loyalist weekly published in Dublin, London and Glasgow.[11] The observation of John Stuart Mill, made in 1829 – 'more affectation and hypocrisy are necessary for the trade of literature, and especially newspapers, than for a brothel-keeper'[12] – may be an overly harsh judgment of the profession, but recognized the fact that as the nineteenth century progressed and the nature of the newspaper business became less politicized and more commercialized, journalists became more malleable in their approach to their work.

Not so in the case of *United Ireland*. The Irish nationalist weekly was relentlessly partisan in both its handling of news and comment. It was largely uncompromising, except when it was required to execute a *volte face* in response to a change in Parnellite policy. *United Ireland* was a journal uncontaminated by objectivity, its columns unleavened with any sense of journalistic distance even at a time of creeping 'professionalization'. Michael Foley contends that the later 1800s marked 'a discernible agreement as to what constituted professional behaviour and a degree of solidarity between journalists'.[13] That was clearly the case, but *United Ireland* and the editors of a number of other nationalist organs remained outside that emerging consensus.

Furthermore, despite its frequent and strident protestations about liberty of expression, *United Ireland* was no more committed to genuine freedom of the press in Ireland than were the two British administrations of the 1880s. Within its own bailiwick *United Ireland* was relentless in defence of Parnellite orthodoxy, often to the point of irresponsibility, in times where journalists were almost as legitimate a potential target of nationalist or agrarian violence as the landlord, bailiff or 'emergencyman'.[14]

According to James Loughlin *United Ireland* had three functions: 'to keep other nationalist papers in line, to confront enemies within and without the movement, and especially to develop the cult of Parnell's personality'.[15] There was a strong element of messianic zeal about O'Brien that caused him, according to T.P. O'Connor, to see people in stark terms as either 'his slaves or his enemies'.[16] Indeed Loughlin contends that O'Brien had a low opinion of the readership of his newspaper.[17] In his *Recollections* he depicted himself as a champion of 'fighting journalism' conveyed through the medium of 'picture writing' easily understood 'by the multitude'.[18] Although regularly included by contemporaries in the officer corps of the early 'new journalism', in reality his florid and allusive style, as well as his didacticism, was far removed from that emerging strain of populist reportage that came to dominate the newspaper landscape after the Northcliffe 'revolution' of the 1890s.

O'Brien waged a ceaseless campaign against opponents, both strident and mildly critical, of whatever philosophy 'Parnellism' espoused at any given time. As his biographer, Joseph O'Brien, has put it, 'no excuse whatsoever would be needed to assail the enemies of the Nationalist movement'.[19] Those enemies included some obvious candidates – the Castle, unionists, and Irish 'Whigs' and some whose transgressions might have been viewed as more venial or, at least, less apparent – socialists and recalcitrant nationalists. Such vendettas were a regular feature of the newspaper, whether or not O'Brien was *de facto* editor. Though a fine journalist in his own right it was Bodkin's mimetic qualities that were more valued in his stewardship of *United Ireland*.

In the same manner as the Liberal and Tory governments dearly wished to 'silence' O'Brien and others, the nationalist press, principally represented by *United Ireland*, aggressively sought to suppress internal dissent within the ranks of nationalism. While O'Brien might well have maintained that he was simply following a censorious template established by Dublin Castle, and that the end justified the means,[20] nonetheless, he displayed an acute desire, if not an actual design, to stifle antagonistic commentary.

United Ireland's frequent attacks on unionist newspapers, either in its editorial columns or in 'The Week's Work', can, in general, be discounted as normal politically and culturally motivated badinage. It was to be expected of the main nationalist weekly that it should take on the chief apologists of the unionist newspaper establishment. For many years, nationally and regionally, the unionist press had been largely unopposed in its propagandizing and special pleading.[21] The expansion of the newspaper business in Ireland in the 1880s had greatly favoured the establishment of a plethora of new nationalist journals. The more enlightened of these might have been expected to advocate an even-handed approach to freedom of speech. After his conviction of its editor, Edward Walsh, under the 1887 Crimes Act, the *Wexford People* had made the case that the suppression of liberty of expression was a threat to all newspapers, irrespective of political ideology.

> The right for which we contend is common property. What is to-day the case of a Nationalist organ may be to-morrow that of a Unionist or Tory contemporary, and he would be the most contemptible of party trucklers who permitted that right to be infringed for the fleeting purposes of politics.[22]

Such sentiments were alien to the mentality of *United Ireland*. Partisanship was more characteristic than journalistic solidarity. O'Brien was, for example, apt to inquire, disingenuously, why unionist editors were not jailed for publishing the same reports that had incurred incarceration when carried by nationalist journals or for comments that might have seen charges laid against a nationalist editor had they been made by one.[23]

Occasionally, however, the newspaper's polemics descended into personal invective or even libellous diatribe. Sir John Arnott, proprietor of the *Irish Times* – dubbed the *Liarish Times* by O'Brien – and its editor J.A. Scott were regular targets.[24] The virulently unionist *Dublin Evening Mail* and *Daily Express* were also subjected to frequent attacks. The editor of the

Mail, George Tickell was once described as 'a small Orangeman ... who keeps a furniture shop in Mary-street, but his spite is the only thing he can contribute to its columns'.[25]

The three Dublin-based unionist newspapers largely ignored the derogatory comments of the nationalist weekly. Had *United Ireland* been a daily paper they might have found it more difficult to remain so detached. The *Daily Express* tended to treat *United Ireland* as beneath its contempt and refused to engage with it, preferring to take issue with the more respectable face of nationalist journalism, the *Freeman's Journal*. The attitude of the *Express* to O'Brien's paper is best summed up in one leader. Reviewing the course of separatism and militant agrarianism through the nineteenth century, the *Express* equated 'the moral scavenging work of *United Ireland*' with the dynamite campaign of Jubilee year. *United Ireland* was compared adversely with the *Nation* of the Young Irelanders. 'The sedition which in 1848 had something chivalrous if Quixotic in it, has become in 1887, a thing that honest men shudder and hold their nose at'.[26]

The *Evening Mail* adopted a similar approach. In 1887, when *United Ireland* published what it claimed was a translation of a cipher telegram sent by Attorney General Peter O'Brien to Crown Counsel Edward Carson concerning the handling of the Mitchelstown case, the *Mail* described the piece as 'a scurrilous article'.[27] It rejected, in slightly contradictory fashion, both the veracity of the telegram – the content of which reflected badly on both lawyers – and the accuracy of the translation. But the *Mail*, with a metaphorical shrug, reserved much of its criticism for the refusal of the *Freeman* to admonish the nationalist weekly.[28]

When an attempt was made on O'Brien's life in the course of his controversial visit to Canada in 1887 to bait Lord Lansdowne as a rack-renting landlord, the *Express* emphasized its 'abhorrence and detestation'[29] of the would-be assassins. It actually described O'Brien as being 'as honest a man as there is in his party', albeit one 'devoured with fanaticism'.[30] However, its London correspondent, Kernaghan, had already written of a near riot at one of O'Brien's Canadian gatherings adding that 'the loyalists of Canada are not so patient and long suffering as the loyalists of Ulster and the people of England ... in Canada the free indulgence in vulgar abuse and repulsive language has brought him perilously near a broken head'.[31]

O'Brien himself was quick to take offence on his own behalf when unionist newspapers, as he perceived it, crossed the line between fair comment and libel.[32] He extracted at least one apology from the *Express*[33] for a series of references in 1886 to the alleged misappropriation of National League funds. The unionist newspaper, which had sought to expose what it called 'the swindlers of the League', did not attempt to justify its claims in court. In 1888 O'Brien secured damages of £100 from the unionist *Cork Constitution* which, he argued successfully, had charged him with making his living from murder and violence. The defendants, in this instance, pleaded that the offending article was 'fair comment'.

Journalist W.J. Ludgate, who doubled as Munster correspondent of the *Times*, had written the piece. In the course of his cross-examination by Tim Healy, Ludgate obliquely adverted to a convention already beginning to gain traction in the journalistic profession. This held that journalists, accustomed to the rough and tumble of commercial rivalry, should, by and large, not sue one another for libel. It was an illustration of increasing levels of collegiality and the growing influence of combination among journalists. Ludgate pointed out that he was constantly being libelled by the nationalist *Cork Herald*, but had always declined to sue for defamation. He had expected similar treatment from O'Brien. He told Healy that 'he didn't think libel case would come forward'.[34]

In an era when the journalistic by-line was still in the future and anonymity was the norm[35] *United Ireland* consistently identified individual correspondents whose journalism aroused its antipathy, and conducted a series of highly personalized campaigns against them. This 'rogue's gallery' featured Patton, Ludgate and Dunlop prominently, but also included W.H. Wilson another Cork-based *Times* correspondent. Most of *United Ireland's* ire was reserved for correspondents who supplied material to prominent English journals. They were described as men 'who slander their own country and people with the zeal of time-serving apostates'.[36]

The journal contrasted the damage done to the nationalist cause by such partisan commentators with the journalism of the likes of W.T. Stead, editor of the *Pall Mall Gazette*, who 'has borne a giant's part of the battle against coercion upon his single shield'. Stead was under the impression that Irish opposition to the 1887 Crimes Bill was not sufficiently vociferous. *United Ireland* ascribed this misapprehension to a lack of coverage in Britain of the opposition to the bill among National League branches. It inquired 'what attention do the Pattons and Dunlops ever allow the English public to pay to the resolutions of all those myriads of men'.[37]

O'Brien had first fulminated against these 'apostates' in a rather sinister editorial in 1884. This concluded with a threat:

> We hereby give public warning that the news agencies, or rather lies agencies, will not be tolerated longer in their present system of secret service to the Government. The men who send these telegrams are known. We have on hand the materials to publish a full list of them, with full particulars of their political and newspaper connections.

United Ireland recommended that the offending correspondents should be warned off, like 'jockeys who misconduct themselves'. It concluded by suggesting, ominously, that 'the Irish public, if they are put to it, will make the one occupation as hazardous as the other'.[38]

One of the particular *bêtes noirs* of *United Ireland* was, as already noted, Andrew Dunlop, a Scottish-born journalist employed initially by the *Freeman's Journal*. Well-known for his unionist predilections, Dunlop was forced off the staff of the *Journal* in 1885 after a prolonged nationalist campaign, led by O'Brien, and based largely on his contributions to the *Daily News*, at that time an anti-Home Rule publication. He spent a year freelancing for the *Journal*, but the clamour continued, so he joined the more congenial *Irish Times*. Even then the pursuit did not abate and in 1889 Dunlop was relieved of his *Daily News* duties, the London paper having metamorphosed into a supporter of Home Rule in the interim. *United Ireland*, leading the charge, in January 1889 had condemned the arrangement whereby a journalist employed by an Irish unionist paper doubled as correspondent of the flagship of Gladstonian liberalism. 'Is it not high time to put an end to so shameless and flagitious [*sic*] a system of imposition?' the nationalist weekly had railed.[39]

Dunlop considered the personalized baiting of O'Brien to be 'a gross breach of journalistic etiquette, and, having regard to the terms in which we were referred to, one which was calculated to endanger our lives'.[40] In addition to being harangued in the columns of O'Brien's newspaper Dunlop also claimed to have been assaulted in the wake of an altercation with the MP himself at a public meeting on the Luggacurren estate of the Marquis of Lansdowne in 1887. Dunlop, by then reporting for the *Irish Times* and the *Daily News*, had recorded the speeches of the local parish priest and of O'Brien himself when, he alleged in his memoir, the *United Ireland* editor demanded that Dunlop leave 'because you are not here as an ordinary newspaper reporter, but as a spy'. Dunlop was then set upon and forced to walk seven miles to Athy to file his copy from the local post office. He was also badly beaten while in the town before being offered RIC protection.[41]

Dunlop, however, was not entirely defenceless and was not above using a journalistic platform to retaliate against the diatribes of *United Ireland*. He wrote an anonymous piece for the *Daily Chronicle* in January 1890 – 'From a Correspondent' – in which he justified the practice of jury packing on the basis that *United Ireland* and other nationalist journals were 'practically telling jurors that it was their duty to give a verdict, not "according to the evidence", as they were sworn to do, but according to their own views of what was "just", which usually meant, in agrarian cases, a verdict in the teeth of the evidence'. O'Brien was cited in the *Chronicle* piece 'as the chief offender in this way'.[42]

Dunlop contrasted the vendetta-style journalism of O'Brien (he made no reference to Bodkin who would actually have been directly responsible for much of the abuse) with that of the Sullivans. He made the point that 'this gutter journalism was never indulged in by the *Nation* or the *Weekly News*, the two weekly Nationalist contemporaries of *United Ireland*'. The *Nation*, he insisted 'although strongly advocating Home Rule and Land Reform, carefully avoided personalities'.[43]

Subject to an even greater level of vilification was Dr G.V. Patton, editor of the *Daily Express* and Dublin correspondent of the *Times*. Within a month of the nationalist journal's inception he was already being abused by *United Ireland*: 'Dr. Patton, who preaches up Irish industries in the *Daily Express*, and preaches them down in the London *Times* is to have a national statue erected to him at O'Connell's feet – convenient to his right boot'.[44]

Patton did not endear himself to *United Ireland* by predicting its demise in December 1881 when it was under threat of suppression. He was, unquestionably, allowed considerable leeway by the *Times* in his reportage, which often reads more like editorial commentary. In a news report on 24 December he referred to the Parnellite paper as 'scattering the most pernicious doctrines amongst the people'.[45] Three days later, again in a report filed as *Times* Dublin correspondent, Patton had gloated about the incipient defeat of *United Ireland*, claiming that 'its strength is greatly impaired, and its tone is that rather of a spiteful but feeble vixen than of the daring outlaw'.[46] While it is important not to import twenty-first-century notions of objective reportage into nineteenth-century polemics, even by the standards of the day, Patton – the correspondent – was given a powerful platform to editorialize.

United Ireland's anti-Patton invective intensified when the Conservative government came to power. Patton was loud in his support for the 1887 Crimes Bill. His espousal of coercion legislation irked Bodkin who wrote: 'If a Coercion Bill there is to be let some Irish member at least draft a Patton Prevention Clause. The outrages he perpetrates in his crape mask are more fruitful of enmity between the two nations than the most revolting feats of his punier brother-in-arms, Captain Moonlight'.[47]

On more than one occasion Patton gave O'Brien and *United Ireland* some cause for its animosity. In a letter to the *Times* in October 1885, for example, O'Brien drew attention to a report of Patton's in which he alleged that O'Brien had made a speech at a public meeting in the presence of the suspended effigies of three 'landgrabbers' and that 'they had formed a topic in his speech'. O'Brien denied the veracity of the report in a letter to the *Times*, adding sarcastically that 'life is not long enough, unfortunately, for any attempt to enable your readers to appreciate the value of the rest of this Correspondent's information about the affairs of Ireland'.[48]

On occasion *United Ireland* would further intensify the personalized rhetoric. After an *Express* attack on Herbert Gladstone in November 1886, in a column in 'The Week's Work', O'Brien turned on the editors of the *Mail* and *Express*, referring to them as 'Irish Tory Quintus Slides'. He compared the treatment of Gladstone to 'the sort of ribald calumny to which the Irish leaders are pretty well habituated … it may be worth consideration whether representatives of the *Express* should not be expelled from all public meetings in Ireland, and Mr. John Robinson[49] or Dr. Patton ducked in the slime of the Liffey the first time he can be laid hands on'.[50]

The American correspondent William Henry Hurlbert also fell afoul of *United Ireland*, who dubbed him 'the bogus American investigator'.[51] In his two-volume study of an Ireland in the grip of the Plan of Campaign, *Ireland under coercion*, the former editor of the *New York World* took an establishment line. He rejected the nationalist narrative of extreme agrarian distress and cited the significant rises in savings bank deposits in areas where the Plan was in operation as proof of the capacity, and unwillingness, of tenant farmers to pay even arbitrated rents.[52] He was also highly sceptical of the nationalist narrative of press suppression, suggesting there were greater abuses of press freedom by the Lincoln administration during the American Civil War:[53]

> Nobody who had not learned from the speeches made in England, and the cable despatches sent to America, that freedom of speech and of the press has been brutally trampled under foot in Ireland by a 'Coercion' Government would ever suspect it from reading the Dublin papers which I this morning bought.[54]

Hurlbert declared himself 'a benevolent neutral'[55] where Irish affairs were concerned, whereas *United Ireland* described *Ireland under coercion* as a 'slanderous book'.[56] *United Ireland*'s animosity was given an added piquancy as Hurlbert had characterized it as 'that dumb organ of a downtrodden people'.[57] Furthermore he accused the paper of being directly responsible for intimidation, citing a court appearance in Ennis of a number of publicans accused of boycotting the police.

> Ten of them signed, in open court, a guarantee not further to conspire … The magistrate tells me that when the ten who signed (and who were the most prosperous of the publicans) were preparing to sign, the only representative of the press who was present, a reporter for *United Ireland*, approached them in a threatening manner, with such an obvious purpose of intimidation, that he was ordered out of the court-room by the police.[58]

The threat posed by Hurlbert was similar to that of Dunlop and Patton, access to an influential audience outside of Ireland. His unsuccessful stewardship of the *New York World* – ended when the paper was purchased by Joseph Pulitzer – was mocked by Bodkin. He was denigrated as 'a clever politico-journalistic hack, his ambitions throughout a somewhat extended career, have ever outrun the appreciation of his countrymen'.[59]

In its defence of Parnellite orthodoxy *United Ireland* also took exception to the independent nationalist line occasionally pursued by journalists and editors with whom it might have been expected to be *ad idem*. Chief among these victims of a form of journalistic Jacobinism was one of the original motive forces behind the land campaign in the west of Ireland, James Daly, editor of the Mayo-based *Connaught Telegraph*. From as early as 1881, despite having obtained £50 from the Land League to secure the future of his paper, Daly's 'locally orientated ideology' was already coming into conflict with 'Parnell's evolving centralised political system',[60] and with the spread of ribbon-feniansim. His support for small farmers in the west was also at odds with the growth of the influence within the agrarian movement of larger graziers and urban professionals. In addition Daly was too closely allied to the renegade Mayo nationalist John O'Connor Power and came to oppose the use of boycotting. Had he remained silent his growing disillusionment would not have mattered. But he had a significant platform in the *Connaught Telegraph* and he was not averse to using it.

Daly was an early target of *United Ireland's* venom. In October 1881, just before the Kilmainham incarcerations, the Castlebar branch of the Land League was persuaded to depose Daly from its vice-presidency and expel him from membership. *United Ireland* approved wholeheartedly of the move, observing 'that branch had the patience of Job'.[61]

Daly's sin was to offend against Parnellism itself. The editor of the *Tuam News*, John MacPhilpin, who had been jailed in 1883 under the Prevention of Crime Act, transgressed because he paid insufficient attention to the sanctity of the Liberal alliance in 1888. In his own newspaper MacPhilpin had, ill-advisedly, drawn attention to the treatment he had suffered in prison in 1883 on foot of the publication of articles condemning three Galway landlords. Far worse, in the eyes of *United Ireland*, was the fact that his untimely denunciation of Lord Spencer had found editorial favour with the *Daily Express*. *United Ireland* observed: 'It is touching to see the communion of souls as to standards of moral elevation between the *Daily Express* man and the editor of the *Tuam News*. In the "good old days" the *Express* would not have recognised for a moment that a publication such as the *Tuam News* had existence.' The piece went on to speculate that MacPhilpin had ulterior motives as his 'hopes of a Parliamentary seat were blighted'.[62]

When the *Tuam News* editor wrote to *United Ireland*, a journal that had itself regularly excoriated Spencer, and attempted to defend himself, Bodkin was dismissive: 'Any man who aids his personal enemies by a revival of ancient grievances … utterly undeserved in Lord Spencer's case – is helping to retard the cause of Irish freedom and the pacification of the country. That is all we have to say to Mr. McPhilpin.'[63] If the editor of the *Tuam News* deserved better from *United Ireland* so did the news-vendors responsible for its own weekly distribution. When two agents discontinued the sale of the newly launched newspaper in October 1881, *United Ireland* went on the offensive:

> Two of our agents have funked. As this is no time for shilly-shallying, and as our duty is too solemn to be trifled with, we must print their names: Patrick Kelly (Rathcoole) and Edmond Flynn (Grangemockler). One of these agents (Flynn) says he cannot get the papers in time. With this explanation we are not satisfied. The other gentleman gives no reason whatever for his stop order.[64]

The effect of the paper's condemnation can be gauged by a complaint sent to Forster by a sympathizer. John Madden wrote from the Kildare Street Club that 'two country agents for the sale of this paper, who seem to have become frightened and desirous of discontinuing the sale of it, are held up by name to the vengeance of the mob for so doing'.[65]

The surrogacy of Henry George

One of the ironies of the journalistic history of the 1880s is that *United Ireland*'s zealous hostility to Patrick Ford and the *Irish World* undermined that journal's influence more effectively than Dublin Castle was ever able to do with its policy of interdiction and confiscation. A collateral casualty in this campaign, which commenced around the middle of 1882, was the American journalist, socialist and economic commentator, Henry George. An aggravating factor was the perceived necessity to undermine the increasingly socialistic tendencies of the virtually untouchable 'Father of the Land League' Michael Davitt. This had to be achieved obliquely, resulting in George becoming a surrogate for the erstwhile Fenian. As Davitt began to re-invent and re-interpret the slogan 'the land for the people' his proxies had to be challenged and enfeebled in order to discredit him.

Davitt had begun the journey to his own particular Damascus in Portland prison in 1882 when, under the 'not too arduous terms of his sentence,'[66] he had re-read George's seminal work *Progress and poverty*, published in 1880. This advocated a policy of land nationalization, confirming for Davitt a conviction of his own that had been forming for some months. Davitt had been impressed with George and his ideas when the two men met through their mutual friendship with Patrick Ford. George was equally impressed with Davitt, but described him to the *Irish World* proprietor, rather ambiguously as 'a very impressionable man.'[67] While in Portland prison the Land League co-founder had abandoned the ideas of peasant proprietary enunciated by that organization and, in a speech in Manchester on 21 May 1882, pronounced in favour of the state ownership of land. In this, and in his call for a measure of compensation for landowners, his template differed somewhat from that of George. With Parnell's authority undermined in the wake of the 'Kilmainham treaty', Davitt's ill-timed intervention 'was perceived by some as a challenge to Parnell's leadership.'[68] The party leader swatted away Davitt's *demarche* – later dismissed as a 'chaotic socialist experiment'[69] – in a June 1882 interview with the *New York Herald*, implying that his old ally would soon return to the fold once he realized that his new philosophy had no traction in rural Ireland.

George also aroused some Irish agrarianist antagonism with his rejection of the validity of certain grievances enunciated by the Land League. In his pamphlet, *The Irish land question*, George had written that 'it is not true that there is – in an economic sense at least – any peculiar oppression of Ireland by England now'.[70] George argued that the Irish land system was essentially the same as that which prevailed in most modernized countries and that, since the passage of the 1870 Land Act by the British parliament, Irish tenant farmers actually held land on better terms than their counterparts in the USA. To him the land war was interesting largely as a laboratory experiment in class struggle.

George was an integrationist, seeking a truer union between Britain and Ireland, and a utopian for whom 'the solution to the Irish land problem was a step in the direction toward universal justice'.[71] So, although clearly identified with George's philosophy, Davitt differed quite radically with him in a variety of respects. Before his departure for the USA in June 1882 Davitt accompanied George on a speaking tour of Britain, where they appeared jointly on a number of platforms. The *Irish World* enthusiastically covered those events, (George was still writing for the newspaper) and the subsequent visit of Davitt to America.

This development posed both a challenge and an opportunity for *United Ireland*. The challenge was how to undermine the deviations of Davitt without damaging its own credibility with outright attacks on such a revered figure. The opportunity was to end any remaining influence of the *Irish World* outside of the United States, following Patrick Ford's post-'Kilmainham treaty' recusancy. The obvious common denominator was Henry George, sometime correspondent of the *World*, whose socialistic pamphlet on the land war had put him at odds with nationalist agrarian orthodoxy.

George had arrived in Ireland in October 1881, partly to view the land war at first hand, partly as special correspondent of the *Irish World*. This was just after the leadership of the Land League had been incarcerated. *United Ireland* had heralded his arrival with the wry observation that 'we trust he is a hardy, thoroughgoing Yank, and that a quadrangular closet in Kilmainham jail will not disagree with his health'.[72] By November the journal was carrying advertisements for *Progress and poverty*,[73] and in December included an article by the great man himself.[74] Relations remained on an even keel for as long as George saw fit to represent the British response to the land war as 'a reign of terror'.[75] The American economist also added to his personal mystique and credibility by managing to get himself arrested on two occasions.[76]

The Irish political establishment was, at first, reluctant to deal directly with Davitt's *bouleversement*. Responding to a speech on land nationalization by Davitt in Liverpool in June 1882, just prior to Parnell's contemptuous rejection of the policy, *United Ireland* sought to square the circle by declaring that 'it conflicts with nothing which the Irish leaders have done or contemplate doing. It stands in the way neither of any process of lowering rents or of enabling the occupiers to purchase out their landlords'. Davitt was depicted as someone involved in an intense psychic conflict:

> Whoever studies his broad and massive scheme cannot even
> pause over its difficult points without feeling that it is one of
> those noble and almost prophetic forecasts of reform with
> which great souls, penetrated with an oppressive sense of
> human misery and a brave faith in a better destiny for man,
> now and again startle a generation, first with the boldness of
> their projects, next with their beauty, and sooner or later, with
> their irresistible truth.[77]

A fortnight later, after Parnell's *New York Herald* interview had greeted
Davitt on his arrival in the US, came the first indication that the 'line' on
his Damascene conversion had shifted. *United Ireland* published a letter
from the highly respected Land League organizer Matt Harris. This was
critical of the principle of land nationalization.[78] It was the first salvo in the
proxy war. In October, as plans were being laid for the establishment of the
National League, the Parnellite journal continued to make light of perceived
differences between Davitt and Parnell in their approach to agrarian issues:
'The question is not whether men differ, but whether they think more of
their differences than the unity and discipline of the National forces.'[79]

Thereafter, when Davitt prominently reiterated his commitment to land
nationalization, *United Ireland* pointed towards the devil at his shoulder.
In a speech in Drogheda in April 1884, in which he renewed his advocacy
of the policy, *United Ireland*, referring to George as 'the Anglo-Californian
adventurer', attacked the new policy enunciated by Davitt, as proxy
Georgism:

> It was harmless until Mr. George ... boldly put forward his
> own fads as a practical programme ... it became a much
> more serious matter when Mr. George stepped upon an Irish
> platform under the countenance of an Irishman of Mr. Davitt's
> position to incite the Irish people to change their counsels and
> discard their leaders.[80]

The following year a further *United Ireland* attack on the land nationalization issue drew a rebuke from Davitt himself in which he characterized the piece as 'ill-tempered and unfair', adding pointedly that 'there ought to be such a thing as consistency even in journalism, and I think I have the right to invite you to give evidence that you are a model in this respect before you lecture the inconsistency of Land Nationalisers like myself'. In response *United Ireland* declined 'to plunge into the sewage of a personal controversy' before remarking sardonically that 'surely it is no more treason for us to differ from Mr. Davitt than for Mr. Davitt to differ from Mr. Parnell, and we certainly admire and respect Mr. Davitt quite as warmly as he admires and respects Mr. Parnell'. Once again, however, the paper chose to leaven its anti-Davitt invective by including George in its commentary. It argued that 'Mr. Henry George's theories should not be allowed to become a bone of contention amongst Irish nationalists.'[81]

The truth was that by 1883 George's interest in Ireland had long since waned and the incompatibility of his ideas and those of Davitt had become apparent to both men.[82] George had tried and failed to shift the debate in Ireland 'from a cultural-religious one … to a socioeconomic one'.[83] By the mid-1880s his retention as a *bête noire* by *United Ireland* was little more than an opportunity for coded attacks on his erstwhile Irish ally.

Of a piece with the campaign against George was the exclusion of the *Irish World* from the Parnellite stable. George's economic ideas dominated the domestic discourse of the *World* while his despatches from Ireland suggested that Davitt's philosophy of land nationalization had attracted more support than was actually the case.

Although one of the collateral intentions behind the creation of *United Ireland* in the first place was to end the need for the widespread importation and distribution of Ford's newspaper, the upstart had initially offered obeisance to its American counterpart. In August 1881 *United Ireland* thanked 'that wonderful Transatlantic Ireland of ours, and its scarcely less wonderful *Irish World*' for the transfer of funds to the Land League. The shift in orientation came in the wake of Ford's declared disillusionment with Parnell when details emerged of the pact between the Irish party leader and the Liberals, which brought an end to the Kilmainham incarcerations. This led to a crucial interruption in funds flowing from America.

In March 1881 Ford had boasted in his paper of his independence when it came to his approach to Irish affairs. He maintained that Irish MPs 'have about as much influence in shaping the policy of the *Irish World* as the members of the Egyptian Chamber of Notables'.[84] He demonstrated that independence, from May 1882, with increasing disparagement of Parnell and acclamation of Davitt. The *Irish World* coverage of Davitt's 1882 tour of the US verged on the hagiographic.[85] *United Ireland* responded by undermining the credentials of Ford's journal, claiming, for example, that many branches of the American League, 'protest against it as unpatriotic'.[86]

Davitt's pivotal Manchester speech of May 1882 received front-page coverage in the *Irish World* in the 17 June issue. In an accompanying leader Ford, conscious of the complexion that was being placed on his altered editorial line, wrote that 'two of our esteemed contemporaries have gravely informed their circle of select readers that the *Irish World* wants to depose Parnell and put Davitt in his place ... what they give out as coming from us is simply the coinage of their own minds'.[87]

In 1891, as the opposing forces of the Parnellite split were gathering, Ford gave an interview in which he reminded readers that the Parnellite newspaper 'was purchased out of funds collected in America, and intended for evicted tenants [which] came absolutely from the pockets of the constituents of the *Irish World*'. He did acknowledge, however, that 'we never subjected the Irish leaders on the other side of the water to any conditions whatever as to how the large amounts of money forwarded by us should be applied'. He also revealed that when Patrick Egan, one of the newspaper's original principal shareholders, had been appointed US Minister to Chile, Egan had made over his *United Ireland* shares to Davitt, using Ford himself as intermediary. However, 'Mr. Davitt was never able, nor did he find it pleasant for him, to assert his rights.' Ford ascribed this to 'the jealousy of O'Brien'.[88]

In 1904, in his autobiographical account of the agrarian and political struggles of the 1880s, *The fall of feudalism in Ireland*, Davitt, in singling out Patrick Ford for his role in those labours, implicitly disparaged the part played by *United Ireland*:

> Mr. Ford has been actively and constantly the most powerful
> support of the struggle in Ireland on the American continent.
> His services to the Irish people in the advocacy of their cause
> in his paper, and in the enormous financial assistance rendered

by its readers and friends to the Irish national leaders, are beyond anything ever done by a weekly newspaper for a great movement.[89]

The cult of personality and personal control

At various times in the 1880s Parnell was either a neglectful or a circumscribed political figure. His career was becalmed in the wake of the Kilmainham Treaty and the introduction of the Crimes Act. His refusal to risk arrest by campaigning in Ireland, and his reversion to domesticity in his relationship with Katharine O'Shea, point to an incipient decline of influence after the Kilmainham interlude. The 1884 franchise extension, and the inevitability of assuming leadership of a large united party, revived his career and advanced his policies. After the failure of the 1886 Home Rule Act he, once again, withdrew into the political shadows until the illusory 'triumph' of the *Times* commission and the enthusiastic renewal of the *rapprochement* with Gladstone. However, even during his fallow periods Parnell could always depend on the weekly beatification of his leadership and public persona by *United Ireland*. As James Loughlin has put it, 'O'Brien and *United Ireland* were at the forefront of a campaign to maintain the psychological reality of his mythic status with the Irish people.'[90]

Parnell himself deftly facilitated his own aggrandizement with a succinct approach to oratory. In this regard either his innate aversion for prolixity, or an acute realization of the value of relative brevity, served him well. A *United Ireland* obituary by the anonymous 'Irish Reporter', referred to his adoption of a 'system of never speaking more than would make about the ordinary column of a newspaper ... One result of this was it developed that method of epigrammatic condensation which made his utterance so strikingly effective and another that he was sure to get a perfectly satisfactory report.'[91] In addition Parnell was noted for cultivating reporters,[92] even ones, like Alfred Robbins, whose newspaper, the *Birmingham Daily Post*, opposed his policies.[93] But antagonistic English newspapers, of which there were many, also played a major role in elevating Parnell to mythic status amongst his own people.

O'Brien's hagiographical treatment of his leader drowned out any potential dissatisfaction at Parnell's inattentiveness to his political duties.[94] James Loughlin has even speculated that the 'cover' provided by *United*

Ireland facilitated Parnell's frequent inactivity: 'It may well have been the case that with *United Ireland* constantly keeping the mythic entity of Parnell before the Irish public, and ensuring that other nationalist papers towed [*sic*] the party line, he felt free to pursue his private interests more fully without political cost.'[95] In establishing the mythic leadership of Parnell the image was of a reticent, reluctant, but passionately committed leader. His 'reticence', by implication, contrasted with the more choleric dispositions of his lieutenants. Occasionally, however, the modest warrior would metamorphose into an Olympian figure, as in one of Bodkin's more purple sallies, an editorial entitled 'Achilles in the field'. This was penned in response to a Parnell speech in Liverpool and written two years before the vulnerable heel of Achilles became apparent.

> Sudden and irresistible as Homer's hero he has sallied out into
> the thick of the fight scattering the enemy before him. Like
> the Homeric hero, he seems to pervade the battle, now here,
> now there, striking along the whole line of the enemy's array,
> invulnerable, in his calm contempt for calumny; irresistible, in
> his pitiless logic and trenchant scorn.[96]

Parnell made practical use of *United Ireland* in that some of the information given to the newspaper for publication about foreign political excursions was actually spurious. It was often 'cover' for a prolonged sojourn at Eltham with Katharine O'Shea.[97] It may be mere coincidence but the newspaper, up to the failure of the Home Rule Bill, rarely availed of countless opportunities to criticize the political allegiances and activities of William O'Shea at a time when its excoriation of other 'nominal' Home Rulers as 'Whigs' was a weekly occurrence.[98]

Parnell also made use of *United Ireland* in a variety of other ways. It afforded him the luxury of witnessing personal attacks being made on his political enemies without he himself having to take responsibility for inspiring them. The incidence of the proposed Chamberlain / Dilke Irish tour of 1885 has already been cited as a case in point. Parnell could privately disown O'Brien's unnecessarily personalized attacks, on Chamberlain in particular,[99] while enjoying the discomfiture of the radicals and aligning himself more closely with the leadership of Gladstone. Davitt blamed

Parnell's influence over *United Ireland* for the entire shambles – 'his reputed organ had nothing for them but the welcome of a threatened horse-pond or the argument of a bog-hole'.[100]

To this notorious incident can be added, as already noted, the splenetic attack by the Parnellite newspaper on Sir Charles Gavan Duffy's support, from Australia, of the 1881 Land bill. Parnell was suitably restrained in his criticism of the former Young Irelander. O'Brien, conversely, poured scorn on Gavan Duffy in a leader entitled 'Knightly counsel' in the paper's third issue.[101]

Despite his denial to the *Times* commission of any overweening or controlling role in the editorial policy of *United Ireland* – he told the attorney general 'Mr O'Brien managed the paper. Mr O'Brien would not allow or would not occupy his post for a single hour if the paper was to be managed by anybody besides himself'[102] – Parnell was quite prepared to attempt to dictate editorial policy. During the brief period of *rapprochement* with the Conservatives in late 1885 agrarian lawlessness was on the rise, jeopardizing one of the most attractive features of the Tory alliance, their willingness to allow the 1882 Crimes Act to lapse. On 17 December 1885 Parnell wrote to Healy, then collaborating with O'Brien in the production of the newspaper, suggesting that it should denounce the spike in the crime figures.[103]

Parnell appears also to have assumed control over at least one aspect of the affairs of *United Ireland*, the disposal of its profits. During the appearance of O'Brien at the *Times* commission on 23 May 1889, the attorney general voiced his assumption that any surplus in the finances of the newspaper was remitted to the National League. O'Brien contradicted him:

> 72037 …the National League has no more to do with the paper than I have – is not in the slightest degree responsible for it, nor me for it.
> 72038 To whom did the profits go then? – To Mr. Parnell.
> 72039 (Mr. Justice A.L. Smith) Personally? – Certainly.
> 72040 (Attorney general) Not to anybody else? – No.
> 72041 To Mr. Parnell personally? – That is to say that I know that the capital was supplied by Mr. Parnell; the profits go to him also, and there were no profits whatever until about 1884.[104]

This does not necessarily contradict other assertions by O'Brien that Parnell had resigned his directorship of the journal in 1883 'to avoid the legal penalties which were then falling in showers upon the paper'.[105] The party leader might well have done so while still retaining a shareholding and extracting a dividend. Neither does it imply that the capital supplied by Parnell came from his own personal resources. In an interview carried by the *New York Herald* on 12 December 1890 O'Brien acknowledged that almost half the shareholding in *United Ireland* belonged to Parnell.[106] In his own evidence earlier that month Parnell himself had accepted the assertion of the attorney general that *United Ireland* was 'the organ of the Land League', agreeing that it had been 'bought with the money of the Land League' while denying that the finance for the newspaper had come directly from the 'Skirmishing fund' in the US.[107] In an interview in January 1891, Patrick Ford, admittedly not the most disinterested source, maintained that 'to my knowledge I can say that not a single farthing of Mr. Parnell's personal money ever went into *United Ireland*'.[108]

Whatever the actual extent of his control and influence, and both he and O'Brien denied its significance, one thing is absolutely clear. After the *coup* in committee room fifteen of the House of Commons in December 1890 Parnell's sudden renewed interest in visiting Ireland began with his re-assertion of his ownership of the newspaper and his repossession of its premises (see chapter 9). The level of control he thereby achieved over the editorial line of *United Ireland* was absolute and continued from beyond the grave.

Notes

1   Irish Loyal and Patriotic Union, *The Real Dangers of Home Rule* (Dublin, 1887), 12.

2   He often shared this role with his onetime employer Patrick Ford of the *Irish World*.

3   See James Loughlin, 'Constructing the political spectacle: Parnell, the Press and national leadership, 1879–86' in *Parnell in Perspective*, D. George Boyce and Alan O'Day (London and New York, 1991).

4   Jurgen Habermas, *The Structural Transformation of the Public Sphere* (Cambridge, Mass. 1991), 171.

5   Robert M. Entman, 'Framing: toward clarification of a fractured paradigm', *Journal of Communication*, 1993, 43 (4), Autumn, 0021–9916/93.

6   Michael Foley, 'Colonialism and journalism in Ireland', *Journalism studies*, vol. 5, no. 3,

2004, 380. Andrew Dunlop, *Fifty Years of Irish Journalism* (Dublin, 1911), 270.

7   Dunlop, *Fifty Years of Irish Journalism*, 276.

8   Dunlop, *Fifty Years of Irish Journalism*, 276.

9   Lucy Brown, *Victorian News and Newspapers*, (Oxford, 1985), 87. She cites, for example, the sale of the *Pall Mall Gazette* in 1880 leading to the departure of reporters with Tory sympathies, and their return in 1894 when the paper changed hands again.

10   Devoy, *Recollections of an Irish Rebel*, 370.

11   Maebh O'Regan, 'Richard Moynan: Irish artist and unionist propagandist', *Eire-Ireland*, 39: 1 & 2, Spring/Summer 2004, 63.

12   Lee, *Origins of the Popular Press*, 25.

13   Michael Foley, 'Colonial and journalism in Ireland', *Journalism studies*, vol. 5, no. 3, 2004, 379.

14   During the land war reporters employed by the Dublin newspapers to record political speeches discontinued the practice of giving evidence in court as to the accuracy of their reports after they were denounced, according to Dunlop 'so strongly as to place their lives in danger' (Dunlop, *Fifty years*, 119). However Davitt represented this as a voluntary act on the part of journalists, even those working for unionist newspapers, unwilling to have their work used in a prosecutorial context (Davitt, *Fall of feudalism*, 415).

15   Loughlin in Boyce/O'Day, *Parnell in Perspective*, 233.

16   T.P. O'Connor, *Memoirs*, 143.

17   Loughlin in Boyce/O'Day, *Parnell in Perspective*, 233.

18   O'Brien, *Recollections*, 360.

19   O'Brien, *William O'Brien and the Course of Irish Politics*, 18.

20   Warwick-Haller, *William O'Brien and the Irish Land War*, 73–4. This is a discussion of the irresponsibility of the journalism of both O'Brien and Healy as against the weight of the forces opposing them.

21   Though *United Ireland* was eminently capable of mimicking some of the less attractive qualities of the unionist press. Note the simian representation of working-class Orangemen in some of its cartoons (*United Ireland*, 5 January 1884–26 January 1884).

22   *Wexford People*, 26 October 1887.

23   *United Ireland*, 8 October 1887, 13 April 1889.

24   *United Ireland*, 10 September 1887.

25   *United Ireland*, 17 December 1881.

26   *Daily Express*, 17 March 1887.

27   *Dublin Evening Mail*, 6 October 1887.

28   *Dublin Evening Mail*, 5 October 1887.

29   *Daily Express*, 25 May 1887.

30   *Daily Express*, 26 May 1887.

31   *United Ireland*, 28 May 1887.

32   This did not just apply to newspapermen. He also took, but did not pursue, legal action against William E. Forster for insinuating that *United Ireland* 'had instigated to crime' (*Special Commission*, 22 May 1889, vol. 8, 152, 71439). In 1889 he sued the Prime Minister, Lord Salisbury, for slander arising out of similar comments relating to O'Brien himself made in a speech at Watford (*United Ireland*, 22 June 1889). A Manchester jury found in Salisbury's favour. A possible reason for his unusually litigious nature was his frequent citation of the unwillingness of others to sue *United Ireland* as a proof of their guilt.

33   *United Ireland*, 8 January 1887.

34   *United Ireland*, 4 August 1888.

35   One of the penal elements of French press legislation prior to 1881 was that contributing journalists should be easily identifiable.

36   *United Ireland*, 1 September 1888.

37   *United Ireland*, 16 April 1887.

38   *United Ireland*, 12 January 1884.

39   *United Ireland*, 29 January 1889.

40   Andrew Dunlop, *Fifty Years of Irish Journalism* (Dublin, 1911), 269.

41   Dunlop, *Fifty Years of Irish Journalism*, 165–9.

42   Dunlop, *Fifty Years of Irish Journalism*, 250.

43   Dunlop, *Fifty Years of Irish Journalism*, 277.

44   *United Ireland*, 17 September 1881.

45   *Times*, 24 December 1881.

46   *Times*, 27 December 1881.

47   *United Ireland*, 12 March 1887.

48   *Times*, 5 October 1885.

49   Robinson was proprietor of the *Express* at that time.

50   *United Ireland*, 13 November 1886.

51   *United Ireland*, 2 February 1889.

52   William Henry Hurlbert, *Ireland Under Coercion* (New York, 1888), vol. 2, 22, 98, 111, 214.

53   Hurlbert, *Ireland Under Coercion*, vol. 2, 22, 111, 83–4, 98. Hurlbert was a Southern Democrat.

54 William Henry Hurlbert, *Ireland Under Coercion*, vol. 2, 111.vol. 2, 22, vol. 2, 98, vol. 2, 83–4.

55 Hurlbert, *Ireland Under Coercion*, vol. 1, 187.

56 *United Ireland*, 25 August 1888.

57 Hurlbert, *Ireland Under Coercion*, vol. 2, 99.

58 Hurlbert, *Ireland Under Coercion*, vol. 1, 274–5.

59 *United Ireland*, 25 August 1888.

60 Gerard Moran, 'James Daly and the rise and fall of the Land League in the west of Ireland, 1879–82', *Irish Historical Studies*, vol. 29, no. 114 (Nov., 1994), 198. Conor Cruise O'Brien refers to it as 'a drastic subordination of the various branches of the movement to central control' (Conor Cruise O'Brien, 'The machinery of the Irish parliamentary party, 1880–85', *Irish Historical Studies*, vol. 5, no. 17 (March 1946), 55).

61 *United Ireland*, 8 October 1881.

62 *United Ireland*, 16 June 1888.

63 *United Ireland*, 23 June 1888.

64 *United Ireland*, 22 October 1881.

65 Madden to Forster, 21 October 1881, NAI, CSORP 1881/36081.

66 Lyons, *Parnell*, 232.

67 T.W. Moody, *Davitt and the Irish Revolution, 1846–1882* (Oxford, 1981), 552. Davitt records in the entry for 13 May in his 1882 diary 'Lent Hn.George £5' (Diary entry, 13 May 1882, MS9536, Davitt papers, Trinity College, Dublin).

68 Carla King, *Michael Davitt* (Dundalk, 1999), 40.

69 *United Ireland*, 19 April 1884.

70 Henry George, *The Irish Land Question: What it involves and how alone it can be settled: an Appeal to the Land Leagues* (New York and London, 1881), 1–2.

71 Michael Silagi and Susan N.Faulkner, 'Henry George and Europe', *American Journal of Economics and Sociology*, vol. 46, no. 4 (October 1994), 499.

72 *United Ireland*, 22 October 1881.

73 *United Ireland*, 26 November 1881.

74 *United Ireland*, 24 December 1881.

75 *Irish World*, 3 December 1881.

76 *Freeman's Journal*, 11 August 1882. Edward T. O'Donnell, '"Though not an Irishman": Henry George and the American Irish', *American Journal of Economics and Sociology*, vol. 56, no. 4 (October 1997), 413.

77 *United Ireland*, 10 June 1882.

78 *United Ireland*, 24 June 1882. Davitt wrote in his diary of Harris's intervention (which

had also appeared in the *New York Herald*), 'These cowardly slanderers had not the manliness to attack me while in Ireland. Now when they stupidly imagine that I am about to be crushed in New York they like so many cowardly curs rush out and bark at my heels' (Diary entry, 23 June 1882, MS 9535, Davitt papers, Trinity College, Dublin).

79 *United Ireland*, 21 October 1882.

80 *United Ireland*, 19 April 1884. In the same edition, in an attempt at ridicule, *United Ireland* wrote that 'the Irish people will have nothing to say to his plans for making the moon into green cheese'.

81 *United Ireland*, 8 August 1885.

82 Silagi and Faulkner, 'Henry George and Europe', 500. In 1884 and 1885 George had seventy-five speaking engagements in Scotland and Wales and two in Ireland.

83 O'Donnell, 'Henry George and the American Irish', 416

84 *Irish World*, 4 March 1882.

85 Davitt returned the compliment in *The Fall of Feudalism in Ireland* when he wrote that 'the *Irish World* has been a tower of strength in every conflict of the past quarter of a century in which the great principle of "the land for the people" was fought for and upheld, and its name and giant efforts in a historic social and national revolution will always be linked with the name and achievements of the Irish Land League' (Davitt, *The Fall of Feudalism*, 715).

86 *United Ireland*, 14 October 1882.

87 *Irish World*, 17 June 1882.

88 *Times*, 3 January 1891. Ford also denigrated O'Brien's potential for party leadership saying, 'he was intended more for guerrilla warfare, not for serious business of this kind'.

89 Davitt, *The Fall of Feudalism*, 715.

90 James Loughlin in *Parnell in Perspective* (D. George Boyce and Alan O'Day, eds), 233.

91 *United Ireland*, 8 October 1891. As against that Edward Byrne wrote of Parnell that 'he was notoriously careless about the reports of his speeches'. (Edward Byrne, *Parnell, a Memoir*, Frank Callanan, ed. (Dublin, 1991), 30). That however, would not preclude his paying minute attention to their format.

92 See Edward Byrne, *Parnell: A Memoir*. J.M. Tuohy (attributed to London Correspondent), *Freeman's Journal*, 8 October 1891.

93 Alfred Robbins, *Parnell: the Last Five Years* (London, 1926).

94 The *Nation*, for one, occasionally adopted a more sceptical approach. 'Mr. Parnell, they [the Irish people] are convinced, is a wise and sagacious champion; they would regard his loss as most serious, but he is not indispensable' (*Nation*, 30 September, 1882).

95 James Loughlin, in *Parnell in Perspective* (D. George Boyce and Alan O'Day, eds), 237.

96 *United Ireland*, 28 December 1889.

97   Robert Kee, *The Laurel and the Ivy* (London, 1993), 373.

98   Dungan, *The Captain and the King*, Chap. 9.

99   Including a reference to his 'sulky antipathy to Irish aspirations', *United Ireland*, 26 December 1885.

100   Davitt, *Fall of Feudalism*, 475.

101   *United Ireland*, 27 August 1881.

102   *Special Commission*, 2 May 1889, vol. 7, 164, 60244.

103   Lyons, *Parnell*, 310. Healy, *Letters and Leaders*, 237.

104   *Special Commission*, 23 May 1889, vol. 8, 200, 72037–72041.

105   William O'Brien, *An Olive Branch in Ireland and its History* (London, 1910), 22. *Insuppressible*, 29 December 1890.

106   *Insuppressible*, 29 December 1890.

107   *Special Commission*, 2 May 1889, vol. 7, 161–4, 60244-60282.

108   *Times*, 3 January 1891.

CHAPTER NINE

Felo De Se:
The Parnellite Split

'The fault of the Irish party began in Committee Room 15 with the language and the method by which the assault on Parnell once begun was carried on.'[1]

(William O'Brien to Michael MacDonagh, 13 January 1928)

Having calculatedly exploited, and then abandoned, what was coyly described at the time as 'advanced' nationalism, in favour of constitutional moderation, Parnell found himself in 1891, much as had Mary Shelley's fictional Dr Frankenstein in the eponymous novel, unable to exercise control over his creation. He was, at a crucial point in his flagging career, incapable of turning the movement he had formed in his image and likeness, away from its innate conservatism. As F.S.L. Lyons has put it 'when in the last year of his life he sought to invoke a more militant spirit, he found in the party he had himself created a vested interest in constitutionalism which it was beyond his power to control'.[2] The party Parnell had largely created then proceeded to consume itself.

The events that flowed from the O'Shea divorce case in November 1890, leading to the decade-long split in the Irish party, also had serious and lasting ramifications for the landscape of the nationalist press in Dublin. The *Freeman's Journal* began its long death rattle. An upstart Healy-inspired project, the *National Press*, was created and later abandoned. The *Irish Daily Independent*, whose successor would dominate the burgeoning commercial market of the early 1900s, was born out of the defection of the *Journal* to the Federationists. And *United Ireland* began its rapid descent into gratuitous partisan vituperation and irrelevance.

As the party split wrought internecine conflict so did certain qualities inherent in nationalist journalism become latent. *United Ireland*, always the assertive policeman, migrated, metaphorically, from a civilian to a military footing, becoming instead a fractious artilleryman. But it no longer had the field entirely to itself. Its belligerence was either complemented or countered by the rancour of the *National Press* and the *Irish Daily Independent*.

The O'Shea divorce proceedings seemed to catch the nationalist press off-guard. The 'triumph' of the *Times* commission, the payment of £5,000 by the newspaper to the Irish party leader in libel damages, and private assurances on the impending divorce case by Parnell to the likes of O'Brien, Morley and Davitt, may have contributed to a sense of complacency. That was shattered by both the result of *O'Shea v O'Shea and Parnell* and the humiliating details that emerged from the unchallenged suit. However, the *Freeman's Journal*, which would remain loyal for the next six months, was quick to rally to the support of the weakened leader:

> Our business with Mr. Parnell is political. The business of Ireland with him is political. He has ably, faithfully successfully served his country ... Is the most important decade in the latter day progress of Irishmen to Home Rule to be blotted out, and, as if it had never been, at the hand of an O'Shea? That ... must not happen.[3]

The initial response of *United Ireland* was, if anything, more muted:

> We have no desire to palliate the grievous sin that has been brought home to the Irish leader by the verdict of a jury,

nor do we affect to deny the profound regret with which the proceedings were watched by the Irish people. It were, perhaps, almost too much to hope in our Leader a man as admirable in the stainless morality of his private life as he is justly renowned for the courage, statesmanship, fidelity, and genius of his public career.

Bodkin, however, despite giving expression to the embarrassment of the Irish people at the personal behaviour of their political leader, had no time for the 'canting hypocrites' calling for his head: 'Of his private life the Irish people have no mission to judge. That they leave to his conscience and his God, who weighs the temptation with the offence. His public career commands their unbounded admiration. It is his public services they will retain, and will repay with loyal support.'[4] The following week, in advance of the crucial Irish party sessional meeting at Westminster, *United Ireland's* support for Parnell was more equivocal:

> If Home Rule is to be still helped by his leadership he will stay; if Home Rule is to be hurt he will go … Whatever else is lost the one indispensable necessity of the situation – a united Irish Party – must be preserved. Disunion or disloyalty is the one crime that Ireland, taught by past experience, will not tolerate in her representatives.[5]

O'Brien, along with Dillon, Harrington and other senior Irish party MPs, was in the US. From there he sent a telegram to Bodkin on 2 December, just before the Irish party meeting in committee room fifteen. The telegram made explicit O'Brien's personal opposition to Parnell's continued leadership[6] but instructed Bodkin, and Edward Donnelly, the paper's general manager, that 'if Irish Party vote for Parnell's leadership, hand over establishment to anybody authorized by Parnell. If Party decide against Parnell, let *United Ireland* strenuously support our views, avoiding all unkind language of Parnell personally, and permit nobody to interfere.'[7]

Bodkin was also coming under pressure from Parnell's acolytes, one of whom, Dr J.E. Kenny MP, wrote to Donnelly the following day, in his capacity as a director of the newspaper. He insisted 'on absolute neutrality

& I told Mr. Bodkin so last week'.[8] The withdrawal from the Westminster meeting of a majority of Irish party members, clarified the position of the parliamentary group and this was reflected in Bodkin's first post-split editorial on 6 December 1890, entitled 'Ireland or Parnell':

> The clouds have lifted. The path of duty is clear at last. No man who keeps his head cool and his heart pure can miss it. Let partisans attempt to disguise it as they may, 'Ireland or Parnell' is now the issue on which Irishmen are to decide … for Ireland's sake, Mr. Parnell must go. It was the Irish party that elected him: it is for them to depose him … The truest and most trusted – the most gifted of his followers – have declared for Ireland against his leadership. The priests and bishops follow emphatically in the same line … no man's personality can be permitted to obstruct the path of Ireland's liberty[9]

Anticipating the opposition of O'Brien, confirmed to him in a cablegram from New York on 7 December,[10] Parnell had tried to pre-empt the antagonistic editorial by invoking his proprietorial rights. He despatched a telegram to Bodkin which read: 'Must insist that your leading article next issue of *United Ireland* being [sic] submitted to me before print, otherwise I must make other arrangements – Parnell.' This was duly published in the 'Week's Work' column with the rejoinder 'there will be no Press censorship in *United Ireland* in favour of any man'.[11] Resisting pressure to use his newspaper to inflict early propaganda damage on Parnell, O'Brien wired Bodkin once again on 8 December: 'Must insist no personalities against Parnell. Don't in any way use cartoons in this controversy. Hold firmly but temperately to Parnell's retirement as *sine qua non*, but remember my injunction, avoid all unkind language of Parnell personally. Write everything yourself.'[12]

Demonstrating the critical importance of *United Ireland* in the political struggle ahead, one of Parnell's first moves on his return to Ireland following the party split was to seize the offices of the journal that had safeguarded and enhanced his reputation for almost a decade, and over which he had notional proprietorial rights. That week Dublin city newsagents had been informed that copies of *United Ireland* would be available on Wednesday 10 December, twenty-four hours in advance of the normal print run 'for an obvious purpose', according to the *Evening Telegraph*.[13] A second set of anti-Parnell editorials was clearly in the offing.

At twenty minutes after midday on 10 December 1890, Parnell presented himself at the front door of the *United Ireland* offices in Abbey street and was refused admission by James O'Connor. After a brief fracas, Parnell and MPs Edmund Leamy (who would take over the editor's chair), William Redmond, John O'Connor and Pierce O'Mahony, as well as Jim Boland of the Dublin IRB,[14] gained entry at the head of a large group of supporters.[15] Bodkin was formally dismissed as editor by Parnell, in his capacity as director of the Irish National Newspaper Publishing Company, and was ejected from the office after being given the option of walking out unharmed or risking defenestration.[16] The current issue of the newspaper, then in preparation, was seized and destroyed. The *United Ireland* offices were left under the control of John O'Connor and Parnell's loyal secretary Henry Campbell. They were, nevertheless, briefly re-taken that night by anti-Parnellite elements before they in turn were forcibly removed. Again Parnell was to the fore in the re-occupation, energized to the point of frenzy 'the habitually placid Irish leader was alarmingly metamorphosed in a public display of wild and violent fury'.[17] In attendance at this second incursion was the fictional Leopold Bloom, who, according to James Joyce in *Ulysses*, handed a grateful Parnell his displaced hat after the office was retaken.

The event itself, and especially Parnell's demeanour, became a central trope in the subsequent Federationist propaganda campaign, masterminded by Tim Healy. According to Frank Callanan, latter-day chronicler of the split, Parnell's obvious passion and dearth of *sang froid* detracted considerably from his lustre and mystique. 'Parnell's loss of composure compromised one of the central attributes of his political repute, that of extreme self-control.'[18]

Bodkin used the *Irish Catholic*'s relatively primitive printing facilities to bring out, single-handedly by his own account,[19] a daily anti-Parnellite organ, called *Suppressed United Ireland*. The referral address for the editor of the paper, still named as William O'Brien, was given as '9 Great Denmark-street, Dublin'. This was actually the home of Bodkin.[20] After three issues, Parnell secured an injunction prohibiting his use of that title.[21] Bodkin immediately replaced it on 17 December with *Insuppressible*, but does not appear to have exercised much personal control over the increasingly virulent content of the paper.

Despite the claim by *Insuppressible*, in its second issue on 18 December, that O'Brien was 'chairman and editor in chief',[22] the real motive force was the mercurial Tim Healy. Healy, using the good offices and facilities of the Sullivan-owned *Nation*, began to set the agenda himself. O'Brien quickly became aware, as he informed Dillon in a cablegram, that 'Healy's influence [is] supreme'[23] where the editorial policy of *Insuppressible* was concerned. The vituperative copy flowing from Healy's pen rapidly served to elevate levels of resentment and tension.

That publication survived for about a month, until 24 January 1891. Demand was brisk and 'exceeded the supply' according to Bodkin.[24] The journal collapsed when O'Brien, embarrassed by its intemperate criticism of Parnell, withdrew his support.[25] Until his repudiation, *Insuppressible,* as had *Suppressed United Ireland*, purported to be 'William O'Brien's paper'.[26] It carried a daily insert on its editorial page entitled 'W[illiam]m O'Brien speaks' over a letter sent by O'Brien to Bodkin on 11 December from New York, in which he had declared that he was 'proud to know that *United Ireland* continues insuppressible'.[27] But his subsequent correspondence with Bodkin makes it clear that O'Brien heartily disapproved of its content, style and direction.

The paper, despite purporting to be under the editorial control of one of the main participants, attacked the negotiations taking place in Boulogne between the Federationists (led by Dillon and O'Brien) and Parnell. Healy was determined to sabotage those talks if he could, and managed to browbeat or charm Bodkin into acquiescence. Writing to his deputy from Paris, where he had travelled prior to the Boulogne negotiations, O'Brien professed himself 'appalled' at what he read in the newspaper. He demanded to know 'in heaven's name who wrote this and published it in my name? The *Times* in its worst hour never published anything more damning … I am afraid you will find that the people who tried to woo you are not as loyal to you as you have been to them. I do not for a moment blame you myself.'[28]

O'Brien was even more disturbed when he received the copy of *United Ireland* from the period immediately after the party split, when Bodkin had still been editor. 'In every portion of the paper I can observe the influence of our friend Tim – the very thing I dreaded all along … the paper was not to be used in any sense for the gratification of personal malice in a crisis involving the very existence of the movement.'[29] The 'malice' to which

O'Brien referred, was not that of Bodkin but of the embittered former acolyte Healy. O'Brien also explicitly warned his former deputy editor that 'Tim is one of the best-hearted fellows in all the world [but] his judgment the very worst in the world.'[30]

In early January Bodkin travelled to Boulogne to consult with O'Brien who made it clear that he wished him 'to moderate the frightful provocative tone of the paper.'[31] Neither that meeting nor O'Brien's subsequent agitated missives to Bodkin had any effect in changing the tone of *Insuppressible*. Bodkin argued, feebly, that he was simply making the paper 'readable.'[32] In mid-January, by which point Bodkin appears to have completely lost control of the editorial direction of the journal, O'Brien was compelled to intervene once again:

> Monday's *Insuppressible* received today, was again most painful reading for me. I am sure you are doing your best in difficult circumstances but I seem to have failed completely to impress you with my position ... I am made to feel responsible for a paper which in every line does its worst to thwart any hope of success by a line of criticism which I have tried to impress upon you is absolutely fatal to our vital interest as well as loathsome to myself[33]

On the day the letter was despatched *Insuppressible* carried allegations of financial impropriety against Timothy Harrington, a senior Parnell loyalist. The allegation, that he had embezzled money from Plan of Campaign funds,[34] marked a new low in the journalism of the anti-Parnellite newspaper and immediately became the subject of a successful libel action. This resulted in the award to Harrington of a modest £5 in damages against J.J. Lalor, printer /publisher of the *Irish Catholic* and the *Nation*.[35]

On 21 January O'Brien decided formally to renounce any connection to *Insuppressible*. This was, in part, a putative concession to the Parnellites in the Boulogne negotiations. O'Brien also offered, subject to a final agreement with Parnell, to decline any involvement in the plans already being formulated for a new anti-Parnellite daily newspaper.[36] When he was sent a requisition by the publishers to make himself publicly responsible for *Insuppressible,* he finally, on 22 January 1891, disassociated himself from the entire enterprise in a formal cable to Bodkin:[37]

> Once I became acquainted with the tone and contents of
> *Insuppressible* I have only been restrained by motives of
> national policy from at once dissociating myself publicly from
> any responsibility for its writings. Since I am now pressed to
> assume such responsibility I regret to be obliged, for reasons
> which it would serve no useful purpose to dwell upon at this
> moment, to request that my name shall not be further used by
> the publishers of *Insuppressible*.[38]

An accompanying letter, for Bodkin's eyes only, was designed to mitigate
personally the public impact of the cable on his former deputy. In this
O'Brien told Bodkin that 'I do most poignantly feel what a thankless and
horrible position yours has been, and there is nothing in this most miserable
business that gave me a more keener [*sic*] pain than to be obliged to add
to your worries … I entirely understand that all the worst parts of the
paper were written not by you but in spite of you.'[39] Bodkin, who appears,
in establishing *Insuppressible*, to have been attempting to satisfy what he
genuinely believed to be O'Brien's aspirations, sent an aggrieved reply:

> I am grateful for the kind expressions in your letter. But you
> have made me an object of ridicule, contempt and contumely
> to every Parnellite in the country & of suspicion to many of my
> friends. All who know I was in Boulogne of course believe that
> I acted in direct opposition to your wishes & fraudulently used
> your name. Whereas you know that it was only at your special
> request I continued the paper.[40]

O'Brien, while sympathizing with Bodkin's plight – 'Nothing in my life
gave me more anguish than to be obliged to take a step which undoubtedly
exposes you to misunderstanding for the moment' – reminded the young
barrister-journalist that the poisonous editorializing of Healy and his
associates, had calculatedly jeopardized the peace talks taking place in the
French seaside resort and constituted an ongoing personal embarrassment:

> Was ever man placed in so cruel a position of misunderstanding
> as I myself personally insulted in every line of a newspaper
> bearing my name, but (what was a thousand times worse)
> obliged to see my own name being employed for the purpose
> of wrecking and inspiring mistrust of an effort at peace on
> which I am convinced in my heart and soul depends the one
> possible hope of extricating the Irish cause from a miserable
> and loathsome chaos . . . apparently the people in command
> were determined that every reference to a possible settlement
> should be made the vehicle of taunts and insults calculated to
> make all reconciliation impossible.[41]

Because of his perceived closeness to Parnell, O'Brien's loyalty to the Federationists was viewed by some as being circumscribed and highly suspect. His 'espousal of an anti-Parnellite *via media*'[42] and his misplaced faith in the Boulogne talks added to his questionable status. Hence the veiled attacks on him in the *Insuppressible* of which he complained to Bodkin. The reaction of John Hooper, editor of the *Cork Herald*, which had taken an anti-Parnellite line, was typical of the attitude of the Federationists to O'Brien until his declaration against Parnell after his release from Galway prison in July 1891. Hooper wrote a sympathetic note to Bodkin after O'Brien's rejection of the proprietorship of the *Insuppressible*:

> He appears to have been completely hypnotised and to have
> forgotten the most elementary facts of his own earlier doings
> during this crisis ... if we had all acted in the beginning in
> the spirit of Christian charity that William is now showing our
> friend, Parnell w[oul]d simply have walked over us & defied &
> laughed at O'Brien.[43]

Even as the *Insuppressible* was being 'suppressed'[44] after 'a career brief and inglorious',[45] plans were well under way for the launching of a Federationist daily paper to fill the gap created by the *Freeman's Journal's* adherence to Parnell. The continuing support of the nationalist 'newspaper of record' for Parnell was largely prompted by Caroline Gray, widow of Edmund Dwyer Gray, and a 45 per cent shareholder in the *Journal*.[46]

In early January an announcement was circulated to potential shareholders in the Irish National Press Company Limited stating that 'the directors will be able very shortly to announce the date of the appearance of the first number of the paper'.[47] Bodkin, despite his *Insuppressible* experiences, opted to assist the new venture as a leader writer. He described it as 'a well-organised, perfectly equipped paper with capital at its back'.[48]

The refusal of O'Brien to take the helm[49] at the new paper left the field open for Healy to direct the editorial policy of the *National Press*,[50] though he acknowledged that Thomas Sexton 'has quietly taken up the editorial position'.[51] Of the total nominal capital of £60,000 just over £41,000 was taken up, although it was claimed at the time that the offer had been over-subscribed.[52] Many of the shares were purchased by the businessman and future *Irish Independent* proprietor, William Martin Murphy MP.[53] When the *National Press* was launched in March 1891, Healy declared, colourfully and vindictively, that 'this is the winding-sheet of Parnellism'.[54] The arrival of the *Press* on the national scene heralded, in the words of Healy's biographer, Frank Callanan, an era of 'chauvinistic populism ... [and] inaugurated a revolution in Irish politics and journalism. The *Freeman's* shrill and *démodé* rhetoric of fidelity to Parnell was no match for the ferocious demotic vigour of its rival.'[55]

The *National Press*, a highly professional 1p daily, with an initial print run of 60,000 and distributed through Easons,[56] continued, rhetorically at least, where *Insuppressible* had left off. But it was without the potentially moderating influence of O'Brien. The most celebrated journalistic manifestation of its harassment of Parnell was the notorious 'Stop Thief' leaders, beginning on 1 June 1891, and continuing on a daily basis for the remainder of that week. In these Parnell was accused of the embezzlement of National League funds. The party leader, it was claimed, had, for a number of years *been stealing the money entrusted to his charge* [their italics].[57] Parnell's unwillingness to sue the newspaper for libel was exploited in further editorials as the week went on. Emboldened by the non-appearance of a writ, on 2 June the *Press* reminded its readers that '"Thief" is an unmistakable word. We called Mr. Parnell a thief. We now repeat the epithet.'[58] On 5 June the *Press* contrasted the alacrity with which Harrington had sued *Insuppressible* for making similar allegations against him, with Parnell's reluctance to challenge 'one of the gravest charges ever made against a public man'.[59] In its issue of 13 June,

United Ireland asked, rhetorically, of Federationist leaders Justin McCarthy and Thomas Sexton, did they approve of the *National Press* articles. It then answered its own question by observing that their silence indicated 'they have enrolled themselves into the "Stop Thief" conspiracy'.[60]

Healy also sought in the columns of the *National Press*, and on the public platforms inseparable from those columns, to undermine the 'myth' of Parnell sedulously cultivated by *United Ireland* and, somewhat less assiduously, by the *Freeman's Journal*. This revolved around, what the newspaper's London correspondent, J.M. Tuohy, suggested were, Parnell's two cardinal attributes 'tenacity of purpose and self-repression'.[61] As Frank Callanan asserts, Healy 'sought unceasingly to find a technique to pierce Parnell's pride and to penetrate the protective carapace of his myth'.[62] The *Press* regularly drew attention, during the rancorous by-election campaigns of 1891, to the disappearance of the mask of aloofness and perennial poise associated with Parnell 'when he ranted from platform to platform, loading the air with personalities'.[63] Healy's imperative was to reduce Parnell himself from a figure of invincibility to one of risibility – 'a disgraced and discredited trickster'[64] – and his 1891 campaigns to the status of 'a bedraggled harlequinade'.[65]

Before long two countervailing but complementary forces took hold and ensured the demise of the controversialist newspaper. The first was the increasing unease of a number of leading anti-Parnellites with the excesses of Healy, the second was the simultaneous and fortuitous financial difficulties of the *Freeman's Journal*.

Primus inter pares among Healy's antagonists was John Dillon. While incarcerated in Galway he had written to O'Brien: 'Loathing is the only word that can express my feeling every time I open the *National Press*. If that spirit is to triumph, national politics will be turned into a privy.'[66]

In mid-August 1891 Dillon warned Bodkin of his opposition to 'an intention of reviving the attacks on Mr. Parnell w[ith] reference to application of funds entrusted. If the *Press* opens up that question again I shall be compelled to make some public statement disassociating myself from this line of attack. And it would be very unfortunate that any such difference in our ranks should be made public.'[67] Healy, for whom the warning was clearly intended, ignored Dillon's opposition and went ahead with supplementary attacks on Parnell's alleged financial improprieties. Dillon responded with a further warning to Bodkin. Expressing astonishment and anger he re-iterated that 'you must see yourself how great a disaster it would be to force O'Brien and me into an open rupture with the paper'.[68] Healy acknowledged in a letter to his brother Maurice – included in his memoir, *Letters and leaders of my day* – that 'Dillon and O'Brien will yet kill the *National Press*.'[69] Ultimately, however, Dillon and O'Brien held their noses and publicly tolerated Healy's envenomed rhetoric. 'A failure of nerve compounded a failure of judgment',[70] in the view of Frank Callanan, and Healy was not publicly upbraided by fellow anti-Parnellites with the moral authority of Dillon and O'Brien.

Coinciding with a growing belief amongst the more moderate Federationists that Healy was getting out of control, were the convenient financial difficulties of the *Freeman's Journal*. The launch of the *National Press* and the *Journal's* advocacy of the Parnellite cause had led to a rapid dip in the latter's regular circulation of over 40,000.[71] This set in motion the newspaper's 'tortuous *volte face*'.[72] Caroline Gray began to vacillate in her support for Parnell. This was especially the case after the return from Tasmania of her twenty-one year old son, Edmund Dwyer Gray Jr, 'justifiably fearful for his inheritance'.[73] Gray Jr quickly wilted under the joint pressure of the bottom line and the crozier. The disparagement by the Roman Catholic hierarchy of the *Journal*, and especially that of Archbishop Walsh of Dublin, had a hugely detrimental impact on its circulation. It was intimated to O'Brien in July 1890, while serving his jail sentence in Galway, by barrister-journalist Edward Ennis, a *Freeman* leader-writer, that the callow Gray 'had been quite converted to our view, and was only deferring publicly saying so until he saw what line we took on our release, and how far we might be able to secure fair play for the *Freeman* from the more embittered of our colleagues who had the *National Press* already in the field as its rival'.[74] The most embittered of those colleagues was Healy, anxious to give the despised *Journal* nothing but short shrift.

To facilitate the switching of allegiance, the composition of the board of the *Journal* was altered at a special general meeting of the company on 21 September 1891. The new board was dominated by the young Dwyer Gray and Captain Maurice O'Conor, soon to become Mrs Gray's second husband.[75] *United Ireland* feigned indifference to the development.[76] The process of Federationist journalistic consolidation was completed in March

1892 when the *Press* and the *Journal* merged into *The Freeman's Journal and National Press*, much to the chagrin of Healy, who was almost as vindictive in his desire to close the *Journal* as he was to obliterate Parnellism.[77]

While the *Journal* disingenuously gloated over the 'disappearance of the *National Press*, and the recognition of the *Freeman's Journal* as the sole organ of the National party and the Nationalists of Ireland',[78] a triumphant Healy declared that the *Press* 'had captured the *Freeman* in the open sea and put a prize crew aboard'.[79] But he had little time to savour victory. Even before the boardroom upheaval in the *Journal* virtually guaranteed the establishment of a single anti-Parnellite daily, there were moves to end the intemperate reign of Parnell's self-appointed nemesis. T.P. O'Connor had written to Bodkin as early as September 1891, suggesting that a coup against Healy was in preparation. The imperative was 'to go for him at once and crush him'.[80] Shortly after the *National Press* and the *Freeman's Journal* amalgamated, Dillon and Thomas Sexton succeeded in ousting the dominant irreconcilables, Healy and William Martin Murphy, from effective control of the new entity.[81]

Not that *United Ireland*, under the editorship of Leamy, was any less caustic and embittered than either *Insuppressible* or the *National Press*. Subsequent to the failure of the Boulogne talks, O'Brien had asked the opposing sides 'to conduct the struggle with decency'. *United Ireland* offered tacit support to his appeal, commenting that 'we earnestly hope that even now the counsel of decency which Mr. O'Brien has offered to all Irishmen will be respected'. However, it simultaneously accused Federationist newspapers of 'squalid vituperation',[82] and did precious little to live up to its self-imposed injunction.

While *United Ireland*, given its self-ordained role of Parnellite *fidei defensor*, might legitimately be excused references to the 'illimitable scurrility of T.M. Healy',[83] less justifiable was the profound narrative shift that saw its editorial commentary almost entirely given over to the abuse of fellow nationalists. The newspaper also evinced a new-found anti-clericalism.

The year 1891 saw a dramatic increase in the number of editorials in the newspaper, from an annual average of 127 over the previous five years to a new high of 159. One-hundred-thirty-seven of those editorials were devoted to intra-nationalist polemics or anti-clericalism. Sixteen of the 159 leaders were denunciations of rival newspapers. However, unlike the

1881–90 period, in this instance the attacks were devoted exclusively to the criticism of other nationalist journals. The main targets were the *Freeman's Journal*, in the wake of the announcement of its apostasy in August 1891[84] and the *National Press*.[85] There was virtually no ongoing editorial analysis of government policy. Intra-party invective largely replaced anti-Castle commentary.

Thirty editorials (19 per cent of the total) can be described as positive in nature. Almost all were in praise of (or in mourning for) Parnell himself. However, such editorials were greatly outnumbered by negative leaders rebuking political opponents. These make up more than a third (34 per cent)[86] of the total number of editorials for the year. Even a leader that began as a bland celebration of St Patrick's Day rapidly degenerated into an anti-Federationist diatribe.[87]

As the year went on the level of invective increased dramatically. Reconciliation was off the editorial agenda after the three Parnellite by-election losses and especially after the death of Parnell himself. The first, black-edged, issue of *United Ireland* after the demise of its leader was highly personalized and vindictive, accusing the Federationist leaders of having 'hounded Mr. Parnell to his death' before concluding:

> Is Mr. John Dillon satisfied now? Is Mr. William O'Brien dead Caesar's Brutus? Are they as happy as Mr. Thomas Sexton, who plotted the Great Betrayal of November last? Shall Ireland exact no punishment for what has been done? Shall this fatal perfidy, this slow torture unto death of our beloved leader go unavenged?[88]

In employing such intemperate language Leamy's *United Ireland* made its own unique contribution to ensuring that the party split continued for almost a decade after the death of its proximate cause.

A different kind of 'slow torture unto death' characterized the nationalist newspaper landscape in the two years following the Parnellite split. The year 1891 was one of newspaper lawsuits. Harrington sued *Insuppressible* for accusing him of financial impropriety. Healy sued the *Freeman's Journal* for alleging that he advised clients in a murder case to plead guilty and accepted money from the Crown for his efforts.[89] Henry Campbell MP, Parnell's secretary, sued the Federationist *Cork Daily Herald* for claiming that he was guilty of 'discharging the degrading duty of hiring horses for the immoral purposes of his master'.[90]

The excesses of the *National Press* – what F.S.L. Lyons characterized as 'endless, monotonous vituperation'[91] – spawned a daily Parnellite rival, the *Irish Daily Independent*, in December 1891. It was edited by Edward Byrne, a Parnell loyalist and former editor of the *Freeman's Journal*. The *Independent*, funded entirely by supporters of the Parnellite faction, announced, without any apparent irony, that 'we promise to make the *Irish Daily Independent* an independent national journal in fact as well as in name'.[92] It had been rumoured that Parnell would simply re-launch *United Ireland* as a daily paper.[93] Instead he chose to start from scratch. In his biography of Parnell, *Enigma*, Paul Bew has noted how, in 1881, the *Nation* 'was pushed ruthlessly aside' in favour of the 'new rising star' in *United Ireland* after 'years of loyal support'.[94] The same ruthlessness was in evidence in the denial of the claims of *United Ireland* to become a daily newspaper, a decade after it had first been mooted, out of a misplaced deference to nomenclature. While the Parnellite 'brand' encompassed the independence from Liberal party domination of those who adhered to its philosophy, no one could have been so deluded as to believe that the new journal was in any sense 'independent' of the Redmonds and the Harringtons.

A confidential Dublin Castle memo – 'History of the Dublin Nationalist Press since the "Split" in the Nationalist ranks' – (undated but written after the end of May 1892) is a twenty-three-page account of this internecine newspaper war. It graphically illustrated the damaging effects of that strife on the status and effectiveness of the nationalist press. It concluded, after dispassionately recounting and analysing the chaotic in-fighting of the December 1890–May 1892 period, that 'its changing policy, bad management, and amalgamation with the *National Press*' had left the *Freeman's Journal* 'in bad odour' and 'diminished in circulation'. *United Ireland* had also declined in readership while 'its leading articles and cartoons are now devoted to denouncing and caricaturing the "Federationists"'.[95] The subtext is one of quiet establishment satisfaction or barely restrained glee at the anarchic disarray of the previously formidable nationalist press.

At the outbreak of these hostilities West Ridgeway had made a telling comment in a note to Balfour. Informing him of the appearance of

Suppressed United Ireland and the travails of *United Ireland* itself, the under secretary had signalled the effective end of the chief secretary's battle with the nationalist press when he remarked, with an air of finality, that 'neither publishes the proceedings of suppressed branches of the League'.[96] Tory victory had ultimately been achieved when the enemy folded its tents and vanished. Like its other nationalist rivals and counterparts the newspaper that had begun life as 'a weekly national monster meeting that cannot be dispersed with buckshot' had turned its own shotgun on other nationalist journals which were apparently equally indifferent, editorially at least, to the latest stratagems of Dublin Castle.

In its final issue of 1891 *United Ireland* welcomed the arrival of the *Irish Daily Independent*, opining that 'in every important particular which constitutes a national organ this *Independent* is all that could be desired'.[97] But by April 1893 *United Ireland* was clearly feeling some pressure from its daily counterpart, because it accused the *Independent* of undermining it. The *Independent* had apparently implied that Leamy's journal 'was absolutely useless as a political organ'.[98] There is a rich irony in the fact that *United Ireland*, which long held the possibility of publishing on a daily basis as a Damoclean sword over the head of the *Freeman's Journal*, was itself destabilized by a daily newspaper brought out by its own side in the midst of the intra-party hostilities. In just over a decade *United Ireland* had gone from being an 'insurrection in print' to defining insularity in print. The paper itself struggled on for a few more years as a partisan battering ram, then gradually discarded its tone of melodramatic recrimination, became a more Dublin-oriented newspaper, before it succumbed to its own irrelevance in September 1898.

By then it had made its peace with William O'Brien by its extensive coverage of the activities of the infant United Irish League.[99] By 23 July 1898 it was prepared to opine that 'the United Irish League has come to stay',[100] and was 'like a memory of old times'.[101] Its final issue, on 10 September 1898, included an editorial on the League entitled 'The New Crusade'. It acknowledged of John Dillon that 'much unreasonable bitterness has been manifested towards him'.[102] It also lashed out for the last time at its wearisome stable companion, the *Irish Daily Independent*.[103] It was not, perhaps, a full circle, but it was, at the very least, a remarkable parabola.

Given the almost simultaneous onset of the so-called 'new journalism' of the late nineteenth century – usually seen as exemplified by Stead's *Pall Mall Gazette* and T.P. O'Connor's *Star* before its apotheosis with Northcliffe's *Daily Mail* – there has been a tendency to align *United Ireland* with this phenomenon. However, while O'Brien's journal may merit inclusion on the basis of its relentless campaigning – a significant feature of 'new journalism' – it falls down in other categories.

Martin Conboy has defined the style of new journalistic writing as 'a concerted attempt to match the content of the papers to the people'.[104] Content, in this instance, should be interpreted in the broadest sense, to include an accessible style of presentation as well as material that was relevant to the readership. Whatever about the editorial content of the newspaper, the literary style adopted by O'Brien and then 'cloned' by Bodkin, lacked a ready accessibility. *United Ireland* was produced and edited by educated men who were not disposed to hide their education. In that sense at least it was the antithesis of the 'new journalism'.

O'Brien was actually indulging in a practice more akin to the 'new/ yellow' journalistic mix of Joseph Pulitzer on the *New York World*. Pulitzer's newspaper was a muckraking, campaigning journal but one that did not necessarily identify totally with the interests of those on whose behalf it professed to fight. As Conboy observes of Pulitzer, 'he was engaging in a much more subtle negotiation between his own campaigning and the projected conflation of this with the will of the people'.[105]

In a sense what these proprietors did (as would William Randolph Hearst with *New York Journal*) was to enlist its readership in the pursuit of common goals. These objectives were more beneficial to the *haute-bourgeoisie* than to the masses but they were, nonetheless, objectives with which the masses could engage and identify. O'Brien did much the same with *United Ireland*. Small farmers were petitioned and cajoled to engage in campaigns that would principally benefit shopkeepers, larger farmers and graziers. Lip service was paid to the needs of labourers but essentially their interests were not paramount. O'Brien used techniques that had already become familiar – obloquy, anathemization, sensationalism, exaggeration, special pleading and disingenuousness – to spice up his oracular prose and maintain a campaigning aura about his newspaper.

Neither did O'Brien succumb, in the 1880s, to many of the popular techniques of the 'new journalism' of the following decade. There was, for example, little or no sports coverage. There was some attention paid to Gaelic games but even this was minimal. The Gaelic Athletic Association was new on the scene and struggled in its early years because of perception that it was a glorified IRB front. Despite his old familial associations with that organization O'Brien, the committed agrarianist and avowed Parnellite apologist was not about to enhance the credibility of the IRB.[106]

United Ireland has to be seen, not within the framework of the development of the practice of journalism in general or even of Irish journalism in particular, but in a purely agitational context. Its journalism was the rhetoric of the platform, stirring, effective and psychologically impactful, but ephemeral nonetheless. Its template was a throwback to the days of Cobbett and O'Connor and, in commercial and journalistic terms, was being superceded by the discursiveness of the 'new journalism'. Like its regional nationalist equivalents *United Ireland* was, in essence, assembled by a single author with a particular agenda. It was far closer to the pamphlet than it was to the *Daily Mail*.

Parnell looked to *United Ireland* in 1890 when he required undifferentiated loyalty and partisan verbal violence. When he needed to reach out to rural Ireland and to revert to the axioms of the 1881–5 period – a narrative encompassing the absolute independence of the Irish party and the destructive intrigues of the 'Grand Old Spider' – it was to *United Ireland* that he turned. But the dramatic reclamation of the offices and presses of *United Ireland* could not compensate for the subsequent loss of the support of the *Freeman*.

Despite certain obvious caveats *United Ireland* had largely been at the disposal of the wider nationalist movement in the 1880s. From the moment at the end of 1890, when Parnell displayed more interest in the newspaper than he had done since the establishment of the Irish National Newspaper Company in 1881, it degenerated into a tool of empty factionalism. In his memoir, *Evening Memories*, O'Brien makes no reference whatever to the decline of his project. The journal that had weathered the best efforts of two coercion regimes to close it down, had, metaphorically, ended up by smashing its own presses.

Notes

1   O'Brien to Michael MacDonagh, MacDonagh papers, NLI, MS 11442.

2   F.S.L. Lyons, *The Fall of Parnell*, 16.

3   *Freeman's Journal*, 18 November 1890.

4   *United Ireland*, 22 November 1890.

5   *United Ireland*, 29 November, 1890.

6   Many years later his wife claimed in a correspondence with an American admirer of O'Brien that had her husband known about the part played by John Morley and William V. Harcourt in the amendment of Gladstone's letter to Parnell he would not have opposed Parnell's leadership. 'I know that the revelation was a cruel blow to William O'Brien. Had he known the truth he would have acted differently.' Sophie O'Brien to A.W. Bromage, 1 December 1951. O'Brien papers, NLI, MS 5924. The demonization of Morley and consequential partial exculpation of Gladstone is challenged by Frank Callanan in *The Parnell Split*, (Cork, 1992), 16–20.

7   O'Brien, *An Olive Branch in Ireland*, 21.

8   Kenny to Donnelly, 3 December 1890, NLI, F.S. Bourke collection, MS 10702 (9).

9   *United Ireland*, 6 December 1890.

10 O'Brien to Parnell, 7 December 1890, TCD, John Dillon papers, MSS 6736, f.44. The cablegram concluded, 'I appeal to you as a leader I have for ten years been proud to follow and as a friend for whom I still feel a warm affection. Can you not see some way by which, while safeguarding your own reputation the country may be saved from the ruin which threatens it.'

11 *United Ireland*, 6 December 1890.

12 O'Brien, *An Olive Branch in Ireland*, 22.

13 *Evening Telegraph*, 10 December 1890.

14 McGee, *The IRB*, 196.

15 *Times*, 12 December 1890.

16 Bodkin, *Recollections*, 174–5.

17 Callanan, *The Parnell Split*, 64.

18 Callanan, *The Parnell Split*, 64.

19 Bodkin, *Recollections*, 175.

20 *Suppressed United Ireland*, 13 December 1890.

21 *Freeman's Journal*, 17 December 1890.

22 *Insuppressible*, 18 December 1890.

23 O'Brien to Dillon, 29 December 1890, TCD, John Dillon papers, MSS 6736.

24 Bodkin, *Recollections*, 175.

25 F.S.L. Lyons, *The Fall of Parnell* (London, 1960), 155–7, 235–6.

26 *United Ireland*, now being edited by Edmund Leamy MP also claimed to be O'Brien's paper, in that his proprietorship was still acknowledged on the back page of the journal on a weekly basis throughout 1891. *Insuppressible*, despite its own dubious claims to having the *imprimatur* of O'Brien, pointed out in its edition of 27 December, that Parnell was 'forging' O'Brien's name as editor of *United Ireland*.

27 *Insuppressible*, 17 December 1891.

28 O'Brien to Bodkin, undated letter, probably 28 December 1890, NLI, F.S. Bourke collection, MS 10702.

29 O'Brien to Bodkin, undated letter, probably 28 December 1890, NLI, F.S. Bourke collection, MS 10702.

30 O'Brien to Bodkin, 29 December 1890, NLI, F.S. Bourke collection, MS 10702. Despite their many differences O'Brien retained what his wife characterized as 'real affection' for Healy (Sophie O'Brien to Michael MacDonagh, 11 March 1928, MacDonagh papers, NLI, MS 11443).

31 O'Brien to Bodkin, 24 January 1891, NLI, F.S. Bourke collection, MS 10702. 'I know you did your best, after our chat in Boulogne, to moderate the frightful provocative tone of the paper, but apparently the people in command were determined that every reference to a possible settlement should be made the vehicle of taunts and insults calculated to make all reconciliation impossible.'

32 O'Brien to Bodkin, 15 January 1891, NLI, F.S. Bourke collection, MS 10702.

33 O'Brien to Bodkin, 15 January 1891, NLI, F.S. Bourke collection, MS 10702.

34 *Insuppressible*, 15 January 1891.

35 *Irish Times*, 11 February 1891. *Irish Times*, 28 February 1891.

36 Miscellaneous notes, 21 January 1891, TCD, John Dillon papers, MS 6736, ff.69–70. A note in Dillon's handwriting records that O'Brien was not 'offered … any consideration whatsoever for withdrawing his name from Insuppressible'.

37 O'Brien, *An Olive Branch in Ireland*, 38–9.

38 O'Brien, *An Olive Branch in Ireland*, 38–9.

39 O'Brien to Bodkin, 22 January 1891, NLI, F.S.Bourke collection, MS 10702.

40 Bodkin to O'Brien, 24 January 1891 [the letter is incorrectly dated 1890], O'Brien papers, UCC, WOB-PP-AC, f.15.

41 O'Brien to Bodkin, 24 January 1891, NLI, F.S. Bourke collection, MS 10702.

42 Callanan, *The Parnell Split*, 155.

43 Hooper to Bodkin, 2 February, 1891, NLI, F.S. Bourke collection, MS 10702.

44 *Irish Times*, 28 February 1891. The wording used, to the amusement of the courtroom, by Justice Harrison in his directions to the jury in the *Harrington v Lalor* libel case.

45 *Irish Times*, 21 January 1891. The words are those of John Redmond, who was defending two men accused of stealing 500 copies of the newspaper and depositing them in Phoenix Park.

46 Felix Larkin, 'The dog in the night-time: the "Freeman's Journal", the Irish Parliamentary party and the empire' in Simon Potter, ed., *Newspapers and empire in Ireland and Britain* (Dublin, 2004), 111.

47 *Irish Times*, 12 January 1891.

48 Bodkin, *Recollections*, 117.

49 O'Brien, *An Olive Branch in Ireland*, 39. Ironically, just over two years previously O'Brien had been offered, and declined, the editorship of the *Freeman's Journal* itself after the death of Edmund Dwyer Gray at an annual salary of £1,200 (O'Brien to Michael MacDonagh, 20 April 1927, MacDonagh papers, NLI, 11442).

50 Healy, *Letters and Leade*rs, 365. 'I have written a great deal for the *National Press*. Wednesday's number had five columns from me – all of which I dictated. The paper is better than the *Freeman,* which is little more interesting than a grocer's circular.'

51 Healy, *Letters and Leaders*, 356.

52 *Daily Express*, 8 May 1891.

53 Donal McCartney, 'William Martin Murphy: an Irish press baron and the rise of the popular press' in *Communications and community in Ireland*, ed. Brian Farrell (Cork, 1984), 31. However Murphy's name does not feature in the initial register of shareholders, which included thirteen MPs and ten Roman Catholic bishops (*Daily Express*, 8 May 1891).

54 Bodkin, *Recollections*, 177.

55 Callanan, ed, *Parnell: A Memoir*, 3.

56 Healy, *Letters and Leaders*, 356–8. Healy claimed a circulation for the *Press* in March 1891, of 34,000 a day, similar to that of the *Freeman's Journal*.

57 *National Press*, 1 June 1891.

58 *National Press*, 2 June 1891.

59 *National Press*, 5 June 1891.

60 *United Ireland*, 13 June 1891.

61 *Freeman's Journal*, 8 October 1891.

62 Frank Callanan, *T.M. Healy* (Cork, 1996), 291.

63 *National Press*, 8 April 1891.

64 *National Press*, 26 June 1891.

65 *National Press*, 5 June 1891. The highly personalized invective would lead to Healy being horsewhipped by a relative-by-marriage of Parnell's in the Four Courts a few weeks after the Irish leader's death (*Weekly Irish Times*, 7 November 1891). Prior to that a bomb

exploded at the offices of the *National Press* on 26 October 1891 (*Freeman's Journal*, 29 October 1891).

66 Dillon to O'Brien, undated, 'Sat', TCD MSS 6736, f.75.

67 Dillon to Bodkin, 14 August 1891, NLI, F.S. Bourke collection, MS 10702.

68 Dillon to Bodkin, 18 August 1891, NLI, F.S. Bourke collection, MS 10702.

69 Healy, *Letters and Leaders*, 370.

70 Callanan, *The Parnell Split*, 155.

71 Mark O'Brien, *The Irish Times: a History* (Dublin, 2008), 26.

72 Callanan, *The Parnell Split*, 160.

73 Felix Larkin, 'Arthur Griffith and the Freeman's Journal' in *Irish Journalism Before Independence: More a Disease than a Profession*, Kevin Rafter, ed. (Manchester, 2011), 178.

74 O'Brien, *An Olive Branch in Ireland*, 55. Ennis, although guilty of a certain special pleading because of his opposition to the *Freeman's* support of Parnell, had often argued that journalists should behave like barristers in being capable of writing contrary to their own political convictions (Callanan, ed. *Parnell: A memoir*, 4).

75 Larkin, 'The dog in the night-time', 111.

76 *United Ireland*, 5 September 1891.

77 Callanan, *The Parnell Split*, 120–1.

78 *Freeman's Journal*, 25 March 1892.

79 Bodkin, *Recollections*, 178.

80 T.P. O'Connor to Bodkin, 17 September 1891, NLI, F.S. Bourke collection, MS 10702.

81 McCartney, 'William Martin Murphy', 33.

82 *United Ireland*, 21 February 1891.

83 *United Ireland*, 28 February 1891.

84 *United Ireland*, 5 September, 26 September, 24 October, 28 November 1891.

85 *United Ireland*, 2 May, 6 June, 13 June, 22 August, 24 October, 28 November.

86 At fifty-four in total – the highest number in any single category in any of the eleven years covered by the survey in Appendix 1.

87 *United Ireland*, 21 March 1891.

88 *United Ireland*, 10 October 1891. The *Freeman's Journal* demanded a retraction by the 'wild writers of *United Ireland*' (16 October 1891) of what it characterized as an accusation of 'murder' against O'Brien, Dillon, Healy and Sexton and for allegedly 'setting' those named and endangering their lives (13 October 1891).

89 *Freeman's Journal*, 19 June, 8 July 1891.

90 *Cork Daily Herald*, 13 February 1891.

91 Lyons, *The Fall of Parnell*, 311

92 *Irish Daily Independent*, 18 December 1891.

93 *Daily Chronicle*, 1 August 1891.

94 Paul Bew, *Enigma: a new life of Charles Stewart Parnell* (Dublin, 2011), 21. Though this is perhaps overstating the loyalty of the newspaper to Parnell, even at that time.

95 TNA, PRO, CO 903/2, miscellaneous notes, series xvi, 'History of the Dublin Nationalist Press since the "Split" in the Nationalist ranks', 23. Interestingly it missed, or ignored, a move by IRB elements of the Parnell Leadership Fund – established to maintain a Parnellite presence in the Press – to exert an increased influence over any new Parnellite daily newspaper (McGee, *The IRB*, 201).

96 West Ridgeway to Balfour, 12 December 1890, BL, Add. Mss 49811, ff.286–9.

97 *United Ireland*, 26 December 1891.

98 *United Ireland*, 6 April 1893.

99 Various *United Ireland*, 1 January–10 September 1898.

100 *United Ireland*, 23 July 1898.

101 *United Ireland*, 27 August 1898.

102 *United Ireland*, 6 August 1898.

103 *United Ireland*, 16 July 1898. 10 September 1898. The latter related to an *Independent* 'special' on British army activities about which *United Ireland* commented that 'it is doubtful if anything so utterly opposed to Irish National feeling has ever appeared in its columns'.

104 Conboy, *Press and Popular Culture*, 52.

105 Conboy, *Press and Popular Culture*, 53.

106 When Parnell's priorities changed in 1891, the 'post-Split' *United Ireland*, edited by Edmund Leamy, was far more inclined to give aid and comfort to the IRB.

Conclusion

It was to be expected that the interaction between the British administration in Ireland and the nationalist press, in a decade of acrimonious civil strife, would be chequered at best and toxic at worst. The relationship was, quintessentially, that of gamekeeper and poacher. There existed, side by side, two antagonistic but complementary feedback loops. *United Ireland* was at the centre of the loop identified by Frank Callanan, in what he calls 'the astonishingly and deceptively fragile *trompe l'oeil* of Parnellism, [where] his coercive power was directed back within nationalism'.[1] In this circle *United Ireland* and many of the regional weeklies were the stern gamekeepers. However, a contiguous loop has been identified by Margaret O'Callaghan. She writes of the administrative ethos and structure associated with Dublin Castle throughout the 1880s as having 'helped to generate what it was predicated upon – rural disorder'.[2] Clearly, in this context the nationalist press was the opportunistic poacher.

In conclusion it may be useful to place *United Ireland* within a wider journalistic context and ask the question, to what extent was Irish nationalist journalism in the 1880s reflective of, or antithetical to, a rapidly changing newspaper industry in the rest of the United Kingdom?

Jurgen Habermas in his influential work *The Structural Transformation of the Public Sphere* writes about the movement towards a mass circulation press in the late nineteenth century and attests that it 'paid for the maximisation of its sales with the depoliticisation of its content'.[3] By the 1880s daily newspapers in Britain were becoming more like their Sunday equivalents, which had long since adopted a 'domestic' over a 'public' model. Sunday publications like *Lloyd's Weekly* and *Reynolds Newspaper* (a radical weekly), with their emphasis on court cases and sensation had been rewarded with circulation figures far in excess of the dailies.[4] A gradual move towards emulation of the Sunday newspaper template by some of the dailies led to a situation where, according to media critic Alan Lee 'the cheap and the tawdry, the trivial and the sensational, kept out of the market place the valuable, the authentic, and the serious'.[5] The process reached its apotheosis with the establishment of the *Daily Mail* in 1896 but before that T.P.O'Connor's *Daily Star*, established in 1888, had begun to revolutionize the style and content of British newspapers.

United Ireland came into being at the start of a decade that witnessed an acceleration of this process of mass market populism. Yet *United Ireland* seems to challenge the entire basis of the thesis of Habermas, one that is supported, to a greater or lesser degree, by most of the leading academic media theorists of the last three decades.[6] *United Ireland* was a mass circulation newspaper that was highly politicized. The received wisdom from media theorists like Raymond Williams, Alan J.Lee and James Curran, is that such journals should not have thrived by the 1880s.

Of course the case of *United Ireland* does not at all negate the notion that by the early part of the decade 'the press had become a business ... almost entirely, and a political, civil and social institution hardly at all'.[7] But why did *United Ireland* buck the prevailing journalistic trend away from political engagement and debate ('delayed reward news') and towards the more sensationalist, recreational mode ('immediate reward news') of late nineteenth-century newspaper journalism? Clearly because Ireland was an exceptional 'market'. While it experienced all the factors contributing to the rapid expansion of the press in the latter half of the nineteenth century – higher literacy, technological advances, the abolition of 'taxes on knowledge' and a good rail distribution network – it had some unique characteristics of its own.

Of lesser importance was the lack of a well-developed 'domestic' mode in Ireland. The new templates being adopted by English newspapers in their own rapid commercialization – an increased focus on sport and entertainment and an increased avoidance of high political debate – did not have quite the same resonance in Ireland. Despite the foundation in 1884 of a populist organization like the Gaelic Athletic Association, Ireland was not yet as well developed a 'recreational' society as England. Ireland of the 1880s was rather more like the England of the upheavals of the Chartist period where O'Connor's *Northern Star* and John Cleave's *Weekly Police Gazette* (which anticipated 'new journalism' by half a century by combining crime reporting with support for radical causes) had combined circulations similar to that of *United Ireland* at its height. In a highly polticized and radically nationalist society there was clearly a market for a highly political and radical nationalist newspaper.

Not that the nationalist 'extremism' of *United Ireland* can be equated with the leftist politics of the mid-century radical journals. By the 1880s the surviving counterparts of the *Public Register* and the *Northern Star*, unable to attract funding from advertisers, had retreated into a high-priced specialist ghetto – Raymond Williams refers to it as the 'pauper press'[8] – often characterized by tedious didacticism. Such was clearly not the case with the mass-circulation *United Ireland*, a journal that, for all its perceived radicalism, was actually characterised by a pietistic social conservatism.

Ireland was also a country well-accustomed to campaigning journalism as an adjunct of mass-movement politics. During the Repeal campaign of the 1840s, three of those tried for conspiracy during the State Trials of 1844, were the newspaper editors John Gray (*Freeman's Journal*), Charles Gavan Duffy (*Nation*) and Richard Barrett (*Pilot*). The weekly purchase of *United Ireland*, which often fetched sums well in excess of its cover price in the wake of the many attempts to seize its print run, was more than just an effort on the part of the purchaser to access information. It was a participatory gesture akin to the payment of the 'Catholic rent' during the Emancipation campaign of the 1820s. Even the 'cover' price of both was the same.

What *United Ireland's* approach masked, however, was the essential misdirection which lay at the heart of much nineteenth-century 'populist' journalism. Just as Hearst and Pulitzer in the USA, as already outlined, enlisted a mass urban readership in pursuit of social goals that were more beneficial to the *haute-bourgeoisie* than to the bulk of their actual readers, O'Brien petitioned, cajoled and even threatened the small farmers and labourers of Ireland to engage in campaigns where their interests were not paramount. O'Brien's anathemizing style was employed selectively. While divisive issues, like the increased ubiquity of relatively wealthy graziers, were raised in *United Ireland*, it was done in a depersonalized fashion. This was in marked contrast to the explicit identification of individual enemies among the landed, political and even journalistic elite. While O'Brien and local proprietor/editors of nationalist newspapers might have harked back to this 'older rhetoric'[9] (the coinage of Patricia Hollis) of radicalism, they managed to eschew much of the actual radicalism of writers like Cobbett. In a very real sense O'Brien operated at the behest of a demanding proprietor in the shape of party leader and part-owner Charles Stewart Parnell. The essential difference was that, while O'Brien was expected to assist Parnell in the pursuit of his agenda (also achieved by misdirection), he was not required to make his 'baron' a substantial profit in the process.

For much of the 1880s the Parnellite movement had a highly serviceable 'special purpose vehicle' in *United Ireland*. It was a remarkably effective instrument until the destructive turbulence of the Irish party split. It was both a victim and a perpetrator of the imposition of 'silence.'

Over a ten-year period *United Ireland* played a crucial role in cementing a nationalist narrative of victimhood – of which it was also a part – and elevating Parnell to iconic status, before descending into irrelevance. Both of its central 'myths', however, were high-maintenance. The prevailing nationalist agrarian conventions did not go uncontested at the time and have subsequently been subjected to rigorous examination and challenge in the twentieth century by the likes of Barbara L. Solow and William E.Vaughan. Parnell himself, despite his own considerable personal and political shortcomings (deficiencies that his acolytes sought to obscure), still awaits a similarly comprehensive deconstructive re-evaluation.[10] Before the vicious intra-nationalist partisanship of the split, *United Ireland* did an excellent job in nurturing and policing both of its prevailing narratives by means of misdirection, belligerent reproach and creative invective.

There is an irony in the blank column displayed by the newspaper, in place of editorial commentary, in the weeks following the arrest of O'Brien in October 1881. It was intended to be a symbolic reminder of the inability of the Liberal government to cope with dissent in Ireland without resorting to crude censorship. This was a form of self-imposed silence that was to be 'more eloquent than tongues of fire'. The newspaper advised that 'from this forth, then, the readers of *United Ireland* must interrogate their own hearts for our opinions'.[11] In truth the readers of the newspaper were rarely afforded an opportunity to formulate opinions of their own on any issue of significance or relevance to Parnellism. *United Ireland's* attempts to quell dissent were often as thorough as those of the two governments it opposed.

Ultimately O'Brien, despite his political loyalty and personal closeness to his leader, was more distraction than defender, more of a red herring than a rottweiler. He enjoyed more latitude than did most of Parnell's other lieutenants. Parnell allowed O'Brien his head because *United Ireland* served his ends well. In its mythologizing of Parnell it helpfully presented him as the radical leader of a quasi-revolutionary movement. He was anything but. The newspaper that more accurately reflected Parnell's own philosophy was a *Freeman's Journal*, intimidated, commercially and politically, into 'deviation phobia'. The *Journal* may have been owned by the Gray family but, after the first appearance of *United Ireland* in 1881, its politics was the politics of Parnellism. While not diminishing the 'bandwagon' effect of Parnell's success, and Gray's own Pauline conversion, *United Ireland* played a significant part in the metamorphosis of the *Journal*.

While *United Ireland's* rigid patrolling of the public expression of the nationalist psyche meant that the *Freeman's Journal* was required to resile from its Whiggish tendencies in 1881, the corollary inherent in the existence of O'Brien's newspaper was that the *Journal* could continue with a moderate editorial line and remain secure from Castle interference. It was not obliged to publish notices of suppressed branches. It was not required to risk the imposition of legal strictures. In commercial and political terms the presence of *United Ireland* meant the *Freeman's Journal* was allowed to occupy an altogether different niche, one protected from the buffeting of coercion. By the late 1880s, in a journalistic sense, everyone had his allotted place on the nationalist side of the argument. The role of *United Ireland* was to reflect the assertive and antagonistic face of Parnellism. The local papers were to act as the National League newspapers of record, and, if necessary, to take the legal consequences of fulfilling that function. The *Journal* was expected to bring the message of Parnell to the Catholic middle class, the class that was destined for dominance in the new Ireland.

In the solar system of late nineteenth-century nationalist journalism, with Parnell at the centre, *United Ireland* was Mars, fiery, hot and inhospitable. The *Freeman's Journal* was Planet Earth deriving more benefits than any other satellite from the light and heat emitted by the celestial body at the nexus of the system. Parnell's intimacy with Edward Byrne and J.M.Tuohy and his acceptance of Edmund Dwyer Gray (senior) within his political circle, testified to his reliance on the constructive support of the *Journal* over the mere political protection and transparent deification of *United Ireland*. From the outset O'Brien's journal had represented a *fauve* Parnellism, in its wildness and chauvinistic zeal. But it was also a *faux* Parnellism, in that it did not reflect the inherent conservatism of the enigmatic Irish party leader. Although 'the *Freeman* was always moderate and cautious to a fault'[12] it was inestimably closer to Parnell's default position on most issues. If, occasionally, it needed to be moved in more radical directions, *United Ireland* could be relied upon to provide the initial impetus. Unionists liked to cite O'Brien's journal as proof positive that freedom of speech would be inhibited in a home rule environment:

> With a Parliament in power, reflecting the opinions of *United Ireland*, there would no longer be any necessity for prudence. The plea that opposition journals lived by 'lying' and by 'lie mintage' would be sufficient. Proof would be considered quite superfluous.[13]

But in reality *United Ireland* would not have been the authentic voice of moderate nationalism in a Parnellite Ireland. That role would have been assumed by the *Freeman's Journal*.

Martin Conboy has written of the phenomenon of vitriolic American 'yellow journalism' that 'the language of colourful insult and simplified villainy was a continuation of folk traditions of mockery and deflation and the role of the individual writer in exposing these to his readers in a voice of individualised outrage was part of the shape of the popular press of the early [twentieth-] century'.[14] Perhaps O'Brien was ahead of his time in some respects at least. His acerbic and uncompromising style served a useful purpose in the rabble-rousing and quasi-legal environment of the 1880s. But the more modern, disengaged, professional mode of the likes of the *Freeman's Journal* was suited to the cool, conservative, centralized, elitist approach of Parnell himself. *United Ireland* was always a useful decoy for Parnell. Occasionally its tub-thumping *brio* and malevolent energy was precisely what he required. But the *Freeman's Journal* more closely reflected his default political style and philosophy. He profited by it to a far greater extent than he ever did from the financial surpluses or the tendentious harangues of *United Ireland*.

Notes

1   Callanan, *The Parnell split*, 3.

2   O'Callaghan, *British high politics*, 2.

3   Jurgen Habermas, *The Structural Transformation of the Public sphere* (Cambridge, Mass. 1991), 169.

4   Raymond Williams, *The Long Revolution* (London, 2001), 198.

5   Lee, *The Origins of the Popular Press*, 212.

6   Alan J.Lee, James Curran, Raymond Williams and Mark Hampton, for example, in works already cited, broadly reject the notion of the educative role of the 'fourth estate' in the late nineteenth century and would ascribe to the view that readers began to demand far less political content and debate while the proprietors, anxious to capitalize on the possibilities of an expanding market, were happy to accommodate them.

7   Lee, *The Origins of the Popular Press*, 232.

8   Williams, *The Long Revolution*, 210.

9   Patricia Hollis, *The Pauper Press* (Oxford, 1970), xiii.

10 However Paul Bew's recent *Enigma: A new life of Charles Stewart Parnell*, a short study of his life, may be a harbinger.

11 *United Ireland*, 29 October 1881.

12 Stephen J.Brown, *The press in Ireland: a survey and a guide* (New York, 1971), 36.

13 Irish Loyal and Patriotic Union, *The Real Dangers of Home Rule*, 12.

14 Conboy, *Press and popular culture*, 69

APPENDIX

United Ireland Commentary, 1881–91 – A Database of Editorials

Introduction

From the date of its inception in August 1881 to its degeneration into blatant partisanship a decade later, *United Ireland* was the most trenchant voice of Irish nationalism. Its wide circulation (rising at its peak to over 100,000 copies a week[1]) afforded it an influence denied even the most popular of regional or local newspapers. Its forthright and caustic commentary placed it in an altogether different category to the other leading nationalist newspapers, the daily *Freeman's Journal*, or the weekly *Nation* who tended towards greater moderation than the Parnellite journal.

Steered by journalists of talent and political commitment like William O'Brien, Tim Healy and Matthias McDonnell Bodkin, *United Ireland* was as loathed in Dublin Castle as it was loved in the nationalist heartlands of rural Ireland. Its weekly clarion call was its leading articles, always carried on page five of the newspaper. What follows is an attempted assessment of the nature of this, generally polemical, resource. The intention is to analyse the content of the weekly editorials and, as a consequence, to divine the preoccupations of a newspaper.

1.2 Main Categories

For the purposes of this exercise the leading articles have been divided into seven categories. These are as follows.

A:British administration in Ireland (excluding coercion legislation and enforcement).

B: Coercion legislation and enforcement.

C: Home rule.

D: Land – agitation and legislation.

E: The law.

F: The press.

G: Irish political activity.

H.Miscellaneous.

1.3 Sub-Categories

Within these seven main categories there is a further division of six into sub-categories. The exception is category B (Coercion legislation and enforcement). The editorial sub-categories are as follows.

A: British administration

A1: Positive

A2: Dublin – negative

A3: London – negative

B: Coercion legislation and enforcement

C: Home rule

C1: Positive

C2: Negative

D: Land

D1: Positive

D2: Negative

D3: Agitation

D4: Labourers

E: Law
E1: Positive
E2: Negative

F: Press
F1: Censorship
F2: Antagonistic

G:Irish politics
G1: Electoral
G2: Nationalist – positive
G3: Nationalist – negative
G4: Unionist

H: Miscellaneous
H1: Foreign affairs
H2: Church
H3: Industry
H4: Miscellaneous

During the period 13 August 1881 (the date of the first appearance of *United Ireland*) to 31 December 1891 – by which time the newspaper was intent on doing little other than discrediting the majority anti-Parnellite faction of the ruptured Irish parliamentary party – a total of 1578 editorials were read and assessed for content. Out of a total of 540 issues of the paper[2] during the period under review at least three contained no editorials whatever. In the case of 1881 a separate, putative, figure has been included of the total number of editorials that might, *pro rata*, have appeared on an annualized basis. Something similar has been done with the figures for 1882 and 1883 to take account of missing editions of the paper.

It is important to note that numerous value judgments were made in deciding into which category a particular editorial might fit. Most decisions were straightforward but a number of leading articles encompassed more than one single theme. In such instances categorization was based on the relative space allocated to the discussion of the different themes. The subject matter that predominated decided the category into which the editorial was placed. Other scholars, however, might have made alternative judgments and assembled the material in a different manner.

No account was taken of overall column length in assessing the relative importance of different subject areas.[3] Such an exercise would have been unnecessarily time-consuming and would probably not have added much to our understanding of the editorial priorities of *United Ireland*.

For the record, editorial lengths varied from as little as a quarter column (fewer than half a dozen) to more than two columns (about the same number). Most editorials were just over a column in length – a column consisting of, on average, a thousand words.

1.4 Sub-Category rationales.

The rationale behind the destination category of individual editorials was as follows.

A: British Administration
A1: Positive

Positive references to figures associated with legislative, administrative and policing activities (but not judicial or legal) connected to the British administration in Ireland, or with British politics.

A2: Dublin – Negative

Includes any negative or critical references to the lord lieutenant, chief secretary, under secretary, other executive figures, the policing functions of resident magistrates, DMP and RIC figures, Castle 'scandals' etc – excludes judges, the attorney general, the solicitor general, Crown prosecutors and resident magistrates in the exercise of the judicial functions.

A3: London – Negative

Includes the royal family and British political figures other than lord lieutenant or chief secretary.

B: Coercion

This includes, in particular, the working of Liberal and Conservative coercion acts of 1881, 1882 and 1887. It excludes actions taken against the press under coercion legislation and references to the prosecutorial and judicial handling of specific coercion act cases going through the courts.

C: Home Rule
C1: Positive
This category includes positive references to all progressive steps towards the introduction of the Home Rule bill and all Irish party initiatives in relation to legislative independence.
C2: Negative
Relating to the criticism or condemnation of negative legislative or political developments and, in particular, the denial of Home Rule in 1886.

D: Land
D1: Positive
Generally refers to Irish party efforts to effect agrarian reforms or carry amendments to agrarian legislation. This category will also occasionally refer to the positive efforts of either British ruling party in relation to agrarian reform.
D2: Negative
This category covers all editorial commentary critical of the agrarian polices of either the Liberal or Conservative administrations. This would include criticism of the terms of the 1881 Land Act, the Land Courts, the handling of the arrears issue, opposition to land purchase legislative provisions etc. It also includes the many negative editorials on landlordism and on individual landlords.
D3: Agitation
This category covers editorial comments on all forms of agrarian agitation or protest and editorial advocacy of agrarian militancy and activism, such as the No Rent Manifesto, the Plan of Campaign, Boycotting etc.
D4: Labourers
This refers exclusively to commentary on agricultural labourers.

E: Law
E1: Positive

Covers the occasional positive comments on the statements, activities and directions of Irish judicial figures.

E2: Negative

Includes adverse commentary on judges, judicial decisions and directions as well as allegations of jury-packing by Crown prosecutors, the use of informers and the suppression of evidence.

F: Press

F1: Censorship

Condemnation of legislative or coercive attempts to control editorial commentary, journalistic activities or the transmission of information by *United Ireland*, other nationalist papers and/or nationalist journalists.

F2: Antagonistic

This category includes critical or negative commentary, often distinctly abusive, of other Irish or British newspapers or of individual journalists.

G: Irish Politics

G1: Electoral

References to general elections, by-elections, Poor Law elections, franchise and boundary issues. (This category also encompasses coverage of post-1886 British by-elections where the 'Home Rule' vote was seen as having had a significant influence on the result.)

G2: Nationalist – Positive

Uncritical, adulatory or propagandistic commentary on nationalist leadership figures. Exhortatory editorials urging increased levels of activism or improved levels of political organization.

G3: Nationalist – Negative

Critical editorials, often abusive in tone, aimed at recusant or conservative nationalist figures such as William Shaw, Richard O'Shaughnessy, Frank Hugh O'Donnell, John O'Connor Power and others.

G4: Unionist

Mainly negative references to Ulster unionist figures (such as Lord Rossmore), members and leaders of the Orange order and participants in the Belfast riots in the wake of the failure of the 1886 Home Rule Act.

H: Miscellaneous

H1: Foreign Affairs

Generally refers to British colonial and/or military adventures or misadventures.

H2: Church

Includes commentary on the interaction of the clergy and hierarchy with high politics and 'grass-roots' activism. It would include some, but not all, of the editorials relating to the controversy over the appointment of Archbishop Walsh as Archbishop of Dublin and becomes more of a factor after the Parnellite split.

H3: Industry

This covers references to various Industrial exhibitions as well as the advocacy of protective tariffs for Irish industries and to trade union activity and industrial training and education.

H4: Miscellaneous

Editorials that do not fit comfortably into any of the above categories.

1.5 Number of Editorials

The earlier years of the existence of *United Ireland* (1881-83) were the most active when it came to the dissemination of direct editorial commentary. Adjusted to take account of the factors outlined above, the average number of editorials per year was 162. During the 'fallow' years of 1884 and 1885, when the intensity of the Land War had diminished and Home Rule was not yet (formally at least) on the Liberal party's political agenda, the number of leading articles declined to an annualised total of 155.

Surprisingly, in the following five years, 1886 (the year of Home Rule), and 1887–90 (the years of a Salisbury-led Conservative administration whose most visible representative was the provocative chief secretary, Arthur J. Balfour), the number of editorials declined still further. The average from 1886 to 1890 was 127 per annum. The decline in the absolute number of editorials from 1884 until the end of O'Brien's interest in the journal in December, 1890, however, does not indicate any noticeable slackening in enthusiasm for the causes taken up by the paper in its early manifestation. The quasi-gossip column, 'The Week's Work' (originally entitled 'The World's Week's Work') – always carried on page four of the paper, and which usually spilled over onto page five each week – was generally even more vituperative than the commentary carried on the editorial page. In addition, in the latter half of the decade, the front page of the paper began to be used for similar purposes. Issues raised on page one, or in 'The Week's Work', would often be followed up on the editorial pages in a more formal, rhetorical fashion.

The decline in the numbers of editorials per week (from anything up to five weekly in the 1881–3 period to an average of just over two in the latter half of the decade) may well have been simply a function of the increasing absences of O'Brien from the newspaper. In the wake of his election to the Mallow constituency in 1883 O'Brien devolved an increasing amount of responsibility for the day-to-day running of the paper to colleagues like ex-fenian James O'Connor and barrister *manqué* Matthias McDonnell Bodkin. During his involvement with the Plan of Campaign, when O'Brien spent much time in jail or avoiding arrest, it was Bodkin who wrote most of the editorials. While O'Brien had an insatiable appetite for the editorial it appears that Bodkin was more easily satiated.

The increase in the number of editorial columns in 1891 is indicative only of the cannibalistic self-destruction of the Irish nationalist movement, as a *United Ireland* under entirely new management and subject to the absolute control of the Parnellites, focused on the perceived depravities of its nationalist enemies rather than the policies of the Tory government.

1.6 Number of editorials per main category

A: Administration 414
B: Coercion 75
C: Home Rule 49
D: Land 272
E: Law 107
F: Press 106
G: Irish Politics 399
H: Miscellaneous 156

Total 1,578

Perhaps the most surprising figure above is the outcome for Home Rule. It is by far the smallest of the main categories with a total of only forty-nine editorials, positive or negative, on the subject over the period of the decade when it became a live issue. Understandably editorials on Home Rule appear with most frequency in 1886, nineteen in all. Most of these were in the first half of the year and by July/August Home Rule had been replaced once again by a preoccupation with the Land, as the Plan of Campaign became established on a number of estates throughout the country.

This is probably a reflection of O'Brien's own agrarianism,[4] of his direct involvement in the Plan of Campaign, of the largely rural readership of the newspaper as well as the crushing disappointment of the failure of the 1886 Home Rule Bill. While the subject of legislative independence did figure in the editorial columns of the newspaper from 1886-1890 it did so in the context of the anticipated defeat of the Conservative government at any subsequent general election and tended to be introduced as an adjunct theme to the dominant topics of eviction, coercion and all-round Balfourian iniquity.

Of some surprise also is the relative infrequency of editorials on the land question. As this category includes direct attacks on landlords and organizations like the Property Defence Association, as well as criticism of the inadequacies of government agrarian policy, the topic might have been expected to figure more regularly.

1.7 Percentage of editorials per category.

A: Administration 26.23%
B: Coercion 04.75%
C: Home Rule 03.10%
D: Land 17.23%
E: Law 06.78%
F: Press 06.71%
G: Irish Politics 25.28%
H: Miscellaneous 09.88%

The figures above illustrate the fact that specific land-related issues (eviction, land purchase, Land Courts etc) comprised less than one-fifth of all editorials. As can be seen in Table 3 (below) the focus on Land issues was far greater under the Tory government from 1886-1890, before almost disappearing altogether after the Irish Parliamentary Party split. When combined with the other, apparently, dominant preoccupation of the 1880s, i.e. Home Rule, it emerges that the Land League / Irish National League's weekly newspaper devoted less than a quarter of its editorials to these two pervasive issues. While it is true to say that much of the coverage in the other categories (administration, coercion, law etc.) is related to or informed by the issues of Land and Home Rule, the fact that these two decade-defining themes are not discussed more regularly and approached more directly is somewhat unexpected.

The subjects that tended to dominate United Ireland's discourse tell us much about the actual rather than the anticipated, or indeed perceived, priorities of the newspaper.

Essentially, O'Brien's paper was rather parochial and custodial in its approach to the politics of its day. The preponderance of antagonistic editorials dealing with the workings of the British administration in Ireland itself (sub-category A2) - numbering 248, almost 16% of the total editorial output – as opposed to the ramifications of the decisions and actions of London-based officials and politicians, suggests the creation or exploitation of a nationalist narrative of victimhood. The number of editorials devoted to attacking nationalist politicians allegedly deviating from the Parnellite line (G3) - albeit almost half of which relate to the exceptional circumstances of the Split - suggests an imperative involving the imposition of nationalist conformity. In this regard it might also be noted that there were more editorials critical or abusive of other newspapers (F2) - 72 in all - than there were about Home Rule (C) - 49 in total - during the entire period under review.

1.8 Analysis of editorials per sub-category
A: Administration
A1: Positive
A2: Dublin – Negative
A3: London – Negative

Table 1

	A1	A2	A3
1881	0	7	7
1882	5	22	8
1883	1	30	10
1884	4	48	13
1885	2	15	25
1886	11	7	12
1887	4	29	21
1888	4	39	10
1889	3	20	8
1890	2	25	10
1891	0	6	6
Total	36	248	130
% Category	8.7	59.9	31.4

[NOTE: Although represented in the tables, for the purposes of this exercise 1891 will be treated separately]

A: British Administration in Ireland (See Table 1)

Only 2.3 per cent of *United Ireland's* total editorial output had anything positive to say about British governance of Ireland. That represents only 8.7 per cent of the number of editorials dealing solely or primarily with the British administration. Almost a third of that number comes, unsurprisingly, in 1886, in the wake of Gladstone's conversion to Home Rule.

Editorials critical of the policies and personalities of the Castle executive – including the lord lieutenant and the chief secretary – comprise almost 60 per cent of the total in this category and 15.7 per cent of all editorials. This is, more or less, as one would expect. What is more difficult to explain is the fact that the numbers of such hostile leading articles reached a peak in 1884, with forty-eight.[5] This can be explained by the continued fallout from the so-called 'Castle scandals', a campaign which *United Ireland* had made its own, the allegations of attempts to cover up the miscarriage of justice in the Maamtrasna trials of 1882, and the paucity of commentary on other issues in a 'valley' period when the Land War had de-intensified and the campaign for Home Rule had yet to begin in earnest. Predictably, the twelve-month period in which far fewer editorials were critical of Castle policy was the Home Rule year of 1886.

Just under one-third (31.4 per cent) of editorials in this category were in the form of attacks on London-based political and administrative figures. This peaks at 25 in 1885 when the Liberal Prime Minister, William E.Gladstone was still the subject of frequent vituperation (this obviously changed dramatically from 1886 onwards) as were colleagues such as the home secretary, Sir William Harcourt and, a particular *bête noire*, even at this early stage in the decade, the Radical leader, Joseph Chamberlain. The baiting of the Birmingham MP must, in some measure at least, have come at the behest of, or been inspired by, Parnell, who had fallen out with Chamberlain over the putative Irish Councils Bill. The similarly high figure of 21 for 1887 reflects a continuation of *United Ireland's* abuse of Chamberlain. For the earlier part of that year in particular the, now, Liberal Unionist, had to share equal billing with Randolph Churchill.

B: Coercion

C: Home Rule
C1: Positive
C2: Negative

Table 2

	B	C1	C2
1881	4	1	0
1882	17	0	1
1883	3	0	0
1884	2	0	0
1885	1	8	2
1886	8	19	7
1887	19	2	0
1888	9	3	2
1889	9	3	0
1890	3	0	0
1891	0	0	1
Total	75	36	13
% Category	N/A	73.5	26.5

B: Coercion – (See Table 2)

The implications and the execution of the three most egregious pieces of coercion legislation, the Protection of Person and Property (Ireland) Act of 1881, the Prevention of Crime (Ireland) Act of 1882 and the Criminal Law and Procedure (Ireland) Act 1887, featured heavily in editorial coverage in the years of their enactment. Discussion of this legislation, *per se*, tended to merge with related considerations in other years. Consequently 'coercion' editorials peak in 1882 and 1887. The apparently low figure for 1881 (4), the year of the passage of the PPP Act, is based on only twenty issues of the paper. It is worth bearing in mind that the total in this category for the three years 1883–5, over 156 issues of the paper, was only six.

C: Home Rule – (See Table 2)

An oddly small proportion of editorial space was devoted to the discussion of Home Rule *per se*. During the Land War and its immediate aftermath, when the national movement was largely placed at the disposal of agrarian interests, the topic was virtually ignored. Towards the end of 1885 it became a live issue in *United Ireland* just as it was on the political stage. In 1886 it, briefly, became a virtual obsession, with more than one-fifth of total editorials in that year (21 per cent) devoted to the subject. The bulk of these were in the first half of the year. The last Home Rule editorial of 1886 was on the 10 July. Once the Conservative government came to power in the latter half of the decade Home Rule was eclipsed as a live topic by more immediately pressing issues. The only context in which it is raised is that of the anticipated defeat of the Salisbury administration or the spate of victories of what *United Ireland* described as 'Home Rule candidates' (Gladstonian Liberals) in a number of by-elections from 1888–90.

D: Land

D1: Positive

D2: Negative

D3: Agitation

D4: Labourers

Table 3

	D1	D2	D3	D4
1881	0	9	12	2
1882	1	10	18	7
1883	0	4	7	3
1884	2	10	1	2
1885	1	6	10	3
1886	11	7	7	1
1887	1	14	7	0
1888	0	17	6	0
1889	2	22	26	0
1890	1	33	4	1
1891	2	0	0	2
Total	21	132	98	21
% Category	7.7	48.5	36.0	7.8

D: Land – (See Table 3)

Almost as surprising is the relative lack of space directly allocated to the other dominant issue of the decade, the land. When *United Ireland* began publication the Land War was at its height. Taking its lead from Parnell and his lieutenants the newspaper opposed the 1881 Land Act and participation on the part of tenants in the arbitrative process engaged in by the Land Courts established under the aegis of that Act. Hence the strong showing of editorials on dedicated land issues (27.4 per cent) in that year. This is not matched in 1882, as the land conflict continued. Fewer than one-fifth of the leaders in that year (18.4 per cent) are devoted specifically or largely to agrarian issues and only a quarter of those – nine in all – came in the first half of the year, prior to the Kilmainham Treaty, seen as having largely ended the initial phase of popular agrarian agitation.

From there the average for the next three years, not the most active in the ongoing land campaign, fell back to about 10 per cent. It was only when the Plan of Campaign was launched in the newspaper, and became a major personal project for O'Brien, that coverage reached the sort of levels[6] comparable to those of the Land War period. Attacks on landlords and Tory land policy equalled or exceeded those on general government policy in the years 1889 (39 per cent) and 1890 (29 per cent).

Not unexpectedly there are relatively few editorials in this category (7.7 per cent) supportive of land legislation or the activities of landlords. Only in 1886, when Gladstone introduced a new Land Bill to accompany his Home Rule legislation, is there any appreciable endorsement by *United Ireland* of British agrarian policy. Eleven of the twenty-six editorials on land in that year were positively framed.

The bulk of the entire coverage in this category, almost half (48.5 per cent), is negative – this was either aimed directly at the incumbent government, its policies and its legislation, at individual landlords like the Marquis of Clanricarde, or at organizations representing the landlord interest such as the Property Defence Association. The growth in the number of negative land-related editorials from 1887–90 was associated with the progress of the Plan Of Campaign and evictions on estates in counties like Galway, Tipperary, Clare and Donegal.

That element of *United Ireland* which was most deprecated by the government, its encouragement of resistance to eviction, of boycotting and its alleged association with intimidation, is reflected in sub-category D3, relating to land agitation. More than a third (36 per cent) of the editorials in the Land category were devoted to coverage of agrarian protest or direct encouragement to participation in such agitation. In the wake of the 1887 Crimes Act, when it became illegal to report on the activities of Irish National League branches in proscribed areas *United Ireland* used its front page to flout (successfully) this legislation. But it also used its editorial columns, in 1889 in particular, to stiffen resistance to eviction on Plan of Campaign estates or in proscribed areas.

By far the least significant sub-category is D4, that dealing with editorials relating to agricultural labourers. Some lip service was paid to the cause of the agricultural labourer between 1881–5 (6.25 per cent of the Land category) while the Liberals were in power and legislation in this area was pending or in the process of delivery. Thereafter the subject was almost completely ignored. Between 1886–91 there were only four editorials relating to labourers. These were mainly admonitory in nature, advising labourers that they should trust the League, trust the farmers and not cause division and dissension by pushing aggressively for the realization of their sectional demands.[7] In its approach to agricultural labourers *United Ireland* therefore reflected the interests of the leadership of the agrarian movement and of the Irish National League. This consisted overwhelmingly of respectable medium to large-sized farmers, merchants and members of the clergy. The newspaper's sentiments are not dissimilar to those of the Sinn Fein slogan before the 1918 general election, to the effect that 'Labour must wait.'

E: Law

E1: Positive

E2: Negative

F: Press

F1: Censorship

F2: Antagonistic

Table 4

	E1	E2	F1	F2
1881	0	5	9	3
1882	0	14	9	11
1883	3	14	5	7
1884	1	14	2	5
1885	0	3	1	4
1886	0	7	1	9
1887	0	7	2	4
1888	2	10	3	5
1889	3	15	0	3
1890	3	5	1	5
1891	0	1	1	16
Total	12	95	34	72
% Category	11.2	88.8	32.1	67.9

E: Law (see Table 4)

Coverage of the law amounts to 6.78 per cent of total editorials.

There was a relatively infrequent but nonetheless consistent polemical argument with the legal authorities in the editorial columns of *United Ireland*. This took the form of criticism of judicial decisions, of the activities of various attorneys general and solicitors general, as well as condemnation of alleged 'jury packing' and of the partisanship of judges and magistrates (stipendiary or otherwise). A particular *bête noire* for the newspaper was the barrister and judge Peter O'Brien[8]. He first attracted the newspaper's attention in 1882 and the phillipics became more bitter as he rose through the ranks to become Irish solicitor general, attorney general and lord chief justice in turn.

One of the few major legal figures to attract occasional positive commentary was the chief baron of the Exchequer bench, Christopher Palles. During the Tory administration, in particular, Palles could not be relied upon by the government to uphold the decisions of JPs and magistrates made at petty sessions or assizes to punish Crimes Act transgressors. This occasionally endeared him to the nationalist press. However, *United Ireland* was capable of turning on Palles when his judgments did not meet with the newspaper's approval.

Concentrated negative attention devoted to judicial decisions coincided with the frequent legal travails of the newspaper itself between 1881 and 1884, and the regular incarcerations of William O'Brien[9], and of other newspaper editors, in 1888 and 1889. The latter period also coincided with the tenure as acting editor of a journalist with a legal background, Matthias McDonnell Bodkin, who later became a judge. The negative editorials can virtually be used to follow the pattern of government prosecutions under the major coercion acts of the 1880s. *United Ireland* was most critical of judicial decisions during the 1881–3 period when the Protection of Person and Property (Ireland) Act and the Liberal government's 1882 Crimes Act were in operation. The graph then troughs from 1884–7 when arrests (and illegal agrarian activity) declined. In 1888 and 1889, when enforcement of Balfour's 1887 Crimes Act was at its peak, the number of *United Ireland* editorials reflected the increased level of police and judicial activity.

United Ireland's animosity towards the legal establishment was reflected in the breakdown of positive to negative editorials in this category, running at a ratio of 8:1 (88.8 per cent : 11.2 per cent). The bulk of the positive coverage comes from the period 1889–90 and much of it relates to the activities of a Wexford County Court Judge (Waters) who consistently overturned the verdicts of Resident Magistrates, especially when confronted with jailed journalists who had, according to the Crown, contravened the 1887 Crimes Act.

F: The Press (see Table 4)

The number of editorials dealing with aspects and elements of the Irish and British press is almost exactly on a par with those related to the law. However, the internal breakdown is striking. Editorials dealing with alleged curbs on the freedom of the press in Ireland (F1) amounted to just over 2 per cent of the grand total (2.1 per cent) while those antipathetic to other newspapers (F2) – mostly Tory or Unionist – were more than twice as frequent (4.6 per cent). This was at a time when there was a prevailing narrative of official censorship of Irish nationalist newspapers. So, when the challenges to press freedom in Ireland were, supposedly at least, acute, *United Ireland* devoted much more editorial space to rancorous observations on the journalistic perfidy of the *Times*, the *Dublin Evening Mail* and the *Dublin Daily Express* than it did to criticism of governmental attempts to shackle the national and provincial press. This disparity is, arguably, even more pronounced in 'The Week's Work' column, where individual Unionist editors, proprietors and journalists were singled out for additional, if less formal, editorial invective.

Ironically this phenomenon was even more pronounced during the period of the Conservative administration when, if anything, Balfour's dexterous use of the Crimes Act (which deliberately lacked a dedicated press clause) against nationalist newspapers was far more threatening than the often half-hearted and hapless efforts of the Liberals. Three-quarters of the censorship-related (F1) editorials were concentrated in the 1881–4 period, when *United Ireland* itself was more directly under attack. During the Balfour chief secretaryship, when the focus shifted to smaller, more vulnerable and less high-profile local newspapers, *United Ireland's* attention was elsewhere, generally excoriating the *Times* or Dr G.V. Patton, editor of the *Daily Express*. It should be pointed out, however, that 'The Week's Work' was more unstinting when it came to the difficulties being experienced by nationalist editors like Jasper Tully and P.A. McHugh.

The latter-day solipsistic newspaper fixation with matters connected to the press itself is far from a uniquely 21st-century phenomenon. Hence it might seem unusual that more editorial space was not allocated to peculiarly journalistic concerns. However, a flexible and more informal column like 'The Week's Work' was, clearly, a more appropriate forum for the propagation of internecine journalistic bile as well as for treatment of the Castle's use of the 1887 Crimes Act against nationalist journalism. The column was frequently used for just such purposes. This may help account for the relatively small number of editorials dealing with press-related matters.

G: Irish Politics
G1: Electoral
G2: Positive
G3: Negative
G4: Unionist

Table 5

	G1	G2	G3	G4
1881	6	4	1	2
1882	10	12	7	2
1883	33	19	18	15
1884	8	7	21	9
1885	23	9	10	6
1886	4	5	0	6
1887	0	8	0	2
1888	3	8	0	0
1889	3	7	0	1
1890	8	18	9	0
1891	10	30	54	1
Total	108	127	120	44
% Category	27.1	31.8	30.1	11.0

G: Irish Politics (see Table 5)
As we have already noted, well ahead of the issue of Land or Home Rule was editorials related to Irish political matters and personalities. Just over a quarter of all leaders fell into this broad category (25.3 per cent).

One sub-element of this category (G1) was discussion of electoral politics.

With two general elections and a large number of by-elections between late 1885 and the final quarter of 1886 precisely 25 per cent of the G1 total was concentrated in this period – although almost one-third figured in 1883.

Almost a third of the editorials in this category (31.8 per cent) consisted of praise poems for members of the Irish Parliamentary Party or Land League/Irish National League leadership (G2). In the first half of the decade most of these would have been written in support of policies and policy switches advocated by Parnell. Others would have been lavish encomiums and endorsements of his leadership. These 'spike' in 1883 around the time of the Parnell tribute and contribute to the cult of personality built up around the Irish leader.[10] However, in the latter half of the decade far more of these laudatory editorials are devoted to John Dillon than to Parnell. This reflects the close collaboration of O'Brien and Dillon in the Plan of Campaign and the increasing invisibility of Parnell and his refusal to support the Plan.

However, on a par, numerically at least, with the applause and commendation of leading figures in the Parnellite movement is the criticism, often amounting to outright abuse, of nationalist opponents of Parnellism. This totals 120 separate editorials, or 7.6 per cent of the overall number, and fully 30 per cent of category G. The principal objects of *United Ireland's* obloquy included maverick or 'renegade' nationalist figures like Frank Hugh O'Donnell, and John O'Connor Power,[11] as well as – up to the general election of 1885 when they were swept from office – members of that group of moderate nationalists inadvertently and ill-advisedly dubbed 'nominals'[12] by Gladstone. These included the leader of the faction, William Shaw and associates such as The O'Donoghue, MP for Tralee, and Limerick MP Richard O'Shaughnessy.[13]

That such a high percentage of editorials should be devoted to the castigation of nationalists refusing to succumb to the dictates of Parnell clearly suggests that *United Ireland* was a self-appointed guardian of nationalist conformity. This 'function' was, in measurable terms, as important as was its anti-unionist rhetoric. The G3 sub-category bears both a numerical and contextual comparison with the anti-unionist journalistic narrative of F2.

The G4 sub-category consists, in the main, of leading articles excoriating individual unionist leaders like Lord Rossmore and the activities of the Orange order. By and large Irish unionists were ignored in the rather fewer editorials from the latter half of the decade. Between 1887 and 1891 they were, for the most part, replaced as objects of hostility by Conservatives and Liberal Unionists (dealt with in A3).

Editorial preoccupation with (principally) Ulster unionists or the Orange order is grouped around the period 1883–6. More than a third of the references in this sub-category (34 per cent) came in 1883 as the Irish Party began to contest elections in Ulster, starting with Monaghan and Tyrone. It then moved in to the 'cat and mouse' period, when nationalist demonstrations were being shadowed by Unionist counter-demonstrations as the Liberal government was being challenged, by unionists, to ban both. The final year in which there was any appreciable coverage was 1886. This was at the time of Randolph Churchill's successful attempt to activate Ulster loyalism against the Home Rule bill and of the unionist-inspired Belfast riots that followed the failure of Gladstone's controversial legislation.

H: Miscellaneous (see Table 6)
H1: Foreign Affairs
H2: Church
H3: Industry
H4: Miscellaneous

Table 6

	H1	H2	H3	H4
1881	1	3	7	1
1882	8	6	18	10
1883	3	9	3	6
1884	5	1	1	2
1885	11	5	0	8
1886	0	0	1	1
1887	0	2	0	0
1888	1	6	0	0
1889	0	3	0	0
1890	0	5	0	0
1891	0	26	0	3
Total	29	66	30	31
% Category	18.6	42.3	19.2	19.9

The final category (H: Miscellaneous) consists of four significant sub-categories that did not fit neatly into any of the previous designations. As a fraction of the total it amounts to less than one-tenth (9.88 per cent) with the majority of editorials belonging in the sub-category of articles primarily dealing with the Roman Catholic church and its interaction with nationalist politics (42.3 per cent).

Almost one-fifth of the leading articles in this category dealt with foreign affairs. However, when taken as a percentage of the editorial total this sub-category (H1) amounts to a mere 1.8 per cent. Clearly *United Ireland*, editorially at least, did not often raise its gaze beyond Irish horizons and certainly did not emulate its compatriot, the *Skibbereen Eagle*, in its monitoring of the Czar of Russia's expansionist policies of the 1850s. Even on the occasions when it did so 'not in single spies but in battalions' – most notably in 1885 – its coverage tended to focus, gloatingly, on English military reverses.[14]

In a sense, foreign coverage of British colonial ambitions and misadventures in places like Egypt or the Sudan stands as allegory for Ireland itself. The military successes, however transient, of figures like Colonel Araby in Egypt or the Mahdi in Sudan are celebrated. Both men act as virtual surrogates for the Irish National League. As with the Dublin Castle 'scandals', when it came to some of their more egregious military defeats, British competence, physical courage and 'manliness' were overtly and subliminally undermined editorially for psychological advantage.

More than 40 per cent of the leaders in category H (42.3 per cent) relate to the interaction of the Roman Catholic Church and nationalism (H2). While many more editorials included references to the policies espoused by nationalistic church leaders like Archbishop Croke of Cashel or Archbishop Walsh of Dublin, or of those opposed to 'advanced' nationalist policies like Archbishop McCabe of Dublin or Bishop O'Dwyer of Limerick, only 4.2 per cent of the overall editorial total related largely or exclusively to the involvement of Roman Catholic prelates and priests in the debates on nationalism and agrarianism or to the internal affairs of the Roman Catholic church itself.[15]

The overwhelming majority of these editorials deal positively with the interaction between the Roman Catholic clergy and the, largely, Roman Catholic nationalist movement. Croke (a close personal friend of O'Brien's) in particular, is depicted as a 'Prince of the Church'[16] despite his single peccadillo in opposing the No Rent Manifesto of October, 1881. There were some implicit, and occasionally overt, criticisms of the sort of ultra-montanism that might cede too much political authority to Rome and thus reduce clerical participation in Irish political matters, but, by and large (until 1891 – see below), *United Ireland* avoided adverse commentary on prominent members of the Irish hierarchy. A notable exception was a final loss of patience with the potent opposition by the Bishop of Limerick, Dr O'Dwyer, to the Plan of Campaign. As O'Dwyer's inveighing against the Plan became more virulent and especially when it was picked up by unionist journals like the *Times* and *Daily Express*, *United Ireland* moved from a position of sublime indifference, through subtle barbs, to outright denunciation.[17]

A significant number of uncategorizable entries (H4) might suggest a newspaper that was capable of dealing with topics outside of the standard, normative or mundane.[18] While the total numbers in this category are similar to those of H1 (19.9 per cent) they are strongly weighted towards the first half of the decade. From 1886 onwards *United Ireland* had found its campaigning voice and was concentrating exclusively on topics and subjects that are relatively easy to categorize. Enthusiasm for the occasional foray beyond the outer limits of utilitarianism was limited to the weekly poem that preceded 'The Week's Work', or reserved for inclusion in *United Ireland's* sister publication *The Shamrock*. Similarly, the newspaper, in its earliest incarnation, made some attempt to reflect an interest, of Parnell in particular, in Irish industrial activity, or, more precisely, the lack thereof (H3). The peak year for leaders on industry/industrialization was 1882, when the Irish Exhibition was taking place. From 1883 onwards the editorial output in this category (two leaders in eight years) reflects O'Brien's agrarianism rather than Parnell's concern with the importance of industrial development.

1.9. 1891 in perspective.

Table 7 – Categories for 1891

A	B	C	D	E	F	G	H	Total
12	0	1	4	1	17	95	29	159

Table 8 - Sub-categories for 1891

G1	G2	G3	G4	H1	H2	H3	H4	Total
10	30	54	1	0	26	0	3	124

In 1891 *United Ireland*, to all intents and purposes, ceased altogether to resemble a newspaper and became, even more completely, a factional Parnellite propaganda sheet. There was an increase in the number of editorials, from an average of 127 for the previous five years, to 159 in 1891. Only thirty-five editorials, however, were outside of categories G or H. Sixteen of those were denunciations of other newspapers. However, in this instance the attacks were devoted to the criticism of other nationalist journals rather than the *Times*, *Daily Express* or *Dublin Evening Mail*. The main targets were the *Freeman's Journal*, following the announcement of its apostasy in August 1891, and Tim Healy's virulently anti-Parnellite *National Press*. There were almost no editorial comments of any kind on the law and virtually none on the land, this at the height of the self-serving Tory policy of political conciliation based on the strategic amelioration of agrarian grievances.

Nowhere is the obsession of *United Ireland* with supporting Parnell against the McCarthyites (dubbed 'The Seceders' or 'The Whigs') more obvious than in Category A, where the total number of editorials is less even than that of 1881, during which only twenty issues of the newspaper appeared. *United Ireland* largely abandoned its anti-Castle phillipics in preference for intra-party invective. Most of the thirty editorials that commented positively on nationalist figures (G2) were in praise of (or in mourning for) Parnell himself. Occasionally other Parnellite leaders such as Redmond and Harrington feature in this column. But the positive editorializing was heavily outweighed, especially after Parnell's death, by the negative editorials berating his opponents. These made up more than a third (34 per cent)[19] of the total number of leading articles for the year.

Criticism of most of the anti-Parnellite leadership remained relatively mild for the first months of the year. This is especially the case where John Dillon and William O'Brien were concerned. Neither had emphatically taken sides by the time of their incarceration in February 1891. Even in August, when both announced their opposition to Parnell after their release from prison, *United Ireland* still referred to them as 'honest men, honourable men, brave men' and held out the hope that they would 'brush aside insidious counsellors'.[20] In the months immediately after the split Justin McCarthy was treated relatively fairly by the newspaper,[21] no doubt reflecting Parnell's personal affection for his former lieutenant. An obvious exception, even in the 'grace period' immediately following the split, was T.M. Healy. All references to Parnell's nemesis were bilious, scathing and highly personal.[22] *United Ireland* also plumbed new lows in its denunciations of Michael Davitt, going as far, on one occasion, as to suggest of Davitt that, 'for nine years now he has been nursing his grudge against Mr. Parnell to keep it warm; feeding his mind on envy; carping, and cavilling without pause at every act and word of the Leader'.[23]

Even overtly neutral headlines, such as two out of the three that year entitled 'The Evicted Tenants', could be misleading. What might have been an old-fashioned piece of O'Brienite Plan of Campaign rhetoric, could turn into an anti-'Whig' diatribe related to allegations being made against Parnell over disbursement of the so-called 'Paris Fund'.[24] Some of the uncritical pieces on Parnell and his lieutenants would quickly turn into vitriolic attacks on his opponents after a few column inches. Even a leading article celebrating St Patrick's Day morphed into an anti-McCarthyite rant.[25]

As the year went on the level of invective was ratcheted upwards. A reading of the frequently venomous commentary in *United Ireland* clearly indicated that reconciliation was not in the air following the three Parnellite electoral defeats and, particularly, after the death of Parnell himself. Editorials that year also reflected some of the alliances Parnell was trying to forge in order to shore up his critical political situation. There was, for example, a new-found admiration for all things Fenian. This included favourable coverage of the return to Ireland of James Stephens[26] and strident condemnation of the death in prison of P.W. Nally[27] There was also evidence of an attempted *rapprochement* with Unionism[28] and with Labour.[29] It is clear from the contents of the newspaper during this period that Parnell was exercising a more direct personal influence on the editorial line than he had been during O'Brien's hegemony. He was certainly spending more time in Ireland than he had during O'Brien's stewardship of his newspaper.[30] A reflection of this re-ordering of priorities came in an editorial immediately prior to Parnell's death. In the issue of 3 October 1890, in an editorial entitled 'What of these, Masters?' doubt was cast on the political wisdom of having prioritized agrarian reform during the 1880s. 'Is the Irish farmer Ireland?' asked a newspaper with a quantifiable record of favouring the interests of the farmer over the labourer, over industrial development and over labour itself. 'Is there no man in this island worthy of the consideration of her politicians but he who rents the soil? For sixteen years we have fought for this man, agitated for him, gone to jail for him, and turned the English House of Commons topsy-turvy for him. Is there no other man?'

United Ireland, clearly a recent convert to class politics, proceeded to answer its own question. 'Ah, fellow countryman, politics or no politics, let us be just. Let us especially be just to our own poor countrymen. The brave fisher folk gazing wistfully at the shoals of mackerel so near, and yet so far beyond their reach; the poor patient Irish labourer in his hovel, the poor Irish labourer who has stood so nobly for Irish nationality, notwithstanding all his poverty; these we do respectfully submit, are as pathetic figures in our national life as any rack-rented farmer. Are they to be left to their fate?'[31] This new line was undoubtedly a function of Parnell's ebbing support in rural Ireland where the clergy had a far greater influence than in the cities. After the death of Parnell *United Ireland* failed to sustain, editorially at least, such an invigorating level of enthusiasm for the 'brave fisher folk' or the 'poor Irish labourer'.

Alongside the 'Seceders' in the *United Ireland* Rogues' Gallery, though only coming in for half the abuse (twenty-six editorials as opposed to fifty-four) was the Irish Roman Catholic hierarchy. Virtually all of the Church-related editorials (H2) were condemnations of the anti-Parnellite stance taken by the entire Roman Catholic hierarchy and most of the ordinary clergy. The single exception was a 6 June leader on Pope Leo XIII's encyclical on the relationship between capital and labour, *Rerum Novarum*. Even the previously untouchable Croke came in for criticism.[32] Attacks on the hierarchy actually tapered off after the death of Parnell. There were only three Church-related editorials in the last three months of the year.

Notes

1   Evidence of William O'Brien. *Special Commission*, vol. 8, 72018, 200. Supported by Accounts for the Irish National Newspaper & Publishing Company, William O'Brien Papers, University College, Cork AA, f.81.

2   A small number of issues, mostly dating from the early 1882 period, when distribution of the newspaper was prevented by the Liberal government, do not survive.

3   It should be noted that this will impact somewhat on any assessment of the overall thrust of *United Ireland's* editorial concerns in that a column which was, for example, devoted 60 per cent to coercion and 40 per cent to land issues will have been categorized under B (Coercion) i.e. the land element will have been entirely discounted.

4   Although not as actively involved in the compilation of the paper from 1886 onwards O'Brien still remained as the legal publisher/proprietor and maintained a close interest in the editorial policy of the paper.

5   Representing an abnormally high 30 per cent of all leading articles that year, the first in which the (adjusted) figure for editorials falls below 200 (158).

6   1886=21 per cent, 1887=18 per cent, 1888=18 per cent.

7   'Stand Together', 22 November 1890.

8   A single example, of many, will suffice. On 2 July 1887, *United Ireland* referred to O'Brien, then Solicitor General, as being 'a goodly, round full-bodied maggot bred in the corruption of the Irish administration'.

9   Though on no occasion during the Plan of Campaign period was O'Brien jailed for activities directly connected to *United Ireland*.

10   James Loughlin, 'Constructing the political spectacle: Parnell, the press and national leadership, 1879–86' in *Parnell in perspective*, Boyce, D.George and O'Day, Alan (eds) (London, 1991), 221–41.

11   Both are criticized in an editorial on 9 February 1884. O'Donnell is referred to as 'a mischievous chief' while O'Connor Power is more of a miscreant, he was described as a 'vulgar apostate'.

12   As in 'nominal' as opposed to 'advanced' Home Rulers.

13   All are regularly recorded as having voted 'for the enemy' on the editorial page in 1882 and 1883.

14   7 March 1885, 'The English as champion runners'.

15   This strain was very much in evidence in relation to the use by the Liberals of George Errington MP in an effort to dissuade the Vatican from appointing Dr Walsh to the Dublin See and later in the decade around the time of the Papal Rescript against the Plan of Campaign.

16   'A brave Irish Archbishop', 19 January 1889.

17   In 'Limerick and its bishop', 30 August 1890, O'Dwyer is described as 'the least among the Irish bishops' and is accused of having 'foully slandered' John Dillon.

18   1 July 1882 – 'The New Impulse to National Literature', 16 September 1882, 'The young men and their mission'.

19 At fifty-four in total – the highest number in any single category in any of the eleven years covered by this survey.

20 *United Ireland*, 1 August 1891.

21 *United Ireland*, 31 January 1891, 'Mr. McCarthy at Manchester'.

22 *United Ireland*, 24 January 1891, 'whose hysterics has become chronic', or 28 February 1891, the 'illimitable scurrility of T.H. [*sic*] Healy'.

23 *United Ireland*, 18 April 1891.

24 *United Ireland*, 10 January 1891. *United Ireland*, 2 May 1891.

25 *United Ireland*, 21 March 1891.

26 *United Ireland*, 3 October 1891, 'Welcome'.

27 *United Ireland*, 14 & 21 November 1891. It should, however, be noted that the death of Nally would have attracted similar treatment in O'Brien's *United Ireland*.

28 *United Ireland*, 28 March 1891. 'Irish Protestants and the crisis'; 16 May 1891. 'Two Letters'.

29 *United Ireland*, 9 May 1891. 'Labour Day in Dublin'.

30 Ironically, up to the end of 1890 O'Brien's name still appeared on the bottom right-hand corner of page eight as the named proprietor, just as it had done since 13 August 1881.

31 *United Ireland*, 3 October 1891.

32 *United Ireland*, 7 March 1891. 'His Grace of Cashel'; 23 May 1891. 'Dr. Croke and the "One Man Power"'.

BIBLIOGRAPHY

MANUSCRIPT SOURCES
National Archives of Ireland

Chief Secretary's Office Registered Papers

1879/10454	1882/8078	1883/1438	1888/7929
1881-36081	1882/8710	1883/1738	1888/9773
1881/42447	1882/9389	1883/13903	1888/26523
1881/43157	1882/15788	1883/ 25743	1890/14986
1881/43529	1882/17524	1883/26909	1897/16306
1881/45842	1882/17681	1883/28833	
1881/47097	1882/19234	1884/512	
1882/149	1882/19499	1884/22154	
1882/3037	1882/19816	1884/24345	
1882/3123	1882/28798	1884/27465	
1882/3283	1882/31460	1884/18324	
1882/4273	1882/33337	1884/27782	
1882/4305	1882/34450	1885/18523	
1882/5269	1882/37374	1887/4363	
1882/5469	1882/39820	1887/18986	
1882/5581	1882/44752	1888/1470	
1882/6000	1882/46849	1888/3076	
1882/6063	1883/157	1888/4483	
1882/6231			

Police and Crime Division Reports, III

Carton 6

Carton 7

National Library of Ireland

F.S. Bourke Papers MS.10702

George Fottrell Diaries MS.33670

T.P. Gill Papers MS.13478

T.C. Harrington Papers MS.8584
Michael MacDonagh Papers MS.11442
MS.11443
Theophilus MacWeeney
Papers MS.21936
Sophie O'Brien Papers MS.5924
P.J. Quinn Papers MS.5930
John Redmond Papers MS.10496

Trinity College, Dublin
Michael Davitt Papers MS.9535Diary 1882
MS.9536Diary 1883
John Dillon Papers MS.6736

University College, Cork
William O'Brien Papers
UCC-WOB-PP-AA
UCC-WOB-PP-AB
UCC-WOB-PP-AC

British Library
Althorp Papers
Add. Mss 76854
Add. Mss 76856
Add. Mss.76860
Add. Mss 76933
Add. Mss 76975
Add. Mss 77060
Add. Mss 77272
Add. Mss 77280
Balfour Papers
Add. Mss. 49688
Add. Mss. 49808
Add. Mss. 49809
Add. Mss. 49810
Add. Mss. 49811
Add. Mss. 49820
Add. Mss. 49826
Add. Mss. 49287
Add. Mss. 49828

Gladstone Papers
Add. Mss. 44157
Add. Mss. 44766
Add. Mss. 44160
Add. Mss 44219

British National Archive / Public Record Office
Cabinet Papers
CAB 37/3
CAB 37/7
CAB 37/8
CAB 37/10
CAB 37/11
CAB 37/12
CAB 37/13
CAB 37/14
CAB 37/16
CAB 37/18
CAB 37/19
CAB 37/20
CAB 37/21
CAB 37/22
CAB 37/23
CAB 37/24
CAB 37/25

Colonial Office Papers
CO 903/1
CO 903/2
CO 904/19

Home office papers
HO 144 72
HO 144 / 102
HO 144/104
A5867

NEWSPAPERS (National/International)

Daily News (London)

Dublin Daily Express

Dublin Evening Mail

Freeman's Journal

Irish Daily Independent

Irish Times

Irish World

Irish Nation

The Irishman

Boston Pilot

The Nation

National Press

Pall Mall Gazette

Standard (London)

Times

United Ireland

United Irishman

Irish local papers

Cork Daily Herald

Cork Free Press

Kerry Sentinel

Roscommon Herald

Sligo Champion

Wexford People

PRINTED SOURCES

A popular and complete edition of the Parnell Commission report. 1890. London.

Special Commission to Enquire into Charges and Allegations Against Certain Members of Parliament and Others. 1888–90. *Special commission on Parnellism and Crime,* vols 1, 7 & 8.

Parliament of Great Britain, (various dates) *House of Commons debates* (Hansard). London.

Public general statutes passed in the thirty-third & thirty-fourth years of the reign of Her Majesty Queen Victoria, 1870. London.

Public general statutes passed in the forty-fourth and forty-fifth years of the reign of Her Majesty, Queen Victoria, 1881. London.

Public general statutes passed in the forty-fifth and forty-sixth years of the reign of Her Majesty, Queen Victoria, 1882. London.

Public general statutes passed in the fiftieth and fifty-first years of the reign of Her Majesty, Queen Victoria, 1887. London.

MEMOIRS AND DIARIES

Anderson, Sir Robert, *Sidelights on the Home Rule movement* (London, 1906).

Anderson, Sir Robert, *The lighter side of my official life* (London, 1910).

Bahlman, Dudley W.R., *The diary of Sir Edward Hamilton, 1880–1885* (London, 1972).

Becker, Bernard, *Disturbed Ireland* (London, 1881).

Blunt, Wilfrid Scawen, *The land war in Ireland* (London, 1912).

Bodkin, Matthias McDonnell, *Recollections of an Irish judge* (Dublin, 1914).

Byrne, Edward, *Parnell: A memoir* (ed. Frank Callanan) (Dublin, 1991).

Davitt, Michael, *The fall of feudalism in Ireland* (London, 1904).

Denvir, John, *Life story of an old rebel* (Dublin, 1910).

Devoy, John, *Recollections of an Irish rebel* (New York, 1929).

Dunlop, Andrew, *Fifty years of Irish journalism* (Dublin, 1911).

George, Henry, *The Irish land question: what it involves and how alone it can be settled: an appeal to the Land Leagues* (New York and London, 1881).

Gladstone, W.E., *Gleanings from past years* (London, 1879).

Gordon, Peter, *The Red Earl: The papers of the fifth Earl Spencer* (2 vols). (Northampton, 1981 & 1986).

Hall, J.B., *Random records of a reporter* (Dublin, 1928).

Harrington, Timothy, *A diary of coercion: being a list of the cases tried under the Criminal Law and Procedure Act – Parts I–III* (Dublin, 1888–90).

Harrington, Timothy, *The Maamtrasna massacre: the impeachment of the trials* (Dublin, 1884).

Healy, T.M., *Letters and leaders of my day* (New York, 1929).

Hurlbert, William Henry, *Ireland under coercion* (2 vols) (New York, 1888).

Hussey, Samuel, *Reminiscences of an Irish land agent* (London, 1904).

Kettle, Andrew, *Material for victory* (ed. Laurence Kettle) (Dublin, 1958).

Le Caron, Henri, *Twenty-five years in the Secret Service* (London, 1892).

Lloyd, Clifford, *Ireland under the Land League* (London, 1892).

McCarthy, Michael J.F., *The Irish Revolution* (Edinburgh, 1912).

McDonald, John, *Daily News diary of the Parnell commission* (London, 1890).

Matthew, H.C.G. (ed.), *The Gladstone diaries* (14 vols). vol. x. (Oxford, 1990).

Moody, T.W. and Hawkins, R.A.J., *Florence Arnold-Forster's Irish journal* (Oxford, 1988).

Morley, John, *Recollections,* vol. 1 (New York, 1917).

O'Brien, Peter, *The reminiscences of the Right. Hon. Lord O'Brien (of Kilfenora): Lord Chief Justice of Ireland* (Dublin, 1916).

O'Brien, William, *Evening memories* (Dublin and London, 1920).

O'Brien, William, *Recollections* (London, 1905).

O'Brien, William, *An olive branch in Ireland and its history* (London, 1910).

O'Connor, James, *Recollections of Richard Pigott* (Dublin, 1889).

O'Connor, T.P., *Memoirs of an old parliamentarian,* 2 vols, vol. 1 (London, 1928).

O'Connor, T.P., *The Parnell movement* (London, 1886).

O'Donnell, F.H., *A History of the Irish parliamentary party,* 2 vols, vol. 2 (London, 1910)

Parnell, Anna, *Tale of a great sham* (ed. Dana Hearne) (Dublin, 1986).

Pigott,, Richard, *Personal recollections of an Irish nationalist journalist* (Dublin & London, 1882).

Robbins, Alfred, *Parnell: the last five years* (London, 1926)

Sullivan, T.D., *Recollection of troubled times in Irish politics* (Dublin, 1905)

Turner, Alfred E., *Sixty years of a soldier's life* (London, 1912)

Tynan, Patrick J., *The Irish national Invincibles and their times* (London, 1894).

SECONDARY READING

Adams, R.J.Q., *Balfour, the last grandee* (London, 2007).

Anderson, Benedict, *Imagined communities: reflections on the origins and spread of nationalism* (London/New York, 1991).

Bagenal, Philip, *The American Irish and their influence on Irish politics* (Boston and London, 1882).

Bew, Paul, *Land and the national question in Ireland, 1858–82* (Dublin, 1978).

Bew, Paul, *Charles Stewart Parnell* (Dublin, 1980).

Bew, Paul, *Enigma: a new life of Charles Stewart Parnell* (Dublin, 2011).

Boyce, D. George and O'Day, Alan, *Parnell in perspective* (London – New York, 1991).

Breathnach, Ciara and Lawless, Catherine (eds), *Visual, material and print culture in nineteenth-century Ireland* (Dublin, 2010).

Brown, Lucy, *Victorian news and newspapers* (Oxford, 1985).

Brown, Stephen J., *The press in Ireland: a survey and a guide* (New York, 1971).

Bull, Phillip, *Land, politics and nationalism: a study of the Irish land question* (Dublin, 1996).

Callanan, Frank, *T.M. Healy* (Cork, 1996).

Callanan, Frank, *The Parnell split* (Cork, 1992).

Clare Carroll and Patricia King (eds), *Ireland and postcolonial theory* (Indiana, 2003).

Churchill, Winston, *Lord Randolph Churchill* (London, 1906).

Clark, Samuel, *Social origins of the Irish land war* (Princeton, 1979).

Cocks, H.G., *Nameless Offences: Homosexual Desire in the Nineteenth Century* (London, 2003).

Comerford, R.V., 'The Politics of Distress, 1877–82' in Vaughan, W.E. (ed.), *A New History of Ireland,* 6 vols, vol. vi (Oxford, 1996).

Comerford, R.V., *The Fenians in context: Irish politics and society, 1848–82* (Dublin, 1998).

Conboy, Martin, *The press and popular culture* (London, 2002).

Cooke, A.B. and Vincent, John, *The governing passion: cabinet government and party politics in Britain 1885–86* (Brighton, 1974).

Crossman, Virginia, *Politics, law and order in 19th century Ireland* (Dublin, 1996).

Cullen, L.M., *Eason and Son: a history* (Dublin, 1989).

Curran, James and Seaton, Jean, *Power without responsibility: the press and broadcasting in Britain* (London, 1991).

Curtis, L.P., *Coercion and conciliation in Ireland, 1880–92* (Princeton, 1963).

Daly, Mary E. and Hoppen, K. Theodore (eds), *Gladstone: Ireland and beyond* (Dublin, 2011).

de Nie, Michael, *The Eternal Paddy: Irish identity and the British press, 1798–1882* (Wisconsin, 2004).

Dicey, A.V., *Introduction to the study of the law of the constitution* (London, 1902).

Dugdale, Blanche E.C., *Arthur James Balfour* (London, 1937).

Dungan, Myles, *Conspiracy: Irish political trials* (Dublin, 2009).

Dungan, Myles, *The Captain and the King: William O'Shea, Parnell and late Victorian Ireland* (Dublin, 2009).

Farrell, Brian, ed., *Communications and community in Ireland* (Cork, 1984).

Fisher, Joseph R and Strahan, James Andrew, *The law of the press: a digest of the law specially affecting papers* (London, 1891).

Foster, R.F., *Paddy and Mr. Punch* (London, 1995).

Foster, R.F., *Charles Stewart Parnell: the man and his family* (London, 1979).

Fraser, Hugh, *Principles and practice of the law of libel and slander, with suggestions on the conduct of a civil action* (London, 1897).

Garvin, Tom, *Nationalist revolutionaries in Ireland, 1858–1928* (Dublin, 2005).

Gilmartin, Kevin, *Print Politics: The press and radical opposition in early nineteenth-century England* (Cambridge, 1996).

Green, William & Manders, Richard, *Law Reports (Ireland) digest of cases, vols i-xx inclusive* (Dublin, 1890).

Groves, Patricia, *Petticoat rebellion: The Anna Parnell story* (Dublin, 2009).

Habermas, Jurgen, *The structural transformation of the public sphere* (Cambridge, Massachusetts, 1991).

Hammond, J.L., *Gladstone and the Irish nation* (London, 1938).

History of the Times: 1884–1912 (4 vols). vol. 3 (London, 1947).

Hollis, Patricia, *The pauper press* (Oxford, 1970).

Inglis, Brian, *The freedom of the press in Ireland, 1784–1841* (London, 1954).

King, Carla, *Michael Davitt* (Dundalk, 1999).

Koss, Stephen, *The rise and fall of the political press in Britain* (London, 1981).

Lacey, Brian, *Terrible queer creatures: homosexuality in Irish history* (Dublin, 2008).

Lawrence, Elwood P., *Henry George in the British Isles* (East Lansing, 1957).

Lee, Alan, *The origins of the popular press* (London, 1976).

Legg, Marie-Louise, *Newspapers and nationalism: the Irish provincial press, 1850–1892* (Dublin, 1999).

Levy, Leonard W., *Emergence of a free press* (Oxford, 1985).

Lyons, F.S.L., *Charles Stewart Parnell* (London, 1977).

Lyons, F.S.L., *The Fall of Parnell, 1890–91* (Toronto, 1960).

McCracken, Donal, *Inspector Mallon: buying Irish patriotism for a five-pound note* (Dublin, 2009).

MacDonagh, Michael, *The Life of William O'Brien, the Irish nationalist: a biographical study of Irish nationalism, constitutional and revolutionary* (London, 1928).

MacDonagh, Michael, *The Home Rule movement* (Dublin & London, 1910).

McDowell, R.B., *The Irish administration* (London, 1964).

McGee, Owen, *The IRB: The Irish Republican Brotherhood from the Land League to Sinn Fein* (Dublin, 2005).

Montgomery Hyde, H., *The other love: an historical and contemporary survey of homosexuality in Britain* (London, 1972).

Moody, T.W., *Davitt and the Irish revolution, 1846–1882* (Oxford, 1981).

Morash, Christopher, *A history of the media in Ireland* (Cambridge, 2009).

O'Brien, R. Barry, *The Life of Charles Stewart Parnell* (London, 1910).

O'Brien, Conor Cruise, *Parnell and His Party* (Oxford, 1957).

O'Brien, Joseph V., *William O'Brien and the course of Irish politics 1881–1918* (Berkeley, Los Angeles, London, 1976).

O'Brien, Mark, *The Irish Times: A history* (Dublin, 2008)

O'Brien, William and Ryan, Desmond (eds) *Devoy's post bag,* 2 vols. vol 2 (Dublin, 1953).

O'Broin, Leon, *The Prime Informer: A Suppressed Scandal* (London, 1971).

O'Callaghan, Margaret, *British high politics and a nationalist Ireland: criminality, land and the law under Forster and Balfour* (Cork, 1994).

O'Day, Alan, *Parnell and the first Home Rule episode, 1884–87* (Dublin, 1986).

O'Day, Alan, *Charles Stewart Parnell* (Dublin, 1998).

Odgers, William Blake, *A Digest of the law of libel and slander* (London, 1905).

Pearce, Edward, *Lines of most resistance: the Lords, the Tories and Ireland, 1886–1914* (London, 1999).

Porter, Bernard, *The origins of the vigilant state: the London Metropolitan Police Special Branch before the First World War* (London, 1991).

Potter, Simon, ed., *Newspapers and empire in Ireland and Britain* (Dublin, 2004).

Rafter, Kevin, ed., *Irish journalism before independence: more a disease than a profession* (Dublin, 2011).

Reid, T. Wemyss, *The life of the Right Honourable William Edward Forster* (London, 1888).

Rodechko, James Paul, *Patrick Ford and his search for America* (New York, 1976).

Shannon, Catherine B., *Arthur J.Balfour and Ireland, 1874–1922* (Washington DC, 1988).

Smith, Anthony, *The newspaper: an international history* (London, 1979).

Solow, Barbara Lewis, *The Land Question and the Irish Economy, 1870–1903* (Cambridge, Massachusetts, 1971).

Steele, David, *Lord Salisbury: a political biography* (London, 2004).

Townshend, Charles, *Making the peace: public order and public security in modern Britain* (Oxford, 1983).

Townshend, Charles, *Political violence in Ireland: government and resistance since 1848* (Oxford, 1983).

Vaughan, William E., *Murder Trials in Ireland, 1836–1914* (Dublin, 2009).

Vaughan, William E., *Landlords and Tenants in Ireland, 1848–1904* (Dublin, 1984).

Vaughan, William E. (ed.), *A New History of Ireland.* 6 vols, vol. vi (Oxford, 1996).

Waldron, Jarlath, *Maamtrasna: The Murders and the Mystery* (Dublin, 1992).

Ward, Margaret, *Unmanageable Revolutionaries: Women and Irish Nationalism* (London-East Haven, Connecticut, 1989)

Warwick-Haller, Sally, *William O'Brien and the Irish Land War* (Dublin, 1990).

Whyte, Frederic, *The Life of W.T. Stead.* 2 vols, vol. 1 (London / New York, 1925).

Williams, Raymond, *The Long Revolution* (London, 2001).

Williams, Robin H., *The Salisbury–Balfour correspondence, 1869–1892* (London, 1988).

Zebel, Sydney H., *Balfour, a political biography* (Cambridge, 1973).

ARTICLES AND ACADEMIC PAPERS

Breen, Thaddeus C., 'Loathsome, impure and revolting crimes: the Dublin Scandals of 1884', *Identity.* no.2. (July, 1982), pp.7–12.

Cooke, A.B. and Vincent, J.R., 'Lord Spencer on the Phoenix Park murders', *Irish Historical Studies*, 18, 72 (September, 1973), pp.583–91.

Curran, James, 'Media and the Making of British Society, c.1700–2000', *Media History*, 8, 2 (2002), pp.136–48.

Dudley Edwards, Owen, 'American diplomats and Irish coercion', *Journal of American Studies*, 1, 2 (October, 1967), pp.213–32.

Foley, Michael 'Colonialism and Journalism in Ireland', *Journalism Studies*, 5, 3 (2004), pp.373–85.

Gill, T.P., 'William O'Brien: Some Aspects', *Studies*, 17, 68 (December, 1928), pp.605–20.

Hampton, Mark, 'Journalists and the "Professional Ideal" in Britain: the Institute of Journalists, 1884–1907', *Historical Research*, 72, 178 (June, 1999), pp.183–201.

Hampton, Mark, 'Understanding Media: Theories of the Press in Britain, 1850–1914', *Media Culture Society*, 23, 2 (2001), pp.213–27.

Jordan, Donald, 'John O'Connor Power, Charles Stewart Parnell and the Centralisation of Popular Politics in Ireland', *Irish Historical Studies*, 25, 97 (May, 1986), pp.46–66.

Larkin, Felix, 'Parnell, politics and the press in Ireland, 1875–1924', The Parnell lecture. *Parnell Summer school*, (August, 2010).

Lyons, F.S.L., 'Parnellism and Crime, 1887–90', *Transactions of the Royal Historical Society*, fifth series, 24 (1974), pp.123–40.

McReynolds, Louise, 'Russia's newspaper reporters: profile of a society in transition, 1865–1914', *The Slavonic and Eastern European review*, 68, 2 (April, 1990), pp.277–93.

Moran, Gerard, 'James Daly and the Rise and Fall of the Land League in the West of Ireland, 1879–82', *Irish Historical Studies*, 29, 114 (November, 1994), pp.189–207.

Murray, A.C., 'Nationality and Local Politics in Late Nineteenth-Century Ireland: The Case of County Westmeath', *Irish Historical Studies*, 25, 98 (November, 1986), pp.144–158.

O'Brien, Conor Cruise, 'The machinery of the Irish parliamentary party, 1880–85', *Irish Historical Studies*, 5, 17 (March, 1946), pp.55–85.

O'Donnell, Edward T., '"Though not an Irishman": Henry George and the American Irish', *American Journal of Economics and Sociology*, 56, 4 (October, 1997), pp.407–19.

O'Regan, Maebh, 'Richard Moynan: Irish artist and unionist propagandist', *Eire-Ireland* 39, 1 & 2 (Spring/Summer, 2004), pp.59–80.

Porter, Bernard, 'The Freiheit Prosecutions, 1881–1882', *The Historical Journal*, 23, 4 (December, 1980), pp.833–56.

Silagi, Michael and Faulkner, Susan, 'Henry George and Europe', *American Journal of Economics and Sociology*, 46, 4 (October, 1994), pp.491–501.

UNPUBLISHED THESES

Ball, Stephen Andrew, *Policing the Land War: Official responses to political protest and agrarian crime in Ireland, 1879–91* (Goldsmith's College, University of London, 2000).

Lucey, Donnacha Sean, *Land and popular politics in County Kerry, 1872–86* (NUIM, Maynooth, 2007).

Index